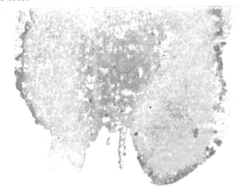

THE MAN WHO MADE THE BEATLES

Also by Ray Coleman

Lennon
Clapton! An Authorized Biography

THE MAN WHO MADE THE BEATLES

An Intimate Biography of Brian Epstein

❑

RAY COLEMAN

McGraw-Hill Publishing Company
New York   St. Louis   San Francisco

1 2 3 4 5 6 7 8 9 DOC DOC 8 9 2 1 0 9

ISBN 0-07-011789-6

Library of Congress Cataloging-in-Publication Data

Coleman, Ray.
  The man who made the Beatles.

  Includes index.
  1. Epstein, Brian, 1934–   . 2. Concert agents—
Biography. I. Title.
ML429.E6C6 1989   338.7'6178454'00924 [B]   88-27223
ISBN 0-07-011789-6

Book design by M 'N O Production Services, Inc.

For Queenie Epstein

Contents

In all unimportant matters, style, not sincerity, is the essential. In all important matters, style, not sincerity, is the essential.

—Oscar Wilde

❏

Aut Vinceri, Aut Mori (Conquer or Die).
—The motto of Wrekin College, Shropshire, England, which Brian Epstein attended from 1948 to 1950

❏

Be a bit tolerant of me at my worst. Really, I don't like, or want, to hurt anybody.

—Brian Epstein's handwritten note to his secretary, 1967

Preface

When Brian Epstein was a fifteen-year-old schoolboy, he wrote home to his parents that he would like to become a dress designer. His mother recognized his artistic interests but privately doubted his determination and patience. "He could never have starved in a garret. And he would have been bored too quickly," she told me.

Such an incident encapsulates vital characteristics of Brian Epstein's life. A hedonist, he loved style and comfort. He did not relish the learning process. Restlessness dominated his life.

And yet Epstein stayed true to that teenage enthusiasm for visual artistry. At twenty-seven, after seeing what he described to me as four "ill-presented, unkempt youths with untidy hair" in a Liverpool cellar club, he masterminded the packaging, promotion, marketing, and media explosion that propelled them into world fame as brilliant songwriters and performers. Instead of designing dresses, Epstein designed the Beatles.

A full quarter of a century after bursting upon the world, the surviving Beatles are often as astonished as thousands of others that their legendary status remains, that their influence and popularity are unequaled in their sphere, that their social importance is still examined. Epstein was always convinced that they had that strength—an almost mystical staying power.

Primarily, it is their work as musicians that endures. But so also does the romantic story of their emergence from Liverpool, which Epstein engineered. When he discovered them, they were seeking a manager and were ambitious to succeed internationally. Their aspirations, he realized, uncannily paralleled his own. He, too, was just then seeking an escape, from what he considered the mundane predictability of managing the record department in his father's furniture and appliance store.

The Beatles quickly became his cynosure, his cause, his obsession. He lived through them. The strategy with which he upgraded the Beatles sartorially and in performance, and the tenacity with which he pursued the elusive recording contract that clinched their success, are demonstrated in correspondence published here for the first time.

This was not a traditional manager-artist relationship but a chemically correct union of two parties who needed each other and happened to meet at exactly the right moment. What proved to be the crucial soundtrack for the 1960s was shaped extensively by Brian Epstein's fantasy as well as by the sounds and message of the Beatles.

The complexities of Epstein's private life are inextricably bound up with his efforts on behalf of the Beatles. As a bachelor, he devoted most of his waking hours to his work. His torturous life as a homosexual, in the years when it was illegal, brought him unremitting anguish. He was a solitary man who shared his dreams, hopes, fears, and problems with no one. He had hundreds of valued acquaintances but very few real friends; his only true confidant lived three thousand miles away in New York.

Nevertheless, he had always wanted to be an achiever, and in the Beatles he found his lifeline. As the Beatles became all-consuming for him, Epstein lost control of his ambitious business operations, partly because of his ceaseless appetite for change.

He died at thirty-two. In five years he had not only launched the Beatles, and many other acts as well, but had realized another of his dreams as a frustrated actor: he had run a London theater. As one of show business's most glittering successes, he had taken the world for his stage.

Epstein's story is of one man's triumphant, but tragic, journey through the 1960s, when both the world of popular music and the youth culture were comparatively innocent. The triumph was self-evident from the euphoria of the music and from historic events. The tragedy, less obvious, was bound up in Epstein's ultimately traumatic persona. Although there were many moments of delirium, the underlying loneliness and tension that dogged his life could never be conquered. Perhaps he was not destined to be a show business elder statesman, for he generated a youthful vitality that mirrored the essence of his era.

"Success gives me an extremely warm feeling," Epstein said to me in Liverpool in October 1963. He spoke of the "tingle" he had felt in the Cavern club on his first visit, and of the Beatles' sense of humor, their enthusiasm, their music, their sound. But at the start of his association with them, he had worried: "I asked myself if I could do for them what a professional manager could do. . . ."

What Epstein did not recognize is that he gave the Beatles precisely what no other professional manager *could:* martyrdom. He loved them as he could love no one else. His private pain became the world's gain; spurred by his inner trauma, he looked on them as his family and plunged totally into converting their boyish enthusiasm into an international artistic phenomenon.

The seeds of this biography were planted during my research for a biography of John Lennon, published in 1985. Epstein's turbulent life and his diligent work for the Beatles seemed to have been glossed over in the hundreds of books on the subject. His autobiography, *A Cellarful of Noise*, published in 1964, was coy, lightweight, star-struck, and told nothing of the real man. As in all the other books, the focus was on the Beatles, their sound, their fans. Who was the man who launched them, molded them? Who had showed the vision?

❑

In researching this first biography of Epstein and searching for motivations, it has been impossible to separate the public face of the man, and his remarkable achievements, from the private person. His natural charm, style, dignity, and politeness scarcely concealed his unease— an inner conflict, a door never opened. He lived and died in solitude. But as a pivot and catalyst of the youth revolution and cultural climate of the 1960s, Epstein had a profound effect on the lives of millions.

When he died in 1967 amid talk that he was losing his grip on the Beatles, the paradoxical truth was that they lost the only person capable of unifying them. "I knew we'd had it when Brian died," John Lennon said to me. By then, however, Epstein had significantly shaped history. And for generations to come, analysts pondering the rise of the Beatles, their timeless music, and the optimism of the period in which it was spawned will find it vital to examine the drama that unfolded largely from Brian Epstein's troubled psyche.

Ray Coleman

Prologue

"Were you born in Liverpool?" a radio interviewer asked Brian Epstein at the peak of the Beatles' success.

"Yes," he replied tersely. "I'd say it was *essential*."

Epstein was sardonically implying that he could not have nurtured and managed a team of Merseyside pop stars unless he could demonstrate a special empathy with their fiercely individual local stance, their endemic outlook, wit, audacity, cheerfulness, and creativity. This empathy could stem only from understanding Liverpudlians, from being born and bred among them.

Paradoxically, the question was perhaps not so naive or rhetorical as it first appeared. Brian was a staunch advocate of his city's strengths but never an obvious, quintessential Merseysider. Though he never received an elocution lesson, his voice carried no trace of the notorious scouse accent. His family background had protected him from the deprivation of the young people he mixed with so freely and happily; to them, he had stepped out of a different world.

The great city, at once so fertile in the arts and so fraught with industrial and environmental decay, had spawned outstanding singers, artists, comedians, playwrights, actors, musicians, and sportsmen long before Brian Epstein mined gold. It was not surprising that its vibrant young people, with their unique blend of musicianship and personality, would make Liverpool the epicenter of popular culture in the 1960s and beyond.

❑

Before meeting the Beatles at the age of twenty-seven, Epstein had led an eventful, if unstructured, life. He hated school, where he was a poor scholar, excelling only in art and drama: "My schooldays were rather sad . . ." He felt uneasy with the drab predictability of selling furniture in his father's store: "I only went into it because there it was, the family business, and I was the elder son." It was simply expected of him.

Seeking an escape that would encourage his predominantly aesthetic nature, he went to drama academy in London. He left after nine months because he was not shining; and he viewed "narcissistic" actors contemptuously. "I didn't enjoy it. I didn't fit in," he said. Also, he felt lonely in London because, he explained, he was shy.

Conscripted into the army for National Service, he loathed the discipline of military life: "If I had been a poor schoolboy, I was surely the lousiest soldier in the world." He was discharged on medical grounds after nine months.

Although he had to confront and combat that series of personal crises, and others more deep, he faced each encounter with a nascent optimism that invariably conquered his palpable air of melancholia. Self-pity was never a trait. In his buoyant determination to enjoy life, he reflected the true spirit of the Liverpudlian.

A chink of daylight appeared when his father mercifully opened a small record department in his furniture store. This was Brian's first life raft, and as he threw himself into running the department, his parents relaxed; perhaps he was settling down after the years of drifting.

By his own admission he had a considerable ego, which needed satisfying beyond the rewards of his eventual success at work; but for now, he earned enough money to indulge in his pleasures: the theater, concert-going, and collecting classical music records. He dressed immaculately and with élan.

According to one close observer, a winning charm is one of the central characteristics of the whole Epstein family. This natural graciousness would merge with Brian's artistic temperament and successful business background to make him, in the late 1950s and early 1960s, a man of both charisma and financial stability. It was an alluring combination.

But two powerful minorities were at work in his psyche: he was a

Jew, alternately passive and proud; and he was a homosexual, alternately reluctant and quietly evangelical, but never happy about it. Fortunately, he had the money to ease his personal pressures. His two-tone blue Ford Zodiac took him to Manchester and to the Cheshire countryside for social forays and fine restaurants. Until the Beatles' success forced him to move to London, he lived at home with his close-knit family, but could afford to rent an apartment in Liverpool to ensure an unfettered private life. It was usually empty.

And there were many solitary holidays. He went to Barcelona, where he adored the spectacle and panache of bullfighting; to Paris and Amsterdam, where his loneliness found temporary respite in the beckoning anonymity.

Life was basically very comfortable, however. And Brian believed that his nonconformist search for a true vocation was not necessarily a handicap, that it might be converted into a strength. If he could not succeed as an actor, he was determined to manage Britain's best-run record store.

Achieving his goal in a three-year span, he left for a five-week holiday alone in Spain in the autumn of 1961. Returning to Liverpool, he was visibly bored and restless. Then fate played its hand. His precision and inquisitiveness paid their dividends. He took a detour, then took a chance, and changed his life.

1

□

ACCIDENTAL DEATH

BELGRAVIA, LONDON, 1967

JOANNE NEWFIELD AND ALISTAIR TAYLOR were not easily shocked by the moods, tantrums, and traumas of Brian Epstein. As his devoted private secretary and his general manager, they both knew that the one certainty about Brian was his utter unpredictability.

But for more than a year they had become worried by his increasing depressions and irrational behavior. He had thrown a full teapot at Joanne, just because she gave him a wrong telephone number. She resigned, he apologized, and she forgave him. Once, with that dulcet-toned telephone style that melted so many of his friends, Epstein had called Alistair: "I've had enough. I'm ending it all. I thought I'd call to say goodbye. I'm going to commit suicide."

Alistair, horrified, tried to keep him talking but Epstein hung up. Speeding to Brian's bedside, Alistair found his boss wide awake and smiling, engaged in reading newspapers and business documents. "What do you want here?" he said, rebuking Alistair for taking an innocent joke seriously.

"You just rang me. . . ." Alistair began, breathlessly.

"Oh, take no notice of that. I'm busy."

As the manager of the Beatles and as a man, Brian Epstein had for

5

six years evoked love, devotion, and seething frustration among his staff, his friends, his business associates, and the artists he managed and befriended. He was both meticulous and capricious; generous and parsimonious; and, exasperatingly, elated one moment and inconsolably despondent the next.

To live and work in close proximity to Brian required cool judgment and inexorable patience. He was a compulsive pill taker who had leaned increasingly on them to get him through the day and night: pills to boost his energy and awareness, pills to get him to sleep, pills to calm his nerves, pills to help balance the pills. His swings of mood and temperament were legendary among his aides, who all sensed his acute loneliness. Despite his influence, wealth, and handsome, debonair appearance, he was a palpably sensitive and vulnerable man.

He was also a dazzling achiever. By 1967, the roller coaster he had begun with the Beatles only six frenzied years before had reached a crescendo with the release of their epic album, *Sgt. Pepper's Lonely Hearts Club Band*. He basked in the reflected glory just as he had always done, with nobody denying his crucial role. But he never overstepped the mark by claiming too much importance.

For the past eighteen months, though, the people around him had been worried. His built-in poise was still there, but he was increasingly restless and unreliable. His secretary and press officer were canceling his appointments and making excuses for him far too often.

This man of precision, so adept at organizing the lives and careers of others, was now disorganized himself. Worse, he would not allow anyone to help him marshal his life. Against mounting odds, with disagreements now occurring about the way he was running his business, the loyalty of his staff remained constant. It was a remarkable demonstration of a man's warmth transcending his many peccadilloes. Yet they all wondered: What news will come with the next telephone call?

❑

At his London home, 24 Chapel Street, Belgravia, not far from Buckingham Palace, Brian was always at his happiest. It was the beautiful town house he had always promised himself. He had furnished it with exquisite taste, spending thousands of pounds on antiques and paintings. These came mainly from Brighton, not far from Brian's rustic country house, Kingsley Hill, near Uckfield, which he enjoyed visiting with friends on weekends.

On Friday, August 25, 1967, Brian was in a particularly cheerful mood. By phone from San Francisco to Chapel Street, just before a flight to London, Alistair Taylor casually mentioned that he'd seen in a newspaper that one of Brian's favorite groups, the Four Tops, was appearing at the Coconut Grove in Los Angeles. Excited, Brian suggested that Taylor stay an extra day in California to see them. "Be sure to give them my love and ask them when they are coming back to appear for me again," said Brian, reflecting on their successful appearances at his London theater, the Saville.

He planned a weekend in the country at Kingsley Hill and had invited two friends, Geoffrey Ellis and Peter Brown, to stay and several acquaintances to visit. Casually chatting with his secretary, Brian asked if she would like to join them, perhaps bringing her friend, the singer Lulu. Joanne politely declined but was reassured by Brian's bonhomie. Only six weeks earlier his father had died, and as well as dealing with his own shock, Brian had consoled his mother and been her perfect host at his London home. Now it was time for a bank-holiday weekend break with his friends in the country.

Dressed in white trousers and a white sweater that sunny Friday afternoon, Brian walked down the steps outside his house to his white open-topped Bentley. As he stepped into the car, he and Joanne wished each other a good, long weekend, and she noted that for the first time in what seemed months, he was relaxed. As he drove off, he turned to smile and wave to her. She would never see him again.

Arriving in Sussex late in the afternoon, he stopped off at Red Tiles Antiques, where he had previously bought several items for his house. Brian told the proprietor, Mrs. M. Rayner, that he would be visiting her again shortly, since he wanted to purchase an item that was her own personal property, rather than something on display. Brian said he would bring the Beatles to the shop, as they were interested in antiques too. "He had a nice personality and charming manners. He was in good spirits," Mrs. Rayner later said.

A local newspaper reporter seeking an interview with Brian about his acquisition of Kingsley Hill, one of the county's finest examples of Queen Anne architecture, was told by a patient Epstein as he strolled around his five acres: "I use this place to get away from things and I am not too keen to have the press around. If you want to give me a call when I return from abroad in five or six weeks, I will try to fix a time for you to see me."

All of Brian's movements and remarks that day, as in the preceding days and weeks, had pointed to his enthusiastic planning of future events.

Even to a secretary trained to expect the unexpected, the telephone call that came on Sunday morning to Joanne's home in Finchley, London, was one that immediately gave her nagging doubts. On the line was Maria, Epstein's Spanish housekeeper at his London house. She apologized for calling on a bank holiday but she was concerned: Brian had returned, unscheduled, to the house on the Friday night, left his car on the street instead of in the garage, and locked himself in his bedroom.

Maria and her husband, the butler Antonio, had knocked on the door that Sunday morning to offer him breakfast. There was no reply. Brian had switched off his intercom so that he could not be contacted. The car was precisely where it had been on Friday night, so he could not have driven off again. Maria thought her boss's behavior unusual; uncharacteristically, he had not been out for *two nights*.

"Look, don't be silly," said Joanne, who had spent a year assuaging worriers. "There's really nothing unusual about Brian being in bed at lunchtime on a Sunday. Just leave him. He's fine." Maria was reassured. But Joanne, putting the phone down, found her intuitive concern increasing. What had happened? Brian had prepared to spend a gentle, full weekend at his country house with friends. Why had he driven back to London a few hours after arriving, and why was he incommunicado? Well, she reasoned, everything could still be fine. He was a solitary man who often turned off his intercom and locked the doors of his bedroom. And yet . . . he usually left a note stating his intentions. Over lunch she told her mother she would have to go to Chapel Street.

First, Joanne telephoned Alistair Taylor. "Maria is worried and I am, a bit," said Joanne. "I'm going over to Chapel Street and I don't fancy it by myself. Will you meet me there?" Taylor, suffering jet lag from the overnight flight from San Francisco, was slightly cynical but, as always, practical and helpful: "Oh Jo, it's probably nothing. But if you're going, okay, I'll be there."

Facing the wrath of his wife for leaving so quickly after the transatlantic flight home, Taylor nevertheless had a strange feeling that he *had* to go. "It will probably be like last time," he said to his wife Lesley as he got dressed. "He'll be sitting up in bed and I'll have wasted a journey. I said to Joanne on the phone that at least we'll face Brian's abuse together."

Joanne arrived first. She phoned Kingsley Hill, Sussex, where Epstein's weekend guests were still in residence. Explaining why she was at Brian's house, Joanne asked why he had returned to London unexpectedly. He had become bored by the lack of action in the country, they replied. And he had insisted on driving himself, in spite of warnings that he might have drunk too much wine.

"Well," said Joanne, "the bedroom's locked, the intercom is turned off. Maria and Antonio are concerned, and now I am worried. I think we're going to break the doors down." Peter Brown advised her not to do that; it had been done before and Epstein had become very angry. Joanne was insistent. Brown believed everyone was behaving too dramatically, she remembers.

"Perhaps I should get a doctor over," Joanne continued to Brown over the phone, "before we knock the doors down." She called Brian's regular doctor. When there was no reply, Brown said they should call *his* doctor, who lived nearby.

When Dr. John Gallwey arrived, Antonio and Joanne went with him to the bedroom doors. Joanne left the line to Peter Brown open, the phone dangling in the kitchen. They knocked again. Reluctantly, Joanne said: "Okay, break the doors down." The two men heaved against the paneled doors, and the frame and doors splintered. The doctor went in first, followed by Antonio. Joanne, now very scared, hung back just outside.

The curtain was drawn, the room was darkened. On the two single beds that had been joined to form one, Brian was lying on his side facing the window. He was dressed in pajamas. Beside him was a pile of opened correspondence, the working script for the film *Yellow Submarine*, and the opened book he was reading: *The Rabbi*, by Noah Gordon. On one bed was a plate holding two chocolate digestive biscuits; on one side table was a glass containing pieces of lemon, and alongside it, several vials. The doctor pronounced him dead.

Joanne ran downstairs to open the front door for Alistair, who had been delayed by the impossibility of getting a taxi from Clapham on bank-holiday Sunday. One look at her face gave him the news he dreaded. Outside Brian's bedroom Alistair noticed the split wood where the doors had been smashed. He went into the room. "The doctor had just reached the bed. Brian was lying there on his side, and it was all so *normal*, that's what sticks in my mind. He was looking terribly white."

As the housekeeper wailed "Why? Why?" Joanne again picked up the phone. She repeated her question several times to Peter Brown in Sussex: "Why did he come back?" Despite the cogency of the reply, Brian's return remained one of several mysteries surrounding that fateful weekend.

The question "Why?" had dominated Brian Epstein's life. Why indeed had he ever become involved with four scruffy, itinerant Liverpool rock 'n' rollers, running against the pattern of his natural taste and his family's background? But now, as the machinery of death moved inexorably into position, there was a more pressing, even less answerable question: How?

❑

At the inquest in London on September 8, 1967, Dr. John Flood, a psychiatrist, told the coroner that he had first been asked to see Brian three months earlier.* His main symptoms at that time were insomnia, depression, and excessive irritability. "He said that he had literally not slept for two or three days prior to our consultation despite the fact that he had taken large doses of sleeping pills."

Dr. Flood had admitted Epstein to the Priory Hospital in Roehampton "for treatment and further psychological assessment," and had discharged him two weeks later in a considerably improved condition. He had treated Epstein with antidepressant drugs: Surmontil and large doses of Librium.

"On the patient's own history and evidence given by his friends," said Dr. Flood, "it appeared that he had been quite significantly depressed for a period of eighteen months or two years. He had previously been under the care of two other psychiatrists but had not

---

*This coincided exactly with the launching of the Beatles' milestone album, *Sgt. Pepper's Lonely Hearts Club Band*.

persisted with treatment. There had been times, however, during the last two years when he had been relatively well.

"After the patient's discharge from the Priory, I saw him on a number of occasions, and his improvement was maintained until the sudden death of his father at the beginning of July.* I saw him on 26 July, when he admitted that he had at times taken large doses of amphetamines and alcohol. On that day he was specifically warned about the dangers of taking sleeping tablets, in particular barbiturates, if he was having any alcohol."

Peter Brown, Brian's personal assistant, told the inquest that on Friday, Brian had appeared "very elated in saying how much he was looking forward to us [Brown and Geoffrey Ellis] coming down to Kingsley Hill, and what time were we going to arrive: in fact urging us to leave earlier than planned." Brian had arrived at his country home earlier; Brown and Ellis arrived at 8 p.m. for dinner.

"We had a normal dinner which three old friends would have, chatting . . . and he was in a very happy, relaxed state." Brown stated that Epstein seemed in "complete control of himself" and was "extremely interested in having related to him business matters which had occurred during the day and asked for a full report on the activities of his artists. He showed no sense of being disturbed in any way and the meeting was a happy and friendly one.

"After dinner we had coffee in the drawing room and while we were having coffee, he made a telephone call." According to Brown, Brian said that he had telephoned a friend in London and that some people might be coming down later, "giving me the impression that it was doubtful if, in fact, they would come, due to the lateness of the hour and the distance that we were from London."

About half an hour after that call, at about 10:30 p.m., Epstein told Brown and Ellis that he "was going out for a little while and that he might even go to London." He then left the room and returned with a jacket on. "We both urged him not to go out at that late hour, and I walked with him to the garage trying to persuade him not to go; and he assured me not to worry and that if Geoffrey and I went to bed that he would be back already in the morning when we got up.

"We were slightly concerned about him," Brown continued, "but

*Brian's father died on July 17.

it was not unusual for him to go off on a whim. After two hours Geoffrey telephoned to Mr. Epstein's London home, where he was told by the butler that Brian had arrived at the house and was thought to have gone out.

"To my surprise, a few people arrived, all except one being unknown to me. We then tried to contact Brian by telephone in London and got no reply. We knew that he was either out or could have returned and turned the telephone off, as he had done in the past. I telephoned on several occasions up to three-thirty a.m."

The next day, Saturday, Peter Brown phoned at around midday. Brian's butler, Antonio Garcia, told him that Mr. Epstein was still sleeping. "We did not call again until Brian called at between five p.m. and five-thirty p.m., apologizing profusely for not returning [to Kingsley Hill] as he said he would, hoping that we did not think he was rude and hoping that we had also been looked after and were all right. He was very apologetic. He said that he had gone to bed late and taken quite a number of sleeping tablets to enable him to sleep, and he still felt drowsy.

"I suggested that, as he felt drowsy, he should come back to Sussex on the train and we would meet him at the station. He said he would probably do that, but he did not feel at that moment even able to do that."

No more was heard from Brian that night. Brown and Ellis assumed he had decided to stay in London.

❏

On Sunday, August 27, 1967, the two men did not telephone Brian, anticipating that he might be sleeping late. They went out to the local pub for a midday drink. On their return to the house, a worried Antonio Garcia phoned to say that Brian had not been out of his room at all the previous day; his door was closed and the intercom was off. "Nevertheless, I was very worried then," Peter Brown told the inquest, "because I thought he had been out during that evening and in fact he had not."

Replying to the coroner, Brown said that Epstein had suffered from glandular fever, which tended to recur and leave him rather weak.

Coroner: Did he find life a strain at times?

Brown: I think he found at times there were pressures.

Coroner: Did this appear to worry him unduly? More than it would an average person?

Brown: He was a very sensitive person. He did appear to get excited about things and very worried at times.

Coroner: What were his habits as regards sedatives and drugs generally?

Brown: He did have a lot of trouble with regard to sleeping, I know, and used to have this worry about not sleeping. He had been taking sleeping tablets for quite a long time.

Brown asked the butler to bang on the door. He said he had already done that when he had been unable to contact him (Brown). He had also spoken to Joanne Newfield, who was en route to the house. "I told Antonio to telephone me the moment Joanne arrived, which she did. I then told Joanne to telephone my doctor and ask him to call me the moment he arrived at the house.

"When my doctor, Dr. John Gallwey, arrived at the house, I told him and advised him to break the door down and hung on while he did this, and Dr. Gallwey then came back and reported to me what the position was."

Antonio Garcia told the inquest that he and his wife Maria had worked as live-in assistants at Brian's house for five months and found him a "perfectly normal person, very kind to both of us." He kept unusual hours, sleeping very late. "On Saturday, 26 August 1967, I went to his room about five p.m. and gave him a meal. He was in bed, using the telephone. He was perfectly normal. There was no one else in the house. About an hour later there was a phone call for him which he did not answer. I went and knocked on the door but he did not reply. I did not disturb him further." Garcia added that he and his wife, who slept in the basement, heard nothing during the night.

"On Sunday, 27 August, he did not rise and so I left it until about two p.m. There was no reply to my knocking. So about two-thirty p.m. I called his secretary. She arrived later and also a doctor. The door to Mr. Epstein's room was locked on the inside and we, the doctor and I, broke it in and found him on the bed. Nothing was touched until the police came." Garcia added that Brian did not always lock the door but he had done so in the past.

The drugs and bottles found in Brian's bedroom at the time of his death were described to the inquest by Police Inspector George Howlett. On a bedside table beside Epstein was a tablet vial, and on a lower shelf was a larger vial containing one yellow tablet, plus an empty tablet bottle marked Librium. On the same shelf was a box containing twelve bottles, one empty coffee mug, and an empty bottle of Schweppes bitter lemon. In a document case were two further bottles of tablets; in a drawer, three more bottles of tablets; and in a bathroom cabinet, eight bottles.

The inspector said there were no suspicious circumstances.

Reporting on the postmortem examination, Dr. R. Donald Teare, consultant pathologist, said that the deceased's blood contained an estimated 168 milligrams of bromide; tests also indicated the presence of pentobarbitone and Amytriptyline but excluded Librium, alkaloids, and amphetamine. The bromide figure in the blood was significant, said the doctor, "and I think it could only be achieved by taking Carbrital [containing both pentobarbitone and bromide] for a long time. The stomach saturation suggests six capsules. The blood concentration about nine capsules but not taken as a single dose."

A raised blood bromide might make a man careless, injudicious, the doctor continued. "He was approaching a state of bromide intoxication. To achieve the blood bromide figure would have taken weeks rather than days." Dr. Teare said that Epstein had no natural disease.

Cause of death was poisoning by Carbrital—a small, lethal dose, not a massive one. The blood concentration indicated repetition, not a single dose. "There was no indication of any other drug at all." His intake, however, would not only make him careless but produce a blunting of the appreciation of the effect of Carbrital, perhaps causing him to take one or two capsules more in a careless way.

Brian's regular doctor, Norman Cowan, told the coroner that Brian had suffered glandular fever in July 1966 upon his return from a trip to the East. He had a slow convalescence; his subsequent depression was reactive to his work load in September of that year.

"He took Tryptizol, Librium, and Carbrital as an hypnotic. He took two tablets of Carbrital at night. I had no reason to suspect he was exceeding this. He had taken amphetamines in the past but very, very little recently. This was not on medical advice. The question of bromide intoxication never crossed my mind," said Dr. Cowan. "In my opinion Carbrital is a very safe hypnotic, widely used."

Dr. Cowan added that he had seen Epstein on August 16, and "he was in excellent health. I had never seen him better."

The inquest heard that Epstein had seen Dr. Flood, the psychiatrist, on May 13, after Brian had previously consulted two other psychiatrists. "At that time," Dr. Flood stated, "his main complaint was insomnia, anxiety, and depression." He admitted Epstein to his care for two weeks, finding him considerably improved upon his discharge from the Priory Hospital. "In my opinion he was not addicted to any kind of drug. He was a man who would be rather careless in using drugs, but I would not regard him in any way as a drug addict."

"With regard to drugs," stated Dr. Flood, "the patient has for at least five years been taking amphetamines in large doses, and he had also been regularly smoking marijuana. He had also experimented with heroin but was not addicted. At times, and in particular over the last two years, he drank excessively and had a tendency to take excessive doses of any drug.

"Since his discharge from the Priory, he had been on Tryptizol, fifty milligrams at night, and Carbrital, two capsules, with a repeat of one capsule if necessary. I gave a prescription for two weeks' supply of this drug on 26 July." Epstein failed to keep an appointment with Dr. Flood on August 3 and was offered another one on August 5, which he could not accept. Dr. Flood went on holiday the following week.

Dr. Flood told the coroner that Brian had "always shown some signs of emotional instability." "The patient was homosexual," he added, "but had been unable to come to terms with this problem."

Recording a verdict of accidental death, the Westminster coroner, Mr. Gavin Thurston, said Brian Epstein's death was due to poisoning by Carbrital, caused by an incautious self-overdose.

The inquest verdict was unequivocal, and to many of Brian's friends it was strangely reassuring that there were no mysterious circumstances surrounding his death. Yet there remains, his mother Queenie agrees, a "mystique" around the events during his last weekend. There are questions nagging away, unanswered: Why did he drive to London after dinner, so late, from his country home? Were boredom, and a need for excitement in London, enough to prompt him to return, unscheduled, from the country? Since he had specifically and enthusiastically invited two senior colleagues to his retreat, what restlessness fired him to drive away into the night, back to the solitude of his London house? That impromptu act alone was strangely out of character for a man whose every move was planned, often in microscopic detail.

The answers are bound up in the enigma of a man whose life's journey had often zigzagged unpredictably, uncharacteristically, infuriatingly, but once with world-shattering prescience. Only six years earlier, as a smooth, successful Liverpool businessman who attended classical music concerts, he had gone off at a tangent, immersing himself in a rock 'n' roll cellar. People who knew him shook their heads in disbelief. But with such alien company, he would quickly change the world. To onlookers, his behavior was as bizarre then as it was in the thirty-six hours preceding his death.

Brian Epstein enjoyed taking people by surprise.

2

□

PRIDE

"A LOVELY BOSS, A PERFECT GENTLEMAN"

"TODAY, MY LOCKS WILL FALL." It was not the direct manner in which most of his fellow boarders at Wrekin College announced their impending haircut. But Brian Epstein did not consider himself "one of the gang." Quietly but steadfastly, he carved for himself a reputation as an individualist.

It was Brian's ninth school when he arrived there at the age of thirteen, and it was to be his final lap. Wrekin, founded in 1880, was a traditional British public school (for 340 boys). Just before Brian's arrival, it had been run as a virtual fortress of strict discipline, but Brian benefited from the more liberal policies of a fairly new headmaster, the Reverend Guy Pentreath, who discouraged the false sense of rivalry among the various school "houses." The new head felt strongly that there had been too much emphasis on sport and not enough attention paid to the arts—music would be encouraged. The school buildings were repainted. But firm rules remained and boys were caned for misdemeanors. Theoretically, it should have been a natural environment for Brian, who was academically weak, disliked sport, and enjoyed drama and music. But the school's wind of change blew too slowly for him.

17

He joined Wrekin in January 1948. Only one other boy, a mild-mannered conformist named Brian Johnson, began on the same day, and Brian was placed into Bayley House with him. Brian lost no time in correcting all sixty boys in his house on the pronunciation of his name: "Not Epst*ine*, Epst*een*," he said curtly. The masters addressed the boys by their surnames; occasionally, as a mark of endearment, a nickname was invented: Johnson became "Johnny" and Epstein, "Eppy," which raised a half smile from him.

The new policy of comparative freedom was not tangible enough for Brian. He disliked the cloistered life, the unrelenting formality, and what he saw as the pretentiousness of Wrekin. He despised the school uniform of black jacket and gray trousers, and though he wasn't lazy, other boys recall him as disinterested in studies. If he didn't think a subject was worth his time, he would hold out against it, even at the risk of alienating the masters. Letters home to his parents, while tolerant of the place, gave the feeling that he was marking time until his education ended. At the school he trod a lonely path and was marked out by others as the iconoclast.

Sunday evenings were devoted to model making. For an hour and a half, boys were encouraged to try their hand at doing something constructive. Alone among the boys of Bayley House, Brian often flatly refused to take part: "Oh, I can't build model aeroplanes!" Instead, he wrote a manuscript on the theater, for which he was soundly rebuked by the master, "Jacko" Frost. To other boys, Brian remarked on the school's comparative disinterest in the arts and music; he thought it was far too science-oriented. To emphasize his point, he wrote an allegorical story about the school, which was passed around. It had an almost biblical tone: "In the beginning there were two gates. One was labelled 'Sports' and the other was labelled 'Arts.' And the citizens were forced through one gate whereas they wanted to go through another. . . ." It was severely frowned upon by the headmaster and by Brian's housemaster.

Despite his individualism, or perhaps because of it, he was popular among the boys. Peter Ward, who was in Bayley House with Brian, recalls Sunday afternoon record sessions with an old wind-up gramophone in one of the temporary classrooms at the college. "We played mostly hits from the 1940s and discussed the artists in detail. Brian would speak proudly of the Jewish contribution to music."

Brian seemed acutely aware of his faith when he arrived at Wrekin. He was apprehensive about having a clergyman as headmaster. Although he attended morning prayers, he excused himself from the Sunday morning services. Once, Brian Johnson asked him for a piece of his chocolate. Epstein gave him a small piece. "Oh, you old Jew!" said Johnson. Epstein swiftly turned it around: "And *you* are a *Christian*!" The sharp rejoinder made Johnson contemplate his pointless jibe.

On the sports field Brian was conspicuously hopeless. The masters and some of the boys criticized his lack of involvement in what they called "manly pursuits." His response was to be the most immaculately turned-out player on the field. After most games, there were fourteen filthy, mud-splattered boys and one sartorial delight: Brian, as elegant as when the match began, even his rugby bootlaces still gleaming white. He was mocked for this but took it all stoically. "I never heard him speak ill of anyone, even his persecutors," says one former classmate.

He used after-shave (called "scent" in those years) and rode out the taunts he received: in 1948 it was not usual for a fifteen-year-old to use it. He spent an inordinate amount of time combing his hair in the changing room and debating whether he needed a haircut. The general pattern was to be "massacred" by Dodds, the school barber. When he went to Dodds, he made sure the haircut met his definite demands. Often, Epstein chose to circumvent the school system. Only prefects had the privilege of going into town to have their hair cut, but Brian, never a prefect, often took a chance and went to town to have his locks styled privately.

Pupils remarked to each other about how Epstein shone on the school stage. Peter Ward remembers directing a play, J. M. Barrie's *The Will,* in which Epstein played an important role. "It won him a part in *Christopher Columbus,* in which he played a cardinal, much to the amusement of all of us who knew of his Jewish background." Brian's penchant for drama made him the nightly storyteller of the dormitory, which he shared with fourteen other boys. When the boys became tired of fooling around, they would elect a speaker for the night and Epstein was the favorite: his love of the theater and his exceptional knowledge of the cinema gave him a fund of stories.

In and out of the classroom, he was continually sketching fashions.

"He was interminably drawing New Look styles," says one old Wrekinian, recalling the ambitious women's styles of the postwar years.

He had arrived at Wrekin College after a bumpy and traumatic pattern of education. "He just did not like school from the start," says his mother.

❏

Queenie Hyman, aged eighteen, married Harry Epstein, aged twenty-nine, at the synagogue on Wilson Road, Sheffield, on September 6, 1933. The couple had met while on holiday at Saint Anne's on the Sea. The wedding also marked the union of two industrious and flourishing furniture firms. Harry worked with his father Isaac in the shop, which the latter had opened in Walton Road, Liverpool, in 1901, as a penniless immigrant. Queenie's family owned the Sheffield Cabinet Company, whose most commercial product, the Clarendon bedroom suite, adorned thousands of British homes.

Queenie was bookish, a shy young girl beginning a fervent interest in the arts, books, music, and the theater. Harry, like so many sons of Jewish immigrants, assiduously applied himself to his lifelong role of ensuring that his Polish father's tenaciously developed business continued to thrive and expand. He became a highly successful furniture retailer when he and Queenie moved to Liverpool upon their marriage. They immediately moved into a newly built house in the suburb of Childwall.

The well-detached property at 197 Queens Drive into which Brian was born was spacious and comfortable. Opposite open fields in an area known as Childwall Five Ways, the Epstein house had five bedrooms and two bathrooms. Twin neatly cropped lawns fronted the marble porch steps, while at the rear of the house was a 100-foot-long garden, with a garage alongside. Inside, the heavy oak-paneled walls gave off a feeling of well-constructed opulence, and a huge, handsome stained-glass mural—colored maroon, green, and blue—overlooked and dominated the landing. In observation of Jewish law, on the doorpost of each room rested a small mezuzah, the wood-encased scroll of the Jewish law, that Brian's grandfather Louis Hyman had provided to mark his daughter's new home.

Off the hall was the morning room, where Brian would in later years sit with John Lennon planning the Beatles' future. In the spacious lounge, the Epstein family would host a morning cocktail party for Paul McCartney on his twenty-first birthday, on the same historic day when the fighting between Lennon and disc jockey Bob Wooler erupted. From the lounge, casement windows led to the garden with its weeping willow tree and lupins.

Upstairs, off to the right, was Brian's bedroom, which overlooked Queens Drive. Here, as a teenager, he kept the room tidy and immaculate, enjoying his high-fidelity audio system, records, and radio. His conservative family were startled when he asked for the walls of the room to be painted purple; it was duly done.

❑

At the Greenbank Drive Synagogue, Harry was a respected, energetic member of the congregation and became a warden. His first son, Brian Samuel, was born on September 19, 1934, at a private nursing home at 4 Rodney Streey, Liverpool, the city's medical equivalent to Harley Street, London. The birth brought Harry and Queenie enormous pride: there was now an heir apparent to the family company. Brian was born on Yom Kippur, the Jewish Day of Atonement, the holiest holiday in the religious calendar.

In a city with high unemployment, Brian lived in comparative affluence and a family atmosphere of unabashed comfort. When Brian was six months old, a live-in nanny arrived. Quickly, Alma Johnson noted that he was a determined child, spotless in his hygiene and dress and, unusual for a baby, rarely crying. According to Alma, "Even as a toddler, playing games in the garden and getting grubby, he'd immediately want to be clean." He was impish, once throwing a young girl's toy pram into a lake. He disliked his nanny's authority. Once when he misbehaved on a bus, she made him get off and walk home. He sulked and walked away from her. "But he never bore malice. It was all over very quickly for him."

His only brother, Clive John, was born twenty-two months after Brian. There were early signs of differences in the brothers' makeup; Brian was difficult to get out of bed in the morning, while Clive was awake and alert at the prescribed times. As toddlers, Brian was demonstrative, Clive better organized, more precise in his dress. "It was Brian who went to school with one sock hanging down, never Clive," says Queenie, reflecting on Brian's switch to a fastidious appearance later in his life. Friends, relatives, and helpers of the Epsteins sagely predicted that Brian would be an actor, because he was so fond of dressing up humorously. Clive, it was forecast, would take over the family business.

At the age of five, just before the Epstein family moved to Southport at the outbreak of war, his mother noticed a squint in Brian's right eye when he was reading. He had an operation to correct it and was "eternally grateful" that this had been done. However, relatives and family friends noticed that a slight imperfection became visible when he was under stress.

When war broke out in 1939, the family evacuated briefly to Prestatyn in North Wales, where Brian went to nursery school. Returning to Liverpool, he went to the kindergarten of Beechenhurst College near the family home. Then, starting in 1940, came a three-year evacuation during which when Harry and Queenie rented a home in Southport as sanctuary from the pounding Liverpool was taking from Hitler's bombs. In the comparative calm of the sedate seaside resort, Brian went to two schools, Southport College and then Croxton, a preparatory school at which he was joined by his brother. Brian registered firmly with his parents and with Alma Johnson that he disliked the Southport schools.

With the war nearly over and the family back in Liverpool, ten-year-old Brian passed a test for entry into Liverpool College, a fee-paying school with high academic standards. He was rapidly convinced that there was an anti-Semitic strain running through it. His parents believed him when the school insisted on Brian's attendance on Saturday mornings, the Jewish Sabbath, when he often went with his father to the synagogue. "They were so adamant and made such a fuss that we thought it best for Brian's sake that he went," recalls Queenie. "But we didn't like it." He was already building up too long a list of schools in his young life, they reasoned.

"What we took as the rough knocks of kids growing up, he took very individually, very personally," remembers Brian Wolfson, a Jew who attended Liverpool College alongside Epstein. "I would not have described the culture of the school as anti-Semitic, but there were six hundred boys, half a dozen Catholics, twenty-five Jews. Life wasn't easy. Everybody regarded him as overtly sensitive, not a very athletic kid, slightly introverted. Not one of the boys; very much a loner.

Knowing him later, I could see the hell he must have gone through as he was growing up."

In his work, he did well in art and English, was consistently weak in arithmetic and the sciences. His parents were not surprised when told, after nearly a year, that he would have to work much harder to remain at Liverpool College. Finally, they received a letter saying that Brian would have to leave. During a math lesson, said the headmaster, he had done a suggestive drawing of dancing girls. Brian contended that it was a theater program in which females were essential; there was nothing obscene about it. But the rift between him and the school was widening, anyway. "We begged them to give him a chance," says Queenie. "He had improved his work in the year he was with them. But they would not hear of it. There was another Jewish boy there having trouble. . . ." Brian left with the firm conviction that his Jewish faith was at the root of the school's complaint.

With his parents now brooding about the problem of their eldest son's school life, Brian went temporarily to Wellesley School, Aigburth. He said the nearby excellent shops were of more benefit to his education than the teaching. "We did not know what to believe," says his mother, "because it was by then part and parcel of Brian's makeup to moan about school."

In Childwall, an area heavily populated by high-income Jews, Queenie ran a kosher home. On Friday nights Queenie lit the Sabbath candles and Harry said prayers; in the kitchen the milk and meat dishes were separated, as were the cutlery and crockery. Jewish dietary rules were observed. On Sundays, Brian and Clive attended cheder at the family synagogue, both for religious studies and to learn Hebrew in preparation for their bar mitzvah at the age of thirteen.

Queenie and Harry decided the damage done at Liverpool College would best be corrected by sending Brian to a Jewish school. Searching through the *Jewish Chronicle*, which arrived each week, Queenie found Beaconsfield School at Frant, Sussex—a £180-a-year boys' boarding school. She reluctantly agreed when Clive insisted on joining his brother there. "Having both boys away together was horrible. I spent my week writing letters and sending tuck parcels," recalls Queenie.

Brian and Clive were soon joined by a younger boy, Malcolm Shifrin, who lived opposite them at 204 Queens Drive. Coincidentally, Shifrin's father was a furniture manufacturer who sold goods to Harry

Epstein. The two men did business together and attended the same synagogue.

At Beaconsfield the signs were that Brian could at last settle into a more stable pattern of education. The school was not an academic hothouse. It tended to nurture the boys in the subjects they naturally liked—in Brian's case, art and drama. He loved horseback riding lessons and chose a book called *Equitation* when he gained a prize for his talent in art. (His parents bought him a horse, which stayed in Liverpool for his return home during school holidays.) Nor was Beaconsfield strongly Jewish: Hebrew was not on the curriculum and most of the staff were Christians. There was a small school synagogue with Friday night services, half in Hebrew and half in English. The new state of Israel was established during Brian's stay at Beaconsfield, on May 15, 1948—a cause for much celebration.

The school tended toward liberal Judaism, and coming from an orthodox family, Brian felt that such an approach clashed with his idealism. On visits home, he was beginning to mildly berate his parents for driving and working on Saturdays. "Either we should do it all properly or not bother. It's hypocritical," he said. Beaconsfield School compounded his irritation by teaching him the wrong portion of the Torah for his bar mitzvah reading.

"When I arrived at Beaconsfield, Brian was quite a personality," his brother recalled. Brian had a good singing voice and was in the school choir—"I don't know why he didn't do anything with the voice." Throughout Brian's school years, Clive was aware of his brother's interest in art. Brian's bedroom chest of drawers was stuffed with books featuring his drawings. "I remember going in to look at them when he was away," said Clive. "They were very modern, all sorts of objects at obscure angles which I'm sure were great ideas. But being younger and totally disinterested in art, I just didn't have the ability to appreciate them."

When Brian joined the cheder (Judaism and Hebrew tuition school) at the Greenbank Drive Synagogue at age nine, the Reverend Samuel Wolfson was superintendent. Discipline was strict. "But I never had to use the stick on him or detain him in class. Harry had instilled in him good discipline, respect, behavior." He was mature beyond his years, inclined to seek the company of boys a few years older. And the Reverend Wolfson observed a penchant for theatricality. "Brian was a good actor with natural talent. At various Jewish festivals like Hanukkah and Purim when we had plays, I always gave him a good part because I knew he would go down well. Even when he was ten, it was clear he would be a *somebody*. He was going to make a name for himself. He did not like to be left out of anything. He stood out as *promising something*."

When the minister discovered that Brian's bar mitzvah training at Beaconsfield was focusing on the wrong portion of the Torah, he decided that a crash course in Liverpool was essential. "He rose to it," says the minister. "At his bar mitzvah he was a bit of an actor. He enjoyed showing everybody he was the man of the moment." After the service there was a family party for a hundred guests at Queens Drive. In his eloquent speech, delivered with theatrical gestures, Brian thanked his parents, in the traditional manner, for supporting and encouraging him.

"If you saw Brian Epstein in cheder, you'd consider him a very nice-looking English Jew, certainly no dunce," says the Reverend Wolfson. "As he got older, the children of his class were not up to his standard. He was popular." As part of their bar mitzvah gifts, Harry enrolled Brian and Clive into the synagogue as members in their own rights.

Even at thirteen, says his Hebrew teacher, it was obvious that Brian had a fertile mind. "Harry wanted Brian and Clive to make their way and not suffer poverty." When the Beatles became world-famous, the Liverpool Jewish community was filled with pride that a local boy was the group's mentor. It was the talk of the Greenbank Drive Synagogue in the early 1960s.

Although Brian was happy in his two years at Beaconsfield, a streak of sadism in the school discipline concerned him and all the boys. The cane was freely used. Those in trouble would be beaten and later their welts would be inspected. One distressed twelve-year-old, who came from a broken home, sucked his thumb: he was made to suck a dummy all day and caned if it was not in his mouth. The proximity of boys sleeping in the same dormitory at the age of awakening sexual awareness was a matter under constant surveillance by the staff. "Teenage homosexuality was widely practiced but was routed out and punished," recalls Malcolm Shifrin. "The most vicious thing I remember was when two boys were found to be involved in mutual masturbation one night. They were actually brought down into the head's drawing room, and the senior classes had to gather round in a circle and watch them caned with their trousers down. I'm convinced Brian was in that dormitory."

"When I first arrived at Beaconsfield," says Clive, "Brian was quite a personality, rated as unusually interesting by his friends there, Martin Rose and Martin Green. For a prep school boy, he thought a great deal more about the lessons, and the value of them, than most of us. When a subject interested him, like art, his application to it was diligent. When he was bored, you could see his mind straying."

With his time completed at Beaconsfield, Brian was firmly pulling towards art and drama. His English was passable but there were problems in almost all other subjects. He clearly needed an arts-based senior school. Although he took the Common Entrance examination for entry to a senior school, his marks were moderate. His parents tried to get him accepted at three public schools—Repton, Clifton, and Rugby—to no avail. Temporarily, they settled on Clayesmore, near Taunton. Within one term Brian was writing letters home, groaning. "He positively loathed it," says Queenie. Finally, after an impressive interview, he went to Wrekin.

Clive arrived at Wrekin a year after Brian, giving him a sense of pride—and the necessity for protecting his young brother. Brian Johnson recalls that within a few weeks of Clive's arrival, Brian said, "Listen, Johnny, the terrible thing is that my brother is totally innocent. He's with that crew in the dormitory—a terrible crowd. Will you help me? We've got to tell him the facts of life." The two Brians sat Clive down in the privacy of the football equipment store and explained to him how babies were born.

The atmosphere at Wrekin did not encourage sexual discussion. In those years, sex was only obliquely referred to in a biology lesson. "It was a male society under pressure because of disciplines around it and the fact that we couldn't go off anywhere other than the school without a pass," says Johnson. As his choice of newspaper or magazine, one boy opted for one on sex and psychology but this was frowned upon by the house master. "Unquestionably there was a certain amount of homosexual activity," says Johnson. The conditions bred it. "The authorities were aware of it, I think, and there was a good deal of strictness to make sure that older boys didn't get together with smaller boys in dormitories. The staff kept their eyes open for it."

In the dining room, however, the boys would debate the physical desirability of the waitresses, young girls from the town. And Epstein was among those who ogled. "He never struck me as being anything other than a person wholesomely interested in the female body," says Johnson.

Epstein's passion for art encouraged him to attend an optional extra class on Tuesday nights. "He was talented in oils and watercolors and also liked sculpture," recalls another student, Keith Arnold. His theatrical flair reached a peak when he produced the school play about Christopher Columbus, showing his imaginative use of scenery and lighting effects. "I realized this was the direction his life would take," says Arnold. "Brian's contribution to school plays showed his style and taste. He had administrative ability, too, and a pleasant way of getting people to do things for him. You did it because you liked Brian." That ability to generate respect was to be a touchstone of Brian's life.

At Wrekin, Brian reluctantly joined the army's Combined Cadet Force. He also became interested in studying the Roman Catholic religion but did not pursue it in any way; increasingly, it seemed that secularism would be his conviction.

❏

Brian wrote home conscientiously every week. One letter astonished his parents. Brian wrote about his career sardonically but with serious undertones. Entering the ministry did not interest him and neither did becoming a law student. He wasn't sure about becoming a businessman of any kind, but he would like to be a dress designer. He was, after all, consistently at the top of his class in art.

To Harry, schooled in diligent, no-nonsense retailing by an immigrant father who had toiled for success, it was too arty to even warrant discussion. Still, he conceded to Queenie, it was a well-written letter; he could see Brian meant it, although he could not comprehend it as a job. Brian's mother, more sympathetic to her son's creative leanings, understood better but thought it impractical: "We had friends in the fashion business but they were no Christian Diors! We weren't very enamored with his idea. Brian was being reared in a business atmosphere, and if his grandparents thought their grandson was going to be a dress designer in those years . . ."

On a visit home, Brian reiterated his interest. Still, Harry was baffled. The thought of his son becoming a professional artist of any description was incomprehensible. "Harry had visions of him drawing on the pavement," says Queenie. At Wrekin, Brian Johnson could see Brian's point more logically: he was a compulsive sketcher of fashions. Several boys believed he was a budding Norman Hartnell. In hindsight, it might have been Brian's correct route. But in 1950 traditional Jewish families with flourishing businesses gave sons fewer chances to assert themselves. They were expected to uncomplainingly follow their father's footsteps in the interest of heredity and security.

In his letter home, Brian tactfully added that if he could not pursue a career as a dress designer or an artist, he would join his father's firm. Although inwardly he was groaning, he reasoned that it was a quick route out of education. Harry would have preferred Brian to stay at school longer, but since his ultimate ideal was to have both sons work alongside him, he agreed to Brian's plea that he be allowed to leave Wrekin at term's end in autumn of 1950.

And so, with no School Certificate (the description in those years for basic academic achievement), the boy who was nearly sixteen left the school he would later describe as "the Wrekin I hate," and on September 10, 1950, he reported for duty at I. Epstein and Sons, run by Isaac with Harry, in Walton Road, Liverpool.

Brian's artistic streak was quickly stifled by his being thrust into the world of business. While Clive remained at Wrekin to excel as a scholar, Harry decided to instill strict working discipline in his elder son. Brian was expected to get to work by 9 a.m. and apply himself fastidiously to stock-checking, furniture display, and sales duties. Grandfather Isaac set a fearsome display of tenacity, sometimes arriving at the shop at 6 a.m.

But the boy who always enjoyed good food and creature comforts decided to make the best of it. His natural charm and impeccable modulation quickly became assets. He persuaded a woman who went into the shop to buy a mirror that what she really needed was a £12 dining table. He rapidly made his mark as a successful salesman; his father believed that both he and Brian had made the correct decision.

Inspired by finding a niche at last, Brian began to assert himself, introducing revolutionary displays of furniture into the windows. The existing ones were disorganized and cluttered, he said. They needed "air to breathe" and should look more natural, he told his father; to attract window-shoppers, the windows should look like living rooms. He rearranged the chairs and tables accordingly.

Grandfather Isaac, who had achieved good profits through straight-forward retailing, would tolerate no such creative revolution. You don't interfere radically with a successful operation, he lectured Harry. Three generations with different ideas were set to clash. So Brian's father decided that his son needed a touch of independence in his training. After two years of fragile relationships at Walton Road, during which Brian had confirmed his aptitude for salesmanship, Harry arranged for him to take a six-month apprenticeship at Times Furnishing in Lord Street, Liverpool.

There he shone. His perfect manner was praised and his originality in window displays welcomed. He was the most elegantly dressed of all the staff and proud of the impact he was making on his seniors. They gave Harry perfect reports on his progress. His salary was an adequate £5 a week. His parents were delighted that at last his life seemed purposeful: he even began taking lessons at home in French and Spanish.

Outwardly, it seemed a time of rehabilitation, but privately, he was uneasy. "I didn't like being at home, being dependent," Brian later told Kenneth Harris in the *Observer*. "I didn't like the atmosphere of middle-class commercialism. Nothing wrong with it. I just didn't like it. But I didn't know quite *why* I didn't like it."

His social life began to thrive, however. Now an affluent and debonair eighteen-year-old, he was perhaps Liverpool's best-dressed bachelor. His thick hair was styled at the Horne Brothers salon, his clothes came from the top tailors, and he found himself popular among girls. He blushed in their company. He mixed in largely Jewish circles, enjoyed the animated company of people his own age at parties and in restaurants and bars.

He established an easy rapport with a neighbor and friend of his father's: Rex Makin, at 199 Queens Drive. Eight years older than Brian, he had an intuitive grasp of the growing pains Brian was experiencing. A Jew who was to become one of Liverpool's most prominent solicitors, the intense Rex Makin had business and religious

links with Harry. Rex was president of the Stapley Home for Aged
Jews in Liverpool and Harry the treasurer. "I think Brian always regarded me as a big brother," reflects Makin. "We had an emotional
affinity. He was a handsome young man, well dressed. Very, very
temperamental. He warmed to me and I warmed to him. Perhaps we
were on the same wavelength. I was very, very fond of Brian. I wasn't
on the same wavelength as Clive.

"Brian was artistic, temperamental, volatile, mercurial, flamboyant.
He didn't fit into his background. That was his tragedy. He talked to
me regularly, and when I got engaged, he wrote me a lovely letter.
He was a very sensitive human being, and in a strange, esoteric way,
my vibrations and Brian's coincided.

"Their father, Harry, was not particularly highbrow. He was a warm,
jolly, fun-loving person who couldn't understand, perhaps, that Brian
was not of the same ilk. But that was never a problem. Every father
loves his son, and to Harry, Brian was always a shining angel no matter
what trouble Brian may have caused him." Harry rejoiced in Brian's
eventual success, although his own favorite music came from the Bing
Crosby era.

Makin adds somberly: "Harry took *nachas* [Yiddish for heartfelt
pride and pleasure] from Brian. He was very supportive of his son.
Harry was a good man. Queenie is a good woman. They couldn't
understand Brian." Occasionally arrogant and rude, Brian "pursued
paths of which I did not approve . . . and he drank too much," Makin
ruminates. "Brian resented his background. He was a very talented
person but a misfit in society. I think drink was a solace to him."

❏

The inner conflict in eighteen-year-old Brian received a further jolt
when he was conscripted for National Service. His preference for the
Royal Air Force was rejected, and in December 1952 he was ordered
into the army for the statutory two years. After six weeks of physically
tough basic training in the Royal Army Service Corps in Aldershot,
Private 22739590 Epstein was designated a documentation clerk.
Being in the army was bad enough; he was bitterly disappointed when
he failed tests for officer candidacy. This piece of self-delusion was
incredible. He loathed the army and all its discipline, had no interest
in physical work, yet firmly believed that his background and com-

posure qualified him for officer status. Disliking military discipline, he would have been weak at instilling it in others.

After being switched from the training center to a "permanent" posting at Taunton, Somerset, he systematically nagged away at his superiors for a more interesting location. Finally, he secured an enviable move to Albany Barracks, Regents Park, London. There, at least, he could pay evening and weekend off-duty visits to his London aunts and uncles. When he arrived, he began a ritual that was to last for his entire period in the army. Every week he telephoned Aunt Frida and Uncle Berrel to inquire who was hosting the traditional Friday night eve-of-Sabbath dinner. "Where are services being held this week?" became Brian's set question—and a family joke.

He was particularly close to his older cousin Peter, grumbling to him about life in the army. In military training he was disastrous, turning right when ordered to go left and once falling over on the parade ground when his platoon came to a halt; in clerical duties, however, he was predictably well-organized and competent.

To Brian, as to all other eighteen-year-olds at that time, National Service was an appalling irrelevance, an imposition on his time. Resenting his role of servility, he was a misfit from the start. "He hated the regimentation," says Queenie. "Brian loved his comforts too much to be in any kind of institutional situation." Apart from the proximity to his family, the only redeeming feature of the daily boredom was that, being stationed in London, he was able to visit the West End regularly for access to the latest plays and films. During these theatrical forays, Private Epstein cut his usual sartorial dash: bowler hat, pinstriped suit, an umbrella. It was hardly the appearance of a private, more that of an off-duty officer.

One Friday, Brian enjoyed the traditional eve-of-Sabbath dinner with Aunt Frida in Marylebone Road, so, again, he was dressed to the nines. His cousins Raymond and Peter drove him the short journey back to the barracks. As he left the car and strode into camp, the sentry, believing his dress to be that of an officer, saluted him. Then the guard commander saluted him. Two private soldiers jerked their heads in the dutiful eyes-right movement accorded an officer, and finally, a clerk on duty in the office said, "Good night, sir."

An officer on duty, however, saw the unmistakable face of Private Epstein. "You will report to Company Office at ten o'clock in the morning, charged with impersonating an officer," he told Epstein. Brian was flabbergasted. It was a trumped-up charge, but such was the speed of the army discipline machine that he was confined to barracks for a week. Not the first time he had fallen afoul of army authority and lost his privileges, it was nevertheless a savage blow, for Brian's tolerance of army life rested on the thread of being able to visit his relatives and wander around London.

The incident did not end there. He was sent for medical and psychiatric tests and finally, after ten months in the army, was told that he would be discharged immediately. After seeing that Brian's nerves had become frayed, the doctors deemed him "emotionally and mentally unfit" for continued service.

The bizarre ejection not only gave him freedom but was softened by the army's reference, his discharge certificate describing him as "a conscientious and hardworking clerk who uses his initiative and can in every respect be depended upon to see a job through satisfactorily without supervision. Of smart appearance and sober habits at all times, he is utterly trustworthy."

In his own words, Brian "ran like a hare" for the train from Euston to Lime Street station. It was January 27, 1954.

❏

Returning to the sanctuary of Liverpool had compensations. At home, his parents had installed a telephone in each of their sons' bedrooms to enhance their privacy. Brian resumed his role as one of the city's charming young sophisticates, noted for his meticulous grooming and gentle voice. He bought classical music records every week, building up a big collection in the cabinet made specially for him at Queenie's father's factory in Sheffield.

And his father's business was flourishing. Harry decided that the pianos and sheet music sold in the North End Music Stores, an annex to his furniture store, should be augmented by records. Who better to mastermind this challenge than his artistic son, who had a strong knowledge of classical music? It would restore a sense of purpose in Brian after the miserable army experience.

The idea was an instant success, the enthusiasm Brian brought to salesmanship being quickly reflected in the turnover. Soon he took charge of another part of Harry's expanding operations: Clarendon Furnishing in Hoylake. He obviously had a creative talent, thought his father. Let him make it work in the more aesthetically conscious part of Merseyside, rather than in hardheaded Liverpool. Again Brian triumphed. He imported "New Elizabethan" furniture from London and showcased it imaginatively. In the postwar years, adventurous salesmanship was particularly welcome in comparatively affluent Cheshire. The Hoylake operation was profitable within a year.

Harry was delighted that his wayward son was at last showing signs of settling down, and enjoying the challenge of the Hoylake shop. To Queenie, Brian was beautiful and dutiful. She always knew, she told Harry, that his good eye for artistic things would bring rewards. His sensitivity and thoughtfulness towards his mother showed every week when he took her rum truffles from Thornton's, the confectioner next door to the North End Music Stores.

Brian's enthusiasm for riding horses, which had begun at Beaconsfield School, proved common ground with his father, who enjoyed an occasional "flutter" and a day at the races. Occasionally they went together to Chester or Liverpool races, where Harry was impressed with Brian's judgment of horses in the paddock. There were also occasional visits to a tennis club, a holiday romance with a girl named Joan Starkey during a family visit to Torquay, and a welcome return to dinner dates in the Cheshire countryside. Brother Clive was now in the Royal Army Education Corps and with his usual diligence had become a sergeant.

Brian had dozens of acquaintances but few close friends. His unease and shyness were always evident at family celebrations and parties. He enjoyed the event itself but was visibly uncomfortable mingling among large crowds, a trait that would linger. Yet his largesse was evident from an early age: at nineteen he gave his book-loving mother, as a birthday present, an annual subscription to Harrods book department, which continued all his life. He enjoyed giving gifts regularly: cuff links to his father, a gold and diamond brooch to his mother, castanets to a neighbor's children after a Spanish holiday. He was a giver who intensely disliked bearing bad or sad news.

His clandestine life as a homosexual troubled him deeply. But he decided there was no alternative but to confront his family and tell them frankly. In what must have been the toughest moment of his life, he chose a Friday night after dinner with his parents and Clive at Queens Drive.

"He told us and I went right up to him and hugged him," says Queenie. Then Brian ran to his bedroom. Harry and Clive were shocked, Queenie less so because, with a mother's intuition, she had had her suspicions for some time. She had never been able to forget her discomfort when, on a holiday in the South of France, during the time that Brian was a student at Wrekin College, the family went to a bar and she got "an uncanny, horrible feeling" about Brian's interests.

Nevertheless, it was "quite a shock," says Queenie. "The night after I went to talk to Brian, Harry went to him. I don't know what transpired, but Harry couldn't quite accept it in the way I did. Harry thought too much fuss was made of it. He said: 'Well, if anybody is heterosexual, they don't talk about having sex all the time. But if you're the other way, it seems to be the main thing in life.'"

After that tearful night, Brian found particular solace in talking regularly to his understanding mother about his inner self. Queenie was the only one who could engage him in therapeutic conversation; the rest of his family were off-limits. "He talked to me. In fact, when he came home I used to prepare to spend the whole night talking to Brian. He arrived perhaps for dinner and would talk to his father about everything, then his father would go to bed and I would spend the whole night talking to Brian, mostly over this subject. What I didn't know about it I read up." She has no doubt that his secret years of homosexuality affected his character and made him "very mixed up." She says: "He wasn't at all happy with it; his love affairs were disastrous. I used to say: 'Honestly, Brian, why can't you find somebody congenial to spend your life with?' I meant a man. I was sure he could find happiness. But he was so unhappy."

Brian's private life scarred him with guilt, although this was rarely apparent. Always impeccably discreet, he appeared to many girls a most eligible bachelor; others, more knowing, sarcastically dubbed him "The Immaculate Deception." Still, he usually seemed comfortable in female company. His frequent blushing could be traced to his lifelong shyness rather than to any self-consciousness about his sexuality. In those years, too, homosexuality was illegal.

He never allowed his nocturnal pursuits to affect his attitude towards work. He was fast developing his grandfather and father's devotion and total commitment to industriousness. His working patterns were punctual and well organized, while his flair for adventurous stock impressed the staid furniture retailers. He seldom mixed business with pleasure. But on a visit to a furniture exhibition in London with Malcolm Shifrin, whose father worked in the same field, Brian did persuade his heterosexual friend to go with him to the Mandrake, a gay club.

❑

Brian's next significant move was fired by an attitude central to his life: As soon as any activity had succeeded or peaked in his mind, Brian became bored. Despite exceptional success as a furniture retailer in his father's new shop at Hoylake, he was restless. The embryonic artist inside him had refused to lie down. He released this creative tension in regular visits to the Liverpool Playhouse, where he would sit in the front row of the stalls admiring and analyzing the excellent repertory players rather than the plot—and wishing he were onstage with them. Just as he had befriended the musicians of the Philharmonic, Brian felt he had to get close to the action at the Playhouse. He particularly admired the warm and vivacious Helen Lindsay, then a rising actress of twenty-five. One night after appearing in a loud comedy, *Sabrina Fair,* she received a courteous note. It displayed more élan than most congratulatory letters from members of the audience. Simply, it said how enjoyable her performance had been, and could the writer please take her out for a drink? Signed, in flowery but distinguished style: Brian Epstein.

Slightly taken aback, Helen went down from her dressing room to be confronted by a formally dressed young man who exuded good manners but clearly seemed reticent. "The first impression I had of Brian Epstein I always kept," she says. "Tremendous shy dignity. He had his head slightly on one side, a tendency to look down rather than boldly forward: very, very sweet.

"What endeared him to me straightaway was a quality of direct sincerity. I didn't think for one minute that he was a creep or trying to waste my time. He wasn't a stage-door Johnny."

Declaring that he was a regular visitor to the Playhouse, Brian said he wanted to discuss the play and asked Helen a little about her work. Could he meet her again? Next day he sent her flowers. She agreed to afternoon tea at Fuller's cafe; it would be the first of many such meetings.

Epstein soon found that he had an addiction to the theater. He went, usually alone, to all the Playhouse productions and was so enthralled by *Hamlet* that he went seven times during the play's three-week run. He especially admired the young Brian Bedford in the lead role. Helen played Ophelia, and by then Epstein, a regular visitor to her dressing room, was fascinated by the intrigues among the repertory players. Because Bedford had come straight from drama school to the starring role, there was much envy from the others: Bedford was triumphing spectacularly. Epstein asked Helen to please introduce him. "They were the same age and he hero-worshipped Bedford," says the actress.

She was impressed by his courage. "However much he liked acting, to knock on the door as he did and get through to me and Brian Bedford was not easy. We were used to getting rid of hangers-on. But he was *so* different." Very soon, the two Brians and Helen became a regular trio sharing after-theater drinks in the nearby Basnett oyster bar. Bedford knew he was going to be a big star; Epstein, starstruck, enjoyed Bedford's anachronistic sense of humor.

"Brian Epstein was potty about Bedford's performance of Hugo Frederick in *Ring Around the Moon,*" says Helen Lindsay. And Epstein's intensity and ability to dissect the drama were astonishing. "He had a very intelligent understanding of what actors were about. He wanted to know how our minds worked, what ruined a scene, how it could be improved." His observations about Helen's performances were pertinent; he listened carefully to Bedford's analyses after each show; he wanted to know what preparation had gone into Helen and Bedford's "thinking themselves into the skin of another person."

Sincerity and total commitment to a serious friendship made Epstein a Playhouse insider. "He soaked up everything like a sponge," says Helen Lindsay. "We enjoyed his company and became very firmly a trio whose interests and outlook were the same. Brian Epstein was very, very determined to become a part of our magic world." He told them, also, that he was very bored with the monotony of his work as a furniture salesman and was ambitious to go onstage. Would they help him audition for the Royal Academy of Dramatic Art, at which Bedford had studied?

Bedford said to Helen: "I really don't think he is an actor. I doubt if he'll get in." Helen was less dogmatic: "Look, everybody hasn't got *your* burning talent. Alan Bates and Albert Finney came from RADA a couple of years before you, but there must have been a supporting team! He doesn't necessarily have to succeed at that level to join the theater." Even so, she doubted his ability: "I was prepared to help but I didn't think he had an earthly chance. He didn't have an actor's temperament."

Bedford said he could not possibly coach him, but persuaded Helen: "He seems pretty determined. You'll be wonderful at it, darling."

"I thought he was barking up the wrong tree, but he was desperate to get away from that shop," says Helen. She told Epstein: "Although I think you're sweet-looking and charming, you haven't got a leading actor's face. You're not going to get the leading parts." Brian would not be deflected and was typically gracious about Helen's willingness to try to coach him.

At home, Brian broke the news of his acting ambitions to Queenie. When there was an impending crisis, or a potential hazard with his father, Brian confided in his patient mother, who would do her best to win over the sceptical Harry. To Queenie, it was an unexpected move but she continued to identify fully with Brian's artistic trends. To Harry, it was another idiotic scheme dreamed up by his impulsive elder son, and just as he was settling down into the rapidly expanding family business. Smoothing his parents' worries, Brian invited Helen Lindsay and Brian Bedford to Sunday afternoon tea with them at Queens Drive.

Helen had a large, sunny flat on the first floor at 61 Hope Street, in Liverpool's bohemian district, overlooking the Anglican Cathedral. Here, every Sunday afternoon over an eight-week period, Brian arrived with flowers or chocolates, planted a kiss on Helen's cheek, and, for about three hours, prepared to enter his dream world.

Brian Bedford and Helen Lindsay knew of Brian's homosexuality, and she was constantly on the lookout for physical manifestations in his early attempts at acting. "It would have to be eradicated if possible, because if it showed in the audition, it would work against him. At that time, there was a different climate of opinion about gays."

Fortunately, Brian was not palpably gay; Helen, in fact, found him "inhibited" on the subject. A much bigger hurdle faced his drama teacher: he was totally unnatural. From the first lesson, Helen thought it would be difficult to get him through an audition. "He just couldn't *move*." Brian was tense and stiff, his movements completely unrelated to his speech. Quickly, Helen decided that he should do as little moving around as possible. He must emphasize his qualities of vulnerability and wistfulness.

"I had a fearful problem trying to figure out some moves that would be natural for him. To stop him from walking like a clockwork soldier. He was erect, but very, very stiff, wooden, self-conscious. His hands were glued to his sides." She worked tirelessly, trying to keep her exasperation down, trying to get him to do basic relaxation exercises. "Loosen up, walk around, touch your toes," she would say. "You must relax, darling. If you don't know what to do with your arms, cross them. And don't stand with the feet together. Put them apart. Keep your movement to a minimum. We'll work on that once they accept you or reject you." It was proving difficult to prevent Brian from physical gestures that had no connection with the speeches. "What *am* I going to do about those arms?" Helen asked herself repeatedly.

Even against mounting negative evidence, the student's ambition could not be curbed. He came to each lesson having learned his lines fully. And he aimed high: Could he go to his audition playing the role of Henry the Fourth or Fifth? he asked Helen.

No, she said firmly. The best chance he had, perhaps the only chance, was to avoid any heroism. Brian had a maturity, a quality of gravity beyond his years, that could be exploited. However insecure he might have been inside, he had dignity. Orally he was fine, with good emphasis, but he did not have the bite or edge in his tone for a major role. Finally, she persuaded him: "You must *not* try to play Hamlet or Romeo or any of the classic parts."

Although Epstein obviously did not have his sights set on becoming an actor in a small repertory company, he agreed that his first objective was to get to RADA; and to do this, he was prepared to submerge his wish for animation. Helen therefore chose for him the Duke of Burgundy's speech at the end of *Henry V*. "I wanted Brian to endow the speech with the weight of the man. He is, after all, a great figure in the French court, much more impressive than the King. And he makes a wonderful speech about the fair and fertile France, trying to reconcile two kingdoms." The scene's quality of benediction would work well for Brian, as would the expression in his clear blue eyes. Their limpidity generated an individual soulfulness.

To the amazement of everyone except the quietly confident Epstein, he passed his audition in London—on his twenty-second birthday, September 19, 1956. Brian was also asked at his audition to read some portions of T. S. Eliot, including an excerpt from *The Confidential Clerk*. He had been privately tested by the director, John Fernald, who coincidentally had formerly run the Liverpool Playhouse.

Burying his sadness once more, Brian's father agreed to pay the academy's fees. He and Queenie bravely waved him goodbye at Lime Street station; Brian left behind the maroon and cream Hillman California car his parents had given him for his twenty-first birthday.

Even his nanny could not understand why he was going to RADA: "If you want to go on the stage, why not be a singer like Frankie Vaughan?"

"No, no," Brian told Alma. "I have to go into acting the *right way*."

Harry repeated his belief that acting was not a "manly" career.

In London Brian sought freedom, acting out the Spartan, independent life of a student after having been so heavily supported by his parents' warmth and generosity. He took a bed-sitter at 83 Inverness Terrace, Bayswater, but Queenie was soon telephoning her family in London to ensure that Brian got good meals regularly. Soon, after scouring advertisements in the *Jewish Chronicle*, Queenie found him better living accommodations with a Jewish lady at 59 Northways, Hampstead, London NW3.

The altercations with his father clearly worried his conscience. Yet he was sure there was no future for him in conventional business or retailing. His feelings of guilt at having virtually fled to RADA were clear in his first letter from the academy, to his brother back in Liverpool:

> Dear Clive,
>   Just a very quick note to apologise for not having written sooner and to let you know that I am settling down quite well.
>   I am very sorry you feel that I am doing the wrong thing but

I want you to understand that knowing how happy it makes M
and D to have me in the business, I would sacrifice my own
ambitions and return tomorrow if I knew of a solution for Daddy
and me to work happily together. But there is apparently no way.
Anyway I do hope that eventually they will feel better about it.
Actually (perhaps naturally) I like it very much here and my
student life is quite exciting.

Frankly I hardly notice the lack of my former comforts.

When are you coming to London?

Hope you are well.
Brian.

At RADA, his contemporaries included names that would one day
shine: Susannah York, Peter Blythe, and Hugh Whitemore. Epstein
was a passive actor not without ability—but clearly not star material.
"Everyone there wanted to be a star," says Judy Coles, another student
at the time. "The standard among men was lower. If he'd been a girl,
he wouldn't have got in, though I wouldn't have said he was bad. He
was correct, wore a suit, whereas other boys were more casually
dressed. He was not extrovert, rather shy, rather like a bank manager.
He was not *obviously* gay as some of the lads were."

"He was always polite, very quiet, rather shy and remote," recalls
Robin Ray, who acted alongside Epstein in *As You Like It*. Brian played
Orlando, while Robin played Oliver. What made Brian different was
that he did not take up with any clique. "He seemed somewhat lonely,
outside it all, with no great enthusiasm for acting or the academy."
On acting ability: "I'd put him very low on the list of students who
were going to make it. He would be hardly a 'probable.' I don't think
it was his buzz at all. But then, RADA could be a very discouraging
place partly because the teachers have decided who will be a star.
Maybe he got a smell and became discouraged," Robin Ray adds. For
whatever reason, Brian was not connected with the mainstream of
academy life.

Surprisingly, he did acquire a steady girlfriend, who was in the same
class of twelve. The adventurously dressed twenty-year-old Joanna
Dunham, a pert, strong personality, was two years younger than Brian
but older and more confident than most of the other girls at RADA.
Recognized by other students as a couple, Brian and Joanna went to
the cinema and art exhibitions together.

Joanna didn't rate Brian's acting potential very high. But she was electrified by his portrayal of Constantin in *The Seagull*. There is a scene where Constantin, after articulating his love and reverence for his mother, is spurned by his lover. He tries to commit suicide but fails, only injuring his forehead. When his mother tries to console him, and is dressing the wound, Constantin goes into a frenzied rage, ripping the bandage off his head.

Brian's immersion in the scene was not merely lifelike, it was frightening. The rehearsal was ordinary. But when it came to the real scene in front of the academy director and others in the class, Joanna says: "It was actually getting rid of something in Brian. I thought: 'Wait, this is not acting.' It was obviously therapeutic to him, slightly frightening to watch." The class was gripped by ten minutes of raw passion. "When Constantin tried to commit suicide, and when he tore the bandage off and raged at his mother, it was all too real," says Joanna. It was, she avers, the high spot of Brian's acting career—probably because he wasn't acting.

Socially, he drank too much. Few RADA students did that: it was the coffee bar era and most days they gathered in a nearby cafe. Brian was not among them. Once, he took Joanna to a party at his cousin Peter's house in Hampstead Garden Suburb. On the way, Brian was swigging from a half bottle of whisky in his pocket. Recalls Joanna: "I was frightfully prissy about it and he got rather drunk at the party. It was frightening, because he slightly changed. He wanted to drive me home but I wouldn't let him. We would have been smashed to pieces. I ran out into the night for a taxi. I thought he had a problem. It certainly turned me off him quite a lot."

Brian never told Joanna of his inner turmoil, and while they were at RADA, she never guessed that he was a homosexual. During their "affectionate friendship," they kissed and held hands. She now reflects that he wanted to tell her everything, "if he felt he wouldn't have shocked me." He wasn't "camp": "There were much campier people at RADA than Brian."

But his work plodded on: he was Proteus in *Two Gentlemen of Verona*, Lilliom in *Lilliom*, the narrator in *The Dynasts*, Posthumus in *Cymbeline*, Lucentio in *The Taming of the Shrew*, Sir Toby in *Twelfth Night*, and David in *Watch on the Rhine*. Just as Helen Lindsay had predicted, he did not secure heavily dramatic roles. His acting stance was indeed "stiff," says Joanna. "I don't think he had much potential. And he realized that."

He also disliked the teachers' discipline. "He resented it, as I did. It was like being at a Victorian primary school. When one of the teachers came in, we all had to stand up and say good morning." At twenty-two, Brian thought he was being made to behave like a young schoolboy, and those miserable days had long gone.

He had told Joanna he hated working in the family furniture business, so she was surprised when he did not arrive for the start of the autumn term in 1957. During his holiday at home, he confessed to his parents that he didn't want to return to London or RADA; he would stay in Liverpool. Another folly had ended. "Although I needed some creative outlet, I realized this wasn't it," he said later. "I was already too much of a businessman to be acting like a student in a duffle coat. And I kept having the feeling that it was rather foolish to throw away the good business career that was obviously on a plate for me, for something so much more insecure.

"My parents' kindness had been wasted [by this Brian meant his father's willingness to pay the fees] and my initiative hadn't come off. There was a sense of let-down, frustration, and only oneself to blame. I'd had my chance to break out. Now I had to accept the result and fit in."

In London, though, he had been able to nourish his growing interest in the world of books, art, drama, music, and the media. When he was not needed at the RADA center in Gower Street, Holborn, Brian had worked part-time as a salesman in the basement section of Ascroft and Dawes, London's first paperback bookshop. Upstairs, a young man also destined for success and fame worked as a salesman: Marty Feldman.

There had been other part-time work at a second-hand bookshop in Moorgate, from which he often joined his cousin Raymond for lunch. "You just couldn't ask Brian if he liked his work in the bookshop," he says. "You could never get deeply into Brian's feelings. He wouldn't answer directly. He'd go quiet, so there'd be no point in asking."

The independence of life away from home, the living in London during the heyday of the coffee bar, had one coincidental offshoot that would shape his life. At one of the drama students' parties he developed a particular affinity with the rock 'n' roll music of American singer

Little Richard, not knowing that within a few years he would be promoting one of his concerts. One of Brian's favorite songs of the period was Little Richard's "Baby Face." (Ironically, Brian would later tell most of his recording artists how much he hated the word "baby" in any song title. It was, he thought, infantile.)

With predictable warmth for a cherished friendship, Brian stayed in touch with Joanna Dunham, sending her flowers on her first nights as she secured success as an actress. Like so many observers of the young man who was now collecting too many failures in his life, Joanna believed that despite his boredom at RADA, Brian had certain qualities that could make him very successful if he found his niche in life.

❑

Despite his evident shyness, there was a hidden assertiveness that Brian desperately wanted to project. He was not prepared to be a *supporting* actor in a small theater company, Helen Lindsay had noted. How lucky he could now return to Liverpool and a new position that his father considered perfect for Brian.

The late 1950s marked the start of the "consumer boom" in electrical goods: television sets, washing machines, and cheaper radios (made possible by the transistor revolution). Harry Epstein decided to expand into this profitable arena. He rented premises in Great Charlotte Street and called them NEMS, the abbreviation for North End Music Stores, which had been an offshoot of the first furniture shop in Walton Road. Brian took charge of the record department, while brother Clive ran the electrical and domestic goods section. Brian was enthusiastic. He even arranged for a star singer, Anne Shelton, to perform the opening ceremony.

He guided the record division into profitability so quickly that Harry was moved to expand even further. A second NEMS shop, with three floors, opened at 12–14 Whitechapel. From Lewis's record department, Brian recruited Peter Brown to manage the Great Charlotte Street shop; he, in turn, would mastermind the new Whitechapel operation. A large crowd gathered for the opening, advertised in the *Liverpool Echo;* this time the performer was a major hit-parade name, singer Anthony Newley.

NEMS at Whitechapel was an instant success. Brian's stock control, his insistence on staff courtesy, and his house rule that no customer should leave dissatisfied, meant that within a year it was the best-run record store in the North.

"A lovely boss, a perfect gentleman," says Beryl Adams, his secretary at that time. He always moved swiftly to overtake her if she was walking into their office, "to make sure he could open the door for me. And he was immaculate. He always looked as if he'd just stepped out of a shower."

"I would have given the world for one of his suits: the way he used to pick a shirt and tie to go with it," reflects John Banks, a senior sales assistant.

To all the staff, he was "Mr. Brian." His brother up on the ground floor was "Mr. Clive," and their father, "Mr. Harry." Beryl, who at twenty-six was older than most of the girls on the staff, noted Brian's punctiliousness. Any letter she typed had to be perfect, and although Brian did not moan about much, his moods were obvious. "He'd go very quiet and you knew he had to be left alone." Like all the staff, she knew of his homosexuality: "But it was very discreet. It didn't bother anyone. Nobody mentioned it."

At NEMS in Whitechapel, Brian was renowned as a keen staff supervisor. This applied equally to their work and their appearance. Although he was quite happy to join the staff for a drink after work, perhaps in the White Star in Button Street or the Beehive in Paradise Street, such sociability was not to be taken advantage of. Next morning, one of those same employees could be sharply rebuked for being five minutes late. "But he wouldn't make a fool of you in front of the other staff," says Rita Shaw, one record assistant.

Every Monday there was a short staff meeting in which Brian emphasized how customers should be approached. "It didn't matter if the customer was a big posh nob or a scruffbag, as we called it," says Rita Shaw. "Brian told us to give him the same service." Brian decreed that the staff should address everyone as "sir" or "madam."

Brian Wolfson,* who remembered Epstein from their days as boys at Liverpool College, continued a friendship with him, observing his "gentle, rather quizzical smile" when he went to NEMS most Saturdays to browse through records. As a stockist, Brian was "very per-

---

*Now chairman of Wembley Stadium and chairman of the Institute of British Management.

nickety; there was a very prestigious streak in him." Wolfson's taste in South American and Greek music intrigued Brian, who regarded those records as his challenge. "I've got the new Los Españoles or Los Paraguayos record," he'd say to Wolfson immediately after he walked into NEMS. Wolfson remembers: "In fringe music he was very good, very eclectic in his awareness."

Among the other customers, there was initially little to identify the rather scruffy, leather-clad youths who regularly came into the NEMS basement. It was a mecca for so many of Liverpool's youth. But Epstein noted that the time they spent in the booths listening to new singles was disproportionate to their purchases. He told his staff to discourage such unprofitable time-wasters, without being discourteous. The girls assured Brian that the youths were particularly knowledgeable about pop and were no trouble.

"We got to know their faces," says John Banks, "and we all said: 'Oh, *he's* come down again. Don't play him a record. He doesn't buy anything. Always listens but never buys.' "

❏

Perhaps subconsciously as a substitute for the theater, Brian was determined to get closer to the world of pop music. He attended a concert at the Liverpool Empire starring Marty Wilde and Billy Fury. At the back of the theater stood their London manager, Larry Parnes. The theater's assistant manager approached him: "There's a young man who very much wants to meet you. He appears to go to all your shows; he's a local chap who runs a record store for his parents and he's very interested in the pop world."

During drinks in the interval, Parnes was impressed by the young man's perceptiveness on aspects of the evening's show. "He remarked on the unusual lighting, the pace, individual artists' performances and their clothes," recalls Parnes. "I was extremely flattered." Epstein told Parnes that running a local record shop was the nearest he could get to joining the pop world; he had originally wanted to be an actor. Brian then asked if he could possibly meet Marty Wilde and Billy Fury. Parnes took him to their dressing rooms, where Epstein enjoyed animated conversations about their work. He and Parnes exchanged addresses and phone numbers.

The meeting with young pop stars several years his junior (he was now twenty-seven), during which Epstein gleaned their views and attitudes, was a significant pointer to his future. By now, the natural record sales detection inside Brian was placing an enormous emphasis on youth. He listened to people between the ages of fifteen and twenty with infinitely more attention and patience than he did to adults. "He would change his opinion or decision if someone of sixteen said some- thing, whereas an older person would have made no impact on him with the same advice," remembers a colleague. For Brian, young people carried the tide. He drew his impetus from them, and it was to prove a crucial factor in his eventual success.

Back in London, Larry Parnes mulled over the possibility of offering the lively young Liverpudlian a job as his assistant. Parnes had gal- vanized the careers of a collection of pop stars and assigned them thematic metamorphoses: Duffy Power, Johnny Gentle, Marty Wilde, Vince Eager, and Billy Fury. He was also partner with record producer Joe Meek in managing the Tornados, whose Telstar record was an international hit. Parnes had an industriousness that Epstein admired—but at the time he had no gaps on his staff. It would be more than a year before the two men spoke again, in much more combative circumstances.

3

❏

PRESSURES

FRIENDSHIPS AND FRICTIONS

CLASSICAL MUSIC WAS ONE OF BRIAN'S MAJOR PASSIONS. In his quest for "the best" in everything, he reserved the finest seats for his weekly visit to the Liverpool Philharmonic, where he began a friendship with the conductor, John Pritchard. And when Malcolm Shifrin, the younger Liverpool boy he had known at Beaconsfield School, returned to the city to live opposite his home, Brian was delighted to discover they had a mutual love of music. At the Philharmonic, they renewed their schoolboy friendship and, inspired by the coffee bar craze of the 1950s, talked vaguely of the possibility of jointly opening a combined cafe and record shop.

Malcolm was one of a coterie of Brian's Jewish friends in the Childwall area, including Brian Wolfson and a doctor's son, Alan Sytner, the original owner of Liverpool's Cavern club when it featured jazz bands. Shifrin, an orthodox Jew, startled Brian with his refusal even to attend concerts or even accept his telephone calls on the Sabbath. But often on Sunday mornings Brian walked across the road to his house for coffee.

After two such meetings, Brian, secure in their rapport, warily broached the subject that was causing him so much pain. They were

47

sitting in the lounge of Shifrin's home discussing a joint trip to London. "When you were in London, did you go to any clubs?" Brian began. "Did you have a good time, go to any interesting places?"

Yes, said Malcolm, he had been to some music clubs, and had been to see an operetta, *The Mikado*. "Things like that," he added, lightly.

Brian pressed him. "Sophisticated clubs? Did you meet any sophisticated people?"

"Yes," said Malcolm. To him, at the age of nineteen, it was a long word that vaguely meant "intellectual."

"Did you have a gay time?" Brian then asked.

"Yes, sometimes, yes. I had quite a few gay times." Shifrin could not detect the theme and had no clue about what Brian was driving at.

Epstein smiled knowingly. "I always knew you were gay, all along," he said finally.

Shifrin was completely baffled. To him, the word "gay" meant happy, exhilarating; it carried no special connotations. Brian's wordplay puzzled him. "What do you mean?" he asked.

Epstein hesitated. "Well, you *are* homosexual, aren't you?"

Shifrin, nonplussed, answered: "No, I'm not."

This unexpected turn put Brian in a quandary. His use of the word "gay" had been a test; it was used only by insiders in those years. To all others, homosexuals were "queers" or "poofs." Brian's questions had obviously misfired. In fact, he had chosen a particularly naive teenager to whom he announced the truth about himself. Epstein perhaps made the mistake of thinking Shifrin was gay because of the company he kept. Without realizing it, Malcolm mixed freely with homosexuals. "I was very backward sexually," says Malcolm. "I just about knew the facts of life but I was unaware of anything to do with sex."

"Well," Epstein continued, now embarrassed and speaking hesitatingly. "What are you going to think of me if I tell you that I am a homosexual?" Brian now had no alternative but to "come out." He knew he risked repercussions, for Malcolm was a valued friend with whom he shared tastes in the arts; their families knew each other; and Malcolm was a devout Jew. He was also, Brian suddenly realized, very naive about sexual matters.

"At the very least," reflects Shifrin, "he might have thought he would lose my friendship. It was not the sort of thing a nice, Jewish, well-brought-up boy in those days would want to be associated with. It's all very different now but in those days it was illegal, although there were people who accepted it and didn't care a damn. But that wasn't my upbringing. So to me, it was quite strange."

As the confession sank in, Malcolm says, "certain things began to make sense" about Brian. Once he had cleared the air, Brian went on to explain the difficult lives of homosexuals. He referred to other Liverpool Jews, known to Malcolm, who had the same sexual preferences. "When he told me that such famous people had been homosexuals," Malcolm continues, "it began to fascinate me." Brian told him of still more Liverpool men whom Malcolm had heard of . . . and slowly Epstein seemed to enjoy the release of talking freely.

Whatever pressures he placed on certain friends and colleagues throughout his life, he was assured their loyalty and respect by his sincerity and openness. Says Shifrin: "He unburdened himself. There would be very few people he could feel he could talk to about it who were out of that world."

❑

Malcolm Shifrin's friendship with Brian was too genuine to be diminished by the news of his homosexuality. While always stipulating that he was not "one of them," Malcolm continued to socialize with him as before. After the Philharmonic concerts, Brian impressed Malcolm with his acquaintances as they adjourned to the Adelphi Hotel for drinks with the conductor John Pritchard and others. Brian and Malcolm went to Manchester together to see ballet. They drove through the Mersey Tunnel to the Continental cinema, Wallasey, to see foreign films that were not readily shown elsewhere. They went to the Edinburgh Festival.

"Once he'd found out that I wasn't gay and that I'd accepted him as an ordinary person and liked him and his friends, he seemed to get a lot of pleasure in showing me off as his non-gay friend to his gay friends," says Shifrin. Brian even gave him a book to increase his knowledge of homosexuals—"definitely a book carried around in a brown paper bag in those days."

There could have been few friends, as distinct from professional colleagues later, to whom Epstein related so securely. It was a clear demonstration that people did not have to be homosexual to qualify for the warmth of his company. More significant, there was evidence that he was a reluctant homosexual, determined to project himself as heterosexual to those who did not know. Inside Brian was a confused spectrum of emotions that his parents recognized and worried about. He often blushed. Friends noticed that he imbibed more than most. "He was far more aware of alcohol and wine at an early age than most of us," says Brian Wolfson. "One was never surprised to see Brian merry, on the verge of giggly, to the point where a smile would become a grin and a giggle." This was unexpected because he wasn't usually a giggler.

Also unexpected, at least to those who knew he was gay, were the several girlfriends he cultivated.

❑

At sixteen, Sonia Seligson was one of Liverpool's most visible young Jewesses. With flowing blonde hair, blue eyes, and exotic hats, she always dressed snappily and trendily; other girls remarked on her audacious clothes. Sonia was a loner, seeking few friends.

She came from a comfortable, middle- to upper-class background, and her parents in some ways paralleled Harry and Queenie Epstein. Frank Seligson was a highly successful Liverpool jeweller, with his life centered on running a thriving business. He had little time for the arts. Ethel, his wife, was an excellent pianist and enjoyed the theater, music, books, and lively conversation.

Academically weak, Sonia had left the highly rated Beechenhurst College in Liverpool at the age of fifteen to pursue a stage career, first getting a job as a student assistant stage manager in Southport, near her home.

Brian Epstein and Sonia Seligson had first exchanged glances in the rarefied atmosphere of the lounge of Liverpool's grand old Adelphi Hotel, where her mother had taken her for tea. Brian was sitting across the room with some actor friends, whose animated conversation attracted Sonia's attention. There was instant eye-to-eye communication, and within a few weeks Brian, having through friends learned the identity of the striking young girl, telephoned her at home. They compared interests, discovered a mutual love of the theater, and casually planned to meet at a Jewish charity event, the Blue and White

Ball. At this event at the Adelphi Hotel, Jewish girls aged about seventeen "came out," rather like debutantes, to the pride of their glowing parents.

On the big night Sonia had influenza; her curiosity to see Brian again, however, proved too strong to resist. "But I didn't stay long because I was terribly shy and we couldn't find each other," she recalls. The next day, he telephoned again to say he had been searching the hotel for her. He set a date to take her to dinner. So began an intense relationship for Brian with a girl four years his junior. It was to last intermittently for two years, with nine months of regular meetings. But it was to end in tears for them both.

"I never had a boyfriend before I met Brian and I was absolutely fascinated by him from the start," says Sonia. "He was so worldly, yet we complemented each other because we were characters who dressed with a certain flair.

"His manners were immaculate and he made a girl feel good. He opened doors ahead of me, knew how to behave, and dressed perfectly, usually in a pin-striped suit. He took a great interest in my clothes and loved me to wear black dresses. He could be quite critical of the way I dressed but usually it was: 'Oh, you look good tonight.' "

At the core of their friendship lay their mutual passion for the theater. Sonia had been a drama student at Liverpool's Crane Theatre, had acted with the Green Room Players, and was now working at the Theatre Royal, Saint Helens. Brian's love of the theater was at its peak. He took Sonia to the Royal Court Theatre every Wednesday, with a routine visit afterward to the Mocca coffee bar, a favorite rendezvous for the city's artists. They also attended Liverpool Philharmanic concerts. Visits to Hoylake swimming pool and regular Sunday morning meetings at Sonia's home, ten minutes' walk from his in Childwall, quickly strengthened their courtship.

With his usual style, Brian gave her chocolates or flowers on most meetings. There was Christian Dior perfume for her seventeenth birthday, and from his shop, he took her an album by a mutual favorite, *Marlene Dietrich, at the Cafe de Paris, London,* and inscribed it: "With all my love, Brian."

Sonia's mother greatly admired her daughter's choice of man. His elegance, exquisite manners, and beautifully modulated voice made him quite a "catch" for any girl. Sonia, however, caught head-on the envy of several local Jewish girls. "I used to find horrible, sarcastic notes in the pockets of my coat. Mostly, the nasty remarks were aimed at me, but then there were a few against Brian. My mother said they were intended to split us up. Very few people disliked Brian Epstein, but they were jealous of him, as people are of people who are successful. I think everybody in the Jewish community was very proud of him because he had a touch of genius about him, even then. So I was treading dangerously, getting all his attention."

The tensions mounting inside Brian rarely surfaced in her company. He was punctual and so was she, and when he was delayed at the store, he would always phone to warn her. "And if he said he would be there in fifteen minutes, he was there in precisely fifteen minutes," Sonia says. The only moment of bizarre behavior she recalls was on a blazing-hot summer's day. Her mother had prepared a lavish picnic for Sonia and Brian to take to the beach at Hoylake. "We were lying there having strawberries and cream when Brian suddenly stood up and said: 'Come on, I want to go home.' For no reason at all. I was very hurt and thought it was something I'd said or done. No, he said, he just wanted to go home right then. He was just restless and didn't want to explain why. So he took us home and went off."

On many weekends Brian flew to Paris alone. "I knew he enjoyed the good life," Sonia remembers, "and when I asked him what he'd done there, he said he'd been to the theater, had a nice dinner, and saw friends. His visits were very frequent." Still, there was nothing untoward, in her view: although she saw him as committed to her, there was a solitary streak in him.

Although Brian told Sonia he had friends in France—"That was the other side of his life," she says—he was jealous of anything she did alone. When she returned from a holiday cruise with her parents, he challenged her immediately. "I hope you've behaved yourself."

"What do you mean?" asked Sonia innocently.

"You know exactly what I mean," he replied. "Promise me you haven't misbehaved."

"No, I haven't."

Nor did he like her visits to Liverpool clubs without him. He was relieved when she explained that she always went to these with her two girlfriends. "I think it was a case of possessiveness rather than jealousy," Sonia reflects.

Brian introduced her to his parents at dinner at the Rembrandt Club. After that formal meeting, she visited the Epstein home often. She became very fond of Queenie, noting the similarity in personality between her parents and Brian's.

"I don't think Clive liked me very much," Sonia says. "Probably because of my very long blonde hair, my heavy makeup, and my rather dangerous clothes. Not the normal clothes that a nice Jewish girl in Liverpool wore in those days. Too theatrical for Clive, I should imagine: I don't think he understood my character. I liked Brian's mother and she was probably very protective of him, as mothers are. His father always showed me great warmth and I always felt at ease with him, possibly because I get on better with males than with females.

"For me, this romance with Brian was a very serious affair. My mother knew how much I loved Brian . . . I just adored him. I knew he was frustrated, working in the family store, but he was making the very best of it and the theater was our hobby together."

When he was not going alone to Paris or driving the thirty-five miles from Liverpool to Manchester to visit the Opera House—again alone—Brian and Sonia were regarded as a united couple. Just as the romance had blossomed as they indulged their strong mutual interest in the theater and the arts, so it strengthened as they stepped out together to parties of mutual friends in the Childwall area. They met at least twice a week.

Sonia had become aware of Brian's enjoyment of drink—usually whisky when in her company. At a party at the home of Malcolm Shifrin, his alcoholic excess pitched him into a crisis. "Brian got very drunk," remembers Sonia, "and he asked me to marry him." She was overjoyed, yet confused in her reaction. They were very fond of each other, and she hoped their love was permanent. But was this the drink talking? Why had Brian not mentioned marriage when he was sober?

She left the party soon after that. Shifrin, gallantly walking her the short distance to her home, said: "Well, congratulations. I hope it all works out." With more knowledge than Sonia about Brian's private life, Malcolm was full of scepticism.

The next morning, Brian telephoned Sonia at her home. "I was very serious when I proposed to you last night," he said in that measured tone she knew so well. "But I think we should take things easy, you know. At a steady pace."

There was no talk of an engagement. "But I was in love with him and I do feel that he was in love with me," says Sonia.

Their dates continued: to romantic settings in the Cheshire countryside for dinner, to as many theater nights as they could manage. And then Brian announced to Sonia that he was going to attempt to become a full-time student at the Royal Academy of Dramatic Art in London. She was not surprised. He was manifestly restless in his father's business, and she saw that he was quickly outgrowing Liverpool. "I knew all along that he was going to do something in the theater." But before he launched himself into training for his RADA audition, he clearly had to resolve his relationship with Sonia.

The only way was a painful confession. Driving her home one night, he parked the car outside her house and announced that they would have to stop seeing each other. There was, he said, no future in their friendship. Sonia, dumbfounded, said: "You're obviously going with another woman."

"No," replied Brian. "I've got to tell you the truth. I'm going with another man." They both wept. For Brian, who was off to Paris the next morning alone, a painful wrench was completed. For Sonia, it was a depressing confirmation of the rumors that she had discounted throughout their romance. She recalls: "He explained his life and said he had to put his cards on the table. Though he loved me, he could not be with me. He broke down and cried a lot."

Sonia was heartbroken. "I never had any other boyfriend before Brian, and to me there was never any doubt that he was a complete heterosexual man when we were together," she says. "We were both loners. We needed each other. He was a super ballroom dancer. The man I knew was a completely normal man, not at all effeminate. I looked up to him. There were malicious rumors among some girls about his sexuality. I ignored them. I put it down to people's envy. Brian said to me that he found most of the Liverpool Jewish girls avaricious and boring, and he was right.

"In those days, sleeping with each other until marriage was out of the question. But he was quite passionate in his advances to me. We weren't intimate at all together."

Shortly after that fateful night when they left each other sobbing, Brian submerged his confession and took Sonia to the Lord Mayor's

Ball at Birkenhead. They had one dance together and did not speak a word. Sonia was still smarting from their official split. Finally, with false confidence from a little too much drink, she snapped at him as he walked away: "I suppose you're going off now with one of your boyfriends."

"It must have been the Scorpio in me, stinging back," she reflects today. It was a wounding taunt she would bitterly regret all her life. "He was very quiet on the drive back. I had said something that had upset him. I could feel the atmosphere. . . ."

Their paths diverged. Under her stage name of Sonia Stevens, she moved upward successfully into the world of theater. Brian went off to RADA and to discover the Beatles. During his RADA period he wrote to Sonia saying he did not feel suited to the acting profession. She wrote back to him with news of her solid progress, notably in Manchester, where she starred with Rachel Roberts in *The Verdict Is Yours*. Brian and Sonia kept in touch by letter, sporadically, for about another year.

By 1963, back in Liverpool, they met by chance at the Adelphi Hotel, where they had first planned to meet nine years earlier. This time, their conversation was mercifully brief. "You're more beautiful than ever, Sonia," said Brian, now on the crest of a wave with the Beatles. "Tell me, are you happy?" Sonia fixed him with a strong stare and an equally piercing reply: "What do *you* think?" His eyes rarely left her during the evening, she says. Despite the bitterness of their parting, Sonia says the magnetism between them remained.

It was the last time she saw him.

"It was one of the happiest times of my life when I was with Brian," Sonia Stevens says ruefully. "I feel he's never actually left me. It's very strange. I feel his presence all the time."

❏

Most nights after he had finished work at NEMS, Brian went for a drink on the way home—sometimes to the Beehive, a short walk away in Paradise Street, but more often to the Basnett Bar, just around the corner from the Liverpool Playhouse. Liverpool had several pubs where homosexuals gathered: the Magic Clock, the Spinning Wheel, Ma Boyles, the Old Dive. But for class and atmosphere, the supreme meeting place was the Basnett. With its oysters and smoked salmon complementing the drinks, served across a long marble-topped counter, the Basnett had the style Brian admired.

The homosexual boss of the Basnett, Alan Isaacs, welcomed Brian to the bar four or five nights each week. "Brian Epstein was always charming to the barmaids," says Monica Shannon, who invariably served him his "gin and tonic, with ice and lemon." "Some people knocked on the counter when they wanted attention. But Brian would just whisper: 'When you've got a moment . . .' I never heard him raise his voice. And he was impeccably dressed." He was a generous tipper, leaving half a crown on the counter each night.

He did not drink much or join the crowd, preferring to stand near the entrance. People sought his company. "He was aloof but polite. Always wore gray suits, and the shirt went with the tie. Though he'd been working all day, his face looked like he'd just stepped out of a shower," adds Monica.

Among the habitués of the Basnett Bar was a dapper young man named Alan Swerdlow. During conversation, Brian saw him as having "overlapping similarities" with himself. He had qualified in graphic design at the Liverpool College of Art, had attended the Quarry Bank Grammar School (alongside John Lennon), and knew the Epstein family as a fellow member of the Greenbank Drive Synagogue. Swerdlow was also homosexual. Alan's artistic flair inspired Brian to ask him to design carrier bags and record tokens for NEMS. Later, when Brian moved into concert promotion, Swerdlow designed the programs, including the one for the Little Richard show at the Tower, New Brighton.

Swerdlow observed, as did many, that Brian was frustrated and bored with his role in the family business. But because of his social status, it was comparatively easy for him to pursue his clandestine life.

"The Epsteins were very well-respected members of the community, held in esteem," says Swerdlow. "And Brian was glamorous, an extremely handsome young man, always well dressed, with a nice car. I envied all that." There was a tacit knowledge that they were homosexual: "In a small Jewish community, there were only a few of us with that, and each knew what the other was doing. We accepted that each other had problems of discretion, a responsibility not to drag too much in front of people's noses. We both knew what the rules were, and that one didn't go too over the top." Swerdlow was interested in gay politics, joining the Homosexual Law Reform Society, which began in Manchester.

"A whole group of the Basnett Bar people used to go to Manchester every Saturday night. It was a question of distancing yourself from home. Brian was more mobile than some of us and was able to spread his wings a bit further afield. Because his profile was so high in Liverpool, Brian experienced enormous pressure in keeping his activities and his relationships private."

Although the Wolfenden Report on homosexuality was issued in 1957, it was ten years before homosexuality became legal between consenting adults. Brian was never an activist or a joiner, according to Swerdlow. "He certainly wasn't a person who would go around with badges, then any more than he would today. But I think he would have expressed a concern today and accepted responsibility."

There was proof for Swerdlow that Brian had more freedom to enjoy his secret. "I decided to go to Amsterdam for a first visit to an acknowledged gay center. And he put me in touch with a recommended hotel and various clubs and pubs. He obviously had been there more than once and was quite well known at the hotel particularly. So he'd obviously had this ability, financially, to get further away from Liverpool than most of the rest of us."

❏

Liverpool in the 1960s was teeming with adult clubs. Among them was The Basement in Mount Pleasant, run by Yankel Feather, a homosexual Jew and an artist whose flat in Upper Parliament Street featured his futuristic life studies. Feather was a forceful, opinionated man, ten years older than Brian, and their relationship proved to be a fractious one. Feather's assertiveness polarized people's reactions. But his perception penetrated the veneer of complicated souls like Epstein.

Brian became a regular at Yankel's club, and it was here that the host noticed Brian's carefree attitude towards homosexuality, which contradicted the impressions of others. In the company of kindred spirits he clearly felt more secure. Once, he arrived with a friend and two dubious boys whose foul language angered the other guests. There were women in the club, and Feather told Brian's friend to remove the boys. "It's very embarrassing. Tell Brian not to bring such people

in here. Even the doorman's complaining. He wouldn't take them to
the Adelphi Hotel, would he?"

Brian's friend smiled. "That's where you are wrong. He would . . .
and we've just been there."

It was an enlightening statement, observes Feather. "I don't know
how his mind worked, but he obviously didn't give a damn what I
thought about him or those boys. He would take them anywhere.
Brian did not mind being homosexual. Because out of the half dozen
Jews in Liverpool he knew who were homosexual, each one was bright
in his sphere, doing something individual. So he saw it as an advantage.
To him, there was something special about it."

Brian's attitude to his Jewishness was different. Feather is not the
only Liverpool Jew who believes Brian found the demands of his faith
a pressure. "Although he obviously loved his mother and adored his
father, the fact that he was Jewish was rather a tragedy to him. He
was certainly a reluctant Jew," Feather says. This view is not supported
by any tangible evidence. Brian was a nonobservant Jew, but his love
of his family circle and his close involvement with relatives—both
endemic to the Jewish faith—were legendary.

He usually attended synagogue on the High Holidays, Rosh Ha-
shanah and Yom Kippur. "That's not difficult, is it?" says Feather
cynically. "If your family is supplying you with all your needs, you've
got to pay." Feather and others maintain that Brian's lifelong aim was
to be recognized as the epitome of the English gentleman. "One of
the ways of doing that would be to get a title. So when the Beatles
were awarded MBEs and he was not, that was the biggest letdown
for him."

Feather and Epstein were never friends. Says Feather: "Our values
were completely different. There was a time when I loathed him and
what he stood for. The only things we had in common were that he
was Jewish and he was gay."

But their paths often crossed. Feather regularly visited the NEMS
store to buy records for his club; here he observed a different Brian,
a man bored, trapped, looking for a way out of the provincial confines
of Liverpool. The professional record store manager contrasted vividly
with the nighttime Brian. Feather lectured Epstein on the danger he
exposed himself to. "I used to philosophize and talk to him like an
old Jewish uncle. When I saw him gallivanting round the town at

night, it used to shock me because he was so attractive and had so much going for him socially. I thought the way he dragged himself down was terrible and I told him. I used to bore him by telling him off about his behavior, telling him to take care. But he didn't care for me much because I stood for everything he didn't want. I wasn't ambitious and I always felt we spoke different languages. He didn't want my warnings. He wanted to live with the security he had as a Jewish boy with the freedom of an Irish navvy."

And there was Brian's loftiness. His behavior in The Basement club often infuriated Feather. The two men once sat talking over Brian's customary double brandy when an irritating Epstein habit caused Feather to explode. "Every time someone walked through the door, he would completely ignore what I was talking about and look over my shoulder, as though I wasn't there, at the new arrivals." Feather berated him: "If you don't want to talk to me, you don't have to. In fact, I'd rather you didn't talk to me ever again if you must carry on with such bloody annoying rudeness, ignoring me when anyone walks in." The rebuke fell on deaf ears; Brian was not easily embarrassed in this situation. When Brian mocked the clothes worn by a youth sweeping up behind the bar, Feather tore into him. "Don't make fun of him. He can't help the suit. When he's got as much as money as you, he'll buy a decent one." Again Brian ignored the taunt. He was rarely drawn into an exchange.

Feather sensed a deep frustration inside Epstein. In mid-1961, Brian told him he was bored and that that contributed to his treacherous nocturnal wanderings. Yankel invited him to his flat in Upper Parliament Street. They stood gazing thoughtfully out of the window and Feather suggested he teach Brian how to paint flowers. Epstein winced. "Oh, no, no, no," said Epstein. "I haven't got a clue. I went to RADA and I failed there. I would fail as a painter. I don't think I have enough interest to be *successful* enough." Feather persisted: Why not try night classes? Then Yankel realized that Brian's use of the word "successful" was the key to understanding his plight. The level of success that Epstein sought was not easily guaranteed to an actor or a painter. He was looking for a bigger break.

Feather strongly resented what he considered Brian's pose as a "pseudo English gentleman," and on this score Brian recoiled from Feather's full frontal attacks. While conceding Epstein's achievements, Feather ruminates that it cost a lot in human terms to create the Brian Epstein the world now remembers. The price included seeing Brian out of his natural habitat—at a midnight coffee stall in Liverpool, for example, lavishing gifts on total strangers. "Whatever forces went into motivating Brian Epstein toward success were the same forces that helped create the Beatles," says Feather.

"But I didn't like him at all. I'd like to think I could find some virtue in the man, something nice to say about him. The only thing I can say is that he was nice to look at. He was always very clean, very well-dressed. He objected to me and my Jewishness, my ugliness. Everything he liked I didn't. That didn't worry me because I had my ideas about him. I found him ineffectual, a very fey Jewish gay. I thought he was very odd. I didn't know *what made him tick*. I mean, most people say they want a good job and good sex and this and that; Brian Epstein never talked straightforwardly about *anything*.

"He was quite outstanding in that I've never met anybody like him. He was not apparent or obvious, and the things he knew he never said anything about. So he was a complete mystery." It strikes Feather as "macabre" that a young man like Brian, prepared to pay the psychological price for practicing homosexuality (illegal in those years), should be capable of living so straight a professional life. "If you're a homosexual, everybody knows it in this world of avarice for money. Anyone who appeared as innocent and simple as Brian would pay heavily. Look, John Lennon wanted fame and stood in the nude for pictures, and he got shot. If you want to go that far, there is a price to be paid."

❏

At his Liverpool tailor, Watson Prickard, Brian was regarded as diffident, well-spoken, and fastidious. "He always looked as if he'd just stepped out of the bath," says George Hayes, who tended to Brian's sartorial needs. "Well-manicured hands, polite, appreciative, but also demanding." His dark blue and gray suits would be made to measure, never "off the peg." He wore Burberry raincoats years before they became popular. Here were bought the polka-dot cravats that were to become his trademark, as well as blazers and even a bowler hat. "He had definite ideas about style, trouser widths, and lapels," says Denis Goodrum, who attended Brian in the same store.

By his mid-twenties, Brian was something of a gourmet and wine-lover. Liverpool, though, was a gastronomic desert. So, on two or three evenings in most weeks, Brian would delight in driving into the Cheshire countryside. There he enjoyed a glass or two of whisky, adventurous cooking (preferably French), fine wines, and the company of a like mind. There, too, he would take the several girls in whose presence he was so relaxed, but to whom he would eventually confess his lifestyle. He was gregarious, worldly, financially comfortable, and he had a droll sense of humor. His ambitions went beyond what he considered the narrow limits of Merseyside.

Brian had a capacity for genuine friendships with men who were not necessarily concerned with his sexual propensity but who were stimulating and who mixed in similar social circles. Among these was Geoffrey Ellis, four years older than Brian, a Liverpudlian who had just returned from Oxford University, where he had studied for the bar. A neatly dressed man whose manners, mildness, and exactness matched Brian's, he had joined the Royal Insurance Company in Liverpool. They met as part of a group of regular faces at the Royal Court Theatre.

Geoffrey was to become a loyal and valued business partner and confidant. Sometimes Brian would organize a group to drive into the country for dinner; on one occasion, Brian Bedford joined him and Geoffrey for an animated dinner discussing the world of theater.

In June 1958, Ellis was transferred by his insurance firm to their New York office. Brian was among the four people who went to the dockside to see him off. The bond between the two men was not to be affected: they corresponded. It was the start of a lifelong friendship with a man who, like Brian, had no interest in popular music. Like other friends, he would later view Brian's flirtation with rock 'n' roll as unseemly at best, and professionally absurd.

❏

With NEMS thriving and his social life enjoyable, Brian searched for an added fillip. He rented a flat at 36 Falkner Street, opposite the Liverpool Art College, close to the flat of his drama coach, Helen Lindsay. But he continued to live at home; the £16-a-month flat was reserved for his private life.

He now renewed a friendship that went back to his childhood. Among the people who regularly bought their records at NEMS was a mild-mannered, domesticated man named Joe Flannery. His father, Chris, was a furniture manufacturer who sold goods to Harry Epstein. Joe's mother ran a small furniture shop in Walton Road, not far from I. Epstein and Sons, the original "flagship" store.

Through their fathers' business link, Joe, three years older than Brian, had known him as a boy when they exchanged visits to the family shops. By the time the teenage Brian began work at the Walton Road store, Joe had opened his own bric-a-brac shop in nearby Kirkdale Road. Sometimes, Brian would walk along to Joe's to eat the sandwich lunch Queenie had packed for him. Occasionally, they would visit the fish-and-chips shop. In Joe, too, Brian found company as a theatergoer. Night after night they reserved the same seats to see Vivien Leigh at the Royal Court Theatre.

A short walk from the theater were the pubs that attracted homosexuals. At the Stork Hotel, which was nicknamed the Pelican, there was quiet discretion; but at the Old Dive, Magic Clock, and the Old Royal, Brian's stylish demeanor and presence were utterly removed from the rougher, tougher homosexual clientele. He nevertheless went to them all, much to Joe's displeasure. After drives into Manchester to the cinema, they would go to a similar pub there, the Dominion.

"We were known as the untouchables because we stayed back a bit," Flannery says. "I was jealous because he liked the rougher type of person, while I was the ideal person to go with him to the theater and spend safe weekends with." Joe resented being discarded.

At Joe's flat, 30 Prince's Road, Toxteth, Flannery, like Yankel Feather, tried to warn Brian of the dangerous aspects of his private life. "He was more daring than me," Flannery states. "There was friction when he left me to look for another partner and I knew where he was going. But I was fighting for him. I was upset that he went off. I couldn't join in on those little excursions for rougher types of people. I regret that about the two of us. If it were not for that, it would have been an ideal live-in partnership for us. I'd say: 'Oh Brian, you've got to be careful. This could be trouble.' " Once, in Joe's car, a nineteen-year-old pulled a six-inch knife on them as they drove back to Liverpool from Southport. He demanded money. Joe increased his speed to sixty miles an hour and said: "If you use that knife on either

of us, my foot goes down on this accelerator and we'll all be dead."
Joe drove like thunder and stopped the car outside a police station,
where the youth got out. Unscathed but shaken, Brian had been given
a tough lesson about the perils he was courting.

When Joe discovered Brian had a private flat, he knew the handwriting was on the wall for their special relationship. Brian developed
a new circle of friends. And Flannery was envious. "I adored him,
but the person I was in love with was now living in another flat. I didn't
want him there. I didn't like him having his freedom." Brian never
slept at his flat, but it represented his crucial independence. And he
dumped Joe Flannery.

4

DISCOVERY

"I'M THINKING OF MANAGING THE BEATLES"

WITH HIS MANICURED NAILS, well-groomed hair, pin-striped gray or blue suit, and polka-dot cravat tucked neatly into his Crombie overcoat, Epstein in 1961 was the least likely person to enter the lives of four leather-clad, street-sharp rock 'n' rollers. He was then twenty-seven, known in Liverpool as the dignified manager of the basement pop record department of his father's NEMS store, which sold chiefly furniture and electrical appliances.

Harry Epstein, a tenacious worker, expected his sons Brian and Clive to follow his example. While Clive concentrated on the merchandising of television sets and washing machines on the ground floor of the NEMS store, Brian was given the stimulating job of bringing classical records into the pop area and increasing sales of both kinds of discs.* This was a relief from the tedium of selling furniture, and though his interest leaned more to Sibelius and show soundtracks than to Elvis Presley, his new job was at least a foot in the door of show business, which he craved.

---

*Clive died after a heart attack during a skiing holiday in Austria on February 1, 1988. He was fifty-one.

His home life was stable, his social calendar full. At NEMS there was unswerving respect for his manners, taste, energetic leadership, and conscientiousness. The female staff were acolytes, the men clones, and they all responded with instant respect to his fussiness. The sales girls were embarrassed if their lipstick was missing or their hair out of place: "Tell me, Rita, would you go for an interview for a new job without your lipstick on? This is a *job* where the public is watching you. . . ." All assistants were expected to be punctual, polite, and particularly positive when dealing with customers.

He was keen on expansion, not only because of the business thrust inbred into the Epstein family but also because of his self-awareness. Before the pop record department came under his wing, he had endured a succession of frustrations, rejections, and traumas; now it was time to redefine his wayward life. He would stamp his authority and style on the management of record sales and make NEMS the citadel for the city's music-lovers—classical, jazz, and pop.

❑

In 1960 an advertisement appeared in the *Liverpool Echo*. "Young man wanted for sales assistant in record shop in Liverpool. Apply in writing to Brian Epstein, NEMS Limited." It caught the eye of a twenty-five-year-old music fan, Alistair Taylor, who was bored with his work in the office of a timber company.

In a long interview, Taylor impressed Epstein with his knowledge of jazz and pop, his orderly manner, and his open enthusiasm. The job was his, said Brian, but he thought Taylor rather mature for the wages he had in mind for a sales assistant. Epstein had an idea: he had toyed for some time with the notion of having a personal assistant. That would mean helping him order records, picking up his briefcase, reminding him that he'd forgotten his pen (and other small aids to memory), as well as helping out at the sales counter when they were busy. For that, Epstein could pay him £10 a week instead of the £8 originally offered.

Taylor accepted immediately. Soon after starting, he became aware that he had joined the best record department in the Northwest of England, perhaps in the country. The methods of operation set up by Epstein were meticulous and exhaustive: there would be the most painstaking inventory control, he said, and for the public, no record would ever be described as "impossible" to get. A customer requesting an out-of-stock record would be told: "It might take a month, six months, or a year, but rest assured that NEMS will get it."

Brian invested the shop with an ambience missing from other, more clinical stores. In the classical department, he displayed potted plants; there were private booths with chairs for listening to samples of new records. Downstairs in the pop section, the listening facilities were more Spartan, with open hooded, plastic-topped booths.

"Brian wouldn't stint," says Ray Cobb, a classical records salesman. "He was interested not just in the business but in the artistic appearance of the place. I could not imagine him spending the rest of his days as an ordinary sales director. There was no way the record side under him would be an extension of the ordinary family business."

Epstein always devised a theme for his window display; it was never simply a row of records. Once when he was promoting show soundtrack music, he placed the album covers alongside wine glasses and fresh flowers. He spent about two hours personally dressing the window each week.

"He seemed a butterfly," says Taylor, "but he wasn't particularly interested in making a success out of his Dad's shop just for profit." What Brian seemed dedicated to, his staff decided, was personal achievement. This was no mundane salesman who bedecked the basement ceiling with album covers and augmented the records with a carefully chosen small selection of greeting cards and paperback books. Here was an *artist*.

An unexpected aspect of Epstein's expertise often astonished his staff: his uncanny forecast of what would sell and what would "stick." He knew little about pop, even less about the jazz records he sold, but he had a sensitive musical ear, one that leaned towards show soundtracks. Yet even with the Top 20 pops list, his diagnosis of potential winners and losers was remarkably accurate. "If an album was selling steadily," says Taylor, "I'd say I thought we should order another box. And he'd often reply: 'No, no, no. That will just tick over now. Order no more.' " He was invariably correct. His pre-Christmas order in 1960 of several thousand copies of the *South Pacific* soundtrack, two full years after its first success, proved commercially correct. Against his staff's forecast, they sold out.

❑

At the dawn of the 1960s, Liverpool was bursting with creative vitality. Youth was not yet the target of the media or the advertisers, and unlike the young people of the two decades that followed, those then in their teens and twenties had little spending power. Instead, they turned their energies to the arts. Musically, the rock 'n' roll of Elvis Presley, Little Richard, Chuck Berry, and Buddy Holly dominated the repertoire of the hundreds of groups playing in clubs, which sold only Coca-Cola or Fanta, tea or coffee. While London listened to the insipid pap of singers like Bobby Vee, Pat Boone, and Eden Kane, and in the provinces a traditional jazz boom was in full swing, Liverpool was witnessing a startling parade of local pop-group talent. The competition for engagements was heating up every week, with high standards in raw rock 'n' roll. The local groups' inspirational sources were American.

It was a world alien to Epstein—his artistic taste was comparatively sedate. But he was gradually becoming proud of his jazz import service supervised by Alistair Taylor, and as his taste broadened, he began to take home records by singers Billie Holiday and Dinah Washington.

It was Bill Harry who expanded Brian's awareness of the burgeoning Liverpool music scene. As a Liverpool College of Art student, Harry had become firm friends with John Lennon and shared his enthusiasm for rock 'n' roll. At twenty-one, in fact, Harry vied with Bob Wooler as the most knowledgeable observer of Liverpool musicians, befriending hundreds of them.

With a taste for journalism as well as pop, Harry had completed a college course on typography and design, and with considerable prescience, he launched his own paper, *Mersey Beat,* on July 6, 1961. Lennon helped to give it early credibility with his famous pastiche entitled "Being a Short Diversion on the Dubious Origins of Beatles." The newspaper, with the delightful stamp of the happy amateur, was the cheerleader of Liverpool pop, with news, pictures, and gossip galore. Harry borrowed £50 to launch it with his girlfriend (later wife), Virginia. They rented an attic office at 81a Renshaw Street to pursue the labor of love. Bill was the publisher, editor, reporter, designer, messenger, and advertisement salesman. Lennon and McCartney chattered away most lunchtimes in his tiny office, with its solitary desk, chair, and typewriter.

For all his artistic leanings, Harry had a commercial streak. He paid careful attention to the crucial matter of distributing his new newspaper. Every fortnight he humped bundles of *Mersey Beat* to twenty-eight points in the city. Music stores were a prime target: Frank Hessy's instrument shop, Rushworth and Dreaper's record store. And NEMS.

"Brian Epstein was a bit more laid-back than the other shop managers," Harry recalls. "Impeccably dressed, so formal. Very polite. I explained the paper to him and asked if he would sell some copies in NEMS." To Epstein, this was simply a matter of helping a young enthusiast promote a subject that he, as a record salesman, knew nothing about. "Right, I'll take a dozen," he said, after Bill Harry's persuasion.

Two days later he phoned Harry and asked him to return to his office. The dozen copies had been sold instantly, a puzzled Epstein told him. Harry said he was not surprised, since NEMS had stocked so few. Brian agreed to replenish his counter with a further dozen. Those, too, sold quickly, but *Mersey Beat* was no big money-spinner. Epstein's profit was half the selling price of 3d. for each copy. Still, he was intrigued. "To tell you the truth," he said to Harry, "I can't believe how well this paper is selling. What is it all about?"

The editor gave Epstein a speedy indoctrination. "What's happening in Liverpool to beat groups now is exactly like what happened to jazz in New Orleans at the turn of the century," he declared. "Everything is happening here, like nowhere in the world."

"You're joking," said Epstein, taking the second dozen copies to the NEMS counter.

"No," said Bill Harry. "We're going to publish a list showing that there are *two hundred and eighty beat groups* in Liverpool. It's unique."

Within a few days, the second dozen copies had been sold. Epstein now capitulated to Harry's enthusiasm, ordering twelve dozen copies of *Mersey Beat*'s second issue. Young fans were going into NEMS not only for records but specifically to buy the paper.

Mersey Beat's front-page story on July 20, 1961, headlined "Beatles Sign Recording Contract," had a picture of the Beatles in Hamburg with the exciting news that they had signed a contract to make four records per year in Germany for producer Bert Kaempfert on the Polydor label.*

The twelve dozen copies sold so swiftly that Brian asked Harry to his office for sherry. "This is remarkable," he said, flipping through the newspaper. He quizzed Bill about the local beat scene and was amazed at all the activity. Harry thought Epstein was interested purely in assessing an advertisement in *Mersey Beat*, which was good news for the financially pressed publication. Next, Epstein surprised him even more: "Can I possibly review records for you?" The prestige of having Brian Epstein of NEMS writing in his newspaper was enough: for Bill Harry, it would bring credibility.

Brian's first reviews concentrated on his own preferences: show music from such musicals as Anthony Newley's *Stop the World, I Want to Get Off!* and *The Music Man*. He also ran through a few classical recordings, showing his strong knowledge of sales potentials. Harry was aghast at his omission of pop. "I thought: 'My God, he just doesn't know what's going on!' " Epstein agreed to Bill's request that, in a newspaper called *Mersey Beat*, his column should concentrate on pop.

His second column touched upon new singles by Elvis Presley and Chubby Checker, and he continued the trend with a comprehensive summary of such prominent names as Roy Orbison, the Shadows, Duane Eddy, and jazzman Acker Bilk. Epstein showed that he was not as naive about pop as might have been thought: he had listened sufficiently to Timi Yuro's new single to describe it as "a lovely tear jerker," and was fully aware that Billy Fury was a successful Liverpool-born singer.

Epstein was so intrigued by the newspaper's contents and its buoyant sales that he asked where these much-publicized Beatles could be seen. Harry said they appeared regularly at the Cavern, a local cellar club.

❏

Although Epstein had heard of the Beatles by name, it was his obsessive business methods that finally ignited his interest.

*The impact of this story, on July 20, 1961, explodes the myth generated by Epstein that he had never heard of the Beatles until the autumn of 1961. *Mersey Beat*, which he must have read, was packed with similar Beatles news for a full four months before he went to the Cavern. And Bill Harry was repeatedly talking about them to him.

On October 28, 1961, a young man walked into NEMS and asked
Brian if he stocked a record by a Liverpool group, the Beatles. No,
said Epstein, he'd never heard of it but he would make inquiries.
With his customary precision and promise, he wrote to himself on his
memo pad: "The Beatles. 'My Bonnie.' Check on Monday."

That day he read through all the record company catalogues, to no
avail. He phoned all his usual channels of information, the record
company distribution points, but they could give no clue. Puzzled, he
returned to other work, awaiting the return of the potential customer,
Raymond Jones.

In the next few days, his staff received two further requests for "a
record by the Beatles." Epstein, reflecting on his own experiences as
a collector, said later: "I disliked most record shops because it seemed
that whenever a record became popular, they were out of stock."

When Raymond Jones returned, asking, "Any luck yet with my
Beatles record?," Brian confessed himself beaten. He asked for more
details. "Oh, it's a German record," said Jones. That was a useful
lead, said Brian. He enlisted Alistair Taylor's help in searching through
the catalogues again. Finally, in desperation, believing that the Beatles
might be German, Brian decided to telephone Deutsche Grammophon, the major German record company, in Hamburg. It was a remarkably diligent and expensive piece of detective work when the
expected result would be the sale of two or three single records costing
just over 6s. each. But Brian's sixth sense for what was important and
commercial was working totally in his favor.

The record men in Hamburg said no, they didn't know of a Beatles
record, but yes, they were distributing a record by a Liverpool group.
The title was indeed "My Bonnie," but the group was named Tony
Sheridan and the Beat Brothers. (Although the musicians were offi-
cially named the Beatles, the German record men renamed them the
Beat Brothers. They feared "Beatles" was too close to "peedles,"
German slang for penis.) Epstein and Taylor were convinced that this
must be the right record and that Raymond Jones was probably con-
fused about the artists' name. "We'll take a box," Epstein told them.
The minimum order was a box of twenty-five singles.

When the records arrived, Epstein, showing intuitive confidence
that he was on to something important, hand-wrote a sign for the

NEMS front window: "Beatles Record Available." Raymond Jones got his copy and the other twenty-four were snapped up within hours. The NEMS staff were flabbergasted.

The same day, Taylor telephoned the baffled sales point in Hamburg and asked for a further two boxes. Within three days of their arrival, those fifty copies had been sold. Epstein, intrigued, wanted to discover more about this freak record, which appeared to be an "underground hit"—long before that phrase became current in the pop world.

Since the opening of the NEMS record department three years earlier, Epstein had gained a reputation for hard-nosed retailing. Now, when it came to a decision on stocking an unknown, foreign-origin rock 'n' roll single, his "feel" was so accurate that all his colleagues were surprised. The record retail network, too, became acutely aware of Brian's judgment. With a routine single he typically ordered two copies for the NEMS branch in Whitechapel, where he was based, and two for the Great Charlotte Street branch. But if he heard a promotional record and believed it would bring brisk trade, he ordered a hundred copies for each shop. Once, he reversed Alistair Taylor's order for five copies of John Leyton's "Johnny Remember Me." When Brian had listened to the demonstration record, he looked at Taylor and said sternly: "Right, I'll have five hundred copies." Taylor, aghast, said it was not a winner. But the EMI salesman left joyfully with the biggest order on his books. And lo, within a few days, the NEMS shop was the only store in the Northwest that stocked the record. It was a number one hit and they sold all five hundred.

So respected did Brian's opinion and accuracy become among the record company and sales people that when area representatives called and he ordered optimistically, they would send the signal back to London, to the sales departments of EMI, Decca, Pye, Philips, and to the Selecta distribution point: "Review the order for this record at the pressing plant. Brian Epstein has ordered a hundred copies for NEMS!" Epstein had no knowledge of the esteem in which he was held.

When Brian scented a potential winner with "My Bonnie," he made an unusual move. Why was the record not on British release? He phoned Polydor, a British division of Deutsche Grammophon. "Look, there's a record out in Germany which you haven't released in Britain.

It's by a Liverpool group and it's a big hit. We at NEMS have already sold nearly a hundred copies. It's crazy that you haven't released it all round your country."

"Forget it, Mr. Epstein," he was rebuffed. "We've never heard of them. It might be a big seller in Liverpool, but in London nobody's heard of Tony Sheridan or the Beatles."

The phone call made Epstein's hackles rise. His judgment and advice had been rejected despite the evidence of his own flourishing sales. He was determined to find out more and prove Polydor wrong.

On his next visit to NEMS with the latest issue of *Mersey Beat*, Bill Harry chatted casually about the city's group scene. Brian asked him for more details on the Beatles.

At this point, the lore of Liverpool divides. Epstein's memories pay little attention to Harry's role in 1961. "I was naive," says Harry now. "He wanted to make out that he single-handedly created the Mersey scene and that nothing happened before he discovered it. It sounds dramatic but it's rubbish. The Liverpool scene was flourishing long before he ever knew about it." Harry argues that Epstein's assertion that he had never heard of the Beatles' "My Bonnie" single before Raymond Jones walked into his shop and ordered it was a piece of theatrical license. "Bob Wooler was plugging the record locally. The Beatles had taken him a copy from Hamburg and they gave me a copy too." With five thousand *Mersey Beat* readers aware of the record on July 20, and asking for it at various shops, it is indeed inconceivable that Epstein had not heard of the Beatles' popularity before October 28, the day Epstein says Raymond Jones walked in and alerted him.

"He smelled the Beatles from *Mersey Beat*," insists Bill Harry. "He was inquisitive, wanted to know what was going on. How could it be that a meticulous man like Brian Epstein did not notice what was on the cover of every issue of *Mersey Beat* from the start of that summer? The Raymond Jones request story which Brian told later was just convenient timing for him."

Bill told Brian that the Beatles appeared at lunchtime most days at the Cavern, a cellar club just three minutes' walk from Brian's Whitechapel shop. Brian said: "Do you think you could arrange for me to go down there?" Certainly, Bill said. He would even tell the man on the door at the club to let him in.

When Bill Harry left his office, Brian enjoyed breaking some news to Alistair Taylor. "Do you realize that group the Beatles are from Liverpool and they're playing regularly at the Cavern? Have you ever been to the Cavern?" Taylor knew it as his regular haunt as a jazz club. He told Brian it had recently switched to a pop policy. Next day, Brian raised the subject again. "Will you come with me to the Cavern at lunchtime and have a bite to eat? I'd just like to see them, see what they're like."

The Cavern was a dank basement in narrow Mathew Street, and 250 footsteps from the front door of NEMS. Brian had no idea where it lay, so Taylor led the way. At about 12:30 p.m. on November 9, 1961, Epstein and Taylor, dressed as usual in white shirts, dark ties, and business suits, strolled across and paid the 1s. admission charge and descended the eighteen steps. They sat on hard wooden chairs at the back of the cellar, in the middle facing the stage.

Among the girls with beehive hairstyles, junior secretaries, and young men who were hard-core rock 'n' roll fans, Epstein and Taylor were like fish out of water. The air was vile, damp, and stale with cigarette smoke, which Brian abhorred. There wasn't a glass of chilled white wine or a civilized sandwich in sight: the teenagers dined frugally on cheese rolls, bowls of soup, lemonade or tea. To Brian, so far from his social class, they seemed like a private clan. He had frequented pubs and clubs in Liverpool many times and understood the special personality of Merseyside people. But he had never mixed with teenagers. Even in his youth he had been a loner.

To Alistair Taylor, the Cavern as a pop club was unspeakable. He detested pop music, though he was content to sell the records as a job. "I was there because Brian really didn't want to be in a place like that on his own."

Yet even to these unlikely patrons' ears, the sound of the Beatles was sensational. To Epstein, attuned to orchestras and the theater, it was the most undisciplined, ragged "show" he had ever experienced. The uncouth Beatles smoked as they played, drank Coca-Cola from *bottles*, and between songs mocked one another and the teenagers who formed their doting audience. "Now we'd like to do a number that John and I have written," said Paul McCartney. "It's called 'Hello Little Girl.' " It was Brian's first clue that there was songwriting energy within the group.

He was flummoxed. They could handle ballads as well as beat, and they included the rousing "Shout," which was later a hit by the singer Lulu. Taylor remarked to Epstein that he was a total convert: "They were absolutely bloody awful . . . and yet they were incredible. They were scruffy, loud, weren't very good musicians, but their soul hit you straight in the chest. It was a physical experience, like someone thumping you." Brian Epstein was transfixed.

The duo from NEMS sat through about five songs, and at the end of the Beatles' set, Brian said: "Let's just go and say hello to them." The band room was little more than a large cupboard next to the stage. Inside were John Lennon, Paul McCartney, George Harrison, and their drummer, Pete Best.

Epstein knocked and put his head inside. "Oh, hello. I'm Brian Epstein. This is my assistant Alistair Taylor. Just came in to see you. We thought you were very good." A Beatle voice replied: "Oh, we know you. You're from the record shop. We go in there." And George Harrison added drily: "What brings Mr. Epstein here?"

Epstein and Taylor adjourned for a proper lunch at the Peacock in Hackins Hey, a nearby mews. "What do you think?" Brian asked Alistair.

"Well, frankly, absolutely bloody marvelous. Incredible. Very exciting."

"What would you think," continued Brian, "if I thought of managing them?"

"*Manage* them?"

"Yes. You see I thought they were *incredible.*"

Epstein had often successfully reversed Taylor's business decisions, but this was preposterous. It was the most bizarre possibility for a successful record shop manager to even contemplate. Taylor was almost too stunned to react, but Epstein continued: "Well, if I do manage them, do you work for me or do you work for NEMS?"

"What a funny question," Taylor replied. "I work for you. Why?"

"Well, if I do this it would mean setting up a separate company. Would you come with me if I did?"

"Yes Brian, I would."

"*If* I did it, and *if* you came with me, I will give you two and a half percent of their earnings." He said it was obviously a salary too.

"Brian, no way," Taylor demurred. "I would want more money, a bigger salary. It's going to cost you a lot of money to get them off the ground, and I have no money to put up. So it would be most unfair for me to take a percentage, anyway." He was twenty-five, newly married, and watching the pennies.

Epstein was phlegmatic. "Very well, that's up to you. I take your point. That's the offer but we'll talk about it further." The lunch ended with Brian saying he had no idea where to begin—"I don't even know what a contract looks like." But clearly he was planning to change the tempo of his working life.

For Alistair Taylor, first witness to the event that was to mark the birth of a legend, the day stands forever as the moment when he turned down the offer of 2½ percent of the Beatles' income.

❏

A major figure on the Liverpool beat scene was missing from the Cavern on Epstein's first visit—Bob Wooler, a twenty-nine-year-old former railway clerk and the club's resident disc jockey. His manner, on- and offstage, was magisterial and authoritative, and his knowledge of pop, particularly the local groups, encyclopedic. His empathy with the young Cavern audience was very strong, and he was to introduce their adored Beatles onstage there 274 times: "Hello, Cavern dwellers, and welcome to the best of cellars."

Like hundreds of local pop fans, Wooler was bemused when he heard of the sudden interest shown in the Cavern's activities by the "posh, upper-class" boss of NEMS. To this day he asks the question that baffles so many: "What *was* Brian doing there?" Wooler was even more intrigued to see Brian arrive several times unannounced, and in the company of Rita Harris, one of his NEMS sales staff. Another assistant, Rita Shaw, and John Banks, in fact, were among the NEMS staff whom Brian canvassed for opinions on the Cavern and the Beatles. Banks twice accompanied his boss to the cellar club; Rita remembers Brian asking all the girls whether they had heard the Beatles and if they were good.

Four weeks after his first visit, Epstein returned to the Cavern alone, looking even more sleek and conspicuous, this time carrying a brief-case. He stayed long enough to listen to the Beatles and confirm his first judgment. Inching his way through the crowd to the stage, he managed to get a brief message across to George Harrison that he would like to see the group back at his NEMS office later; perhaps he could help them, he added mysteriously.

John Lennon was wary. He said to Bob Wooler as the show ended: "Will you come to NEMS with us? We're going to see a fellow called Brian Epstein. Will you come with us and give us your opinion of him?" Wooler, a cautious man, father figure to hundreds of Liverpool musicians, agreed. "Well, okay, I'll come down. We've got to be suspicious of all these people."

It was Wednesday, December 3, 1961, a half-day closing at NEMS. Lennon, Harrison, McCartney, and Best first went for drinks at the Bridge pub with Bob Wooler. Young though they were, they were sceptical of business relationships, having learned some of the ropes in Hamburg, where they were popular. How, they wondered, could a record shop owner advance their careers?

They sauntered nonchalantly across Whitechapel to NEMS. Epstein, who had been busy working alone on Christmas orders, unlocked the door to let them in. He had been waiting at the counter on the ground floor, among the refrigerators and washing machines, to see their arrival. For the Beatles this was a strange scenario: the pop department in the basement was their regular place for listening to the latest American pop records; now they were virtually summoned to the shop by its boss.

Epstein, in turn, was now vaguely identifying them as the rather uncouth youths who would loiter in his basement for too long. When the Beatles drifted into NEMS after their lunchtime sessions, "they used to drive us crackers," says Rita Shaw, "wanting way-out American music." Most of the NEMS team were expected to remember the catalogue numbers of the most requested records; the Beatles' inquiries not only didn't register in their memories but also were missing from the record company lists of available discs.

Three Beatles arrived late for the 4:30 p.m. meeting, irritating the punctual Epstein. Paul McCartney was missing, having gone home to have a bath; he was thirty minutes late. The atmosphere was apprehensive on both sides. Then Lennon broke the ice, realizing Brian's bewilderment at their arrival with Bob Wooler, whom Epstein had never met until that moment. "This is me Dad," said John, raising a flicker of a smile from the diffident record shop manager.

The talk was nonspecific, Brian telling them of the remarkable, speedy sales of "My Bonnie," and asking if they had a manager. No, they said, most of the administration was done by Pete Best. Epstein said that to be honest, he had no experience of such things—"but I'd like to look at your affairs." The Beatles were noncommital. Reflects Wooler: "They were very cagey. He was a totally unknown quantity because he had no experience of pop music except selling records." They all adjourned to a milk bar and talked vaguely of contracts and ambition.

Finally, after about ten minutes of polite exchanges, Brian, rather shy as always, said: "Well, I'd like to meet you again." The Beatles said simply that they would go away and think about his idea.

Much later, Wooler casually mentioned to Epstein that the first meeting must have been very strange for him. "They asked me to come along for the ride and they talked about you, Brian, afterwards."

"Oh?" said Epstein anxiously. "What did they say?"

Wooler replied that the determined Beatles had not inquired whether Brian was genuine. They had made no personal observations of any kind. What they asked, and repeated in several ways, was entirely practical: "Is it going to amount to anything?" They had heard promises and theories before. They really wanted hard action and wondered if an inexperienced man could provide it.

Brian, aware of the status difference between him and the Beatles, was concerned to hear this. He mused that what the Beatles felt made complete sense, that perhaps more subtlety was needed in his next communication with them, for they clearly had greater empathy with Wooler than with him. He was determined that neither Wooler nor anyone else should accompany the Beatles to the next meeting. But Wooler was to prove his irreplaceable link with the group, for a few days later he gave Epstein a nugget of information that John, Paul, George, and Pete were not providing at that ultracautious stage: they actually were looking for a manager.

❑

When Brian asked the Beatles how they had been running their affairs, they mentioned the name of Allan Williams as someone who had got them work in Hamburg and promoted concerts for them on Merseyside. A sharp-tongued promoter with a keen, intuitive eye on the commerciality of rock 'n' roll, Williams had been the manager and agent of the Beatles for nearly a year up to the spring of 1961. But after a row with them over a commission he claimed was due him for their residency at the Hamburg Top Ten Club that autumn, he had concluded that the Beatles were unreliable.

Williams had been entrenched with the Beatles socially as well as professionally. He ran the Blue Angel club and the Jacaranda Coffee Bar, haunts for Liverpool's teeming rock population when they were not playing or when they wanted to catch up on essential gossip. Although by the late autumn of 1961 there were rumblings around Liverpool of Epstein's interest in the Beatles, Williams was nevertheless surprised when the suavely dressed man arrived early one evening at the Blue Angel and introduced himself to Williams at the reception desk. There were only a handful of people in the club, but Brian was embarrassed lest they should hear what he said. Williams did not know him, but knew of his professional reputation at NEMS and of his byline in *Mersey Beat*. Consultation was a characteristic that was to mark Epstein's life, sometimes, but not always, to his advantage. This night, Brian was careful with the buccaneering, street-sharp Williams, who he knew had managed the Beatles—four young men who were slightly apprehensive of getting involved with him (Epstein). "I hope you don't mind me asking you, Allan, for a bit of help. I'm thinking of managing the Beatles," said Brian.

Williams was not completely surprised at the news. His reaction was succinct. "They're a fantastic group—but they'll let you down. My advice is: don't touch them with a fucking bargepole. They have a track record of being late, especially Paul McCartney." Here, Williams had struck an uncomfortable truth; Paul had been late for that first meeting at NEMS. Epstein interjected defensively that they hadn't let him down yet; he explained that he was meeting people before he actually did anything with the Beatles and that he valued Allan's opinion. Williams emphasized his conviction that the Beatles were untrustworthy. Brian was troubled by this, since unreliability was a trait he loathed.

"They're ruthless," Williams said. "When it comes to contracts, be careful what you're signing. Make sure you can get out any time you want to." But he could sense Brian was fixated by the Beatles and that nothing could deter him. "So that was me off the scene," he says ruefully.

❏

As a solicitor and friend and neighbor of the Epstein family, Rex Makin had grown used to Brian's restlessness and capricious ideas. He was not the family lawyer, but his offices were next door to NEMS. He had a particular affinity with Brian, "a peculiar, very intimate relationship. He confided in me. I saw him in stress, in distress, when he was exhilarated, when he was normal."

The Brian Epstein who went to see Makin at his office in December 1961 had another surprise. "He said he wanted to have an unbreakable contract with a shattering group who were going to be absolutely unique in the world," Makin remembers. The lawyer wearily reacted to another of Brian's foibles: "Brian, there is *no such thing* as an unbreakable contract! Any contract that has been written is pulled by a coach and horses." Makin would not draw up a document for him, telling Brian flatly that he would not take the responsibility. "If you trust them and they trust you, then that's fine. If they don't trust you, well, then you've had it, mate." Epstein berated Makin for such superficiality. He was deadly serious, he informed him. "Oh, another thing," said Makin, unmoved. "Just settle down." Perhaps, reflects Makin now, he was cruel to Brian.

The cynicism of Rex Makin would not deter Brian, who then phoned David Harris, another solicitor who was also a friend of the Epstein family, particularly of his brother Clive's. At twenty-six, Harris was assistant solicitor with the law firm of Silverman, Livermore. Surprised by the call, Harris laughed at the mention of a pop group called the Beatles. Although the two men were from the same social framework, "Brian and I were not friends," says Harris. "Even then, there was nobody in Liverpool quite like him. He didn't seem to *have* any close friends: he was artistic and not part of the young bourgeois Jewish community in which we moved. He may well have despised us. We were all academics, intellectual snobs proud of going to university."

Epstein spoke purposefully to Harris about what the contract should establish. It was crucial for him to be perceived as treating the Beatles fairly, not taking advantage of them. "He had great agonies over whether he was seeking to charge them too much," says Harris. "He was concerned that their parents or guardians should be involved or that they should consult their own lawyers. He was acutely aware that since he came from a different backround, he had to demonstrate honesty and good faith." In this respect, Epstein probably patronized the Beatles, who were street-sharp. But his concern for the small print of the contract was enormous, says Harris.

Brian wanted the contract drawn up before Christmas 1961, because that would be a busy time in the NEMS record department. He wanted no diversions, and besides, it was important to impress the Beatles with his momentum.

The first contract, effective from February 1, 1962, was for a five-year period, but the Beatles or Epstein could each end the agreement by giving the other side three months' notice. It was particularly fair. "If he had really wanted to be nasty and tied them up, he could have made the termination clause one way only," Harris points out. Brian took 10 percent of the Beatles' income up to £1500 a year. If they each earned more than £1500 a year, Brian's percentage went up to 20 percent.*

Brian later said several times that his percentage was 15 percent during his first management year, when he lost money on the Beatles. "They had to earn £100 a week before I could earn more than fifteen percent," he said. All his artists joined him on similar terms. But Epstein said the percentage he took was difficult to view "in oblique terms," because his management service gave much more than that of the traditional show business manager or agent. In return for which, says Harris, "he did everything."

The contract cost Brian a mere £15. In it, he undertook to get the Beatles work; to guide and advise them in all professional matters; to employ subagents in any part of the world; to undertake all necessary advertising and publicity for the artists. A vital part of the contract called for Brian "to advise the artists on all matters concerning clothes, makeup and presentation and construction of the artists' acts."

Epstein was in a hurry, but the gentlemanly public-relations instincts deep inside him dictated pristine etiquette in dealing with the

*By 1963, when the Beatles earned big money, Brian's commission was 25 percent, the figure at which it remained.

Beatles' parents or guardians. After all, they were young men who would be involved in "employment" or partnership with him. He was also aware that, with his image as a leading city businessman who ran a company and a car, he could expose himself to charges of exploitation: Paul was nineteen, John twenty-one, George eighteen, and Pete twenty.

When the Beatles mentioned to their relations the arrival in their lives of a man named Epstein, there were undertones of anti-Semitic resentment. These were short-lived when Epstein visited all the Beatles' homes in turn. With his personable approach Brian was able to persuade their families that he would do his utmost to elevate the group and treat them fairly. Paul's widower father Jim, especially, was impressed by Brian's clear sincerity and businesslike determination; he fondly remembered learning to play piano on a second-hand instrument he had bought from NEMS at Walton Road. Queenie and Harry welcomed Mr. McCartney to Queens Drive and got along perfectly. Lennon's Aunt Mimi clung to a new hope that her errant nephew might now have some prospects after squandering his years at grammar school and art college in favor of a guitar. When Brian visited John's home, he invariably arrived with chocolates or a potted plant for Aunt Mimi, who, noting that he was an established and successful Jewish businessman, declared him "nice and bright."

Brian thoroughly immersed himself in "talking tactics" with the Beatles and their families, and there were reciprocal trips with John at his home at 251 Menlove Avenue. Clive recalled many such meetings at the Epstein home, only a mile away, Brian and John animatedly talking of a master plan. At that early stage, Lennon did not oppose the sanitization of the Beatles' image; Epstein was able to convince him that it was to their advantage to hoist themselves out of Liverpool to national exposure.

Epstein, concerned for the Beatles' security, learned that they were earning 75s. each for every Cavern session, higher than the normal rate because of their audience-pulling power. But they were having a financial struggle. Worse, they appeared to Brian to be rudderless, and despite their parents' friendly encouragement, he was aware that the Beatles were finding it hard to justify spending so much time in rock 'n' roll, which offered them an unpredictable future.

Quickly seeking to impress them with his seriousness about their career, Epstein crossed the road from NEMS to Frank Hessy's instrument shop. From the manager, Bernard Michaelson, he learned that the Beatles' debts on hire-purchase payments for their instruments totaled a massive £200. Epstein settled that sum immediately with a personal check, securing Lennon ownership of his precious Hofner Club 40 guitar, Harrison possession of his Futurama guitar, and amplification equipment for McCartney. It was an important manifestation of his faith.

❏

As David Harris drew up the contract, Brian decided another formal meeting with the Beatles was essential to prepare them for the signing. The next Wednesday, December 10, they met again at his Whitechapel office, this time with Alistair Taylor present. There was nothing to sign yet, said Brian, but the contract would soon be ready. He spelled out to them what was involved; what percentages he proposed to take; how much he hoped that they would all be successful together and reach the top. It was at that meeting, Epstein later told the author, "that the idea of management occurred on both sides." John Lennon, in just as much of a hurry as Epstein, said: "Right then, Brian, manage us. Where's the contract? I'll sign it." Paul McCartney astutely asked for confirmation that the relationship would not affect their music. Then he added: "I hope we make it as a group. But I'll tell you now, Mr. Epstein, I'm going to be a star anyway."

The formal signing of the contract on January 24, 1962, took place not at Brian's office but in a fourteen-room Victorian house at 8 Hayman's Green, in the residential suburb of West Derby. Here, at Pete Best's home, the embryonic Beatles had built up a loyal following in a coffee bar basement club called the Casbah, run by Pete's mother, Mona. The four Beatles signed the contract and Alistair Taylor signed as a witness, but Brian did not sign that first document. Later, when the Beatles had left, Taylor felt exposed, having been asked by Epstein to witness his signature, which wasn't there. "I asked him why," Taylor remembers, "and he replied: 'Well, if they ever want to tear it up, they can hold me but I can't hold them.' "

Later, hearing of Brian's decision, Allan Williams deduced that Epstein had wisely acted on his warning. If anything went wrong, he had the route out of their association which Williams had urged him to guarantee himself. "He could have walked away at any time," Williams points out, "and that had been my advice to him."*

❏

NEMS had rapidly expanded to nine Liverpool record shops, boasting a total stock of half a million records. The city-center bases in White-chapel and Great Charlotte Street had been augmented by smaller branches at 44 Allerton Road; 90 County Road; 2 Marian Square, Netherton; 37 St. Mary's Road, Garston; 25 High Street, Runcorn; and 6 Central Way, Maghull, while the original "flagship" remained at 62-72 Walton Road, Liverpool. Brian took all his responsibilities se-riously, but mentally he was pulled from the daily commercial routine by his passionate determination to lift the Beatles out of their treadmill of club work. Since he ran a record store, the Beatles expected action: their immediate dream was a British recording contract that would lift them out of the Liverpool group maelstrom. They knew they were good; now they wanted money and national fame. The contract with Brian signed, their psychological pressure on him increased. All his waking hours were now centered on the challenge he had set himself.

The sudden incursion by respectable Brian Epstein into the "lout-ish" world of youthful rock 'n' roll was stupefying to many local ob-servers. At Beaver Radio, the hi-fi and record shop just a few doors from NEMS, sales representatives went in and told Walter Beaver: "I don't know what the hell Brian Epstein's playing at. We can't do any business with him nowadays because he's fooling around with these idiots." Although Epstein was still keen to be seen as the city's premier record industry figure—with Walter Beaver, he formed the Liverpool branch of the Gramophone Record Retailers' Association, attracting nearly a hundred national record dealers to an inaugural meeting at NEMS one Sunday afternoon—his mind was clearly on other matters. Beaver remembers that Brian's father "got very annoyed and said: 'It's disgraceful, the way he's carrying on with these yobboes.' "

Beaver mentioned the general scepticism to Brian: "I believe your family are not very pleased with you." Brian answered: "I don't know what they're moaning about. At least it keeps me out of mischief two days a week."

*A second management contract, running for five years, was drawn up on October 1, 1962. Epstein did sign this.

"But his own family and everybody in the trade thought the fellow was mad," says Beaver, "and he was going to ruin the business and himself. It took a lot of time before they all felt proud of the fact that he had created something out of nothing."

Beaver, as a competitor, saw Brian grasping the record business very quickly. "His musical knowledge was excellent. But the downfall of it was that he overbought drastically. The only place to buy singles was NEMS: they had every single, and some in colossal quantities. They finished up with literally hundreds of thousands of completely unsaleable singles." It was, however, that very expansiveness that gave Brian and NEMS a golden reputation, and that same vision convinced him the Beatles would successfully break the rule that said that show business had to emanate from London.

Brian now realized he was up against the critical test of his life. He had to show his sceptical family and staff that the talent of four scruffy lads from the Cavern was not just exceptional but world-beating. Deep inside, he had no doubt that their vibrant act was a winner. Now he would have to satisfy the cynics, and himself, by delivering them out of Liverpool.

The Beatles were a heaven-sent anchor on which to pin his hopes of fame by proxy. With a belief in them that sparked an epic struggle for their golden break, Epstein was driven to acts of ruthless determination. The Beatles became his alter ego, while to them he was the best possible chance of a successful route out of Liverpool, which they had craved long before they dreamed of making hit records. Just like the three hundred other rock 'n' roll groups in the city in 1961, they wanted to turn professional as musicians. They were the cream of a fiercely competitive scene, but their treadmill of one-night stands gave no guarantee of a future, much less fame. Then along came a gentleman from a different world, a man with money, class, and an unshakable conviction that they deserved his energetic support. At a moment of desperation for both parties, the Beatles and Brian Epstein found each other.

5

❑

PASSION

THE BATTLE FOR A RECORD DEAL

BASHFUL AND SENSITIVE IN PRIVATE, Epstein had a remarkably tough veneer in business. Assertive and commercially orientated by dint of his father and grandfather's examples, he had learned to take some knocks in life—in his early school years, in the army, and at RADA —and he realized the need to bounce back quickly from rebuffs. But managing a pop group was swimming against the tide, wildly uncharted territory. And yet this *had* to be successful for him.

Fortunately, his success in establishing the excellence of the NEMS record shops, and his doctrine that no customer would leave dissatisfied, were the exact ingredients that guaranteed the Beatles' breakthrough. There was another crucial factor: his realization that he could not face his father if his exhausting campaign for the Beatles failed. As an eldest son, a hallowed position in a Jewish family, Brian carried the weight of family pride.

Around Liverpool he faced whispering and mockery as he set about revamping the Beatles. People tended to disparage his optimism, but they could not deflect his steely determination. "Every insult to Brian was taken as a compliment," recalls Yankel Feather. "If people did not agree with him, he attributed that to either their lack of knowledge of the subject or their plain ignorance. You could not insult him."

Epstein had two major, simultaneous tasks: to assert himself on Merseyside, where the Beatles were working successfully in clubs and ballrooms; and to interest a record company in his group.

Seeking a boost for their income from live shows, Brian telephoned promoter Larry Parnes in London in March 1962. Their conversation backstage at the Liverpool Empire had, he said, helped inspire him to become manager of a Liverpool pop group. Parnes remembered Epstein's act as the Silver Beetles, which had toured Scotland in 1960 in one of his package shows with the singer Johnny Gentle. Brian said he was confident that they would have a record deal soon. Would Parnes be interested in booking them for a series of Sunday concerts he was staging in Great Yarmouth that summer?

The cautious Parnes replied that he might be interested. "How much do you want a night for them?" Fifty pounds, said Epstein. "That's too much, Brian, for one night. They're not known! They may have a record coming out, but there's nothing to say it's going to come into the charts. I'll give you twenty-five pounds a night for them."

Two weeks later, Epstein went to Parnes's Marble Arch offices. He was buoyant. He said he intended to sign other acts, and expected them to be successful. Privately, he was very keen to impress the Beatles with a rewarding summer season. "If you take the Beatles for these thirteen nights," said Epstein, "I'll come down to forty-five pounds for them and I'll give you first option on a five-year contract to promote all my artists worldwide for, say, twenty weeks a year at an agreed fee going up annually for each of the artists, including unknown ones. And we'll take it from there."

Parnes admired Brian's optimism and confidence that his artists would have international appeal, but how could he be sure he was investing in artists with any drawing power? It would be better, said Parnes, to spread the agreement to thirteen weeks in the year rather than hold the Beatles to a summer season. "If they make it big and your other artists do, too, they're not going to be very happy later if you've done a set-price deal." Epstein disagreed: "If you give them their first breaks, they'll be very, very happy." Parnes, maintaining that £45 was too much, now offered £35 for the Beatles. Epstein left Parnes to reconsider that offer.

At 6:30 p.m. one Friday night, the phone rang in Parnes's office just as his secretary was preparing to leave—not just for the night, but permanently. Parnes was preoccupied. She answered the phone and, cupping her hand over the receiver, told Larry it was Epstein from Liverpool. Parnes told her to deal with it. Epstein said she should relay his final offer: the Beatles for £40 and the five-year contract. Parnes, distracted and awkward, said: "Tell him I'll go to thirty-seven pounds, ten shillings." At this, Brian contemptuously hung up. The two men never did business together but socialized in London.

Epstein faced a truly daunting task in getting the Beatles a recording deal. Though he understood how to sell records, he had no knowledge of the mechanism of creating them. His insight into the consumer aspect of pop had been limited to short conversations with singers Anthony Newley and Anne Shelton when they visited NEMS. His purist view was that if he had a saleable commodity, then people would quickly snap it up to claim a piece of the action. That was the way he operated, and he assumed everyone else would jump at the golden opportunity he had uncovered with the Beatles. He did not realize he was about to encounter the arbitrary judgment of the British record industry, still steeped in pre–rock 'n' roll conservatism.

Typically, he decided from the start that he would go for the biggest and the best. He chose EMI Records, which, with justification, described itself as "the greatest recording organisation in the world." As a retailer Brian knew of their prestige, impact, and power to distribute records. In his role as boss of NEMS, Brian arranged a meeting with Ron White, marketing manager of EMI in London. Since he bought lots of records, Brian said he felt justified in requesting an additional discount. White replied that EMI did not give discounts, whatever the quantity bought. "He accepted that quite gracefully," White remembers. "He was always a very polite gentleman. He then asked if, while he was in my office, I would mind listening to a record he'd got with him."

Brian's grooming, quiet confidence, and style gave White the strong impression that "he ought to have been doing something other than running a record shop. He could have been in industry. I certainly felt he was not fulfilling all his abilities.

"He was a very good, enthusiastic dealer, devoted to the record business. He never took advantage of any relationship that he had established with anyone. I'm not suggesting he was a pushover. He wasn't: he knew exactly what he wanted and was determined to get it. But he did it with kid gloves, whereas others might well have got out a cosh and hit you over the head. He was easier to deal with than a lot of lesser managers, who were hardheaded and unpleasant. I trusted him. I was never aware of him going back on his word. But he was also a good businessman, looking for his discounts."

Brian, of course, had used his entree as a respected record retailer to get himself heard and to give the Beatles a platform inside a record company office. That request for additional discounts was a ploy he would use several times to gain attention.

For White, Epstein then produced the single Polydor record of Tony Sheridan with the Beat Brothers singing "My Bonnie." "I asked what I was listening to," says White. Epstein answered: "Well, listen to the backing group."

"It's difficult to listen to a backing group when you've got a solo singer upfront," White recalls, "especially when the backing group sounded well laid-back. It really was impossible to make a judgment. But Brian was determined, totally involved with his act. He brought me a picture of the Beatles in leathers to show what they looked like. He had an air of confidence and style. I said I'd take the record round to our artists and repertoire people and ask them to make a decision."

Well, thought Brian, this was a start.

At the same time, White said he assumed that the Beatles were contracted to Polydor, the name on the label. Yes, said Brian, he had a copy of that contract, but it was in German and he could not understand it, still less tell EMI of the ramifications if they wanted to sign the group. As a gesture of help for a good retailer, White offered to get the contract translated in-house. Brian left London for Liverpool happy with the good faith of the honorable Ron White. But this was not enough for him. He felt he should generate some publicity for the group.

Next, he wrote to the *Liverpool Echo* asking for attention in the column "Off the Record," written by "Disker." Surprisingly, the reply came not from Merseyside but from Tony Barrow in London.

Disker was his pseudonym. A Liverpudlian who had moved south to become a full-time sleeve-note writer for Decca Records, Barrow replied courteously but firmly: his *Echo* column dealt only with singles reviews. "If they get a contract and when they've got a record released, of course I'll do a local interest story. Keep me posted."

This was Epstein's first real contact with anyone on the "consumer" side of the music or media business. Hitherto he had known only record retailing or marketing men. Hungry for as many new contacts as he could muster, on his next visit to London he dropped in at Barrow's office at Decca's Albert Embankment headquarters.

While EMI had made the running in encouraging young British talent, the boss of Decca, Sir Edward Lewis, had gained an enviable reputation for moving quickly to acquire American pop acts. While awaiting EMI's decision, Brian decided to bring Decca firmly into the picture.

To Tony Barrow's office he took an acetate recording that he said was part of a soundtrack for a television documentary at the Cavern. This was untrue, merely a hype and an excuse for its appalling quality. The fans' screams and the Cavern echoes were discernible, but the ability of the Beatles was impossible to evaluate. When Epstein coolly informed Barrow that this unknown Liverpool act would one day be as big as Elvis Presley, whose records were then distributed in Britain by Decca, a colleague in Barrow's office winced and looked askance at Barrow, wondering why he was giving any time to a manifestly idiotic hustler. Barrow, however, was tactful, because he knew NEMS was a big record store in Liverpool.

When Brian left the office, he lifted the internal phone to Decca's marketing manager, S. A. "Steve" Beecher Stevens. Barrow explained that a prominent Liverpool record dealer was touting a group called the Beatles: Perhaps Decca might want to audition them? Beecher Stevens was inclined to listen, like his counterpart Ron White at EMI. Although they were not technically in the business of talent hunting, NEMS and Epstein were significant names on Decca's and EMI's sales representatives' reports. Stevens and White instinctively knew that Epstein would use all his influence with every record company to make inroads for the Beatles. They did not want to be seen as disinterested, thus incurring the displeasure of a man who controlled a big outlet for their records.

❏

December 1961 was a heady, frantic month. Brian juggled the signing of the Beatles with his EMI and Decca visits while coping with the record shops and his puzzled father, looking for record company interest even before the Beatles had fully committed themselves to him; such was the ardor of his belief in them. At Decca, Brian had excellent relationships with two executives: Arthur Kelland, the regional sales manager based in Leeds, and Colin Borland, assistant to Beecher Stevens, the London marketing chief. Again using his influence as a retailer, he phoned both men to say that the Beatles from Liverpool could be their British "answer" to American pop dominance of the best-seller charts.

He asked Arthur Kelland to arrange an appointment for him in London to negotiate extra discounts for the records his shop bought from Decca. Provocatively, Brian said he thought other dealers might be getting preferential treatment. This was untrue, but Kelland politely referred him to Colin Borland in the head office.

On regular visits to Liverpool, Borland had been impressed by Epstein's enthusiasm and candidness: "I'm a failed actor and I've *got* to get the shops moving well." The Decca men thought him "too nice" for the rough-and-tumble of retailing, but like the entire industry, they admired his techniques; and his rising sales graph made beautiful reading. Though Brian had delegated many decisions to his shop manageress, Josephine Balmer, he earned Borland's respect by often telephoning him in London to ask precise reasons for Decca's pressure to display promotional material on certain artists. "Why *should* I give you my window display? Are you going to do a big advertising campaign?"

And Borland always found Epstein convivial company. Unlike many provincial shop managers, Brian never opted for the most expensive restaurants when Borland visited Liverpool; he was happy with a simple trattoria. Borland now suggested lunch to discuss the request for discounts.

To his surprise and that of Beecher Stevens, when Brian arrived at their London office on December 1, 1961, he immediately dismissed the topic of discounts. That, he implied, was merely a ploy to discuss something infinitely more important. It was the same tactic that he had used with Ron White at EMI. "What I'm *really* interested in is getting records made by a group I'm managing." He produced a copy of a Liverpool pop paper, *Mersey Beat,* which featured a picture of the Beatles. "We were well aware," says Borland, "that this was the most important thing that had happened to him for a very long time."

Epstein's first proposal was revolutionary and showed a visionary commercial streak that was unlike anything happening in the pop record business in 1961. He wanted Decca to make a record that would be exclusively licensed to him, perhaps on something called NEMS Records.

Borland said this would be difficult. If Decca recorded the Beatles, then as a major trading company they would have to make their records available to the whole retail trade. Brian said he was prepared to make the deal viable by personally buying five thousand copies. Even with a discount, that would have cost him £1050, an astronomically high figure in 1961 but an indication of his unshakable confidence. Conceding that the record would have to go on general sale, he added: "All right, if I'm giving you this nice big order, I want the records first and I want to be allowed to sell them where the Beatles are appearing." It was, says Borland, a big gamble that Epstein was prepared to take to demonstrate his enthusiasm.

To any record company, Epstein's offer would have been very attractive. A guaranteed sale of five thousand would get things off to a flying start: some singles did not get that many pressed as an advance, or sell that number in total. Next, Brian played Borland and Beecher Stevens the Polydor single, "My Bonnie." Listen to the backing group, Brian urged them. Like Ron White at EMI, the executives found it hard to isolate them from the vocalist.

Still, Brian's offer of five thousand sales was music to the ears of salesmen. Borland lifted the phone to Dick Rowe, the company's head of artists and repertoire. This resulted in another lunch, a few days later, in Decca's senior executive club on Albert Embankment. Rowe joined them at the coffee stage. Well aware of Epstein's status, he listened to his enthusiasm and said he would start wheels moving. He delegated the next step to his young A&R assistant Mike Smith, who confirmed to Brian that he would travel to the Cavern to judge the Beatles' potential. It was a triumphant breakthrough—a London record executive was on his way to Liverpool! Brian could scarcely wait to return home to break the news to the Beatles, who were equally excited.

Meanwhile, Brian was taking few chances. He was strategically playing EMI off against Decca, ingenuously planning for at least one of them to remain a possibility. On December 8, 1961, five days before Decca's Mike Smith was due to see the Beatles at the Cavern, Epstein wrote this energetic letter to Ron White at EMI:

Dear Mr White

As I'm somewhat disappointed at not having heard from you with regard to the matter we discussed last week, I thought I'd write again and attempt to impress you once again with my enthusiasm for, and belief in, "The Beatles."

If I didn't mention that they were so much better in reality than on the disc it was because I may have assumed that "you'd heard it before."

This point has been confirmed during the last few days by various persons that I'd persuaded to come from London to see them. Earlier this week the group were seen by representatives of Deutsche Grammophon* (in connection with the record they are issuing in January) who were very impressed, and now feel that the release will be worth summoning all the efforts and promotional activities that D.G. can muster in this country.

Next week the Group will be seen by A&R men from Decca. I mention this because (as you may appreciate) if we could choose it would certainly be EMI.

These four boys who are superb instrumentalists also produce some exciting and pulsating vocals. They play mostly their own compositions and one of the boys has written a song which I really believe to be the hottest material since "Living Doll."

This is a group of exceptional talents and appealing personalities. I look forward to hearing from you.

Yours sincerely,

Brian Epstein

P.S. With regard to the German contract they had signed (a copy of which I left with you) I understand that if pressed Deutsche Grammophon in Germany would probably be willing to negotiate on their breaking same at an earlier date than stated.

---

*Polydor Records' German parent company.

That letter crossed with a letter from White to Epstein dated December 7:

Dear Mr Epstein,
    I return herewith the original of the contract you gave to me in confidence a few days ago and thought you might like to have a translation to save you the bother of having it done.
    Now that I see their contract expires quite soon with Kaempfert I will certainly ask our Artistes Managers if they are interested in the group. I think you should note that it is necessary to give three months notice of termination before 30th June 1962 if you are to obtain their services.
    Please feel assured that I will have the material assessed very carefully and will write to you again as soon as possible.
                            Yours very truly
                            R.N. White,
                            General Marketing Manager, EMI Records.

At EMI's Manchester Square offices, Ron White was getting negative responses from the recording managers who were paid to have "ears" and make commercial records. There were four house producers, then described as A&R (artists and repertoire) staff men. Norrie Paramor, a respected orchestra leader, supervised the careers of Cliff Richard and the Shadows (together and as separate acts), Frank Ifield, and others. He listened to the Beatles' record and told White it was probably all right, but he had the Shadows at the peak of their career; he really didn't need another group like them.

White then offered it to Walter Ridley, who recorded Frankie Vaughan, Ronnie Hilton, Alma Cogan, and Joe Loss. Ridley said the record was difficult to judge, especially when he was asked to separate the backing group from the lead singer. The sound didn't interest him particularly.

The third A&R man, Norman Newell, as well as being a successful songwriter, recorded stars like pianists Russ Conway and Mrs. Mills plus soundtracks for the London theater musicals. From what he could detect, which wasn't much, he told White that Epstein's group sounded a bit like the Shadows. And he wouldn't want to compete in-house with Paramor.

The fourth A&R man, George Martin, was on holiday, so White could not offer the record to him. Had he not been away, it is possible that history might have taken a different course. The rejection of the Beatles by three of his colleagues, whose work was aimed more directly at the young pop market than his, might have colored his view.

Brian's salesmanship technique combined a thick skin with undeniable flair and energy. Only a month after he had first seen the Beatles, he had them under contract, had secured at least the attention of two major record companies, and had a London talent scout en route to the Cavern. But just before Christmas, Brian's EMI hopes capsized. He must have felt he had overplayed his hand with Ron White by mentioning the Decca visit to Liverpool, because on December 18 White replied to his heavy overture:

> Dear Mr Epstein
> Thank you for your letter of 8 December in connection with "The Beatles."
> I am sorry that I have been so long in giving you a decision but I have now had an opportunity of playing the record to each of our Artistes Managers.
> Whilst we appreciate the talents of this group we feel that we have sufficient groups of this type at the present time under contract and that it would not be advisable for us to sign any further contracts of this nature at present.
> Please accept my sincere apologies and also thanks for letting us have the opportunity of first refusal. I return the original of the German contract herewith. With best wishes for Christmas and the New Year.
>
> Yours sincerely,
> R N White*

Brian was now aware that he had inherited big problems. He had a categorical "No" from EMI and also the complication of extracting the Beatles from a contract with Polydor Records.

Their German record deal turned out to be a licensing arrangement

---

*This letter, published here for the first time, contradicts the theory advanced for twenty-five years that Decca preceded EMI in rejecting the Beatles. In fact, EMI's rejection here, confirmed by three senior producers, was even more devastating than Decca's eventual rejection, since EMI was Epstein's preferred home for the Beatles.

to Polydor by a noted bandleader. Bert Kaempfert Produktions had signed the Beatles to a contract from July 1, 1961, for one year, renewable for further periods of one year. The agreement called for four songs to be recorded per year and gave the German company world rights, as well as exclusivity for ten years from the date of recordings.

There was provision for DM25 a day for living expenses when the group was recording in Hamburg, and, surprisingly, first-class rail fares. The royalty, however, was iron-fisted: 5 percent of the *wholesale* price. This contrasted with the traditional deal offered by major British record companies in those years: "We usually gave five percent of the retail price," says Ron White. "If the record sold for five pounds, the shop paid one pound for it, the artist got five percent of one pound." The German deal was much lower: it was 5 percent of the price Polydor charged to the dealer. For foreign sales, the Beatles received a paltry 1 percent of the retail price. Companies like EMI paid 50 percent of their receipts on overseas sales, "and *that* was subject to criticism for meanness!" says Ron White.

While gaining the Beatles' confidence and beginning the task of raising their fees for live performances, Brian sounded out Kaempfert's attitude toward his legal right to "kill" the deal on three months' notice. He wrote to Kaempfert on February 20, 1962, optimistically saying he hoped to generate British record interest. Brian asked the German for the Beatles' freedom. Luckily, Kaempfert was a fair, conciliatory man, a successful musician who did not wish to stand in the way of the Beatles' possible success. "I do not want to spoil the chance of the group to get recording contracts elsewhere," Kaempfert wrote to Epstein, "but I do think that we should have the chance to make recordings with the group for the Polydor label whilst they are in Hamburg." The trade-off was simply that when the Beatles visited Hamburg in April 1962, they would make records for Kaempfert/ Polydor to complete their commitments in Germany. Epstein, mightily relieved, agreed. The way ahead for a British record deal was painlessly secured.

❑

All hopes were now pinned on the visit by Decca's Mike Smith to the Cavern and on the hope that the trip would produce a London audition. Still, Brian kept up his frenetic activity: when visited by representatives of Deutsche Grammophon's London office, who were intrigued by his enthusiasm for "My Bonnie," he pressured them to release it as a single in Britain. They agreed and the record was scheduled for release on January 5, 1962. It was important for the Beatles to see he was moving on all fronts.

On December 13, 1961, amid enormous local excitement, Mike Smith went to Liverpool. First, he was taken to dinner by Brian Epstein. At the Cavern he was mightily impressed by the Beatles' performance. Brian was thrilled. When Smith invited the Beatles to a London audition on New Year's Day 1962, Brian firmly believed they were on the first rung of a ladder to the top.

In London, while Brian visited his Aunt Frida and stayed overnight with her, the Beatles stayed at the Royal Hotel, Woburn Place. Next morning, amid snow and ice, they went to Decca. They were punctual for the 11 a.m. appointment; Mike Smith was late. Epstein, a lifelong stickler for punctuality, was peeved at what he regarded as inferior treatment.

The audition passed uneventfully. The Beatles reluctantly listened to Brian's advice about some of their repertoire; he wanted them to play a little "safe," with the accent on melodic ballads. John Lennon said they should do their usual Cavern act, a strong dose of raw rock 'n' roll, but they conceded to Brian's knowledge of salesmanship. Brian was particularly glad when Paul sang the pretty ballad "Till There Was You" from the show *The Music Man*.

❏

Back in Liverpool, Brian's lengthy phone conversations on booking arrangements, proposed visits to London (Ray Cobb observed Brian's looks of exasperation when he kept returning empty-handed to Liverpool from visits to record companies in London), and negotiations for the Beatles to audition for BBC radio in Manchester, were taking priority over his work in the record shop. Harry Epstein visited the Whitechapel store about twice weekly, bringing the payroll down from the original store at Walton Road. "He was never one for showing his worries to the staff," says Ray Cobb, "but I think he was very alarmed at Brian's involvement with the Beatles." He confronted Brian several times, saying: *Do you know what you're doing?*

"Harry used to get very uptight," says Alistair Taylor. "He felt

Brian was neglecting the business, which he wasn't." When Alistair told him where his son was, sometimes in London hunting a Beatles contract, Harry once snapped: "This is absolute nonsense." Brian assured his father that the Beatles really were worth pursuing and that he would "resolve the business." Sometimes Brian was so tired from "doubling up" in his work that he overslept, missing his father's automatic lift by car into work; on those days, he caught the tram into Whitechapel.

Over drinks at Queens Drive, Queenie said to Brian's friend Geoffrey Ellis, when Brian was out of the room: "You know, Geoffrey, Brian said to me that the Beatles were going to be bigger than Elvis Presley. Isn't it ridiculous? But we've got to let him get it out of his system." However, Rita Harris, a NEMS salesgirl whom Brian had been dating occasionally, taking her to Halle Orchestra Concerts in Manchester, delivered an ultimatum. She would not be relegated to second place behind the Beatles, who were taking too much of his time. Brian was now too hooked on the Beatles to even consider a choice.

❑

To the men at Decca, there was no great rush for deciding whether to move ahead with Epstein's Beatles. An immensely thriving company, its studios jammed with established artists, Decca put its musical emphasis firmly on show business professionalism rather than on energetic rock 'n' roll. A Liverpool entrepreneur with a guitar-led group sounding "vaguely like the Shadows" was not of critical importance.

Dick Rowe kept Epstein waiting for weeks, an agonizing period for Brian and the group. Finally, a phone call from Beecher Stevens invited him to London. Brian was pessimistic; there had obviously been no immediate excitement at Decca over the audition tape.

To ease what would inevitably be a painful confrontation, Dick Rowe and Beecher Stevens again took Brian to lunch in their seventh-floor Albert Embankment executive club; the date was February 6, 1962. Over coffee, after what must have been one of the longest meals of Brian's life, Rowe broached the subject of their rejection of the Beatles. "Not to mince words, Mr. Epstein, we don't like your boys' sound. Groups are out; four-piece groups with guitars particularly are finished."

Brian's fury at such a denigration was camouflaged by his genuine optimism and belief in the Beatles. "You must be out of your minds," he retorted. "You get these boys on TV and you will have an explosion. They will be bigger and better than the Shadows. I am completely confident that one day they will be bigger than Elvis Presley."

This was sheer heresy! Not only were Presley's records distributed by Decca, but for Brian to line up an unknown Liverpool group alongside the King of Rock 'n' Roll confirmed to these show business veterans that Epstein had lost his balance. The men of Decca stonewalled. "The boys won't go, Mr. Epstein. We know these things. You have a good record business in Liverpool. Stick to that," Dick Rowe finally advised.

Brian fought hard to rebuff their negativism. He reiterated that he was determined to prove them wrong, because the Beatles were very special, the best in Liverpool, where competition was intense.

It would have been terrible psychology to send Epstein away empty-handed. Although the men at Decca had rejected the Beatles, they still needed NEMS as a valued retail outlet. And Brian was an influential voice among retailers nationally. Rowe and Beecher Stevens stared at each other, wondering how to appease him. At last Rowe said: "I have an idea. You know who might help you? Tony Meehan." Ironically, he was a former drummer with the Shadows but was now making a name as a Decca artists manager.

Well, thought Epstein, here was *something*. It was a curious suggestion, and although he was irritated by Decca's continued procrastination, he agreed to stay overnight in London and take advantage of this first concession. Brian then learned he would have to pay £100 for the benefit of Meehan's advice on making a Beatles record. Already aggrieved at Decca's rejection of the audition tape, he now felt he was being treated condescendingly. To be asked for money upfront was indeed an insult, but not quite as final as EMI's letter of rejection.

His worst fears were confirmed at Decca's West Hampstead studios the next day. "Tony," said Rowe after Brian had waited a patient half hour for their attention, "take Mr. Epstein out and explain the position." Meehan knew the ropes of the pop scene, having met other managers with sky-high aspirations. His message was terse. "Mr. Epstein, Mr. Rowe and I are very busy men. We know roughly what you

require, so will you fix a date for tapes to be made of these Beatles?
Telephone my secretary to make sure I am available."

It had been an empty rendezvous. That chilly February day in
1962, Brian left London brooding on the fact that he had been to
Decca so many times and emerged with very little hope. The future
looked bleak. Failure stared him in the face, and he did not relish the
task of breaking the news to the Beatles, now eager for positive news.

On his return to Liverpool, he decided to reject the offer of Tony
Meehan's services. It was clear that Decca did not favor the Beatles
and that all their talk amounted to a dead end. Viewing their proposed
olive branch as grudging at best, he wrote to Dick Rowe and decisively
closed the door himself. In a letter dated February 10, 1962, he wrote:

> Dear Mr Rowe,
>   I am writing to thank you for your kind offer of co-operation
> in assisting me to put the Beatles on records. I am most grateful
> for your own and that of your colleagues' consideration of this
> Group and whilst I appreciate the offer of Mr Meehan's services
> I have decided not to accept.
>   The principal reason for this change of mind is that since I saw
> you last the Group have received an offer of a recording Contract
> from another Company.*
>
>   Kindest regards,
>   Yours sincerely,
>   Brian Epstein.

Thus ended the Beatles' tenuous link with Decca. Or so both sides
thought at that moment. Within two years EMI's production facilities
were to become so stretched that Decca helped them out in a reciprocal
arrangement, to cope with the unprecedented demand for pressing
Beatles records.

But there was no disguising Epstein's present dilemma. Within two
months he had been rejected by the two giants, EMI and Decca. He
was visibly dejected and began to be thankful that he had not signed
that management contract with them. At least if he could not get them

*This was untrue, clearly an attempt by Epstein to make the Decca men regret their
coolness and change their minds.

the big breaks, they were free to find another manager. Told of Decca's rejection, Lennon icily remarked that they should never have listened to Epstein's advice on their choice of songs for the audition. It would be the last time he interfered with their music, he averred.

While contemplating his next move on the recording front, he decided to consolidate the Beatles' live appearance schedule. Fiercely protective of their unique name, Brian began to enforce rules that would shape his future policy. He reacted strongly against a Manchester group called the Measles, who also played Liverpool's Cavern. Their name was too close for comfort, and he raged to Bob Wooler about the publicity campaign for them, which traded on the Beatles' popularity. "THE -EA-LES are coming your way," proclaimed posters and leaflets. "Cheap," protested Epstein, demanding their withdrawal.

The first booking he fully arranged for the Beatles, through local promoter Sam Leach, on February 1, 1962, was at the Thistle Cafe, West Kirby—at a ten-mile distance from Liverpool and the Beatles' regular venues. Brian plumped for a special promotional theme to mark his first outing with them: he persuaded the owner of the hall to describe the night in newspaper advertisements and onstage as "The Grand Opening of the Beatle Club." Since it was not an established pop place, the appendage was meaningless, but it showed Epstein's early promotional zeal. The Beatles' fee was £18 and Brian's percentage was 10 percent—mere "petrol money," as he later described it.

Now he began the process of elevating their status by pressuring local promoters for improved treatment of the Beatles, plus higher fees. At the Aintree Institute, where he received the £15 fee in the kitchen in bagged silver coins, Brian expressed horror. It was, he maintained, an insult to him and the Beatles if he accepted such treatment: important artists should never be paid in ready cash. He told promoter Brian Kelly that he and the Beatles would like to be paid in a "civilized manner, in pound notes." Then, wearing gloves and overcoat, he stalked off in a huff, saying: "Send me a check." The message began to spread on the pop grapevine on Merseyside: the Beatles were being changed. Nobody could have predicted the extent to which Epstein would orchestrate their next, incredible step.

Strong and abrasive characters though they were, and he loved them for that, he decided that as manager he had to smarten them up, get them out of leathers, and make them more accessible to a wider public. Everyone who knew them thought it would be a Herculean task, but Brian was adamant. Their music was their own; it would remain intact. But he knew more than they about self-projection. He insisted they cut their stage repartee, their drinking and smoking on the stand, and totally sharpen their professional attitude. This met with a muted response, and Brian realized he would have to swing the leader of the group to his viewpoint very quickly.

Although they worked as a cooperative, the Beatles had metamorphosed from Lennon's grammar school skiffle group, the Quarry Men; it was he who had recruited McCartney. So Lennon was the leader. And having drifted away from a promising art college future to burn his bridges with rock 'n' roll, he had the most to gain from the Beatles' success. Brian invited him to his home for strategy meetings, explaining that better appearance could only enhance his opportunity to raise their fees and "present" them to London. The music would be unaffected and the end would justify the means, Epstein added. A dubious Lennon was finally convinced, somewhat reluctantly.

Next, Brian took them to Beno Dorn, an outfitter in Birkenhead, where he invested in £40 mohair suits for them. Getting the Beatles into suits, as well as tightening their stage act, was one of Brian Epstein's amazing achievements. A large part of their success in Liverpool and Hamburg had been traceable to their earthiness. "Nobody could understand how he got them to conform," says one local musician, Rod Pont. "I remember talking to them in the Cavern band room when they first wore those dark suits with very narrow lapels. They had their arms in the air making sure there was enough room, and they obviously felt uncomfortable.

"Yet, rebellious though John Lennon was, he still conformed to Epstein's demands! I could never understand how Brian got him to accept that outrageous behavior and casual dress would not necessarily contribute to their success. There's no doubt about it: John was the leader, the boss man of the Beatles. Paul would fall into line. But really, how Epstein ever persuaded Lennon to put on a suit I shall never know."

Others on the sidelines were equally aghast. A fifteen-year-old schoolgirl, Shelagh Carney,* who helped run the Beatles' fan club, was "hit like a brick" when she saw the changes in the Beatles activated by Brian. "They had looked so rough until then. Suddenly they looked steam-cleaned, from their skin and shiny hair to their fingernails and their clothes." Staring at their slightly aloof manager in his office, where she sifted fan mail, Shelagh observed where the boys' grooming came from. She was startled to note that between the bottom of his trousers and the beginning of his beautiful toe-capped leather shoes, "he wore sheer black nylon socks. I remember thinking: gosh, such wealth and prosperity!"

The changes were palpable. The Beatles had an assertive manager pushing for better fees, and a new mode of presentation. The key difference between their pre-Epstein years and what followed was that he honed a raw, rugged group of rock 'n' rollers into a mature, palatable, and commercial entity.

Fired and inspired by their ebullience and razor-sharp wit, Brian was increasingly in love with their act. He grew to admire their off-stage personalities almost as much as their performances. Their debunking humor checked his own stuffiness. Brian decided he could not give up the fight for a record contract. He would have to visit London for a final onslaught on the labels, major and minor.

But the rebuffs continued. At Pye, he met artists manager Alan A. Freeman, a warm, benevolent man who had more empathy with his top singers, Petula Clark and Lonnie Donegan, and jazz trumpeter Kenny Ball than with rock 'n' roll. Brian's tape from the Decca audition was not considered good enough; Freeman said he might consider a better presentation. Next, Brian tried Oriole, a lively little independent. Morris Levy, its boss, was out when Epstein called and Brian's time in London was limited. He was concerned about his father's irritation at his absences. A phone call to Philips asking for a meeting with an executive brought an empty response. "Write in," said a secretary, coldly.

"Look, really, Brian was a fool," reflects one top music industry figure. "He was so naive about the way the business ran, even in those days. All he had to do was invest a little money in studio time

---

*Now Shelagh Johnston, one of six qualified Beatles guides appointed by the Merseyside Tourist Board.

and get a few good tracks made to tout around. He should have had a perfect sample to play. Instead, he relied on that lousy sound, which didn't even present the full scope of what he was selling. The Beatles were effectively a backing group on some of his demonstration samples."

Alternating with the negative reaction from record companies was Brian's other pressure: he had to keep showing the Beatles he cared about their live appearances. He secured them a BBC radio audition in Manchester, which they passed.

Then, in midsummer 1962, he finally decided that it was not enough to be a casual manager. He launched NEMS Enterprises, a new company that would be the umbrella for his show business activities. It was a signal to everyone that he was deadly serious about pop music and saw his future as a manager. Harry Epstein, perhaps fearful of a bad division in the family, told Brian that he would need the business acumen of his brother Clive in the business to ensure its success. Clive became joint director with a 50 percent share.

Still, the once-or-twice-weekly visits continued by train from Liverpool to London. They were tiring and dispiriting. The Beatles met him at Lime Street station with the same question: "Have they signed us yet, Bri?" After one such frustrating journey, they adjourned to the all-night Joe's Cafe, their regular haunt in Duke Street. Epstein gave them his grim news: rejections everywhere. Lennon drily suggested trying Embassy, then a low-price budget label with no prestige, run by Woolworth's. It cut the ice and raised a laugh but reminded Brian of the desperation facing him.

Meanwhile, Allan Williams's declining relationship with the Beatles took another turn when he banned them from his Blue Angel club. It was a devastating blow to their social lives, denying them access to drinking with other players after Cavern sessions. The ban was Williams's retort to the disputed issue of a commission due him from the Beatles' German work.

The group gave Epstein the job of getting them reinstated at the Blue Angel. Brian's charm cajoled the prickly Williams. "They're very, very sorry for what happened between them and you," Epstein told him. "They'd love to come back. They're outside, waiting. They've got no social life. . . ." It worked, and their relationship with Williams was partly healed. The Beatles recognized the smooth persuasiveness of their new manager—if only he could use that asset to transport them to London, to a record deal, and beyond. They knew their music was good. And they desperately wanted to burst out of Liverpool.

"The Beatles had placed their absolute faith in Brian getting them a contract in London," says Bob Wooler. "He was their guardian angel and benefactor, but until he had secured that contract he was not much different from any other manager waving promises. Disillusionment was setting in and their parents were asking why they didn't get proper jobs." Wooler is certain that if Epstein had not been successful around that time, they would have split.

What gave Epstein the edge over other contenders in gaining the Beatles' confidence was certainly his background. Though Brian did not come from an endlessly rich family, he seemed in the millionaire league to the impoverished scufflers on the Liverpool rock 'n' roll scene. The Beatles' families recognized his natural air of command. And he drove a Ford Zodiac, totally beyond their reach. "To all of us, he was *wealthy*," says Bob Wooler. "But the Beatles were cunning. As with everyone they dealt with in business, whether he had money or not, he had to prove himself."

During his period of battling for a record deal, Epstein was a forlorn figure, the Cavern host recalls. Wooler commiserated with him when he returned so often from London empty-handed. "Well, you *tried*, Brian! There's always another record company. . . ." But he was inconsolably despondent; time was running out if he wanted to keep his credibility. Wooler could also see and hear the pressure Brian faced at home and at NEMS for wasting too much time; and he heard the Beatles repeatedly asking him the embarrassing question on his return from London: "Any luck?"

The Beatles occasionally mocked his gloss behind his back, at the Cavern and in the pubs. Epstein realized this but never chastised them. To Wooler, he said once: "They can be very hurtful at times, can't they, Bob?"

"Because of his homosexuality he was able to put up with them and swallow his pride," says Wooler. "If he was not homosexual, the Beatles wouldn't have happened. They gave him a lot of trouble, but to Brian, because of what he was, they were everything; he did not want to know failure and was prepared to tolerate anything to achieve success. Yet he wasn't sure he could do anything for them. It was a period of great uncertainty and tension for him. Whatever anyone said later, Brian was going through hell from the Beatles and his family."

Despite all the anxiety, and because of the adrenaline it released, Brian enjoyed the role of manager. How he relished flamboyantly reaching for his diary when Wooler and other promoters asked if the Beatles were free for engagements! He would then flex his muscle and say airily, "Ah, I see they are free a week on Friday," before asking for high fees. He showed his support by attending most of their performances, preferring to arrive unexpectedly for their shows at the Cavern. "Don't let the lads know I'm coming," he would tell Wooler. The compere would face the same question from the Beatles when they arrived to set up their equipment: "Is Eppy here? Is he coming?"

If the record deal was an obstacle, there had to be tangible benefits from trusting him and relinquishing their scruffy appearance. They had a foothold in Hamburg, where they earned good money at the Top Ten Club. A visit to Liverpool by the club owner, Peter Eckhorn, had the sole purpose of signing the Beatles and other groups for appearances in Hamburg in mid-1962. But in his first encounter with their new manager, Eckhorn was aghast at the demand for much more money than they had previously received: Epstein wanted DM500 for each player per week. Eckhorn offered DM450, a substantial increase, but Epstein said he would let him know. The club owner returned to Germany with no contract.

Three weeks later, another promoter flew into Liverpool. Horst Fascher was seeking the Beatles for a new, larger Hamburg venue, the Star-Club. He, too, was surprised at the sudden arrival of the well-spoken Epstein in the Beatles' lives, but was happy to negotiate with him. Brian again asked for, and this time received, the DM500 per person per week that Eckhorn had been unable to match. It was a lucrative deal, for the Beatles were scheduled for seven weeks in Hamburg from April 13 until May 31, 1962.

Brian was proving that he was capable of exploiting the Beatles' commercial strength. As a grand gesture, typical of the style he was injecting into their lives, he told them that they would never again travel by train and ferry to Germany. He would arrange a flight from Manchester.

As he increased their earnings from appearances and raised their spirits, Brian decided on a final trip to London for an appeal to every record company he could reach. On May 8, 1962, he spent an emotionally charged, sleepless night at the Green Park Hotel before heading the next morning for the HMV Record Shop in Oxford Street.

There, the general manager was an acquaintance, Robert Boast, with whom Brian and fifty other enterprising record retail executives had visited Hanover and Hamburg a year earlier for a sales training course organized by Deutsche Grammophon. "We recognized each other," Boast recalls, "and he told me he'd had an exhausting time going to Decca in the hope that he could get the opportunity to promote the Beatles. Could I listen to his demonstration and see if there was anyone at EMI with whom I could put him in contact?"

Brian's chief reason for visiting the HMV Shop was to equip himself with better samples of the Beatles' music. He was armed only with reel-to-reel tapes from the Decca audition, and he had heard that HMV had a section that, for a fee of £1 10s., transferred tapes to acetate records. These, he reasoned, would be easier to play to record company men, and he certainly needed more than one copy.

Asked to listen to Beatles music, Boast confessed that it was not to his taste. Unaware of the rejections Brian had faced from his company, however, Boast said that "someone in EMI ought to listen to what Epstein has to offer." He then asked his private recording engineer, Jim Foy, to listen to the music and perhaps advise who in the record division might be approached.

When he went downstairs to the cutting department to transfer the 7½-inch reel-to-reel tapes to lacquers, Foy was impressed. With Brian's permission, he telephoned the only man he knew who might be able to assist. Sid Coleman, who had an office on the fourth floor of the Oxford Street store, ran EMI's music publishing arm, Ardmore and Beechwood.

When Brian played him the tape in his office, he asked: "Have you taken these to anybody?"

"*Everybody!* But I'm still trying."

"Have you taken them to George Martin?"

"Who's George Martin?" asked Brian.

"He does comedy records," Coleman replied, adding that he also headed the Parlophone label within EMI.

Coleman phoned Martin and asked if he would meet Epstein. Martin agreed to see him the next morning. He was a tall, well-spoken man and, like Brian, urbane and precise. He was also atypical of the hustling pop industry, from which he stood apart. A former student at the Guildhall School of Music, Martin at thirty-six had established himself at EMI as the recording manager of the zany "Goon Show" stars Peter Sellers and Spike Milligan and top ballad singer Matt Monro. And more important, for the teenage market he had no artists under his wing who could be considered counterparts to those handled by his A&R colleagues Paramor, Ridley, and Newell.

The night before he met George Martin for what would be the clincher, Brian was uncharacteristically hesitant, almost a beaten man. From his London hotel he phoned his Aunt Lorna and Uncle Berrel. "Could I come to see you?" he asked, looking for company to distract him from the worry. His uncle answered: "We'd love to see you, Brian, but the children [Brian's cousins Basil and Doreen] aren't in." Brian nevertheless sought solace by going to their home in Ingram Avenue, Hampstead. There was a weight on his mind.

He was disheartened, he said, by all the rejections. The Beatles were a wonderful act but he was getting nowhere on the record front. "What shall I do? Shall I give it all up? I've got one more appointment in the morning. Or should I go back home? I really don't know what to do for the best." Queenie recalls that her brother told him: "Oh, just keep that appointment."

When Epstein arrived next morning to see George Martin at EMI's Abbey Road studios, the self-preservationist in him prevented any mention of his previous rejections by EMI. He was privately perplexed to have an audience with an open-minded EMI executive when Ron White had already delivered a firm written refusal. This was like reentering EMI by the back door.

As always, his personality helped him. George Martin and his eloquent secretary, Judy Lockhart-Smith, immediately considered him "unusually smartly dressed, quite unlike the average person who brought in a demonstration record." Epstein was anxious for real action but Martin's cool authority invited no tough sales talk. "He didn't press too hard," says Martin.

"He really believed they were great because he knew the Beatles as people. And it wasn't until you met them that you knew they were great. They didn't come across on those songs." Taking a chance on the very raw material, Martin told Epstein: "Okay. Bring them down to London and I'll give them a test." Brian grinned. It was the second big chance since he had committed himself to the Beatles.

A totally different and more dramatic story, conceivable in view of Brian's utter desperation, comes from Alistair Taylor. He says Epstein finally blackmailed EMI into giving the Beatles a recording deal. "Brian threatened to withdraw his business from EMI if they didn't give them a recording contract," says Taylor. "It was as simple as that. He went to every record company. That's why they went to George Martin on Parlophone, which was unheard of as a pop label.

"EMI took them on sufferance because Brian was one of their top customers. I saw Brian in tears, literally, because Martin promised to phone back and day after day went by and George Martin was never available, always 'in a meeting.' I saw Brian thumping the desk and in tears because George Martin hadn't phoned him back."

Taylor says Epstein talked to him of how NEMS as a shop would jettison the EMI labels HMV, Parlophone, and Columbia. "There wasn't much on the actual HMV label that worried us, and we could get Parlophone and Columbia from other sources when needed." The plan was therefore to not carry regular stock from the company that Brian so wanted to accept his Beatles.

Brian's obvious desire to sign with EMI was more understandable than his anger with Decca. Throughout all the publicity he generated about his ordeal in getting a record contract, Epstein never released the dramatic truth: that EMI had originally rejected the Beatles before George Martin's acceptance. He gave credence only to the story of Decca's ineptitude. Even in his autobiography, Brian whitewashes EMI by ignoring the early rejection, pretending that all was sweetness from the start, while castigating Decca—actually the *second* company to turn him down. Yet Epstein, who had a superb memory, would never have forgotten Ron White's letter or the worry it had induced. He chose to forget the bad news for expedience, so that no feathers were ruffled. Everything was going too well with EMI by the time he told his story of the battle for a deal. And by then he needed to bury the earlier problem to secure a good relationship with EMI, thus protecting his other artists' careers. The Machiavellian streak that had surfaced with his upgrading of the Beatles' visual appeal, and with the powerful arguments he used to win them esteem and more money, was now apparent.

George Martin's offer of a test–cum–recording session sent Brian into a paroxysm of delight. Leaving Abbey Road studios at midday on May 9, 1962, he headed for the post office on Wellington Road to telephone his mother with the great news. "It was such a relief: we could hardly believe it after all the disappointments," she says. Brian then sent two telegrams. To the Beatles in Hamburg his message read: "Congratulations boys, EMI request recording session. Please rehearse new material." The second, with Epstein's omnipresent eye for publicity plus the need to blast the news around Liverpool, went to Bill Harry at the *Mersey Beat* newspaper: "Have secured contract for Beatles to record for EMI on Parlophone label. First recording date set for June 6." The apocalyptic news was greeted on Merseyside with delight tinged with sorrow. Epstein, it was apparent, had indeed "done the job" and the Beatles were on their way out of the city.

❑

Bob Wooler was one of the first to know of Brian's elation that the EMI contract was clinched. Brian knew Wooler was keen to announce the big news over the Cavern microphone. But he banned Bob from saying anything: Epstein wanted everything signed and sealed first.

The Beatles-Martin-Epstein axis connected from the start. The Beatles respected the fact that Martin was the producer of two of their beloved Goons, Peter Sellers and Spike Milligan. On their first meeting on June 4 at EMI's Manchester Square office, where the musicians were required to sign a contract, George Martin quickly recognized their "tremendous personality and charisma," which Brian had identified. Their irrepressible humor struck a chord. Then, there was a natural empathy between Epstein and Martin that transcended business. After the test on June 6, the party adjourned to the Alpino restaurant in Marylebone High Street. "Okay, I like you and we'll make some records," Martin told them.

He was investing chiefly in their vitality, because original rock 'n' roll groups did not exist on records in Britain in 1962. Elvis Presley, Little Richard, and other American acts were countered in Britain by Cliff Richard, Tommy Steele, and the highly packaged stable masterminded by Larry Parnes, featuring Joe Brown, Marty Wilde, Billy Fury, and many others who sang the songs they were given without a murmur.

So Martin's views were colored by the musical climate. "It was something very new. When I first listened to them, I tried each voice in turn, wondering which one was going to be my Cliff Richard. Paul was the prettiest, John the most off-beat, and I didn't think George's voice was as good as those two. It wasn't until they started together that I suddenly realized they should be recognized as a group."

Financially, EMI had little to lose: "To say I was taking a gamble would be stretching it because the deal I offered them was pretty awful." It was, in fact, the standard deal for new artists making a debut record. In those days, a debut was marked by a single rather than an album, so the remuneration was always expressed in currency terms instead of percentages.

Epstein accepted EMI's basic offer: a penny a single. EMI paid all recording costs, so there were no levies against the penny, but there was no advance payment. "They were very happy to get it," says Martin, "but looking back, that penny was split five ways." The deal guaranteed the Beatles only four songs to be recorded each year. It also bound them exclusively to EMI for a one-year contract, with EMI having the option to three further options of a year each. So from EMI's view, they were tied up for four years.

From a meager bunch of Lennon-McCartney songs offered by Epstein for their debut single, George Martin chose "Love Me Do" and "P.S. I Love You." For a record aimed at the charts, the Beatles had an unusual sound quite unlike anything the 1962 British pop scene was accustomed to. Few artists wrote their own material. There were wafts of original rock 'n' roll creativity from America (Elvis Presley, Buddy Holly, Little Richard). But in Britain, popular music was firmly dominated by carefully honed love songs from professional writers in Tin Pan Alley, virtually a music factory. (Martin originally wanted them to record a song called "How Do You Do It" as their debut. He had obtained this from one such writer, Mitch Murray.) The Beatles hated the vapidity of this scene. Their rock 'n' roll thrust was tilted toward overthrowing the Establishment. That tenet was lost on Brian, who had a healthy respect for successful entertainment.

Every Tuesday at the EMI Records offices in London, the repertoire meeting chaired by the pragmatic Ron White sat in judgment on the commercial prospects of the records sent along by the company's four trusted A&R men. One record acetate of each imminent release would be sent to the meeting; when it went onto the record player, no artist's name was mentioned to the dozen sales-oriented men present. When the single stopped playing, they were usually given a piece of paper with the name of the act they had heard. Rather like judge and jury, they would then issue their verdict on the record's future.

When George Martin's "white label" record of "Love Me Do" was played, as was customary, three weeks before its release, EMI's cynical head of promotion, Arthur Muxlow, looked quizzically at Ron White. The two men nodded; they thought it sounded good. Their view was not shared by the other people present. To their ears it was far too irregular. They voted it a miss. They opined that it was "just another record." White said, however, that they should back Martin's judgment and support the record.

Back in his office, White's memory began working on the curious name he had heard somewhere before. The Beatles? He checked his files. Yes, it *was* the same group that Brian Epstein had played rough cuts of several months earlier. And it *was* the same group that three of his A&R men had rejected. Now, George Martin had evidently seized them, and presumably contracted them, and *recorded* them! Epstein, an experienced and highly respected retailer, would think EMI a bewildering company with which to do business.

"I was embarrassed," says White, "at having sent a letter which purported to turn them down on behalf of the entire A&R department. I suddenly found George Martin hadn't been a party to that." White wrote to Epstein on June 26, 1962, after first hearing of Martin's signing:

Dear Mr Epstein,
   I was nonplussed and somewhat embarrassed to see details of a contract going through for "The Beatles" especially in view of my letter to you of 18th December 1961 when I told you that our Artistes Managers did not feel that we could use them.
   I hasten to say that I am very pleased that a contract is now being negotiated as I felt that they were very good but our Artistes Managers who heard the record felt at that time that they had the greatest difficulty in judging their quality from the record.
   George Martin tells me that he has been suitably impressed with them and has made certain suggestions to you which in his view may improve them still further and it is for this reason that he has offered a contract.

My only reason for writing is to endeavour to explain what must appear to you an anomaly in our organisation. I can assure you that our Artistes Managers did hear the record but I know you will appreciate that even Artistes Managers are human and can change their mind!

> With best wishes,
> Yours sincerely,
> R. N. White

To White's relief, Brian was unruffled by the episode. With the efficiency and courtesy that had marked his campaign for the Beatles, Epstein answered on June 29, 1962, after first hearing of Martin's signing:

> Dear Mr White,
>   Thank you very much for your letter of the 26th instant regarding The Beatles. In the circumstances, your attitude and remarks are greatly appreciated. As you will probably realise it is a great pleasure for me to be associated with EMI in this manner. I am very much looking forward to the issue of the group's first disc which I expect should be towards the end of August—although I have not heard from George Martin recently.
> > Thank you again, kindest regards,
> > Brian Epstein.

Marshaling his Liverpool forces to ensure that "Love Me Do" was a winner, Brian dispatched his family and friends to record shops in the city and told them to ask if it was in stock. "Will you help me create a demand for the record?" Brian asked his mother. Brian said she did not look like a genuine pop fan, so she should explain the record was for her niece. Later, from her holiday in Majorca, she wrote a request to BBC radio's "Housewives Choice," signing herself "Alice." (During all this frenzy, Brian found time to see his parents off on holiday, taking them to the airport.)

Brian received his first copy of "Love Me Do" during the Jewish New Year, when relatives were visiting his home. "Take it off!" said an aunt from genteel Southport. "What a *noise*!" She preferred Andy Williams. But Brian's young cousins were intrigued by the unusual sound.

Clive, too, was sceptical. "Brian has gone mad," he said to his mother. "He says there is going to be a *Beatle cult*!" Around his family, as well as to record company chiefs, Epstein had talked of a group that would be "bigger than Elvis."

Brian was rumored to have stocked ten thousand copies of "Love Me Do" at his Liverpool shops. But even if that sky-high figure were sold, the record could not have topped the national best-selling lists from sales in one city; the chart positions were decided on a "weighting basis," which excluded an uneven sales barometer from one outlet. Adamantly denying that he had bought the disc in bulk to force it onto the charts, Brian said: "I did no such thing, nor ever have. The Beatles progressed and succeeded on natural impetus without benefit of stunt or back-door tricks."

Coming from the giant EMI organization, "Love Me Do" commanded the attention of lively, thrusting London show business agents. The unusual sound caught the interest of one such impresario: Tito Burns, a former accordionist-bandleader, by then the personal manager of Cliff Richard.* He telephoned Epstein in Liverpool asking about the group's availability for live shows. As "Love Me Do" nudged onto the national charts at 48, Brian wrote to him on October 24, 1962:

> Dear Mr Burns
> Further to your telephone call here today I am enclosing details of the Beatles' availability this year.
> Although there are a few dates committed in January and February I have no doubt that it will be possible to postpone or cancel them. You will understand that I am naturally anxious to obtain good work for the boys, although of course one night stands in ballrooms, etc., would probably prove more lucrative.† I would be prepared, however, to accept a fee of £250 per week for anything that you may have in mind for January, February. As we have been inundated with inquiries, etc., during the last few days I intend to be in London next week when perhaps we could meet.
> Yours sincerely
> Brian Epstein.

*Ironically, Cliff Richard and all he represented as a custom-built pop singer at that time were one of the Beatles' first targets in their jibes against the show business establishment. "He's so bloody Christian," taunted John Lennon.
†Epstein was referring here to Burns's ambitious suggestion of a concert tour for the Beatles.

Epstein's mention of fees of £200-plus per week seemed low, demonstrating that he was not a manager who always sought quick, easy money. His national strategy was to get maximum exposure for his act, in the conviction that once they were seen, their fortune would follow. Other managers grabbed big fees and their percentages as fast as possible. With Epstein, longevity of the Beatles' career was paramount, especially now that they had a foothold on the record charts.

Tito Burns thought no more of that letter. He told his secretary to file it away. Within five months, however, Burns would be in touch with Epstein again as the Beatles soared to the top with their second single and all the signs were that they would be a huge act.

Promoter Larry Parnes, whose 1950s pop influence paralleled Brian's emergence in the 1960s, now wrote to Liverpool offering the Beatles a tour. On November 10, 1962, Brian replied to him:

> Dear Mr Parnes,
>   . . . Yes, we are very interested in your tour and would assure you that we would be delighted to be associated with one of your shows.
>   The group's fees for the tour as specified in your letter would be £230 per week. You will appreciate they would be able to earn appreciably more if they were working one nighters in ballrooms but I am quoting this fee because I am keen that they should do the tour and that it should prove acceptable.
>   The boys record again in November for release in January. The disc will receive maximum publicity, exposure, etc., and there is no reason why it should not prove a smash hit (although I still think that their present disc Love Me Do will go further).

Parnes's response was an offer of £140. Epstein replied to this on November 15:

> Although for many reasons I would like to accept I cannot agree to your suggested price to the group of £140. I doubt that the gain in experience and prestige will compensate the too considerable financial loss. Could you consider £200 per seven-day week? At this fee of course your suggested proviso could not be included in the contract. If you can agree to this I will be prepared to give you an option on the group for another six-week period within the next eighteen months.

A smiling baby in his Liverpool garden. *(Alma Johnson)*

Brian at three years old. *(Queenie Epstein)*

Brian with his mother Queenie and brother Clive (left) at their Liverpool home when he was eleven. *(Queenie Epstein)*

Thirteen-year-old Brian at Beaconsfield School in 1947; he is standing immediately behind the headmaster. *(Clive Epstein)*

Wrekin College, 1948: Brian is standing, sixth from the right, in the back row. *(Clive Epstein)*

In 1952, the year of the Coronation of the Queen, soldiers were given dress uniform; Brian is pictured here during a weekend visit home to Liverpool from his London barracks. *(Queenie Epstein)*

Brian at his most romantic: holding hands over dinner in the Cheshire countryside. Brian, aged 18, is with Sonia Seligson, aged 16, at the George Hotel, Knutsford, on one of their many dates in 1952 during an intense romance. *(Sonia Stevens)*

A holiday romance at the Imperial Hotel, Torquay, 1954. *(Queenie Epstein)*

Solitary man: Brian, aged 21, on holiday alone in Venice. *(Queenie Epstein)*

Seeds of success: Long before the gold discs arrive, Brian has framed a black vinyl copy of the Beatles' debut single, "Love Me Do," in his Liverpool office in March 1963. *(Rex Features)*

With his parents outside their home at 197 Queens Drive, Liverpool, in 1963.
(Queenie Epstein)

After the wedding of his brother Clive to Barbara Mattison at Greenbank Drive
Synagogue, Liverpool, on September 14, 1963: Best man Brian is flanked by
Billy J. Kramer and Gerry Marsden. *(Universal Pictorial Press)*

A pensive Brian, arms folded in his frequent stance, watching the action in a London television studio, December 1963. *(Universal Pictorial Press)*

In Liverpool's Cavern club on January 22, 1964, Alun Owen, Lionel Bart, and Brian are looking for an actress to take part in the Bart-Owen play Maggie May. *(Syndication International)*

On the threshold of a dream: Brian with
his lawyer David Jacobs at the London
airport on February 7, 1964, waiting to
board Pan American Flight 101 with the
Beatles on their first visit to New York.
(London Features International)

Relaxing in Miami, February 1964:
Brian is reading the *New York Times*
account of the Beatles' tremendous U.S.
reception at their first concerts there.
(Rex Features)

With Ringo, George, and John in Miami
(The Photo Source)

Immaculate and happy, at London
airport before flying to America with
Gerry Marsden, March 31, 1964.
(Rex Features)

At his happiest among his artists, seen here at the Palace Theatre, Manchester, on April 21, 1964. Front row: Tommy Quickly, Cilla Black, Billy J. Kramer; right, the Fourmost; center, the Dakotas and the Remo Four. *(John Topham)*

Arriving back in London from Australia on April 22, 1964, with Gerry Marsden, Derek Taylor, and George Martin. *(BBC Hulton Picture Library)*

Celebrating Cilla's 21st birthday, May 27, 1964. *(BBC Hulton Picture Library)*

A picture of the Beatles is the solitary decoration in Brian's spartan office at Sutherland House, next door to the London Palladium, in 1964. *(Rex Features)*

George Martin, John Lennon, and Ringo Starr with Brian at the Abbey Road recording studio, 1964. *(Clive Epstein)*

One of Brian's favorite pictures of himself, which was distributed by the Beatles' American fan club in 1964. *(Queenie Epstein)*

Backstage with John Lennon
in 1964. *(Rex Features)*

Relaxing with a whiskey in his first
London home, Whaddon House,
Knightsbridge, on July 27, 1964.
(BBC Hulton Picture Library)

Beatles pictures look down on Brian at breakfast in his Knightsbridge flat; this was taken on October 6, 1964, to coincide with the publication of his autobiography, *A Cellarful of Noise*. *(The Photo Source)*

Leaving London with singer Tommy Quickly for a promotional tour of America, November 25, 1964. *(Press Association)*

Two British pop czars of the 1960's: Brian with Andrew Oldham, who shaped the image of the Rolling Stones. Brian is interviewing Oldham on NBC's *Hullabaloo,* December 19, 1964. *(The Photo Source)*

Everybody's idea of a perfect best man, this time for the wedding at Caxton Hall, Westminster, London, of Ringo to Maureen Cox on February 11, 1965. *(Camera Press)*

Fulfilling an ambition, Brian produced Alan Plater's play *A Smashing Day* at the New Arts Theatre in London. He is pictured here with two of its actors, Hywel Bennett and Michael Blackham, on February 12, 1966. *(BBC Hulton Picture Library)*

Brian was the British interviewer of pop stars for the American NBC television show *Hullabaloo*. He is pictured here in February 1965, pensive in Shepperton Studios during filming, interviewing Chris Curtis of the Searchers, and signing autographs.
(Rex Features)

Parnes's proviso suggested that if the Beatles' next single after "Love Me Do" reached the Top 10 in both the *Melody Maker* and *New Musical Express*, they would receive a fee of £230 per week. If the same release reached the Top 3 on either chart, this would be increased to £300 per week. Epstein never reached an agreement with Parnes.

The financial return did not matter enormously to Brian, even at that embryonic stage. What concerned him was his adoption of a position, and how people perceived him as a result of his excellent judgment of the Beatles. His family and his contemporaries were suddenly aware that his resourcefulness had been a perfect move of self-determination.

It was, however, a radical move for all the family to accept. In the 1960s, as his cousin Raymond Weldon points out, "you just didn't *leave* a high-powered furniture business to manage a pop group!" But once Brian had made the switch and shown it to be fruitful, he was respected. "We began to realize he was doing something special. Brian was completely different from the whole family, but with parents like his, it hardly surprised me on reflection. Auntie Queenie was and is a very intelligent, very modern woman, and Uncle Harry was ahead of his time, modern-thinking."

Under the sagacious chairmanship of Sir Joseph Lockwood, EMI Records had a dominance in classical music but a staid, if successful, pop image, despite the company's nurturing of Cliff Richard since his 1958 hit "Move It." Sir Joseph applied pressure on his staff, upgrading the importance of his recording managers and encouraging competition among them—which partly explained George Martin's desire to trump his colleagues running the Columbia and HMV labels. Sir Joseph was determined that EMI should overtake Decca as the champion of pop in Britain, and with Epstein's Beatles he quickly achieved his goal. The EMI Press Officer, Syd Gillingham, was instructed to make Epstein feel important from the start: he recalls being reminded by his seniors that as well as being manager of the Beatles, Epstein was a significant Liverpool retailer.

Immensely proud of the breakthrough with a debut single, Brian took one of the first pressings of it to Yankel Feather in Liverpool's Basement club. Feather, predictably unimpressed, told Epstein he had once turned John Lennon away from the door of his club: "I thought he looked like a hoodlum." He had also heard that Lennon was among the musicians accompanying a stripper in a Liverpool club. Brian did not react. Showing Feather early photographs of the Beatles, Epstein met another curt response: "Don't get involved with them. They look like little nothings." Feather and others in the club who heard "Love Me Do" were scathing. "Oh, it's like an Arab dirge. I can't see anybody enjoying this. It's awful." But the Epstein-Beatles link was now the talk of Liverpool.

"Love Me Do" was a minor success, peaking in the national charts at 17. It bolstered Brian's confidence, but it was a long way from the world status that he had assured so many people the Beatles would reach.

George Martin, too, now felt the need for a substantial hit to prove that the provincial young men he had signed were worthwhile. Worried about the poor commercial prospects of Lennon-McCartney compositions, he scoured Tin Pan Alley for stronger material and finally approached Epstein with a professional composition. Hmm, said Brian, it sounds good. But the Beatles remonstrated when he played them a demonstration tape. Epstein phoned Martin. Diplomatically rephrasing the Beatles' condemnation of the song, he said: "The Beatles like what you've found, but they would really very much like to record their own songs, George. Do you think you could see your way . . . ?" Martin answered: "If they can give me anything as good as that, we'll go ahead." The Beatles returned with "Please Please Me." A Lennon composition, it was a slow dirge and as such Martin doubted its potential. Lennon had based the title on the Bing Crosby oldie "Please" and the vocal on Roy Orbison's falsetto style. Martin said it could work only with changed rhythm, increased tempo. The Beatles agreed. Recalls Martin: "I knew it was a hit. At the end of that session I said to them: 'You've got your first number one.' And it was."

"Please Please Me," the second single, sounded hot, but Brian's promotional instinct told him it needed a big kick to launch it. So much was at stake. Had not George Martin conceded his request for Beatles-written material? If their second single did not take off, the effect would be demoralizing to the Beatles and he would suffer with them. Brian went to London for a "tactics" meeting with Martin.

Brian knew a little about music publishers who printed sheet music and took percentages for licensing the songs. But he had been in too much of a hurry to concern himself with that subject with regard to the debut single. On Martin's suggestion, "Love Me Do" and the reverse side of the record, "P.S. I Love You," had been published by EMI's Ardmore and Beechwood, partly as a reciprocal gesture to Sid Coleman for introducing Epstein to Martin. Brian told George he was dissatisfied with Ardmore and Beechwood's work. Getting a record launched was tough: the national media were not attuned to pop, and radio play was very limited. And EMI had done little to promote "Love Me Do."

"When I introduced to EMI a group called the Beatles, they were really narked," says Martin. Arthur Muxlow, who ran the promotion department, was an old-guard traditionalist who saw no future in the group. So Martin was not surprised when Brian said he would give the next Beatles song to a publisher who would generate interest aggressively, work for his percentage, and help the record take off. He had met someone from Hill and Range, the company that published the Elvis Presley catalogue. He wanted to give the song to them; what did George Martin think?

Martin's advice was sound and succinct. "It would be better if you gave this material to an English company rather than an American-owned company. And give it to someone who is very hungry, who will *work* for you. Hill and Range don't need you. They've got Elvis Presley. You'll just be another pea in a very large pod."

Epstein said he knew nobody else. Could Martin recommend someone? George had three names. Although two worked for American publishers, they were honest, hardworking people. They were Alan Holmes, who ran Robbins Music, and David Platz at Essex Music. The third suggestion, a wholly English company, was a newly independent publisher, Dick James. "I knew Dick would break his neck to pick up that record," recalls Martin, "but I said, 'Any one of those three would do a great job for you, Brian.'" Inclining to Dick James because of his British operation and his track record as a performing artist, Epstein did not arrange to see Holmes or Platz.

George Martin and Dick James had a close affinity. When Martin was asking around London's music quarter for new material, it was James who came up with "How Do You Do It." Their association dated back eight years to the time when James, a dance band singer, had been recorded by Martin—the million-selling hit "Robin Hood," a television theme song. So when George phoned Dick to say he was with a man named Brian Epstein, who wanted to talk with him about the Beatles, James knew he would not be wasting his time. He was already "sold" on the Beatles from George Martin's talk of "Love Me Do" and "How Do You Do It." George put Brian on the phone, and the two arranged to visit James's office in Charing Cross Road at 11 a.m. next day.

Epstein set up another appointment to precede it: to meet an executive at Francis, Day and Hunter, an EMI subsidiary. That night he returned to the Green Park Hotel, Mayfair, feeling optimistic. But when Brian arrived for his 10 a.m. appointment, he was asked to wait in the reception area. By 10.25 a.m. he asked why he was being kept waiting; a secretary said her boss had not yet arrived. A bad omen, Brian decided. If the man could not honor an appointment, they had no future together, he told the receptionist. That said, he marched out.

He arrived at Dick James's office at 132 Charing Cross Road twenty minutes early. "I'm sorry I'm early, I'll sit and wait," he told the receptionist. She alerted James, who bounced out of his office and jovially ushered Brian in.

On those two different treatments of the punctilious Epstein, a fortune was lost and won.

❏

Dick James had a perfect pedigree for his role as publisher and plugger. He had left school at fourteen, resolute in his determination to be a singer, and within three years was singing professionally with dance bands, having changed his real name of Isaac Vapnick to the more snappy Al Berlin and, later, Lee Sheridan. He had first joined publisher Sidney Bron (actress Eleanor's father) and had a hand in writing hits, notably Max Bygraves's novelty "I'm a Pink Toothbrush, You're a Blue Toothbrush." He had a fine ear for hit songs. A year before meeting Epstein, he had branched out on his own as a publisher, having stopped touring so that he could see more of his wife Frances and young son. And now, at forty-four, James was hungry for success.

James had been encouraged to listen to the Beatles by his son Stephen. At home the previous night, he asked the sixteen-year-old if he had heard of them. "Oh yeah, they're great," Stephen replied. " 'Love Me Do' is a hit. It would be good if you could sign them."

When Epstein sat down in his office, James said he was "interested in whatever you've got." Impressed by his undivided attention and fresh enthusiasm, Brian took from his briefcase an early pressing of "Please Please Me," the Beatles' next single. When the record stopped, James was almost speechless.

"That's a number one," he said simply.

"If you can make it number one," said the elated Epstein, "you can publish it and have Lennon and McCartney on a long-term contract." That was a tall order, said James, but he would get to work. "Do a great job," Epstein continued, "and we will do something together." Wait, said Dick James, while he made a phone call.

It was a vitally important move. James telephoned a friend, Philip Jones, producer of a major network TV series, "Thank Your Lucky Stars." "There's this amazing group from Liverpool called the Beatles," Dick enthused. "They've got a new single coming called 'Please Please Me.' I want them on the show on Saturday."

Jones had his rules. "I can't book them unless I hear it." James said he would play it on the phone to him; he put the receiver next to the record player. "That sounds pretty good to me," said Jones. "Okay, you've got them on the show this Saturday."

Brian was both impressed and ecstatic as Dick replaced the telephone and looked up at him. "Make sure the boys are free on Saturday; you've got the show: 'Thank Your Lucky Stars,' " said James.

The loss of publishing the Beatles' music by his wholly owned company Ardmore and Beechwood was bad news to EMI chairman Sir Joseph Lockwood. Epstein had slipped through the net too quickly for EMI to pitch in with an offer. "I don't blame Sid Coleman, because he published the first two songs without a contract. He wasn't getting any support from either the record producers or the solicitors," says Sir Joseph. He resented the loss of a vast amount of profit, which went to Dick James. "I have every confidence in George Martin; I think he just didn't want our own music publisher breathing down his neck," he reflects.

"Please Please Me" was the first of seven number one hits that Dick James published through Brian Epstein within the next year. It was also the first step six men took on the road to becoming millionaires.

6

❏

POWER

ENTERING THE BATTLEGROUND

BRIAN'S ZEAL, SPEED, AND RESILIENCE in projecting the Beatles, once
he had secured their management contract, were based on his philosophy as a salesman. He had always asserted that if customers were
provided with efficiency, courtesy, and something they needed, the
vendor would reap the results and word would spread. That theory,
which in turn meant he did not overpitch his financial demands too
early, combined with his doggedness to conquer on many different
fronts. In effect, he had set off half a dozen fireworks at once: the
record contract campaign, the Beatles' fresh appearance, radio and
television appearances, higher fees in clubs and ballrooms, media publicity, and the demand that they receive star treatment, thus elevating
their local status.

He applied steadfast persistence to getting them a television
debut—long before they had achieved success as a recording group.
In one foray, in the spring of 1962, Brian's approach showed remarkable chutzpah. From his Whitechapel office he telephoned
Associated-Rediffusion, an independent television station in London, and asked to speak to "Miss Vyvienne Moynihan, manager of
light entertainment."

120

"You won't know me," he intoned. "My name is Brian Epstein. I would very much like to come to see you to discuss a group I manage."

At thirty-eight, Vyvienne Moynihan was used to uncouth phone bullying from tough pop managers. Here, she thought, was something off-beat: a voice that spoke the Queen's English, even though it drifted into just another attempt to get a television booking.

"Well, do tell me where your group is performing. One of our people will go out and check them over," she replied.

"Well, I don't honestly think that's a very good idea," Epstein countered.

This intrigued Miss Moynihan. "Everyone was getting down on their knees, begging us to go everywhere. Even Andrew Oldham threw his hat in and crawled in on all fours for the Rolling Stones." However, she told Epstein categorically: "That is the way we do it. I'm sorry, you must understand that we can't book people blind. . . ."

Brian interrupted her: "Oh no, no, no. I don't wish to do that. I've never managed anyone before, but these people are really rather special and they are soon going to be making a record and I think it will be quite sensational. They've been working at the Cavern in Liverpool and before that they were working in Germany. . . ."

"Well, wouldn't you write in?" said the TV lady.

"No."

She recalls: "I thought: that's funny, what's this guy about? So I said: 'What are you doing on Thursday afternoon?' "

Fine, said Brian, but could they meet during the latter part of the day because he had to get down from Liverpool.

"Heavens, I wouldn't dream of bringing you down from *Liverpool* just on spec. I mean, next time you're in London, why don't you give me a ring?"

"I would rather make an appointment now." A meeting was set for 11 a.m. two days later. "Will you be free for lunch afterwards?" offered Brian.

"No."

"I mean, after we have discussed our business."

"Look, Mr. Epstein, we don't really *have* any business. You want to discuss with me your new group which is *possibly* going to make a record and hasn't done anything. Let's just meet, certainly. . . ."

The well-groomed man who presented himself at her office two days later completely disarmed Vyvienne Moynihan. Her background in the theater made for an easy introduction. She had studied at the Guildhall School of Music and Drama before acting in repertory, then branching out into stage management, direction, and business management.

He told her of his RADA background. Recalls Moynihan: "He was absolutely charming, self-composed, determined, well brought up, nervous about his own ability, but driven on with the Beatles thing because he was *sure*. He struck me as a young gentleman with a mission. I began to desperately hope, for his sake, that these blokes were anything like as good as he thought they were. Because he told me he was now giving them a salary."

She asked if he had a contract with them. "Well," said Brian, "we shook hands," adding that their relationship was based on complete trust. She thought privately: "Very strange. I hope they don't rough you up too much, Brian, because you're rather nice."

Subject to agreement by the show's production team, Vyvienne agreed that they could talk of an appearance for the group on an important weekly magazine program, "Tuesday Rendezvous." Brian invited her for lunch at the Savoy. She demurred, accepting a sherry across the road at the Waldorf Hotel. On his return to Liverpool, he sent her pamphlets and articles about the Beatles.

By then, the agents, promoters, and managers who phoned the television studios every day were talking to Vyvienne and her colleagues about the Liverpool group, the Beatles. One of them was Arthur Howes, soon to promote their concerts. When the day came, on December 4, 1962, for their trip to London, Brian introduced John Lennon to Vyvienne. "Hello, this is our first London gig," said John.

"Yes, it's live. I'm sure it's going to do well," she said.

"Oh, it will go well, all right. He [Brian] is very keen on this, you know . . . us making it in London."

The interaction between the group and Epstein in the studio was noticeably different from that of other acts and their managers. Says Vyvienne Moynihan: "When Brian spoke, they listened. They didn't necessarily agree but they didn't disagree publicly. At first I thought that was probably because they hadn't made it at that time and they were beholden to him for the security of a small salary. But basically it was his style. They never, ever, really understood him but they liked him and respected him."

❑

Brian quickly discovered that being a manager was not merely a business role. He would need diplomacy to survive a big crisis in the Beatles story.

To Epstein's astonishment, George Martin told him at the Beatles' test session that when it came to actually recording, he would not use drummer Pete Best. "He can't keep time," said Martin. "He's not a very good drummer and we need one to bind this group together. I'll book a session drummer. It shouldn't affect you. You can do what you like with the group."

Martin was implying that the handsome Best, who attracted female fans, seemed an integral part of the unit and could remain for live performances. "I didn't realize," says Martin, "that the Beatles were thinking of getting rid of Pete anyway, and what I said was the catalyst for firing him. In my mind it wasn't an important decision. He was not an important member of the band. He was good-looking but he didn't say anything.

"At the test session, Best had been almost sullen. He had the moody good looks of James Dean, but he virtually was in a corner all alone. He didn't have the charisma of the other three, who were laughing and joking. The most damning thing, though, was that he didn't contribute anything lively to the group. The group weren't swinging."

When Brian told the Beatles of George Martin's decision, it confirmed their instincts. Their hot favorite as their new drummer was Johnny Hutchinson of the hugely popular Big Three. "He was first choice," says Cilla Black. "Johnny Hutch was renowned as *the* drummer with *the* band in Liverpool. But he must have thought that because the Beatles were going to be big, he didn't want to be part of them as he had the Big Three." More likely, John, Paul, and George thought his personality too strong. They were sacking a popular, good-looking guy in Best, leaving the band's front line unchallenged. His successor would need to be more acquiescent than Hutchinson. John, Paul, and George told Brian they thought Ringo Starr, then drummer with another local group, Rory Storm and the Hurricanes, would suit the chemistry of the group better.

Next day, Lennon told Epstein that he would personally recruit Ringo if Brian would fire Best. On the morning of August 16, 1962, after a sleepless night of worry, Epstein faced Best in his Whitechapel office. It was not unusual for Brian to ask to see him; before Epstein's arrival as their manager, Best had often been the group's "link man" in administrative matters.

Best was surprised by Epstein's demeanor. His talk was superficial and he exchanged pleasantries. This was quite uncharacteristic for a man who usually went straight to the point. Finally, Brian blurted it out: "The boys want you out and Ringo in. The boys and George Martin don't think you're a good enough drummer." Epstein, clearly uneasy about plunging the knife, was brutally frank. Best was mortified.

There was little to add. Ringo was already signed, Brian continued, but there were three more shows before he could join the Beatles. With his quaint idea of "business as usual" even in this tense situation, and with little concern for Best's feelings after two years in the group, Epstein expected him to be at the remaining shows before departing the Beatles on a date decreed by their manager.

He was stunned by Best's nonappearance that night at the Riverpark Ballroom, Chester. In Epstein's world, a diary engagement was always to be kept. He failed to comprehend how shattered Best had been by a method he considered sly. Best was deeply hurt that the Beatles, particularly Lennon, had not shown the guts to confront him personally and explain the firing. And he never understood, even a quarter of a century later, why he had been sacked after two years of musical success and personal harmony.

Pete Best never appeared with the Beatles again. Epstein, who did not relish the animosity he had been forced to cause, tried to heal the wound by offering him the drum chair in the Merseybeats, a rising local group he was considering for management. Pete Best refused and joined the Lee Curtis All Stars, managed by Brian's friend Joe Flannery.

Rumors about Best's overnight exit began to percolate through the Liverpool pop circuit. Shortly after the sacking, Brian had a dinner engagement with Bob Wooler and Ted Knibbs, the manager of singer Billy Kramer. In their alcove at the Cabaret Club, the three men discussed the vagaries of the mushrooming local beat scene. Wooler, with his shrewd knowledge of how to promote groups, if not himself, was at his most loquacious, championing Brian's cause with the Beatles and also providing Brian with valuable information. Epstein frequently hosted such occasions, partly for social reasons but also to solicit advice that could lead to his next move.

As the night wore on, Wooler became increasingly confident and liberal with his views. As well as being the éminence grise of Liverpool pop, he was a member of Liverpool Press Club and wrote for *Mersey Beat*. He had strong connections with the *Liverpool Echo*. Reminding Epstein and Knibbs of his journalistic interests, he suddenly announced: "I am going to tell the *true* Pete Best story." There was a pregnant silence.

"You can't do *that*," Epstein said.

Wooler and Epstein's exchange implied that there was more to the sacking of Best than had been admitted. Wooler was defiant. "I *am* going to do it." Red-faced and fuming with fury, Epstein repeated: "You can't do that. You just can't."

The two men squabbled for several minutes over whether Wooler was ethically entitled to write a story. Finally, Epstein called the waiter, paid the bill for all three dinners, and stood up. "I'm sorry, I must say goodnight, gentlemen."

Knibbs berated Wooler for overstepping the mark. What had happened between Best and Epstein and the Beatles was none of his concern, Knibbs argued. Wooler maintained that "the truth" should be told. But by the next morning, Knibbs had convinced him by telephone to call Brian and pacify him by saying he did not intend to write an article. Epstein, not a man to bear grudges and realizing his need of Wooler's friendship, accepted his spirit. The night was gone if not forgotten.

Johnny Hutchinson "sat in" with the Beatles during the period in which they were waiting for Ringo. "But the Beatles did not like his attitude, and Brian was frightened of his belligerency," says Wooler. "The Beatles, especially Paul, did not want a drummer who was too clever." They were now sure they wanted a drummer who would happily assume a subordinate role, allowing the front line of Lennon and McCartney to dominate.

Ringo Starr proved to be a perfectly capable drummer, driving the group well and pleasing George Martin. He was passive, nonthreatening to John and Paul, and his droll sense of humor coalesced with the group's. Epstein admired the Beatles' choice, but he was worried about the fans' reaction to the decision to get rid of Best. After a Cavern session by the Beatles, he asked Wooler for a drink later. The pubs closed at ten o'clock but Brian said he knew a place that would accommodate them. Together with McCartney and Harrison, Epstein and Wooler adjourned to the Old Dive. Brian was friendly with the landlord; the side door opened after three familiar knocks on the window.

In the pub's back room, Paul and George did most of the talking about Best's leaving the group. "Brian was mostly listening and watching," says Wooler. "I was bitter and contemptuous about it. I said: 'I see no reason why he should go.' Brian asked me how the fans would react. I said they'd be amazed." The meeting was an abortive attempt to "soften up" Wooler, a key link between the Beatles and their supporters, but he left them all in no doubt that he disapproved.

Epstein had indeed administered an unpopular blow to Beatles fans, and the unlikely "posh" man who was taking them upward to fame became hated, pilloried, and spurned. He did not dare go near the Cavern for a week until the club manager, Ray McFall, gave him a bodyguard. Even then, Brian was physically knocked about in scuffles with Beatles fans, who now believed he was wrecking their band. Convinced he was right in smartening them up, Brian instructed John to tell Ringo he should shave his beard and tidy his hair to become a Beatle.

Pete Best fans bearing placards proclaiming PETE IS BEST and PETE FOREVER, RINGO NEVER marched outside NEMS. Bruised inwardly as well as visibly, Brian was remorseful, full of guilt, about the brutal exit of Pete Best. He extended the hand of friendship by sending him a birthday telegram for his twenty-first birthday, three months after the sacking, on November 24, 1962. "Congratulations, many happy returns, all the best, John, Paul, George, Ringo and Brian." Performing ruthless acts of surgery was never easy for Brian. It always caused him inner turmoil to be the blushing bearer of bad news.

By then, "Love Me Do" had been released and Brian was about to return to Hamburg with the Beatles for another season at the Star-Club. The machine was in motion, and after a year's dramatic initiation into the Beatles' world, Epstein felt reasonably secure.

❑

Brian set about his command of Liverpool's beat scene with a ruthlessness that belied his outward passivity. His smooth approach sometimes concealed a deviousness that punctured his more sensitive victims. One of these was Sam Leach, a jittery twenty-seven-year-old promoter of pop dances who had presented the Beatles in Merseyside ballrooms and clubs for nearly a year before Epstein arrived in their lives.

Like Brian, Leach saw the unique potential of the Beatles. And he wanted to get them on records. By late 1961 he had mooted the idea of his own label and asked the Beatles to launch it. They agreed but said they were tied up with a German record deal.

The day after Brian's first visit to the Cavern, on November 9, 1961, the Beatles played at a Sam Leach promotion at the Tower Ballroom, New Brighton, a regular venue. A few weeks later, a telephone message at Leach's home from Paul McCartney asked him to contact John and Paul "urgently." At the Kardomah Cafe, Lennon and McCartney were frank with Leach. "Look," said John, "we know we've got an unwritten handshake with you, but we've been approached by this Brian Epstein and he's got real money. Have a look at him and see what you think." The three went together to Brian's office in Whitechapel. John and Paul quickly disappeared to check out the records and then went away, leaving Leach alone with Epstein.

"As soon as I met him I liked him. He was a nice fellow, obviously green about the music business but eager to learn. But he was obviously wrapped up with the Beatles. And since he had money, money was an easy teacher," Leach says.

Paul and John bobbed in and out of the office as the two men weighed each other. Leach faced a dilemma: he did not want to lose the Beatles. Instinctively, he wanted to advise them against Epstein. "But I couldn't. It would have been selfish to put them off." Instead, Leach tried a ploy he thought might work: he mentioned that he was thinking of starting a record label. Why didn't Brian and he do it jointly? Brian immediately said no. He had bigger plans, he replied tersely.

"I wanted a link with him," says Leach, "because here was this rich man who loved the Beatles, like me. I thought I could talk him

into putting money into the record label, and that way we'd work together. He pooh-poohed the idea. It was disappointing but I was glad
for the Beatles: I told Brian they'd be a big group." Leach knew at
that point that the race was over. He had earlier tried, without success,
to get financial backing from a top industrialist for his record label
idea. The man refused when Leach arrived at his office with a Beatle.
"He said he wasn't having anything to do with teddy boys."

Epstein showed neither guilt nor sympathy when he realized he
had wrested the Beatles from a disappointed man. Says Leach: "He
believed he was doing them a favor and he would get the reflected
glory. I don't believe, though, that deep down he thought they'd be
as big as they became. He claimed he did. But it was the biggest
shock in the end. He'd nearly given up when it all started happening."
To the Beatles, once the die was cast and Epstein had become involved, Leach said: "He's the man who will get you there."

Leach had no inkling of the bumps that would scar his relationship
with the new man in the Beatles' lives. Confident though he was,
Epstein saw people like Leach as a threat. At that stage, Sam knew
more about the Beatles than he did; he understood their music better;
and as a "street person," he had a good rapport with them. All Epstein
had to offer was his power base, and the seemingly impossible dream
of rising above the Liverpool crowd and getting a record made. Epstein
realized, however, that he had enough of a problem getting established
with the Beatles; he could not be undermined in any psychological
sense by their old friends. He systematically set about wearing down
the authority of people like Sam Leach.

Brian began the pressure on Leach at the first Tower Ballroom show
he attended. There, groups usually shared dressing rooms; Brian told
Sam this was not good enough for the Beatles. From now on, they
would require their own private room for changing. Leach protested
that this was an impossible precedent: Rory Storm and Gerry and the
Pacemakers would not tolerate that. In the bar, with the Beatles present, Epstein insisted that Liverpool's top group deserved star treatment. McCartney agreed, but John was embarrassed: "That'll *do*,
Brian. . . ." Epstein's face reddened as he pulled John aside to explain
the tactic. Eventually, Leach capitulated to Epstein's quiet but re-
lentless pressure: the Beatles were special. Their private room was

not luxurious, but a point had been scored. It was Brian's first, small but significant step in asserting his authority.

The Beatles' world in Liverpool was far from tranquil, a fact that Brian was quickly forced to learn. At the Tower, fights among the crowd were frequent; once, a table flew through the air as Brian drank in the bar with the Beatles and Sam Leach. Epstein was nervous but kept his cool. In his soothing voice he offered a round of drinks to a few people who had been shaken up. Gradually, Brian discovered the abrasive drinkers who sought out the Beatles and who often challenged them to fights. In the Zodiac club, the Boomerang basement club, and in Joe's Cafe in Duke Street, Brian was alarmed when he saw his new "boys" running into tough people who said such things as "Okay, you can *sing*, but can you *fight*?"

With his deceptively gentle dominance, Epstein next set out on a stealthy takeover of Sam Leach's franchise for Tower Ballroom concerts. His initial thrust was to put the Beatles second on the bill to bigger, professional artists from London, established artists like Joe Brown and Screaming Lord Sutch. Epstein asked Leach to meet him in the Kardomah Cafe to discuss plans for joint promotions at the Tower.

Leach saw his chance. "Okay, let's go fifty-fifty. You put the money up and I'll do the promoting." Brian said no, his brother was a partner in his newly formed NEMS Enterprises, and Clive would get a percentage. Would Sam be prepared to accept a third of the profits?

Leach balked. "The Tower was my place and I was making a living there," he says today. He had built up the audiences to between two and three thousand an evening; he was a proud individual who enjoyed presenting pop shows in his own way. Now he feared that with two Epsteins muscling in, he would be told which acts to present, and how to do it.

Sam, in fact, was mystified by Brian's sudden announcement of his brother's involvement. "I have a mother-in-law, a wife, a dog, and a cat, and they're going to be on twelve and a half percent!" Sam told an unsmiling Epstein. Beyond the money problems, Leach feared the Tower would become a showplace for any Epstein act and that he would be stopped from booking any name that didn't help Brian's long-term plans. He could not allow that, and so he shook his head.

Red-faced and vexed, "like a spoiled child not getting its own way," Brian said to Leach: "You're making a big mistake, as you'll see." Leach countered with this suggestion: Why didn't they form a new company simply for Tower promotions?

No, said Epstein. And his gambit continued. "What would you say to me if I asked you for eighty pounds a booking for the Beatles?" Sam said he could not afford that: "As it is, I'm struggling to put shows on every week."

Epstein, testing him, said he just wanted Sam's reaction. But Leach was riled. "Don't try that on me," he said curtly. He believed Brian was pushing his luck with a piece of silly blackmail. "He knew how much I needed the Beatles and he knew I couldn't afford eighty pounds a show."

A cunning compromise was reached that satisfied Brian's pride and allowed Sam to continue booking the Beatles at £40. If anyone ever asked questions, Leach would *pretend* to be paying £80. That enabled Brian to quote the figure and refer anyone to Leach if he doubted the new price. On the basis of that wily strategy, an uneasy truce was declared. The two men parted, Leach now aware that the Beatles' new manager was devious, determined, and learning very quickly.

Leach's promotions for the Beatles included a show at the Rialto and two at the Tower, New Brighton. The first problem came just before the show at the Rialto, located in the tough Toxteth area, where the Beatles were apprehensive about violence, especially in the wake of the Pete Best sacking. Leach said they should not worry: he would give each of them a bodyguard. In any event, it was too late to cancel. He had the posters out and there would be more trouble if they didn't appear. McCartney said if Sam promised their safety, they would go on.

"But Brian was also worried about the toughness of the place. It wasn't that dangerous," says Sam Leach. "There was a strong black population, and they were all worried about black girls' liking the group and that could cause trouble with the black guys."

Epstein was firmly against the Beatles' playing at the Rialto, which Leach saw as part of an attempt to drive a wedge between himself and the Beatles. To Brian's dismay, John and Paul overruled him. McCartney said the Beatles were too well known not to play, and Lennon added: "We can't pull out. We're billed." So the Rialto show of September 6, 1962, went on. There was no trouble but it was not a financial success. Epstein had been humiliated. The Beatles had swung behind Leach rather than him. Brian then decided he had to chop their link with Leach. It would be difficult because the boys were loyal, having worked for him for eighteen months. Brian set about turning the screws with blistering treatment of a man he now considered an adversary.

The Beatles' fee for the Rialto show was £30. Brian's NEMS Enterprises had sold tickets for that and other Leach shows. At the Rialto, Leach gave Brian £11 in partial payment. "Look, Brian, I can't give you all the money now. I'll give it to you tomorrow." The next show was to be at the Tower.

Brian pulled a face as the two men bristled in the Rialto band room. "If you don't pay the money tomorrow night," he said, "they won't go onstage. I'll see you in my office tomorrow." Epstein's peremptory tone warned Leach of problems. The thunderbolt came next morning in Brian's office.

"Sam," he began. "We have only eight pounds from ticket sales in the agency for tonight at the Tower. We haven't taken much money." It was a strangely negative stance. Sam Leach shot back: "You know quite well, Brian, that you'll sell plenty today." Brian answered: "No we will not. The Beatles won't go on tonight. I'm taking the tickets out of the agency." Leach argued that at least £30 worth of tickets would be sold by NEMS for the show; the Tower was always a guaranteed seller and Brian knew it. But Epstein shook his head.

Leach immediately recognized the thin end of Epstein's wedge; he was clearly starting to edge out anyone close to the Beatles whom he saw as influencing them. Epstein then pointed out that Leach owed him £19. "They're not going to play unless you have that money now."

The sensitive Leach was baffled. Why, he asked Brian, had he sabotaged ticket sales for a show that night? Why such harsh treatment when the money would certainly arrive? Brian was tart: "I'm not having the Beatles' name besmirched. You haven't paid them for last night. They're not playing the Tower."

By late afternoon, McCartney had joined the fray. He pleaded with Brian to let them go on. They could not cancel an advertised appearance and they could not let Sam Leach down, he said. Although

Lennon was the leader, Paul was always more concerned with public relations and presentation. With difficulty, he persuaded Brian to let them go to the Tower that night in the hope that the Epstein-Leach deadlock could be broken.

It was a night of fog and rain. The crowd was small. Perhaps word had spread that the Beatles were not going to appear. Perhaps the Pete Best sacking had kept loyalists away. In the best show business tradition, Leach begged them to go on, despite the friction. Lennon, McCartney, and Harrison, already faced with the uncertainty of a new drummer, were torn between three loyalties: to their new manager, to an old promoter friend, and to their fans.

It was a contest Epstein vowed to win. As the night wore on and the start of the show neared, Leach had some box office takings: he offered Brian the £19 owed from the previous night's show at the Rialto. But now he also owed the fee of £35 for this night's show. Brian said: "I want the full nineteen pounds and thirty-five pounds for tonight in pound notes, that's fifty-four pounds, before they go on-stage." Leach pleaded that they always had latecomers arriving at eleven o'clock and that they would boost the takings.

Then a disc jockey announced to the crowd that the Beatles would not appear because they had not been paid. "Paul, John, Brian, and I were in the box office," Leach remembers. "Clive Epstein was there too, wanting them to appear. I was devastated. People were beginning to ask for their money back. There was chaos. Even then Paul and John were still arguing with Brian, saying they'd known Sam too long to do this."

Paul then said: "Play and we'll take a chance." He volunteered to Brian his slice of the Beatles' pay that night to pay Sam's debt. Epstein said that was an unfair solution he could not accept. Why should Paul be penalized for a bad debt? Says Leach: "He was adamant."

Meanwhile, the manager of the Tower Ballroom, Jesse James, said that if the Beatles did not honor their advertisements and go on, they would never appear there again. Paul was very close to disregarding Brian's wishes and getting onstage. And John would have followed. Seeing this, Epstein issued an ultimatum to them both: "You went against my wishes last night by appearing at the Rialto. Do it again —and it's all over for us." It was a test of his strength.

At that point Sam Leach moved in to call a halt to the argument.

He told them to leave the box office. "I didn't want to be responsible for a split between the Beatles and Brian, because he had a lot to offer them and he was so far down the line. I told them they'd have to do what their manager said, and they left."

Amid much acrimony, the Beatles did not appear and the two sides parted. To Sam Leach, the final insult was a report from his sister-in-law Vera that Ringo, the new boy, had the nerve to walk around with a placard that said: NO PAY, NO PLAY.

Epstein and Leach were now bitter rivals. At the root of Brian's discontent was his knowledge that while he could put on Tower shows on Thursdays, Leach had the crucial Fridays—with bigger crowds—sewn up. And Sam was determined to keep them going. Brian decided otherwise.

When Leach booked the prestigious American rock star Little Richard, he proudly advertised the October 12 concert in the *Liverpool Echo*. But Brian trumped him. Leach had offered £350 but Epstein moved in with £500.* "It was obviously a plan to row me out of the Tower, but I didn't dream he would do that to me, I was so green," says Leach. "So when I lost the Beatles, I lost the Tower. Brian lost money on the Little Richard show, which gave me some satisfaction. He squeezed me. No doubt about it. Maybe he thought it was necessary because I was standing in his way. I didn't dislike him as a person. But I hated what he'd done to me."

By late summer 1962, with the Beatles signed to a recording contract and Pete Best sacked in favor of Ringo Starr, problems surrounded many of their appearances. Best's popularity caused fans to camp out in the garden of his West Derby home as a gesture of support. Epstein had to run the gauntlet of anger from fans throughout the city; they fiercely resented his intrusion and his rearrangement of their heroes. The general air of uncertainty hit attendance at some of the Beatles' shows. Sam Leach, still loyal despite some misgivings about Brian's methods, offered a ray of hope during these difficult weeks. He booked the Beatles for a Merseyside rock festival spanning six venues in a week. Epstein was delighted with Sam's commitment, especially when

---

*Epstein placed the Beatles second to Little Richard on this show, his most ambitious to date as a promoter. The twelve-act bill whetted his appetite as an impresario and he rebooked the influential U.S. star for the Liverpool Empire on October 28.

Leach plastered five hundred posters on the hoardings, reasserting Brian's claim that they were "the North's top group."

"I felt sorry for Pete Best but Ringo was more in line with the Beatles," says Leach. "But there were some bad scenes. Brian was threatened, George Harrison got a black eye. There was a lot of trouble around. And the fans were starting to stay away from the shows." Epstein had not warned Leach of the Ringo-Best switch, and Leach was angry: "I have six shows booked for you this week and it's special. Couldn't you have left the change of drummer until the following week?" Epstein apologized, saying he had not thought of it that way. But after what followed, Leach had cause to wonder whether it was another ploy by Brian to force a confrontation.

Sam Leach's emotional link with the Beatles was not to be severed. In 1963, when they had "Love Me Do" released, they played at the city's Grafton Ballroom. Paul dedicated "Hippy Hippy Shake" to Sam's wife Joan. Recalls Leach: "I was very proud but shattered." He said to the four Beatles in the dressing room: "I see, lads, you're on your way now. Remember me when you're up there. Best of luck."

"You'll be there with us," John said. George, always the most money-conscious Beatle, laughed and said: "You still owe us nineteen pounds, you know."

Leach took it to heart. "Lads, if I owe you nineteen thousand pounds, there's nothing I can do. I'm having a hard time."

Leach took the view that he was not going to pay Brian that £19 on principle. Because of Epstein he had to refund more than that in ticket repayments. He still felt he owed the Beatles money, though. By June 1964, Sam had made a profit from the publication of a booklet, *Beatles on Broadway*. The first check he drew was to NEMS. Brian wrote thanking him, saying it was not necessary, "but I appreciate it was important to you and the Beatles send their regards by way of return."

Leach philosophizes on his battle with Brian: "No hard feelings, because although at the time it was painful, business is business, and he was good for the Beatles. Maybe if I'd have had the Beatles, they'd still be playing the Cavern. But Brian would be alive and so would John."

❏

By mid-1962, when his Liverpool work for the Beatles was at its most frenzied, Brian went to Allan Williams to discuss a joint promotion at the Tower Ballroom, New Brighton, on July 27. Brian asked to see the promotional posters. Joe Brown, then riding high in the charts, was top of the bill. The Beatles were second. But Brian, with his promotional flair, insisted that the Beatles be billed as the "sensational" Beatles, with the adjective printed in red. Allan Williams agreed. Even more colorful scenes awaited them at the show.

Fighting broke out, and amid ugly battles bricks were hurled. The bouncers shielded themselves with dustbin lids. Brian, coming down the stairs to the front hall of the Tower into the thick of the battle, saw one bouncer battering one boy. Epstein, horrified, shouted: "Don't hit that boy. Stop!" When the bouncer turned to Epstein and told him to get lost, Brian said: "But I'm the promoter."

"I don't care. I'll smack you as well if you don't get out of the way," said the fighter.

Williams recalls: "People were battling for their lives, and it was the first time Brian had seen a proper fight like that. The Beatles were used to it, but Brian, as a very sophisticated, gentle person, was completely out of his territory." He was astonished that the police were not on hand to quell the riot. "The police reasoned they weren't going to be there as unpaid bouncers," explains Williams. "They weren't going to be booted and kicked around when the promoter was making a profit. If you were a good promoter, you made sure that your main cover was that you had adequate security. Also, if you called the police, it was a black mark for the next show. The magistrates would note, when you asked for a license, that there was a police objection on the grounds of violence last time. So you tended to handle it yourself—part of the risk.

"Brian was grabbed and physically shaken by all this. I had to get him out of the way or he would have been badly hurt." Epstein, scared by the fighting, hated the Beatles involved in such ugliness.

This very protectiveness, his defense of the Beatles, endeared him to Williams as his perfect successor. "He came to the Blue Angel one night in a foul mood. I asked him what the matter was and he said: 'That's the first and last charity show we'll ever do.' They'd just played the Grafton Ballroom. 'We were treated so badly,' Epstein said. 'There was no hospitality and the backstage treatment of the Beatles was appalling.'

"He was furious at the way they'd been handled. He loved them. He worshipped them. He was a Beatle. One day they may accept that their success was due to him." Such realism springs truly from the man who, realizing what he had lost, hurled a cushion and a few expletives at his television set when he saw the Beatles appear on the Royal Variety Show in 1963. "It might as well have been a brick," says Allan Williams. "That moment really got to me. . . ."

The insidious jibes and sarcasm directed at Brian by the Beatles would have crushed most men. In the tiny Cavern dressing room, the Beatles often mocked his demeanor, pulled faces behind his back, mimicked his immaculate speech, his enunciation, his precise arrangements. He was a sensitive man, but when he walked away from the scorn that nobody else would have tolerated, he earned their respect. Epstein and the Beatles were no ordinary business partners. He admired them so much that he would endure anything: their mockery, their pressures, their lampooning of all he stood for. He took the insults because he craved their affection. Once ensnared, he could not reject them, because they became his family. And he slowly learned to enjoy their quirky, debunking, uniquely Liverpudlian sense of humor. He decided that the rock 'n' roll group whom his social circle might denigrate as loud yobs were not dullards but sharp, quick-witted, perceptive.

"Brian wanted very much to be accepted by them as more than just a manager," says Ric Dixon, a club owner who saw them together early in their partnership. "I remember him at the Floral Hall, Southport. Standing by the stage, he was living every moment. To Epstein, it was like food and wine. He breathed every note, every minute. When I first spoke to him, he was quietly genteel. I thought he was an actor; all the mannerisms were there. The Beatles were what he wanted to be himself, but had no hope of being."

Dixon recalls visiting NEMS at Whitechapel to talk about booking the Beatles into Manchester's Oasis club. Brian made a theatrical gesture out of phoning Paul and John: "You're number three in the charts with 'Please Please Me.' Not the Liverpool charts, Paul, the *national* one!" Epstein was still busy getting dates for the band at the Oasis and the other places which Dixon booked for, such as Southport.

"The first time the Beatles played the Oasis there were thirty-seven people there," says Dixon. "It cost *me* money. Later, we crammed about twelve hundred into the place, and the capacity was about five hundred. There were about five thousand people queuing, four or five deep, right round the block and in the surrounding streets."

The hastily arranged bookings and Brian's inexperience combined to bring the Beatles less money than they could have commanded for such shows. "If the record went from fifteen up to ten in the charts, the contract should say the price went up," says Dixon. "Everybody had chart clauses. But Brian didn't seem to know what these were all about. He never seemed to ask for the clause."

For the Beatles, it was enough to see that their bandwagon was rolling, that their faith in this most unlikely mentor had paid off. With the achievement of a record deal, and his physical battering in the Pete Best sacking, Epstein had immersed himself into their inner sanctum. When he was with them, they noticed, he submerged his high-income, upper-middle-class family background. He was great company and they trusted him implicitly. The superb relationship was achieved without any maudlin speeches; and while Brian was impressed with the maturity they showed at not mentioning his private life, they were baffled by the girlfriends who would be his "dates" for nights at the Cavern. His discretion as a homosexual was admirable, they thought; but they were not alone in noting a propensity for female company. And his relationships with women seemed so normal.

❏

Long after he had told his family about his homosexuality, Brian actively pursued women. They admired his élan. Dashing and poised, he stood out, his quiet voice carrying no trace of a scouse accent. But some found that gentleness in contrast to his hot-bloodedness when aroused. Nor was he always discreet in his advances.

Vera Brown was among the sixteen-year-olds who went into Brian's Whitechapel store asking for records to be played but rarely buying them. He would order his staff to eject girls who were bopping around the basement counter. But as he moved into the young people's environment, the pert and strikingly blonde Vera, like the other girls, would say hello to Brian in the coffee bars. "He'd say hello in reply, but he didn't seem friendly. A bit stuck-up," she says.

When Vera's sister Joan became engaged to promoter Sam Leach, the girls' mother threw a party on March 17, 1962, at the family home in Huyton. Epstein and the Beatles, Rory Storm, Bob Wooler, and other local musicians were among the guests. A drunken John Lennon caused riotous scenes that night. He brought screams of horror from Vera's mother Dolly, who found him lying fully dressed in a bath full of water, his face covered. He was pretending to be dead. Next he cracked eggs straight from the fridge over the beehive hairstyles of all the girls. Brian, embarrassed by Lennon's behavior, apologized to the party's hosts. But his mind was on other things.

The less predictable big event taking place in that Liverpool house was the hot pursuit of Vera Brown by Epstein. She was operating the bar from a tiny converted cloakroom, where she supervised the crates of beer, the wines and spirits. Brian repeatedly asked Vera to dance; she said she preferred to serve drinks. So Brian lifted the small bar shelf and joined her behind it. "Let's dance in there, then," he said.

"He seemed to me a very exciting person," says Vera. "It was the first time I'd seen him really relax and enjoy himself. He was getting quite fresh; every time I had to bend down to get some bottles, I was on top of all the crates . . . and it's very hard for me to believe he was anything other than heterosexual. It's still very difficult for me to think of the Brian Epstein people think of. Everybody at the party saw Brian and me necking. They were surprised. I wasn't." Bob Wooler, visiting the bar to replenish his glass, said sarcastically: "I hope I'm not disturbing you two."

"I don't think I was the only girl Brian had mad necking sessions with," says Vera. "It just seemed impossible. He was far too experienced and in control. He didn't seem the shy person I thought he looked. He quite shocked me. He was quite comfortable, and I know for a fact that Brian Epstein had been with women before. I'd say he was a better necker than anyone else at that party. Not much at dancing, but good at necking."

While Brian always had perfect manners in company, Vera says he "wasn't always the complete gentleman" and remembers that "I had a few bruises on my back from the beer crates in the larder when he wouldn't let me up. I was screaming the place down. I think he must have found very few times in his life when he could be himself. I felt quite natural and at home with Brian; I met him in a mad, sexy mood.

Believe me, he was well up on what to do and how to go about it. A man who'd never been out with a girl wouldn't have the chat, or knowledge of how to neck, like Brian Epstein did. He was quite confident and sure of himself. I thought he was fantastic."

To Vera, the experience was the start of what could have developed into something significant if she had allowed it. When people whispered to her that she clearly didn't know Brian's sexual preferences, she laughed them away. "To me he was the complete man. A very sexy man.

"He may have wanted to hide something, using me so that he was seen as normal," says Vera Brown, "but he could have fooled me if that was so." There had been two homosexuals at the party who appeared to be from a lesser social class—"down market," says Vera—and Epstein appeared to want to keep them at a distance.

"At this time he'd assumed the role of father to the Beatles. He wrote a beautiful letter to my mother, apologizing for some of the antics at the party." In thanking Dolly for an enjoyable evening, he asked if he would pose any problem if he asked Vera out; he greatly enjoyed her daughter's company. Brian had a fine communication with Dolly, who, as well as being a lecturer at Ruskin College, Oxford, was a gifted poet. Brian had helped her finish a poem at the party, and sent her a book of poems as a thank-you gift.

Vera assured Brian that she was free to meet him occasionally, and he now pursued the friendship, telephoning, writing letters, visiting the house. Vera's mother gave photos of her daughter, then working as a photographer's model, to Brian. Brian and Vera went on to rendezvous several times. Their usually clandestine meetings were sometimes in the most bizarre settings—inside the classy Liverpool jeweler Boodle and Dunthorne—or in coffee bars, where their tête-à-têtes were visible. Always, Brian was conscious that he had too high a profile to go unnoticed. "It wasn't intense," recalls Vera today. "It was sneaky because I was married. We couldn't see each other every day and build something up. The intensity of it all lay in not getting caught.

"I felt relaxed with him. He liked me and I liked him. I was married but separated at the time, and I didn't believe in adultery; otherwise, we would have had sex. I got frightened because I didn't want to get Brian into trouble. I liked him too much to get him into something he didn't deserve. He was very emotional. He always gave the impression of being cold and icy, but he was very softhearted, very tender, very gentle, and he had a lot of feelings. And he was all man, I don't care what they say. He was very forceful. I was naive, I was married, and I didn't want any problems. I was a terrified flirt, but I didn't want it to go any further. But he would have done. There's no doubt about it. People who saw him know he was quite keen."

When Vera's sister married Sam Leach, Brian said he could not attend the Catholic church but would accept the reception invitation on condition that he sit next to Vera. There, at the Crown in Lime Street, Liverpool, Brian gave a pop-up toaster as a gift to Sam and Joan. And he resumed the warmth in his friendship towards Vera. But she now told him firmly that she was married. It was the painless end of another apparent endeavor by Brian to confront and challenge his sexual instincts.

❑

Meanwhile, Brian was ebullient as word spread that the Beatles were special.

Among those interested in the group was an aggressive dance promoter in Sheffield. Peter Stringfellow ran his Black Cat club in a church hall, where the girls repeatedly asked him to book the Beatles on the strength of their "Please Please Me" success. Intrigued, he discovered that their manager was a Liverpudlian and phoned him to ask for a booking. "I'm pretty new at all this," Brian told him, "but I'm going to ask you for fifty pounds for an engagement."

Stringfellow dismissed the idea. "That's the top price for the *major* bookings!" he told Epstein. "I only pay that for the likes of Screaming Lord Sutch and the Savages." Epstein politely told him he had quite enough work for the Beatles and that there was no point in continuing the conversation if Stringfellow rejected his fee.

"I called him back a few days later," Stringfellow remembers, "and he said the money had gone up to sixty-five pounds. I said it was out of the question. I'd never paid that to anyone. He said the Beatles' demand was increasing by the day and he wasn't prepared to undersell them. Meanwhile, the kids in Sheffield were talking about them more and more, and I had to satisfy my regulars. I returned to Brian on the phone, offered him the sixty-five pounds, and he said the fee had now gone up to a hundred pounds. I told him I couldn't possibly make money on that.''

They compromised at £85. No contract was signed until the eleventh hour, just before the promoter was swayed by police advice to move the venue from the church hall to the Azena Ballroom in the interests of security. Stringfellow had cajoled his girl fans with newspaper ads saying, "Believe it or not, we've got the Beatles," and he sweated over losing money on the night. The agreed fee, he believed, was extortionate. However, the show on February 12, 1963, was a riotous success, and Stringfellow and Epstein forged a friendship. No contract had been signed by the time the group took the stage, but to Stringfellow's surprise, Epstein honored his telephone agreement, a reassuring act in a business not known for acts of honor.

It was to be another year before Stringfellow and Epstein met again, this time in Brian's London office. Stringfellow and his brother Jeff petitioned Brian to take the Beatles to Sheffield during their concert tour. Epstein, impressed with their energy, agreed to the Beatles' visiting Sheffield on November 9, 1964, and gave the Stringfellow brothers the job of compering the show.

Stringfellow was a lively provincial entrepreneur, and Epstein, with an eye to establishing a comprehensive team, offered him a full-time job as a concert compere with his NEMS organization. But by then, Stringfellow ran three successful Sheffield clubs—the Black Cat, the Blue Moon, and the Mojo—and was slowly on his way to his own show business success story. Twenty years later, he would be the millionaire owner of London and New York nightspots—Stringfellow's and the Hippodrome. He reflects on his experiences with Epstein, whom he admired as "completely honorable in a cutthroat business," and on the sound advice Brian gave him: "Peter, if you come to work for me as part of my team, you will have to get rid of your clubs. You will have to choose, one or the other. I'd like to have you as a regular compere for my shows, but if I were you, if you own something that's going to develop, then it might be wise to stay with it." This desire to nurture, to advise, and to informally "direct" the careers of people he respected, coincided with Brian's belief that talented people should immerse themselves in creativity. It would always bring more rewards, he said, than thinking only of "profit for profit's sake."

7

◻

EMPIRE BUILDING

HIRINGS AND FIRINGS

THE BEATLES WERE AWARE of Brian's sexual leanings from their earliest days with him. Not only were they immune to the unkind whispers, but they were defensive and protective of the man they quickly came to respect. As early as February 28, 1962, a mere three months after Brian's first visit to the Cavern and a month after they had signed their first management contract with him, a solicitor's letter was sent on Epstein's behalf. It went to a Liverpool man who in the Kardomah Cafe, Church Street, had allegedly been heard uttering an innuendo about Brian's motivations in his management of the Beatles. The letter demanded an apology and a guarantee of nonrepetition of the remarks, which were considered by Brian to be "highly malicious and defamatory."

Bob Wooler, reflecting on Epstein's first visit to the Cavern, says: "I honestly feel that if Brian had not been homosexual, if he hadn't had this drive within him, there would not have been the same dedication. His motivation was *paramount*. A homosexual cannot indulge, or doesn't wish to indulge, in certain procreation. So a male homosexual goes and finds an image, and they are then his creation. The

Beatles existed as an entity before Brian Epstein, but he created them. He was driven on by this: 'They are *mine*.' "

The Beatles and their girlfriends were always a matter of concern to Epstein. Such was the case when John Lennon told Brian that his art-college lover, Cynthia Powell, was pregnant and that they would have to get married. Believing the Beatles' "availability" to girl fans was vital, Epstein immediately banned John and Cynthia from talking about her pregnancy or the marriage. Brian took command. Determined to ease their problems, he proceeded to arrange the wedding for August 23, 1962, at Liverpool's Mount Pleasant Register Office. As he hosted a lunch after the ceremony in Reece's restaurant, he told John and Cynthia of a special facility available to them. They could have free, unlimited use of his private flat at 36 Falkner Street, opposite the art college. It was both comfortable for them and practical for Brian, who could not imagine the leader of the Beatles living in Cynthia's cheerless bed-sitter in Garmoyle Road. It would be terrible for their image.

"They'd never had a manager before as serious as Brian," says Cynthia. "It was a shock to their system. If John didn't get up in time for a meeting or a journey with the Beatles, Brian would come to Aunt Mimi's house, where I lived with John, and Brian would make quite sure John was out of that house in time. John wasn't used to being told what to do and how to do it. There was a bit of a fracas until they all eventually accepted Brian's new system." Eppy, so nicknamed early in his association with the Beatles and their entourage, told them bluntly that good organization and punctuality were essential if their ambitions were to be realized.

Epstein's urbanity and class were, however, attractive to Lennon. "John aspired to Brian's finesse," says Cynthia. "John's first tremendous boost to his confidence came from his first big wage packet with the Beatles in Hamburg. When he met Brian and they began to climb, his excitement was terrific because this was in his own town and country." And Brian was an upper-middle-class Liverpudlian. Contrary to some theories about the Beatles in Liverpool, Lennon had a perfectly comfortable upbringing, and apart from the differences of age and income, there was not a colossal gulf in Brian's and John's backgrounds.

One marriage within the Beatles was enough, however, before they conquered London. Brian suppressed any evidence that Paul Mc-Cartney had a "steady" girlfriend. Iris Caldwell, attractive blonde sister of Rory Storm, whose group had spawned Ringo, was Paul's date for about a year during the early period of Brian's stewardship. She had trained as a dancer and worked as a showgirl at holiday camps and on variety shows, even appearing at New Brighton's Tower Ballroom alongside the Beatles. "Epstein was not very pleased that I was going out with Paul," Iris said.

While Brian thought a Beatle's image could be affected by marriage and fatherhood, his next move proved wildly indiscreet and potentially dangerous. On April 8, 1963, Cynthia gave birth to Julian, and Brian was named his godfather. Shortly afterward, Brian invited John to join him alone on a holiday in Spain. Lennon had been working hard, writing songs and touring Britain. He needed a rest, and Cynthia relished some time alone to adapt to life with a baby. John accepted and flew to Barcelona on April 28 for the twelve-day break.

John made it clear to everyone that he was a woman-chaser, a hundred percent heterosexual. But it was inept of Epstein to risk the whispering that was bound to ensue from such an expedition by a manager and a solitary Beatle. It was one of the few times when Brian's perception of public opinion faltered, for the Spanish trip fueled rumors in Liverpool of an Epstein-Lennon relationship. Paul McCartney's theory is that "John, not being stupid, saw his opportunity to impress upon Mr. Epstein who was the boss of this group . . . he wanted Brian to know who he should listen to." Lennon knew that Brian held him in awe, regarding him as a genius.

On their return to Liverpool, Brian and John decided to deal with the gossip decisively. At McCartney's twenty-first birthday party on June 18, Bob Wooler and Lennon were seen chatting together and within minutes the Beatle had pummeled the Cavern compere to the ground. "He called me a bloody queer, so I bashed his ribs in," John later told Cynthia. Epstein, no less angry but sensing the need for repairing all wounds, physical and oral, drove Wooler to hospital for treatment of torn knuckles and for shock. Next, Epstein moved swiftly to prevent the friction from escalating. Through his solicitor friend

Rex Makin he paid Wooler £200 in damages and insisted that Lennon sent him a telegram of apology.*

The rumors were quelled. But nothing could prevent the attack on Wooler from reaching the *Daily Mirror*, whose pop reporter Don Short, in a first recognition of the group's burgeoning importance, published a back-page story headlined: "Beatle in Brawl Says: Sorry I Socked You."

Since the deaths of Epstein and Lennon, many with no access to, or observation of, both men in their lifetime have peddled the assumption that Brian and John had a sexual liaison. This is despite the lack of any evidence, despite firm declarations of John's heterosexuality from Cynthia and many other women, and despite the statement by McCartney that he "slept in a million hotel rooms, as we all did, with John and there was never any hint that he was gay."

Brian possibly had a homosexual fascination for Lennon but it could never be reciprocated. And since Epstein was not a predator, that eliminated the likelihood of such a link. More than anyone, Epstein saw the Beatles as an indivisible unit. He would never have risked so profoundly changing his relationship with them, individually or collectively. Nothing mattered more to Brian, after his devotion to his family, than the entity of the Beatles.

In 1964 Brian said: "Paul has the glamour, John the command." His intuitive knowledge of the extraordinary chemistry of the Beatles was vitally important to the whole story, and on that he never faltered. It is extremely doubtful that he would have compromised his position.

"His obsession with the Beatles was much stronger than anything else and he wouldn't have done anything to frighten John off," says Wendy Hanson, Brian's personal assistant. "John certainly wasn't gay. He was a womanizer. And Brian was a very sensitive person; he'd never push himself on anybody."

❑

Not everyone applauded Brian's arrival on the pop scene. To the sixteen-year-old girls, the "boppers" who formed the core of the Cavern "dwellers," the posh Epstein's ejection of the handsome Pete Best

*The original telegram, sold at a Sotheby's auction of Beatles memorabilia in 1984, was bought by a collector for £550.

and the sudden smartening up of the Beatles were heartbreaking. Further, Brian's expansion and management of other top local acts came with bewildering speed.

Because it was so well stocked with records, and because of its proximity to the Cavern and the city center, groups made NEMS a mecca. It became the hub of an explosion that, within two years, would reverberate around the world.

To Brian, the groups appeared to have a friendly rivalry. Once at NEMS, when Brian asked Gerry Marsden why he wanted obscure discs by Fats Domino and Arthur Alexander, Marsden replied that with a busy band playing the clubs of Merseyside and Hamburg, he was always trying to extend his list of songs. Brian quickly discovered that Gerry enjoyed big popularity at the Cavern and was impressed to discover that he had a massive repertoire of 250 songs.

Gerry and the Pacemakers had an appeal different from that of most groups: their leader, a nineteen-year-old former railway apprentice, cultivated a boy-next-door aura. Although they played rock, they were less aggressive and threatening than the Beatles or the Big Three. Yet Marsden's sunny disposition concealed a sharp competitive edge. When Brian visited Gerry at the Cavern, the singer was pleased to be able to tell him he was leaving for a few weeks' work in Hamburg, the mandatory sweatshop for all Liverpool groups. "Would you like me to manage you?" asked Brian, simply. Gerry, ever cautious, said they could chat on his return.

"When I got back from Hamburg I went to see him in his office," says Gerry Marsden. "We never anticipated making records; I actually just gave Brian the diary and hoped for more *money*! But within about four weeks of us signing with Brian, the Beatles did have a contract, and as we'd been battling with them in Liverpool for years, we thought we'd like one as well." Sure enough, Epstein said it would happen. He was telling people: "The Beatles are recording, and Gerry, my second signing, will be next."

So Marsden offered no resistance when the Epstein formula was applied to his group's appearance. "The jeans and tatty shirts onstage had to go. We were told to wear suits. And he said if I must smoke, I should stop the Woodbines and start filter tips. We did tend to listen to him because he never said anything without a reason. He was constructive. He cared about us from the start. I took a great deal of notice of him where I wouldn't give the time to others. He had no pop music in him but he could tell a good song, and he had definite opinions on which of our songs should stay in the act."

Headstrong and argumentative, Liverpool rockers were poor listeners. But Brian could diffuse their anger and petulance with calm moderation, soothing explanations. "I'd steam into his office to strangle him and come out apologizing after a real *chat*," says Gerry. "In those days we never *chatted* to anybody. We went in and smacked them in the mouth. Brian took a lot of the aggression out of us. He slowed us down, told us to relax, talk to people."

As with all his new signings, Brian moved quickly and tactically. On December 9, 1962, he persuaded George Martin to see the Beatles live for the first time, at the Cavern. While Martin was visiting Merseyside, Epstein took him across to the Majestic, Birkenhead, where Gerry and the Pacemakers were appearing. They had a lively potential and Martin soon recorded them. What followed was a best-selling British charts record that has never been beaten: Gerry and the Pacemakers topped the British hit parade with their first three consecutive singles: "How Do You Do It," "I Like It," and "You'll Never Walk Alone."

On the day his debut disc reached number one, Gerry Marsden could not resist a tilt at the Beatles, his old rivals. Visiting Brian's office, he found Lennon and McCartney. Winking at John, Gerry said: "What's it like, then, being Brian's number two group?" Lennon was dismissive. He regarded the Pacemakers' music as "bubble-gum junk."

❑

If Brian sometimes left himself exposed to criticism for inopportune business dealings, his promotional flair was unique among managers. On January 13, 1963, Brian traveled to Birmingham with the Beatles for the recording of the next week's major ITV show "Thank Your Lucky Stars." It was to be the premiere of "Please Please Me." Among the dressing room throng was a wiry, ginger-haired young man with brown horn-rimmed spectacles who said he was publicizing Mark Wynter, a singer on the show. His name was Andrew Loog Oldham, and his capacity for projection and self-publicity immediately impressed Epstein and anyone who would listen. An antiestablishment thinker,

Oldham recognized the Beatles' unique personality. He told Epstein that they should be publicized as cheeky, youth-orientated opponents of the show business status quo.

Brian was so convinced that he hired Oldham to handle press relations for the group, with particular emphasis on their new record. But shortly afterward, Oldham discovered the Rolling Stones and determinedly cast them as opposites to the Beatles: the Fab Four were anodyne, cuddly moptops whose appeal spanned the generations, while the Stones would be unkempt, angry young men whom parents hated.

The grand strategy worked to both groups' advantage as Oldham and Epstein became friendly rivals for the attention of the nation's youth. They even agreed to plan "no clash" on the release dates of Beatles and Stones records. If records came out in different weeks, Epstein firmly believed, young people would not have to choose between the two groups. They could both then top the charts instead of fighting each other.

❏

Just as the Beatles were about to begin their concert tour with Helen Shapiro, "Please Please Me" rocketed to the number one position on the national charts. Brian, ecstatic, gave the news first to the group and then to the man who had been their strongest link with their Liverpool fans: Bob Wooler. Announcing the news to the Cavern audience just before they took the stage, Wooler was surprised at the silence. Here was the news the audience dreaded. They deeply resented the export of their group into the arms of the nation's fans. Indeed, it was the start of an exhausting year in which Epstein worked the Beatles around Britain amid scenes of fan mania not witnessed before or since.

On another tour around Britain, which saw American singers Tommy Roe and Chris Montez replace Helen Shapiro, the Beatles were unstoppable as their personal energy, musical harmony, and abrasive characteristics enraptured Britain. In the wings at each show stood their manager, immaculate, arms folded, eyes riveted to the stage, carefully monitoring the tiniest detail: a misplaced microphone, a seemingly uncomfortable chair for the drummer, John wearing trousers that were very slightly short. The applause for his Beatles, he told Arthur Howes, was more than for the bill-toppers.

Epstein, who only a year earlier had emerged triumphantly from his battle to secure them a record deal, now implemented the second phase of his ambition to make them world-beaters. True to his family-bred ethic of hard work, Epstein gave himself and the Beatles no time whatsoever to bask in glory or even to reflect on what was happening so quickly. The diary of engagements he accepted for them was grueling. It was planned not to capitalize financially but to gain recognition, exposure, and credibility for the original sound with which the Beatles were bombarding the theaters and the airwaves.

There was no time for delusions of grandeur. While working on a big national breakthrough, Epstein plugged away at their Liverpool origins. He organized Mersey Beat Showcase Tours, running coaches for local fans to see the Beatles and other acts—Gerry and the Pace-makers, the Big Three, and Billy J. Kramer—in cities in the Midlands and the South. But for national tours, as a gesture of thanks for his early faith, he allowed Arthur Howes to handle the bulk of the Beatles' touring arrangements. That dedication to loyalty, to the repaying of favors, was central to Epstein's method of working.

Danny Betesh, a mild-mannered Manchester area promoter, had always impressed Brian with his quiet efficiency and enthusiasm, and Brian developed a particularly strong relationship with him. Anticipating the success of Brian's Beatles around the time of "Love Me Do," Betesh had asked if he could promote them on a national tour. Brian, by then committed to Arthur Howes, said they were not big enough to be top of the bill; Danny should return to him when he had a major attraction to headline the tour. Betesh flew to America in an attempt to book guitar star Duane Eddy. When that plan fell through, he signed singer Roy Orbison, a major artist who had nine hits.

All was set for the nineteen-city tour opening at Slough on May 18, 1963, a package show in which the Beatles were projected as second from the top of the bill; there were seven other acts. "But when tickets were about to go on sale," says Betesh, "it was quite obvious that the Beatles were becoming enormously popular. It would be hard to put them second on the bill to anyone. So we switched the billing. Roy

Orbison understood. All the tickets sold out as quickly as they could physically pass them over the counters." In most towns the shows had sold out within hours, hardly surprising in view of the entertainment value: 9s. 6d. was the top price.

By April 3, Gerry and the Pacemakers had reached the number one position with "How Do You Do It." Although the group had no hit when Betesh's tour was in the planning stages, Brian had negotiated them onto the bill. Knowing the Beatles and Orbison would attract big crowds, he was keen for "exposure" for Gerry. By the time the tour began, Gerry was celebrating three weeks at the top of the charts, and Epstein was being hailed as the manager with the Midas touch. Gerry closed the first half of the show, Orbison bravely accepting the spot just before the Beatles—the position every artist dreaded, since the fans were always by then feverishly anticipating the group.

Says Betesh: "I liked to do business with him: he was a man of his word. A yes was a yes, a no was a no. And he was decisive." Watching Epstein checking out the Beatles from the side of any stage was, Betesh avers, "just like watching a proud father."

❑

Brian's pride in the visual appeal of all his acts was a paramount priority, and his attention to the Beatles' appearance never wavered. Their suits had to match Epstein's dictum: the Beatles could be outlandish and unorthodox but must remain smart. As he masterminded the Beatles' look, the latent dress designer in Brian Epstein sprang into action. It was a delicate operation. He had to retain the raw, earthy attraction that had riveted him at the Cavern while he simultaneously switched their clothes from jeans and black leather bomber jackets to something more conservative for adult consumption. He asked Larry Parnes for advice on outfitting his stars.

All the pop stars of the 1950s had been clothed by show business tailor Dougie Millings and his son Gordon at 63 Old Compton Street, Soho: Cliff Richard and the Shadows, Marty Wilde, Tommy Steele, Billy Fury, Eden Kane, and the stable operated by Parnes were among eighty pop names under their sartorial wing. On his first visit to London to meet with Millings, during which he ordered a charcoal-gray pin-stripe for himself, Epstein pooled his, the Beatles', and the tailor's ideas to produce the collarless jackets. "We did five hundred variations for the Beatles eventually," recalls Millings. "Four in the set, and we always made spares. On some of the black velvet suits they had three or four different shades. There was always an extra one for John, who either got thin or fat or split his trousers running from the theater. The only complaint from the Beatles was that the trousers weren't tight enough."

From twelve-ounce mohair and worsted material, Millings created a style applauded by Epstein and envied by other stars for its simplicity and uniqueness: a four-button, high-buttoning jacket in dark gray, with black velvet collar and no outside pleats. There were eight-inch side pleats on the jacket, cut with a tubular look, the shoulders as narrow as each Beatle could carry. The skintight trousers were so close-fitting that the Beatles could not sit down in them. For future emergencies, Brian ordered multiple suits in each of several colors that he himself chose: silver-gray, blue, navy blue, beige, and black.

❏

Liverpool buzzed with speculation: Whom would the unlikely Svengali sign next? At NEMS in Whitechapel, there was a domestic question: How much longer could the family business contain such rapid growth, and how long could Brian remain there? Epstein's sights were firmly set on empire building.

There was a period when any young man with a guitar who also shopped for records at NEMS believed he could be the next candidate for Epstein's magic wand. And every day Brian ventured out from behind his glass-encased basement office to talk to them all. His next interest in a Cavern group, however, was to be halted by his own rigorous, unyielding demands.

Rod Pont, who led his band under the name of Steve Day and the Drifters, was surprised one day when the "gentleman" boss of NEMS walked over and asked what record he was buying. Pont had chosen a single by an act named Dr. Feelgood. Epstein immediately said: "Oh well, would you do me a favor? Would you please not perform the flip side?" Why, asked Pont. "Because it's called 'Mr. Moonlight' and I've got it mapped out for John to do with the Beatles."

Epstein had seen Steve Day and the Drifters' smooth act at Cavern lunchtime sessions but had been too busy launching the Beatles and signing Gerry and the Pacemakers to pursue them. "I couldn't comprehend what he was doing on the beat scene anyway," says Pont, a middle-class man who lived on the Wirral. "I could understand him selling records or washing machines, but I remember thinking he would find it difficult to communicate with people running the clubs. I couldn't see the Beatles being successful under him because he wasn't the sort of promoter we groups were used to dealing with. God knows what Brian was doing mixed up in rock 'n' roll. He was totally alien to it."

Steve Day and the Drifters' immaculate stage uniforms, the band in cherry-red suits and the leader in emerald-green, instantly impressed Brian. Their act, too, was professional; and he saw no need to tamper with their appearance.

As a trial, he offered them a date at the Locarno, a ballroom in West Derby Road where he was hoping to secure plenty of work for his acts. Rod Pont, used to running his semiprofessional band on the telephone, was baffled to receive a letter from Brian with specific instructions about time of arrival, duration of the sets—every moment of the evening planned. "This efficiency stunned me." Disaster struck when the band's Humber Super Snipe saloon broke down in the Mersey tunnel. They arrived at the Locarno forty-five minutes late.

Scrambling onstage to do three songs, Pont was horrified to see Epstein in the audience. He was not expected, but had arrived to check the act with a view to management. It was one of the first bands Brian had booked into the hall; he felt let down. He rounded on Rod Pont. "What happened? You were told *specifically* to be here at half past seven."

"We had a breakdown in the tunnel. We left our homes in sufficient time. . . ."

"You know the perils of the tunnel," Epstein snapped. "You should have set out half an hour earlier to anticipate any holdups or breakdowns."

The heated row continued. Pont was not in awe of Epstein. Was Brian accusing him of lying? Epstein angrily replied that he was unimpressed with their failure to be punctual. Pont retorted that if Brian questioned his honesty, he could forget it. "Brian wasn't the sort of fellow you could use bad language to, unlike some promoters." It was, predictably, the first and last show Epstein offered to Steve Day and the Drifters. "I didn't like the clinical way he just cut people off like that. We remained friendly, but we never ever worked for him again," says Pont.

To Epstein, the Cavern now seemed a bottomless well of great artists. The Beatles and Gerry and the Pacemakers were absorbing his time, but he had no doubt that Liverpool was teeming with talent. Epstein's third Cavern act, signed at Lennon's urging, would prove a short-lived but significant milestone, a classic example of how his enterprise, energy, and enthusiasm could be canceled out by his own obduracy.

The Big Three were rugged rock 'n' rollers whose popularity, particularly at the Cavern, nearly matched the Beatles'. Cilla Black and Bill Harry sang their praises; their own song "Cavern Stomp" was a huge hit; and the surging sound was capped by a powerful animalistic presence. The Big Three drummer, the abrasive Johnny Hutchinson, believed his group was better than the Beatles—"a bunch of wimps." The other two, guitarist Brian Griffiths and bass guitarist Johnny Gustafson, also regarded the Beatles as "college boys" whose credentials were not quite faithful to rock 'n' roll. "The Big Three were down-to-earth, working class, tough, scruffy," says Gustafson. Part of the Big Three's appeal lay in their unkempt look. "We dressed in rags and tatters: Griffiths used to wear his dad's docker's belt. I sometimes hung around in a pyjama jacket."

Epstein moved in carefully. He tried out the Big Three on a shared bill at Southport, where the crowd had gone specifically to see the Beatles. The response was excellent. In the dressing room Brian said he would like to manage them. "For anyone on the Liverpool scene then to be offered management by Brian Epstein," says Gustafson, "was a very big deal, the passport to riches and fame. He had the voice of authority, someone who could talk proper, like, y'know?"

But when Epstein invited them to his office to complete the arrangements, he stunned them with his caveat. Without mentioning the Beatles, he told the Big Three that they must immediately drop their disheveled appearance, which went against his policy, and wear suits and ties. What was good at the Cavern wasn't a certainty for the rest of Britain, he told them. Nicotine-stained fingers, Epstein told Brian Griffiths, could be improved with a pumice stone. And could he please not chew his nails? Finally, criticizing their tatty shirts, he said he would pay for new outfits, which they could choose. He encouraged them by saying he had great hopes and plans.

"Surprisingly," Gustafson says, "Johnny Hutchinson, the hard man of the group, was the one who fell into line. He made us wear the suits and put the shirts on. But eventually that fell away. The suits got wet, we left them behind somewhere, and the jeans went back on. Brian found out when we were on tour and there was hell."

Epstein secured the Big Three a recording audition with Decca, a company now regretting its loss of the Beatles and thus particularly watchful of other Liverpool talent. Towards the end of a five-week stay in Hamburg, the Big Three received a telegram from Epstein saying they had come in second to the Beatles in *Mersey Beat*'s readers' poll; and they had a Decca test on the day of their return. Epstein's progress had again been swift.

But his timing of the test appalled the group. Exhausted from the punishing Hamburg schedule, as well as excesses of pleasure, the Big Three flew straight from Germany to the London audition. "Hutchinson had some semblance of a voice but mine was a croak," says Gustafson. "Brian *insisted* I sang. I'll never forget seeing the people laughing at me in the recording booth." With more willpower than strength, the trio staggered through their classic, "Some Other Guy."

Back in Liverpool, they were surprised and elated to hear they had passed the audition. Happiness turned to horror when they were told that the test version of "Some Other Guy" would be released as their debut record. It was the worst performance of the song they could recall. A proper session to rerecord it was essential, they angrily told Epstein. They went "berserk" in his office but to no avail. Brian had too much on his mind to enter into a battle with Decca executives, who were happy with the music. He was doing well for the Big Three, raising their income from the £10 at the Cavern to between £20 and £30 for each appearance—"absolutely astounding money for us," says Gustafson. The record was released and was a minor hit.

With both their stage outfits and their debut record now causing tension after only two months of his management, Epstein introduced a third confrontation. He appeared not to perceive the rock 'n' roll strengths of the Big Three, wanting to soften their look and their sound. He imposed his own choice of songs on them. "He'd give me a bunch of records and say which ones he wanted us to record," says Gustafson. "When I played them, I thought, Oh my God, awful pap. The problem was he fantasized about his ideal possessions. No way did it coincide with the musical content of the band he was managing." On tour, the group ignored his instructions about the songs they should play.

Brian's curious weakness at this stage coincided with the national habit of pigeonholing the "Liverpool sound." To him, all the city's groups had to fit into a neat three-guitars-and-drums lineup. The Beatles, as market leaders, had to be slavishly copied. So Brian applied the same cleaning-up tactics to Gerry and the Pacemakers, the Big Three, and all his artists.

He misfired again with the Chants, a black vocal group that needed instrumental backing. Brian banned the Beatles from accompanying them, declaring that it was beneath their status. But they did so, once, at the Cavern. It signaled the quick end of Brian's interest in the Chants, who, as the Real Thing, would later form part of a long-running success story. What Brian failed to absorb was that Liverpool offered a variety of music, not only Beatles-styled rock 'n' roll but also good-quality folk music (the Spinners) and country and western (the Hillsiders.) It was not until Brian reached London in 1964 that he seemed able to pull himself out of the straitjacket of Liverpool rock, a narrow vision he had done more than anyone to perpetuate.

With the Beatles charging ahead, Brian flexed his muscles and became more assertive. He believed his fortnightly investment of £10 for a NEMS advertisement in *Mersey Beat* entitled him to reciprocal editorial favors. And Brian knew how to oil the wheels: returning from a weekend pleasure trip to Amsterdam, he took Virginia Harry a box of liqueur chocolates. She was mightily impressed by this suave man who gave her a lift home from Beatles shows in his flashy Ford Zodiac. "I thought of him as in a class beyond me. But he seemed so shy. He hardly spoke in the car, as if he was embarrassed."

Brian wanted to court the Big Three with evidence of his promotional expertise: he would grandly announce his management of them in a half-page advertisement in *Mersey Beat*. Calling at the paper's offices, he told Bill Harry that he wanted the front-cover picture in the same issue. Bill Harry guffawed when Epstein's photos of the new-look Big Three landed on his desk. "It was like taming wild animals! Their casual look in jeans and open shirts was important. Brian had them in horrible mohair suits, looking constrained, embarrassed. It was yucky."

Harry was not intimidated by Epstein's new influence or swayed by his charm. What Brian wanted was impossible, he said: he had other plans for his paper. Epstein was livid. His power over *Mersey Beat* was to be an important tool in persuading groups that he had leverage. Bill Harry, guarding his editorial independence, told Brian he would never bow to such pressure. "I have *created* this paper and I'm fair to the groups."

Brian flew into a fury. If the Big Three were not featured on the cover, he would withdraw all his advertising—and NEMS as a vital sales point for the paper. Virginia joined in the row. "Don't talk to us like that. You can't dictate . . ." Brian stormed out.

The next day Bill Harry received a formal written complaint from Epstein. Virginia, he wrote, had behaved with "appalling rudeness" and he demanded an apology. He had visited *Mersey Beat* to discuss business and had been met with a rebuff not only from the editor but from his *secretary*!

Harry was having none of that. With the anger of a zealot, he dug in with a two-page typewritten defense, saying that they, the creators of *Mersey Beat*, would run the paper their way. He operated as editor independent of advertising pressures: if Brian wanted to threaten and virtually blackmail, there would be a complete breakdown in communications. Where Brian had tried to be a business bully, Bill Harry now retorted with the logic and idealism of youth. His extra asset was a good reputation among musicians, some of whom at that stage mistrusted Epstein as "Mister Big."

The editor won this skirmish. Brian telephoned immediately upon receipt of Harry's letter. "I'm glad you wrote. You are right. Come round and have a sherry with me, Bill."

Brian's acquisition of the Big Three was a valuable addition to his stable, but his subsequent loss of them was a dent in his artistic prestige. Bill Harry remembers a fracas between Epstein and the group towards the end of their relationship. In the Grapes pub in Mathew Street, one of the group was drunk, ranting about their emasculation at the hands of Epstein. "I'll fill him in . . . he's got to get us out of this. . . I'm gonna smash him up." Brian heard the venomous remarks across the crowded bar, and left. Shortly after that, he and the Big Three had a showdown.

In Liverpool, many observers had confidently expected the group to capitulate to Brian's demands: he had so much to offer. But finally Epstein would accept no more disobedience. As their diary of engagements increased and he could not attend all their shows, he heard tales of how they had repeatedly rejected the suits and ties he had so generously bought. Then, one Saturday, there they were before his eyes on the major television show "Thank Your Lucky Stars," spurning him yet again. They were dressed in jeans and polo-neck sweaters and playing *borrowed guitars*. "He went crackers," says Gustafson.

Epstein immediately called them to his office and fired them for "unruly behavior." Says Gustafson: "He was absolutely adamant. But we thought doing it his way would be selling out. With us, there was a spirit of give and take, but there wasn't enough give from Brian. Brian's discovery wasn't to his liking and neither was ours. He was niggly about unimportant things."

The gentleman in Epstein reigned. Although the group had to leave him, he referred them to his friend Danny Betesh. For a few months his more conciliatory style allowed a good relationship, but the Big Three disintegrated after an internal row.

In the Epstein–Big Three clash, both sides lost. Three headstrong rockers proved unmanageable by a man intent on stubbornly imposing his set of rules; and a Liverpool act that should have gone on to national success failed to jump the crucial hurdle. "Brian and the Big Three didn't know each other," says Gustafson. "He should have seen from us that not all acts were wine and roses."

❑

During his management of the Big Three, Brian had vaguely heard of Swinging Cilla. She had made her singing debut under that name with the trio at the Zodiac Club in Duke Street. A nineteen-year-old docker's daughter, training to be a shorthand typist, Priscilla Maria Veronica White was well known among the local beat groups, occasionally helping out as a cloakroom attendant at the Cavern.

At Brian's store, asking to hear records in the listening booth but never buying them, she was often told to leave. With the little shorthand she had learned at commercial college, she wrote down the words to current hits while she listened, so she could sing them with any group that allowed her to get up onstage. Since the age of eleven she had had a burning desire to be a stage star.

The first group Priscilla had sung with was Rory Storm and the Hurricanes, and thus her closest friend in the Beatles was the drummer, Ringo Starr. She was therefore amazed when Brian Epstein approached her in the Cavern and said: "John Lennon has told me about you. He says if I'm looking for a girl singer to sign, it should be you." Lennon, then gaining real influence with Brian on whom he should sign, had seen "Swinging Cilla" several times with the Big Three, his favorite Liverpool group. She was inclined to sing standards like "Autumn Leaves" and "Lavender Blue." John thought she had a special style. Brian asked her to audition for him in a Beatles show at the Majestic, Birkenhead. "I was very, very nervous and not professional," says Cilla. "I'd never done anything like that before and this was with the *Beatles*, who were on the brink of stardom, and their *manager*, who was really like a film star to me. He was immaculate from head to toe, like Cary Grant—real silk scarves and Cashmere overcoats, which you just didn't see in Liverpool."

After the show Brian was politely noncommittal. It was obvious she had failed the test, however, for she heard nothing more from him for nine months. Then one night in the Blue Angel club, Cilla needed little persuasion to sing with a modern jazz group led by a noted local pianist, John Rubin, whom Brian knew. After she sang "Bye Bye Blackbird," Cilla discovered that Epstein was in the audience with Bob Wooler. "I'd like to sign you," he said simply.

Cilla, "over the moon" with excitement, heard Wooler say to Brian: "Oh Brian, you're very silly. She'll never make it." Says Cilla: "I thought to myself: Please don't say that! I failed the first audition. I don't want to blow it a second time." Epstein asked Cilla to visit him at his office.

There he declared that he would like to design clothes for her in leather. The latent fashion designer inside him still yearned for this outlet; Cilla was excited. "He had impeccable taste, and I thought leather would be great, as we only ever wore imitation. But he never really got round to it."

Brian's first priority, though, was to convince Cilla's father to sign a management contract for her, since she was under the age of twenty-one. And a mistake in her surname in *Mersey Beat*, which announced her as Cilla Black rather than White, seemed worth adopting, Brian told them: it flowed better. Cilla's father needed convincing. But on September 6, 1963, at his house at 380 Scotland Road, he gradually warmed to Brian's convictions and persuasiveness. He agreed that his daughter should be launched as Cilla Black. Epstein had succeeded where several visiting managers from London and elsewhere had failed. The fact that the White family owned a piano bought from NEMS was strongly in Brian's favor, as was his background. "Obviously, Brian came from a family which had more than two halfpennies to rub together, and I'm sure this influenced me Dad," says Cilla.

The day he signed her was frantic. At lunchtime and at night, Brian attended celebrations to mark his parents' thirtieth wedding anniversary, telling them of his exciting acquisition. As if to lay the ghost of her unsuccessful audition, Brian had planned Cilla's professional debut with the Beatles again, this time at the Odeon Cinema, Southport. Proudly, he drove his parents there to demonstrate his latest talent. With exceptional accuracy, Harry Epstein predicted: "She'll be the next Gracie Fields." Says Cilla: "Actually, Brian really did think the sun shone out of my eyes." The admiration was mutual.

Brian chose good songs for Cilla and her record career blossomed. "Love of the Loved" was a minor hit. Still visiting NEMS to buy records, she pounced on Dionne Warwick's "Anyone Who Had a Heart" as a potential song to cover. When Epstein returned from his first American trip with the same record, he was delighted that their views coincided. Brian was less pleased when George Martin said it was "an excellent song, perfect for Shirley Bassey." Brian was furious: "No way, it's for *my* artist, it's for Cilla!" He and Cilla won their point and took it to number one. The next song, "You're My World," helped establish her as a creditable ballad singer, a previously unrevealed aspect of her talent.

Although he undervalued her Liverpudlian sense of humor, which endeared her to the beat groups and would later dominate her career, Brian saw in Cilla a hugely popular world-class singer. "Brian had the sense to see in Cilla something that I originally hadn't seen," says George Martin. "I thought she was this dolly rocker from Liverpool, good and different but not in any way a ballad singer. She was a miniskirted little girl with a brassy voice. He opened my eyes to Cilla's dramatic potential. He had a great sense of vision in the artists he handled."

❑

At the Queens Hall, Widnes, the Beatles shared the bill with a rising group named Billy Kramer and the Coasters. Epstein went along with Bob Wooler. When Brian asked some fans what they thought of the Beatles' show, he was perplexed when some replied that they had not come to see the Beatles, but to see Kramer. Driving Wooler home, Epstein asked him: "Bob, do you think I've made a mistake? Should I have signed Billy Kramer instead of the Beatles?" No, said the wise compere: "The Beatles will do it for you." That night, though, Kramer's act and personality fired Brian's interest. It had to be his next signing, he decided. Kramer was handsome and well-built, with a stage presence not unlike that of pop stars Billy Fury and Vince Eager, so skillfully managed by Larry Parnes in London. Epstein, intrigued, envisaged a potential male solo star to contrast with Cilla.

A few nights later outside the Iron Door Club, Epstein bumped into Ted Knibbs. A boilermaker by day, he was Kramer's manager, although no contract existed between them. At fifty-six, he was a benign friend of the pop scene and frequented the Old Dive pub, where he had seen Epstein long before his Beatles association. "Ted, I'd like to have a talk with you. What's the chance of my taking over Billy?" Epstein began.

Knibbs was receptive. "Well, I think we have got as far as we can as amateurs. . . ." Inside the "Nemporium"—pun-loving Bob Wooler's name for Epstein's (the "Nemperor") office—Knibbs needed little persuasion from Epstein that his clout would benefit Kramer's career. "It was simply psychology," recalled Knibbs. "He pointed out that he had done well for the Beatles, his list of acts was going to expand, and it was not in Billy's interests to be left out. Brian at that stage had the Beatles, Gerry and the Pacemakers, and the Big Three. I couldn't disagree." Epstein said he would pay Knibbs sixpence to the pound out of Kramer's earnings.

"Okay by me," said Knibbs, "but I have to see the lads first. They might think I'm throwing them overboard."

That formality completed, Knibbs returned to Epstein to say that Kramer was prepared to give up his work on the railway but that his backing group, the Coasters, were less happy about turning professional. Brian was sure that hurdle could be overcome. He then revised his financial offer to Knibbs. As a management transfer fee, would Ted accept £50? In 1963, that was a substantial cash offer, which Knibbs accepted. Epstein immediately handed over £25 in his office, saying "Now I owe you twenty-five pounds." That debt was never paid, but Knibbs bore no grudge. It was, he remembered, pure forgetfulness rather than an intention by Brian to pay him less. "I wasn't in pop for the money, anyway," says Knibbs. It was just as well: Brian's original idea of paying him a percentage was forgotten too.

Others were less charitable to Epstein and his evident plans to build a show business empire. They whispered that Brian had "bought Billy Kramer for fifty pieces of silver."

❑

Billy Kramer was flattered. His parents had bought their first three-piece bedroom suite from Harry Epstein at Walton Road. For a nineteen-year-old who augmented his real job as a railway worker with pop singing, the approach from Brian was a pleasant shock.

Epstein next saw Kramer, whose real name was William Ashton, at the *Mersey Beat* awards presentation, where Billy had won third prize in their readers' poll. Walking down Mathew Street, the two met. "You look a bit down," said Brian. "Let's go for a drink in the Grapes." Kramer was morose because he was facing a crunch decision: as an indentured railway apprentice, he feared he might have to pack in his lucrative rock 'n' roll gigs and go to Crewe or Derby to study diesel electrification.

Brian said he was too talented to drop music. He would guarantee Billy £50 a week to turn professional. Brian would not take his commission until Kramer had earned that figure; and if he earned less, Brian would make it up out of his own pocket. "You have a lot of potential and I think I can do a lot for your career."

"To be approached by somebody who was managing the Beatles was a big deal to me," recalls Kramer, who accepted immediately. John Lennon, who had just become a father, injected the "J" in his stage name to mark the birth of his son Julian. Epstein and Kramer both agreed that Billy J. Kramer had a good flow, and the career was launched.

Kramer was not the speediest of thinkers, but he had a robust voice and Epstein saw him as a natural Liverpool response to Elvis Presley and Cliff Richard. But first, he told him, he would have to dress differently. The gold and pink lamé suits were to go, in favor of conventional mohair and knitted ties. "And you speak so badly," Epstein added. "You must have elocution lessons." Epstein drove him to a woman teacher, but on leaving her house, Kramer said it was the first and last session: "I'm not going through with it, Brian. People take me for what I am or let's forget it." Shortly afterward, the Liverpool accent became fashionable and his broad scouse accent was never criticized again.

Brian had another problem, however. As Knibbs had warned him, some of Kramer's backing group did not want to take the chance of turning professional; as always, Epstein had neither the time nor the inclination to change their minds. He spoke to his Manchester friend Danny Betesh, who suggested that the Dakotas should be recruited as Billy's accompanists. It was an unhappy union; they were too well-established to submerge themselves as a backing group. Tensions built up.

Epstein's relationship with Kramer lacked the warmth that he so relished in connection with his other artists. John Lennon, who praised Billy's voice, sent him a tape of his song "Do You Want to Know a Secret?" Billy tried it out onstage but was bemused when Epstein said it would be his first single. "Don't you think we should find a *good song*?" asked Kramer. Brian was aghast at the insult to his treasured songwriters. It went to number one, the first of three songs by Lennon-McCartney that did well for Kramer. The next confrontation arose when Kramer felt he was being pigeonholed into a cozy image. He wanted more accent on his rock 'n' rolling, but Brian refused to change a winning formula. Brian did not sign any act until he was fairly sure he could get a record deal, and when he had proved a capable salesman of their talent, he felt he was entitled to pass judgment on their songs, style, and appearance. ("I took Billy J. Kramer reluctantly," says George Martin, "because, although he looked very good, I didn't think he had a very good voice.")

Next, Brian proudly announced that he had booked Kramer for the major TV show "Sunday Night at the London Palladium," on which he would sing his new single, "I'll Keep You Satisfied." Kramer argued that he was not ready for such an important show. "Come back in six months. I've had no TV experience to do that." Brian insisted: "It will do *so* much for your career." The nervous Kramer did not sleep for weeks. On the big night, Brian arrived at the dressing room with a white suit specially made for Billy by Douglas Millings, the London show business tailor, to whom Brian had given Kramer's measurements. Billy protested: "I had a suit made specially. . . ." Brian would have none of it: "*That* doesn't suit the occasion."

There were constant lectures from Epstein to Kramer about his weight. From a physical job on the railway to the comparatively pampered life of show business, Kramer had quickly ballooned to 230 pounds. It was "terribly important," said Brian, in one of his favorite phrases, "to lose weight." He was so worried that he invited Kramer to relax and talk it through at his home in Queens Drive. There, he persuaded Kramer to go to a health farm. It worked.

The slender rapport between artist and manager was finally punctured when Kramer flatly rejected two further songs by Lennon and McCartney. To Epstein, this was heresy. Dick James phoned Kramer to warn: "This will do you *so* much harm." Defiant, Kramer went ahead and recorded "Little Children." It was successful, but his tenuous relationship with Epstein plummeted. Driving down Park Lane, London, Epstein said to Kramer: "You had that song up your sleeve all the time, didn't you?" The singer, basking in the success of a hit he alone had chosen, said: "I'm learning fast."

But, Epstein pointed out, he had tacitly insulted the two biggest songwriters in the *world*.

It was the point of no return. The two became distant, and relations went even more sour when Kramer said to Epstein: "Look, I know you're a very busy man and your empire has grown. Isn't it time each artist had a personal manager to look after their affairs, with you at the top to vet everything?" Brian curtly disagreed.

"I thought a lot of Brian. And think of the pressure he was under at the age of twenty-eight. He took over the world of pop. But he thought I was ungrateful, that I'd had lots of success through his management but didn't appreciate it."

8

❑

MIGRATION

THE LEAVING OF LIVERPOOL

IN LONDON'S SOHO, as Beatlemania engulfed Britain, the moguls of popular music exchanged gossip every day over lunch in a Jewish restaurant called Isow's. The biggest question buzzing around the tables was: Will it last? It was a fair question in 1963, when little was expected of a pop career beyond a few hits.

Nobody could be blamed for failing to predict that, a quarter of a century later, the Beatles would dominate the compact disc charts; that thousands would attend regular annual Beatles conventions throughout America; that, even with John Lennon and Brian Epstein dead, the media would continue to clamor for a Beatles "reunion"; and that the group's *Sgt. Pepper* album, on its twentieth anniversary, would eclipse all other contemporary rock. Not even Brian Epstein knew the icon he was creating. . . .

With the triumphant acquisition of a Beatles recording contract, Epstein decided that NEMS as a retail organization could no longer contain his activities. On June 26, 1962, three weeks after the Beatles' first visit to EMI's recording studio, Brian and his brother registered NEMS Enterprises Limited. At Harry Epstein's suggestion, Clive, with his business acumen, was appointed company secretary, with the brothers owning the £100 company equally. NEMS Enterprises, launched "to carry on the business of theatrical, concert, variety agents," was the start of a convoluted business structure that found Brian directly involved in sixty-five registered companies within five years. NEMS Enterprises became the main operating company for the Beatles and all his other artists, and Brian reveled in the stance of impresario that the company immediately gave him.

❏

"Can *anything* be more important than this?" Euphoria was not part of Brian's makeup, but the sight of the Beatles' second single, "Please Please Me," at the top of the music papers' best-seller lists in the spring of 1963 was special. Beaming, he walked around the NEMS offices: it was the first real justification to his family and the cynics in Liverpool for spending so much time away from the record shop.

"Once we had our first number one under our belt with 'Please Please Me,' " says George Martin, "Brian and I worked out a grand plan of campaign. A single would be released every three months and an album every six. I quickly realized I had to have an album. I knew the boys had a big repertoire from the Cavern and from their knowledge of American records. I said: 'I'll just record everything you've got.' That's how the first album was made. We started at ten in the morning and finished at eleven at night. We recorded eleven tracks." Brian was present throughout.

Brian's new office for NEMS Enterprises, on the top floor at Whitechapel, was a hive of activity. Telephones rang nonstop; every post brought thousands of fan letters (some in the form of cardboard hearts); and an air of pandemonium shattered the store that had once merely sold washing machines, television sets, and pop records in the basement. Brian was gleeful over the fees he could now ask for the Beatles: for big dates, he pushed their rate to £200. Beryl Adams, his secretary, was amazed to find that at the end of a Beatles week she was now putting £50 into each of their pay envelopes instead of the old average of £20.

In August, NEMS Enterprises moved from the Whitechapel record store into a first-floor office above a magic shop at 24 Moorfields, close to Liverpool Exchange station. Here, Brian could expand more naturally, without the distraction of record retailing. The move symbolized, too, Brian's statement that he was a full-time manager. In less than two years he had grasped his opportunity, reshaped his life, and begun a fast-expanding empire.

Building up his staff was another urgent priority, since the Beatles, Gerry and the Pacemakers, and Cilla Black would cause too much pressure for the present team. (When interviewing potential employees, Brian often asked about their religion; it appeared to make no difference in his decision to hire, but several of them thought it a curious personal quirk.) His staff quickly grew from three to ten, plus nine road managers. The speed of events brought an immediate need to streamline the primitive bookkeeping. An accountant, Peter Bevan, called in to establish a management and agency booking system, discovered Epstein coping with nightly fees that jumped from £250 to thousands within a few months. "In the early days, Brian had been on the phone pleading with the established entrepreneurs to take one of his acts: the Beatles, Billy J. Kramer, Gerry, Cilla. Within four months, Brian didn't have to ring anybody. They rang him. He was calling the tune entirely."

If he was going to operate a successful organization, however, he would have to learn to delegate. He was working seven days a week and into most nights, checking and telephoning, negotiating better fees, planning new records, and always keeping an eye open for further ways to expand. His temper was often frayed: when a secretary used her initiative and opened a bank account for one of his artists, Brian was furious. He alone could make such decisions.

Freda Kelly was another who felt the sting of Epstein's anger. Head of a local fan club, Freda was close to the group and Brian knew it. She was always visiting their tiny Cavern band room, asking them for 5s. to answer fans' letters. When Brian opened NEMS Enterprises and gave her a job, he gained control over the club: "Eppy said if we gave him the fan club subscription money, he'd pay the bills," says Freda. She was to become a loyal, trusted employee, but working at NEMS was not without bumps. When Brian's secretary, Beryl Adams, was away, Freda had the job of working Brian's dictating machine. The tape once stuck with thirty of his letters. "When he arrived, some of the Beatles were with him," recalls Freda. "He threw his coat on a hanger as usual. I walked over and told him I'd had an accident with his letters tape." Epstein raged: "You stupid girl! You're sacked!"

Lennon burst out laughing at Epstein's tantrum. He thought the incident was hilarious. "When John laughed, Eppy laughed," says Freda. "I kept my job. Eppy dictated the lot again that night after hours."

❏

With his rising roster of artists, Epstein needed press representation and a London anchor. He turned to the punctilious Tony Barrow, who had impressed Brian at Decca with his highly organized mentality. Over lunch at Wheeler's in Soho, Epstein was determined to swing Tony over to his team. Without knowing his Decca salary, Brian offered to double it. Barrow would join him as press officer for the Beatles and whatever other activities NEMS began. And he would open a London office, coordinate the national media, and plan for the inevitable move south.

At Decca, Barrow earned £15 a week. He asked for a percentage of NEMS profits in addition to a salary. Epstein shuddered at the thought. "It would be very small if I did agree to it," he said, brushing the request aside. Barrow accepted £32 a week and joined him on May 1, 1963, becoming one of Epstein's longest-serving employees.

Brian always had difficulty relating salaries and expenses in Liverpool to those in London. He described prices in the capital as "preposterous." As his first job, Barrow was told to find a London office. When he telephoned Brian with some possibilities, Brian immediately rejected them as too expensive. And yet he had told Barrow to find a "prestigious" location. Finally, with the help of Dick James, Barrow found space at 13 Monmouth Street, Covent Garden. A single first-floor room above a bookshop that sold sex magazines, it was devoid of atmosphere; the previous tenant had been pianist Joe Henderson. Basically, Brian intended it as a press office and interview point for journalists, now crucial to Brian's vision of his future growth. Liverpool economics again applied when Barrow hired a secretary and, later, when Brian moved permanently to London: his salaries for office staff never matched London rates.

The first London office was primitive, with only two telephones—and rarely any time when they were free for incoming calls. But to Epstein in 1963, it was a vital beachhead for his inexorably growing stable. He had a *West End office.*

❏

"If you're not queer and you're not Jewish, what are you doing coming to work for NEMS?" Only the vicious tongue of John Lennon could have delivered a remark of such stunning and unanswerable directness. Epstein and the Beatles had been to EMI Records in Manchester Square and had adjourned to a nearby pub, the Devonshire Arms. Tony Barrow was being introduced to the group he was about to represent. It was the first confirmation he had that Brian was homosexual. Numbed into silence by Lennon's broadside, Barrow was getting a foretaste of the irreverence that would mark out Lennon as the vitriolic Beatle, the counterpoint to McCartney's acute sense of charming projection.

Lennon seemed to enjoy telling people of Brian's homosexuality. In Liverpool one Saturday morning, when the Beatles arrived at NEMS with their road manager, Neil Aspinall, to collect their itineraries, John sidled over to Freda Kelly and the conversation turned to Brian. "Don't you know he's bent?" said Lennon. "Put you on a desert island with him and you'd be safe."

Brian withstood all the whispers and the few taunts to his face because, in the opinion of Barrow, "he had all the graces and charms of an educated person with a good family background." It was simply "out of order" to respond angrily, or offer a riposte. Inwardly, however, the sensitive Brian was often hurt. He paid heavily for his recognition of Lennon's genius, for the Beatle's volubility on Epstein's sexual preference was to be a recurring theme over the next five years. John's merciless exploitation of anyone's minority status found Epstein an easy target.

One time at EMI's Abbey Road recording studios when the Beatles were recording, Brian came in from a dinner date and joined George Martin in the control room. The intercom was on, and Epstein remarked to Martin that there appeared to be some sort of flaw in the voice of Paul McCartney when he sang "Till There Was You." John overheard this and declared icily: "We'll make the money. You just go on counting your percentages." Deeply offended, Brian left the studios in a rage.

Later, John explained it was meant only as a bit of fun. But the effect on Brian, not for the first or last time, had been withering. Lennon was, conversely, the only Beatle who fully grasped the extraordinary qualities in Epstein that had been the group's springboard to success. Alone among the Beatles, he saw that they and Brian, needing each other, had been drawn together at a perfect moment. But he would not be subservient. Anyone working closely with Lennon learned to live with his caustic tongue. In the company of a genius, Brian felt, he should learn to take the knocks.

Brian was so determined to integrate himself into the rock 'n' roll coterie that for a few weeks he occasionally discarded his formal attire and wore either a leather or a black velvet jacket, a polo-neck sweater, and black trousers. It was a mistake he would regret. In and out of the Cavern, everyone on the pop circuit sniggered at his silly attempts to join the crowd to which he patently did not belong. The garb rebounded on him comically when he went seeking bookings for his acts. At the Orrell Park Ballroom in Bootle, the doorman refused to believe he was the manager of the Beatles and would not let him in because of his casual dress. He quickly reverted to suits and ties.

At the Cavern, after his initial visits to observe the groups, Brian rarely mingled with the fans. His aloofness made him stand out. To be less noticeable, he went straight to the tiny dressing room. At ballrooms, he moved among the crowds to ask their views on other groups.

❏

In the years before pop music became a big industry dominated by corporations, it was packed with young entrepreneurs. One, Sean O'Mahony, worked with the publication *Pop Weekly*. When O'Mahony left the magazine to set up his own *Beat Monthly*, he phoned Epstein with an idea for a special article on the world's top groups, including the Shadows and the Beatles. Epstein enthused; he even agreed to a readers' competition in which the winner would meet "the boys." O'Mahony, a keen new publisher looking for groups who would help him sell magazines, was impressed with a report that five hundred fans had been turned away from a Beatles show in January 1963. This was unprecedented for such a new group. When "Please Please Me" rocketed up the charts, lights started flashing for the opportunistic Sean

O'Mahony. An avid record watcher, he knew from "chart intelligence" that when a debut record was a small hit and the second a number one, something very special was happening.

Epstein agreed to meet O'Mahony on his next London visit. Over drinks at the Westbury Hotel, O'Mahony found Brian more like an accountant or doctor than the usual huckstering pop manager. Brian told O'Mahony what he was telling everybody: "The Beatles are going to be *very*, very big."

Keen on growth of his small publishing operation, O'Mahony told Brian he would like to start a magazine exclusively on the Beatles. It was a revolutionary idea. Only fan club magazines with restricted circulations existed at that time. O'Mahony was proposing a mass-sale monthly that would project the Beatles and also be profitable. Brian coolly said he thought the idea worth pursuing; he "would certainly talk to the boys about it." The Beatles' canny reaction was to ask to see O'Mahony when they next went to London. They wanted to know whether they could get along with a man who would be such an important link between them and their fans.

O'Mahony went to a BBC studio where the Beatles were broadcasting on "Pop Go the Beatles." He told them he would need to meet, interview, and photograph them regularly but would try not to intrude too much on their schedule. "Paul McCartney asked most of the questions," says O'Mahony. "His main concern was what I was going to put into the magazine to fill it every month. Rather funny in view of subsequent events."

Epstein confirmed by phone that the deal was on, but they had to agree on financial splits. What kind of deal did Epstein want? asked O'Mahony. Brian answered that he would like 50 percent of the profits. It was not a clever request. In calculating "profit," a publisher can offset all kinds of expenses before the balance sheet shows black. Brian would have been better advised to have asked for a royalty on each copy sold. But Epstein, the record retailer, was used to talking in terms of profits. O'Mahony knocked him down to 33⅓ percent for the Beatles, and the deal was set. Brian asked for creative veto over the content of the magazine, and for a period he wanted to see all the material before it was published. That stopped very quickly as Brian and the Beatles became too busy.

The Beatles Monthly Book was an immediate success. The first issue sold 111,000 copies, the second reached 200,000, and by the sixth issue the magazine was selling 350,000. Though it was a wonderful platform for the Beatles, Brian had surprisingly placed no expiration date on his agreement with O'Mahony. Nor had he limited distribution to Britain. The deal was completely open-ended in O'Mahony's favor.

But Brian was delighted. The ball was rolling for him, and *The Beatles Monthly Book* was a powerful asset. He asked O'Mahony to lunch at the Westbury. What about a special monthly magazine on Billy J. Kramer, his latest star? he asked. O'Mahony said he would prefer to take a chance on Gerry and the Pacemakers, who had better visual appeal. The venture was disastrous. Only ten thousand copies of the first print run of ninety thousand were sold. "I had to stop it. Brian took it very well."

❏

Spurred by his boundless enthusiasm for nurturing new talent, his enjoyment of empire building, and love of his work, Brian added more and more artists, or "artistes," as he called them. It was impossible for him to cope with so many fast-moving careers. Inevitably, there were casualties.

Not surprisingly, bands that regularly played at the Cavern had a sentimental attraction to Epstein. The next group he set his sights on, the Fourmost, contrasted sharply with the Beatles. They wore suits onstage, traded heavily in comedy and repartee, and belonged more to the world of cabaret than to the rock 'n' roll arena. Show business was, to them, a profitable hobby. Academic high-fliers, they were on course for professional careers such as accountancy and architecture.

Their career plans, in fact, caused problems for Epstein. Cautiously protecting their chosen careers after years of study, they demurred about a dozen times before his promises of much bigger money and a secure future, with records to be produced by George Martin. "Brian was always in awe of our band's education because he said he was a bit of a dunce," says Billy Hatton, the Fourmost drummer. "He couldn't understand why people like us wanted to make fools of themselves onstage." Once they were in the fold, however, the Fourmost quickly confirmed the judgment of Epstein and George Martin with a hit single, "Hello Little Girl."

But the relationship deteriorated after they had their third hit, "A Little Loving." As it soared up the charts, the group was booked into a variety show at the London Palladium featuring Cilla Black, Frankie Vaughan, and comedian Tommy Cooper. Epstein anticipated that this coup would establish the Fourmost in a show business league different from that of any of his other groups. And when Brian Epstein, the man with the Midas touch, made predictions, people nodded and accepted. But the show, expected to last seven weeks, ran for six months. The group was therefore trapped, unable to capitalize on its hit record by charging extra money for concert appearances.

Hatton and the other three members of the Fourmost—Brian O'Hara, Mike Millward, and Dave Lovelady—raged at Epstein in their dressing room. How could their manager behave so ineptly? Why was there no protection clause in their contract? Great though the Palladium was for prestige, they were losing thousands of pounds in potential concert fees, they bellowed. His face red with anger and embarrassment, Brian had little defense. He tried to calm them. The Palladium season, he argued, was important as a career builder; but that cut no ice with young men eager for immediate cash. "And none of my acts, including the Beatles, have *ever* spoken to me like this," said Brian. They replied curtly that their fury was justified, but Brian never forgave them.

"He felt crushed by the verbal hammering we'd given him," says Hatton. "Even though we'd never have made it without him, I think Brian was far too sensitive to be a good business manager. He was very upset that one of his acts should have a go at him as we did, questioning his ability. And really, if you weren't Brian's friend, he couldn't function as your manager."

Relations never recovered from the confrontation. Brian delegated contact with the players to others in his organization.

❑

As one of Britain's dynamic young meteors, Brian was now courted by hustlers from all spheres of the media. Ernest Hecht, a driving Czech-born publisher who had quickly come up with a Beatles picture book, had gone on to publish similar titles on Brian's fast-moving stable of artists. Now, like several publishers, he sought Brian's autobiography.

It was already a remarkable tale. Only two years earlier he had been an unknown Liverpool shopkeeper. He had marched into show business, taken control of an empire led by the Beatles, and spearheaded a revolution in which youth had gained its voice.

Hecht's track record as head of Souvenir Press was impressive. As the first publisher to capitalize on the interest in pop, he had brought out both manager John Kennedy's story of the rise of Tommy Steele and Cliff Richard's *It's Great to Be Young*. Now it was Epstein's turn, but Brian, always "too busy," stalled Hecht for months. Finally, again impressed by an entrepreneur's persistence, he accepted a £2000 advance for his autobiography, which turned out to be *A Cellarful of Noise*. Souvenir Press controlled newspaper serialization and world rights, which a more sought-after, financially assertive author might have fought to reserve. Brian, however, liked the idea for its aesthetic, potentially historical value. His income from it came in a very poor second in importance.

"I liked him but he was impossible to do business with," says Hecht. "He drove me mad. He was terrifyingly vain, had more than a touch of arrogance, but in spite of the fact that he had an offer from a publisher much bigger than me, he accepted. He trusted me." It took Hecht three months of phone calls and meetings at NEMS's Monmouth Street office and in Liverpool just to tie Brian down to a writing and publishing schedule. "He was procrastinating," recalls Hecht with a weary smile. Epstein's caravan of stars was moving so quickly that he often appeared distracted in these meetings.

However, there was a reason for Brian's apparent tardiness. He was worried about who would ghostwrite the book for him. Brian first suggested Godfrey Winn, the prominent writer with the *Daily Express*. "Far too pricey and the wrong image," said Ernest Hecht. Brian, in turn, rejected Tony Barrow as being "too close." He certainly wanted an established name to write his story. How about Beverley Nicholls? Hecht said he would send a potential writer to see Brian for his evaluation.

Tony Stratton Smith* was a former *Daily Express* staff writer who had become a successful author, particularly adept at ghosting celebrity

---

*He later became the founder of Charisma Records, a highly influential record label in the 1970s which launched the careers of Genesis, Julian Lennon, and many others.

bios. At Hecht's expense he flew to see Brian, who was staying in the penthouse suite of the Amsterdam Hilton during a short business trip abroad. Brian received the talkative Tony with his traditional courtesy, and after a day spent avoiding the subject of the book, they adjourned to dinner. Stratton Smith, a bon vivant, was impressed: Epstein chose the Black Sheep, the most expensive restaurant in a city he knew well from his solo sojourns. He pored over the wine list. Stratton Smith had just returned from Brazil, where the bossa nova rhythms were being launched. Brian was fascinated and the conversation flowed.

After they had exchanged ideas for the book, Brian casually asked Tony when he could begin preparing it. Not for six months, or three at the earliest, he answered. (He was writing *The Rebel Nun* at the time, and it eventually became a success.) "Six *months?*" the now-impatient Brian exploded. Couldn't Tony shelve his current project? The autobiography of Brian Epstein was much more exciting and, he believed, urgent: "The faster my book is out the better!" Stratton Smith disagreed. Another six months of Brian's life would strengthen the story. He replied stubbornly that he would be happy to write Brian's book but not until he had finished his current work.

Epstein was visibly upset. After dinner the two men went to a couple of bars that Brian knew. The business of the biography was left "open." Next day, as Tony flew back to London, Epstein phoned Hecht to say he was not prepared to wait three months, let alone six. He would have to find another writer immediately.

Back in Liverpool, meanwhile, Epstein found himself a national media hero, described by newspapers as the new Svengali—not surprising, with Gerry and the Pacemakers ("I Like It"), Billy J. Kramer ("Do You Want to Know a Secret"), and the Beatles ("From Me to You") occuping the first three positions in the national charts. The Manchester offices of Britain's daily papers were instructed to go out and get exclusive interviews not only with Epstein's interesting artists but with this mysterious, scarcely known manager who had masterminded an apparent shift in pop's emphasis from London to the Northwest. Brian politely declined most of the interviews, since he wanted to reserve most of the story of his rise for his imminent biography. But he was finally won over by the intrepid Derek Taylor, show business reporter for the *Daily Express*. Although based in Manchester, he had the distinct advantage for Epstein of having been born on the Wirral.

A theatrical, slightly conspiratorial man, Taylor had been an early convert to the Beatles story, reviewing their concerts favorably. That impressed Epstein, who also warmed to the reporter's knowledge of the theater. Taylor, in turn, was quickly impressed by Epstein's honesty of purpose. Brian told him he had seen a lot of raw deals since entering the music business. "Jealousy, dissatisfaction, sharp practice. I want none of it," he announced. On the Beatles' future, Taylor reported him as saying succinctly: "Whatever happens to popular music, whatever happens to beat groups, the Beatles are in the business for life." Describing Epstein, Taylor wrote: "Were it not for his buckled shoes and the royal blue initials on his white shirt, he could be in shipping or cotton. Or the bank, with an eye on the managership."

The interview took place twenty-four hours after the punch-up between Lennon and Bob Wooler at McCartney's birthday party. Considering the pressure he must have been under to play down the adverse publicity surrounding the Beatle, Brian kept up a remarkably cool performance, eased by the rapport he had quickly achieved with Taylor. He asked if the reporter had any suggestions for a ghostwriter for his autobiography. Derek responded that he himself might well be interested.

Brian engaged him at a fee of £900 and informed Ernest Hecht. With his personal letter offering him the job, Epstein enclosed an advance of £250. With only £2000 coming up front from Hecht, the autobiography was clearly not going to be written for profit but, rather, to satisfy Brian's ego and to place his rapid rise on the record.

Interviewing was set for April 1964 at the luxurious Imperial Hotel, Torquay. Brian spoke to Taylor with disarming candor about his family background, his troubled school years, his discovery of his artists, his philosophy as a manager. But he felt uneasy not talking about his homosexuality—a barrier that had to be crossed before it impeded the interviewing process. Over lunch Epstein came out with it. "Did you know that I was queer?"

Taylor said no. As a journalist he was not easily surprised, and his quiet understanding relaxed Brian. "It had become inconvenient for him to lie; he was not a deceitful man, but brutally frank. Until that moment he was very cagey. There was no in-between situation. He was cautious and careful until he knew it was going to be OK. Then it was right out in the open. I didn't find him sly, except that he wasn't going to tell all to a *Daily Express* reporter on first meeting. I found him extremely vulnerable, sensitive, and really rather sweet."

Once he had broken the ice about his homosexuality, Brian talked about it jocularly. "I found him very easy and amusing on the subject," Taylor says. "He was very free with all sorts of jokes." Epstein said he was glad Taylor was not a homosexual, since that made the working relationship much easier.

Taylor detected a man who "liked a good time in many different ways." The best way, above all, was taking care of the Beatles, "his primary need throughout his life, all he wanted in the end."

Predictably, Epstein's homosexuality was not mentioned in his autobiography. The only reference to any relationship was a passing mention of Rita Harris, the NEMS assistant whom he had escorted several times and whom he described as having lost out when he became frenetically involved with the Beatles. Taylor doubts if Epstein would have allowed the book to mention his sexual preferences even if the social climate had been more liberal than it was in 1964. "He would have had to ask permission of people; he was a consulter of people. I don't think he would have made any kind of public statement without asking everybody, not only the Beatles but the Rustiks (a group he signed later) and the Fourmost. And a lot of them would have been very cross if he had not asked them, because if he hadn't it might have been assumed that he was somehow involved with them. Among acts, it wasn't talked about much."

Just before the book's publication, Brian turned his attention to its promotion. Over lunch at the Ivy restaurant in London, he told Hecht that his book would have to be strategically advertised; only a full-page display on the front of the *New Musical Express* would suffice. And he wanted a hand in its design. Hecht relented. There should also be some plugging of the book on Radio Luxembourg, said Brian. When he later produced his visual idea for the press advertisement, it was so low-key that Hecht was alarmed. It said simply, "Brian Epstein," and showed the cover of the book. "But where does it say," asked Hecht, looking for maximum impact for his investment, "that this is a sensational book everybody will love?" Brian recoiled from such hard-sell technique: "No, no. This is *tasteful*." Hecht said a £500 advertisement should be more than tasteful. It should *sell*.

On publication day, Hecht hosted a champagne lunch at the White

Tower, London. He told Epstein he had managed to get him on Granada TV in Manchester to promote the book. Impossible, said Brian, he *had* to be with the Beatles on the first night of their tour, which opened in Bradford. Hecht had a phone brought to the table to impress on Brian the importance of his appearing on the TV show. He then made a charter flight available after the Manchester TV show so that Brian could get to the Beatles concert.

As he toured with his stars, Brian kept an eagle eye on the book's availability in shops throughout Britain. He chastised Hecht when it was not visible; monitored his royalty statements carefully; and asked about income from serialization in the *News of the World*. "I don't believe the money would have made any difference to him but it was important to his ego," reflects Hecht. At NEMS in Liverpool, both city center shops had huge displays of the book, and sales were healthy.

Even for 1964, when pop celebrities were never projected in a poor light, *A Cellarful of Noise* was a vapid autobiography. It bore signs of being thrown together too quickly and prematurely, with no real feel for Brian's life and his prodigious work pattern. Its main attributes were a touching naiveté and a true reflection of Epstein's faith in his artists. Against that, it suffered badly from a lack of human grit.

The merciless streak inside Lennon, which exploited anyone's clear vulnerability, caused a ripple when Brian was preparing the book. Asked by Brian for a title for the autobiography, John said: "Why don't you call it 'Queer Jew'?" When Epstein told him he had decided on *A Cellarful of Noise*, Lennon countered with "A Cellarful of Boys." Brian rode out such taunts with aplomb. Singer Alma Cogan, a friend of Brian's, phoned him on receiving her copy and said cryptically: "I thought it should be 'Cilla-full of Noise'. . . ." Brian was not amused.

Epstein understood the waspish words from Lennon and was now accustomed to his vitriol. As an art-college student, Lennon had mocked cripples in the Liverpool streets; as a Beatle visiting Hamburg, he had taunted the Germans. In 1962, after a Cavern session, a drunken Lennon had adjourned with Paul and Epstein to the Blue Angel and was loudly heard shouting: "Hitler didn't finish the job." Mercifully, Epstein did not hear him. Paul McCartney diplomatically sought to quiet Lennon's outburst.

When Brian heard jibes about his sexuality or his Jewish faith, he rarely responded. He was capable, if caught in the right mood, of camping it up, playing along with the joke. "Dreadful! How *could* you?" he said to Lennon after the "Queer Jew" joke. Says Tony Barrow: "Outwardly, he rarely acknowledged that he'd heard such remarks. He tried to ignore them and passed on to something else, or literally physically turned his back. I saw him do that many, many times, particularly with the Beatles and Gerry."

Epstein believed that only his "inner circle" knew of his homosexuality. He thought it stopped there, that the switchboard girl and junior office staff had no idea. "I don't think he realized that we all knew how many other homosexual people he was involved with in his business," says Tony Barrow. "As for hiring of staff, what John Lennon said to me upon our introduction—'If you're not queer and you're not Jewish, why are you joining NEMS?'—proved to be pretty accurate. They weren't all Jewish, but that was the ideal combination of the two things that were very close to his or his family's heart. If he could find somebody who was gay who could do the job, he would choose them. If he couldn't, then as second best he'd choose somebody for whom he had admiration or whose work he respected."

Like Cilla, Billy J. Kramer believes Brian's secrecy was a mistake. "It wasn't talked about among the acts. It was a hang-up to him and he wasn't open about it. If he had been more open about it to his artists and said, 'Look, I'm gay,' my attitude would have been: Well, as long as you don't bug me, it takes a lot to make this world go round. That's fine. It wouldn't have bothered me. I think he was frightened of being up-front." Many of Brian's other artists and friends believe he was petrified of being publicly revealed as a homosexual, chiefly because the resulting publicity would have rebounded against his artists and affected their careers; this, after all, was the early 1960s, when homosexuality was still illegal. The Beatles, particularly, who were embraced by all levels of society internationally, could never be exposed to such adverse publicity.

London show business moguls, who had served up a rigid diet of safe popular music by American artists, tilted their heads at the unorthodox impact being made by this suave, elegant, unlikely manager—a novice in the entertainment world—who came from so-provincial *Liverpool!* At the time of his ascent, the show-biz hierarchy cruelly regarded him as "the very lucky son of a rich father," says impresario Tito Burns. "In this business, everyone needs a bit of luck. You don't walk in and say:

'I've found a star.' The general feeling in the business was that Brian didn't even know what he had in Liverpool and it overtook him. The Beatles would have been big despite Brian, despite any agent, despite any manager. The moment their records came out, they were destined to be big stars. They were so compellingly different."

The smug show business verdict on Epstein, echoed by Burns, overlooked Brian's vision of the Beatles in their raw Cavern days and the changes he imposed on them. His belief in a rock 'n' roll group, unfashionable in the entertainment world, was ignored and so was his exhaustive determination to get them a record deal. What the hard-headed businessmen had failed to detect was the one quality that most of them lacked in their pecuniary orientation towards artists: Brian's dedication and devotion to the Beatles, driven by his need of them as a *cause* in his life.

By the autumn of 1963, with four major acts securely on the way to splendid careers, Brian could be forgiven for believing in the in-fallibility of his judgment. Within a year of their debut single, the Beatles were the cult heroes he had predicted to his brother Clive. Writing in *Fabulous* magazine on January 25, 1964, he glowed with pride at the achievements of Liverpool pop groups, pointing out that in the past eleven months eleven records made by the city's groups had topped the "hit parade." He had been associated with nine of these. The other two singles had come from his favorite non-Epstein group. If he could retrace his steps and add one more Liverpool group to his stable, it would be the Searchers.

"People in the business say I made a quarter of a million pounds last year," he continued. "I shall be lucky if I keep a fraction of this sum in the bank after paying a staff of twenty and settling the year's enormous expenses: office rents, travelling and a hundred and one other costs."

❑

Not everyone involved in the Liverpool stampede applauded Epstein's methods. Local fans not only resented Brian's "cleaning up" of their acts, but derided their move to London. "He didn't care about the people of Liverpool," says Bill Harry. "Once he'd made it with the Beatles, he used people, threw them away like used tissue. He turned a really nice scene into something nasty, vindictive, back-biting. His

ego took over. He was interested in his prestige and image." Bill and
Virginia Harry condemn Epstein for bleeding Liverpool dry, putting
nothing back into the city that had given him everything, for turning
his back on the people who had shaped the very scene he exploited.

The symbiotic relationship between Harry and Epstein, with its
roots in the *Mersey Beat* newspaper, turned bitter in 1964, soon after
Brian decided to buy a financial stake in the paper. The shares in
Mersey Beat had been held by Ray McFall, the owner of the Cavern,
who had put up the working capital to bail Bill Harry out of trouble.
Epstein paid McFall £2000 to acquire majority shares. Brian dispatched
his friend and solicitor Rex Makin to give Harry the news, assuring
him that he "realized he had created the paper and that he would
continue to have editorial independence."

Epstein by then had delusions of grandeur, says Harry. "He was
devious. He sent notes to the Beatles and other groups saying: 'I'll
get you on the cover of *Mersey Beat* and your fees will go up.' And
then he used to get the proofs of *Mersey Beat* in advance, from the
printer in Widnes. So he was no longer genuine, he was two-faced."

Brian's editorial grip on *Mersey Beat* increased. He installed a managing editor from London named Brian Harvey, and moved Harry to
plush offices in Hackins Hey, Liverpool. The paper now had pictures
printed in color; it was published weekly instead of fortnightly; and
the circulation climbed to seventy-five thousand.

It soon became clear that Brian saw his acquisition as a national
publication rather than a Liverpool-only paper. Bill Harry was told
that whoever was atop of the national charts *must* be the featured cover
picture. Gradually, his autonomy as editor was eroded. "It was a one-
man paper, and all Brian had bought was me," Harry now reflects. The
paper's name was changed to *Music Echo*, a title Bill Harry created.

His unease ended in a showdown, and Harry, complaining of too
much Epstein interference, walked out. A few days later, Clive Epstein phoned him saying Brian was upset and wanted to offer him a
job; would he please call him. Harry refused. "I said I'd never work
for him after he'd ignored all his promises and assurances. I had been
told the paper was still mine and that I had a secure job for life! But
his word wasn't worth a spit in the wind. What annoyed me was that
I'd created a unique concept and Brian Epstein tried to turn it into
an ordinary music paper. I resented this: I started the paper, wrote

it, designed it, and made it successful." After helping Epstein find the Beatles and other acts, Harry "didn't expect to be treated like a serf." In fact, Epstein believed his changes showed astuteness and realism. The Liverpool pop scene was drained by then and *Mersey Beat* would, he felt, perish in its old guise. His surgery was a genuine rescue attempt.

But the paper Harry left, which was showing a profit, soon began losing money. *Music Echo* had not merely diluted its Merseyside appeal but had entered a fiercely competitive music-paper market, fighting the *Melody Maker, New Musical Express, Disc,* and *Record Mirror.* Within two years *Music Echo* was a drain on even Epstein's resources. The title was bought by the publishing giant IPC and merged with *Disc,* a weekly pop paper of which I was then editor. It was launched as *Disc and Music Echo* on April 23, 1966.

Brian's company had a 50 percent share in Disc Echo Limited, an IPC subsidiary. As with *Mersey Beat,* he sometimes tried to impose his power or veto on the editor, asserting that his artists should have the front-page spot. Fruitless attempts at such interference became a running joke between Epstein and the author. But he also made some constructive suggestions and was immensely proud to have an investment in a London-based pop weekly.

There should have been enormous benefits from being part-owned by the manager of the Beatles. But Brian proved to be not merely a sleeping partner; he was self-conscious about his involvement with *Disc and Music Echo* lest it damage his relationships with other media outlets. After a few more skirmishes concerning more prominence for some artists, particularly his unsuccessful ones, he laid low.

❑

Liverpool was still awash with hundreds of pop groups, and because of his achievements Brian had the option on the best of them. But he always described the outstanding Searchers as "my group that got away." Next to the Beatles, Cilla, and Gerry, it was the perfect unit for him to mold to perfection. To powerful melodies and distinctive vocals they added a stage presence that gave them a tight show long before their professionalism secured them long-standing success as live performers. John Lennon said their first number one hit, "Sweets for My Sweet" in 1963, was "the best record to come out of Liverpool."

He told Epstein that here was a group that needed no cosmetic work but was "ready to go." But by then, Brian had missed the opportunity to sign them. He had his chance early in 1962, when he met them in the Grapes pub. Brian wandered along with them to the Cavern to see their act. But some of the group were drunk, remembers John McNally, Searchers founder and guitarist. Brian passed on them.

Shortly afterward, the group arrived in London under the aegis of Tito Burns, who had taken over from their original manager, Les Ackerley, proprietor of Liverpool's Iron Door club. Ackerley had approached Burns, believing they needed representation in the capital. With the Searchers and Brian both disappointed that they had slipped through his net, it was surprising that neither Chris Curtis, their drummer and leader, nor Epstein made any attempts to wrest control from Burns. The root of the puzzle was traceable to Epstein's demand for unity among his groups. Word reached him that personality clashes were rife within the Searchers: Curtis was falling out with Tony Jackson, the guitarist whose vocals gave the group its distinctive sound. And Brian did not want the job of referee. In London, however, Brian did consolidate a particularly close friendship with Chris Curtis. And the two had a joint partnership in song publishing.

"We were the last band to really make it out of Liverpool, and we always regretted not being part of Brian Epstein's stable," says McNally. "We felt out of the mainstream, seeing his list of acts in the papers with ours missing. It was sad."

But even to be coveted by Brian was fame of a kind. The closest Epstein got to the Searchers, professionally, was to ask Lennon and McCartney if they had a song with which to lure such excellent musicians. John and Paul suggested "Things We Said Today," which Brian excitedly offered to the Searchers when they met in Birmingham for a television show. He was miffed to find the song, perfect for their melodically powerful style, relegated to one of their B-sides.

❑

The Man with the Midas Touch. Mister Beat. The King of Liverpool. The Fifth Beatle. The epithets bestowed on Brian Epstein by the media could have turned a conceited man's head. But Brian was far too busy and self-composed to wallow in self-aggrandizement; in fact, he seemed unable to stop and take stock. His huge appetite for expansion, his sincere enjoyment of his management role, and his immodest belief that he could do a fine job for whomever he represented became the problem of his life. He became obsessively keen on signing new acts when the stable was already too large; managing the Beatles alone could have been a full-time occupation. But his addictive personality—"one more throw of the dice" was his unspoken philosophy—would ultimately prove a handicap. To many Merseysiders, Brian had expanded far too quickly and it was unthinkable that he should take on even more acts.

Yet Brian felt he should continue to nurture Liverpool's music. Tom Quigley was a freckle-faced seventeen-year-old who first caught Brian's attention when he opened a Beatles show at the Queens Hall, Widnes. (The opening spot of the show was for newcomers.) Quigley commanded the fans with his group, the Challengers. He sang breezily, had an impish sense of humor and a cheerful presence. Brian noted that the girls in the audience liked him, and he believed there was "something there to develop." He spoke to Quigley but promised nothing.

Quigley told Bob Wooler at the Cavern soon afterward that he was urgently awaiting an offer from Epstein, but it was a year later, with his business more secure, when Epstein offered him a salary and the now-traditional inauguration: a new suit, a new hairstyle, and clear instructions to smarten his demeanor. His previous suit, Brian noted, "had quite obviously been bought cheaply and off the peg." He renamed him Tommy Quickly, echoing the images of speed and power that Larry Parnes had invested in such acts as Vince Eager, Marty Wilde, and Billy Fury. The Challengers, his backing group, were dropped.

Epstein launched Quickly with a grand strategy. The promotional material talked cozily and confidently of the boy who was "freckled, kind to his dog Arthur and who's going to be a star." But Quickly was to be Epstein's bête noire, and probably his most costly failure with an act in terms of time and effort, not to mention money.

With George Martin busy, and spurred by a determination to spread his wings to other record labels, Brian asked Dick James to suggest a recording home outside of EMI for Tommy Quickly. From his huge number of business contacts, James quickly arranged a lunch appointment at the Trattoria Terrazza in Soho and introduced Brian to Ray

Horricks. Brian was impressed: Horricks had recently switched to Pye Records from Decca, where he had produced all of Anthony Newley's string of hits; Brian recalled that Newley had opened his NEMS record shop back in Liverpool, and he admired the man and his work. To link up with his producer would be a coup.

Horricks was keen on the chance of producing an Epstein artist. "If Brian's picked him," he told Dick James, referring to Quickly, "then I'm definitely interested." He had no problem in persuading the head of Pye, Louis Benjamin, that Tommy Quickly should be signed.

The investment that Epstein lavished on Quickly knew no limits. He attended most of his recording sessions; he hand-wrote letters of thanks and encouragement to Horricks; he donated a Lennon-McCartney song, "Tip of My Tongue," as his debut single. Epstein pulled out every piece of ammunition in his armory to ensure that the fans knew of Quickly. The singer had massive audience exposure. He went on three Beatles tours, two Billy J. Kramer tours, a Gerry and the Pacemakers tour; and there was a promotional tour of the United States costing $30,000. Within eighteen months of his first record, Quickly had released five new and lively singles—and all had flopped.

Brian was horrified and dumbfounded. For the first time his commercial judgment had been rejected by the public, which would not be browbeaten into elevating all his acts to the hall of fame. Quickly's shows were popular, but the yardstick of real success was the record charts, which Quickly never entered. In Brian's office Quickly's name became taboo. Staff members who asked questions or sympathized were ignored . . . and an Epstein silence spoke volumes for his feelings.

Yet Quickly had a loyal following, and in a 1965 interview with the author, he made light of his string of record misses: "I want to be in this business forever. I don't want to be a pop star for today and then get forgotten. That's what hit records are all about." He denounced the competitiveness of the music scene, but it was clearly a case of sour grapes. Nothing could conceal the harsh truth; talented though he was, Quickly was Epstein's first artistic failure.

"Tommy had an ingrained professionalism but he knew his place with Brian," says Ray Horricks. "He was very hardworking, very self-confident." His act carried a touch of vaudeville, which the Beatles loved; he used a bowler hat. His natural stagecraft caused Epstein to believe that time alone would prove him right, and that Quickly would transcend pop.

Brian continued to praise him when forced to discuss Quickly, talking of his "fresh, vital personality, warmth, artistry, individuality." Finally, his career petered out when he indulged in too much drink and became hopelessly unreliable. He commited what to Brian was a heinous crime: he arrived late for some shows.

❑

The move to London on March 9, 1964, was planned with military precision—the regimentation of Alistair Taylor and Tony Barrow combining with the panache of Epstein to make it a grand event. While Liverpudlians jeered at Brian and the Beatles "defection," the departure from Liverpool was accepted as inevitable by Harry, Queenie, and Clive Epstein, who continued to run the thriving stores. Brian's commuting had become too great a strain.

(Before Brian's migration south, his father mused over dinner one evening on the family surname, people's pronunciation of which varied between the preferred Ep*steen* and the generally favored Ep*stine*. Anyone who knew the family instinctively called them Ep*steen*. Perhaps, said Harry, Brian would like to consider changing his surname for business. It might make life easier in London, eliminate the need to correct people. Brian would not contemplate it. As well as his pride in the name, he said, it sounded positively Jewish, and in the world of show business, that would be advantageous. In London, however, he tired of correcting people who automatically called him Ep*stine*. Stoically, he always pronounced his name as he had always done.*)

With the grandiloquence that was to characterize the new image of his organization, Brian wrote personally to all his performers. Eight acts—the Beatles, Gerry, Billy J. Kramer with the Dakotas, Cilla, the Fourmost, Tommy Quickly, a rugged instrumental group named Sounds Incorporated, and the Remo Four—were at that time under his direction. Every artist in each group received this letter—headed

---

*In an ironic twist, two years after the death of Brian, Paul McCartney married New Yorker Linda Eastman, whose father, lawyer Lee Eastman, had changed his name from Epstein.

only by Brian's tastefully embossed initials—with his or her name handwritten by Brian, who then signed the letter personally:

> Thought I'd write you a note to give you a few details about our move to London. First of all I want to make it quite clear that the principle [*sic*] reason for the departure from Liverpool is that I am anxious to make quite certain *that Nems Enterprises provides the finest and most efficient management/direction of artistes in the world.*
>
> I have been concerned for some time that the success and expansion of the business has often meant that I have been necessarily absent from our office, and on the other hand unable to attend important engagements in London, because it has been necessary for me to be in Liverpool at the office. Furthermore, the separate location of the press office, and its cramped premises has not helped general liaison. All this should be improved by the centralisation of all our divisions in the heart of London (next door to the London Palladium).
>
> The telephone number of the new office is REGent 3261. There are ten lines and the telephonists have been instructed that our artistes' calls are the most important of all, and must be treated accordingly. For important calls after hours and at weekends we are installing an "Ansaphone" service which will advise you which member of the staff is "on duty", and at what number they can be located. In a nutshell Nems Enterprises is open to you every hour of every day and night! My own personal number is [here he handwrote his number]. (Please treat as strictly confidential.)
>
> Attached is a list of important personnel for your information. Each have various specific duties, but remember that basically they all have your general welfare in mind.
>
> If you haven't been in to see us at the new offices yet I hope you will soon. I hope you like them and also very sincerely that you will feel and enjoy the benefits of our new set up.
>
> With best wishes.

To all his new staff Epstein wrote this letter:

> Welcome to the new offices:
> Attached is a copy of a letter which is being sent out to all artistes. I hope you will note its most important message: *"that Nems Enterprises provides the finest and most efficient management/*

direction of artistes in the world." This must be without question our principal aim and should be borne in mind by all staff.

Alistair Taylor will be advising you of the details of operating the new offices, but I would like personally to point out one or two things.

First of all as our organisation is very much in the public eye, it is most important that we present the best possible "front." By this I mean that *all* visitors must be treated with utmost courtesy. That work must be carried out smoothly and efficiently without fuss. And most important, that the offices themselves must be kept tidy and clean at all times.

Another matter which I must ask you to treat with considerable care is the question of divulging to unauthorised or persons outside the organisation information concerning the company. It is strictly out of order for anyone to discuss with the press any business (however slight or remotely connected) whatsoever. Your adherence to this ruling is of great importance.

I really hope that you will be happy and as comfortable as possible in our new surroundings.

> With best wishes for the future
> Brian Epstein

On their arrival in London, Brian impressed his entourage with his thoughtfulness. He gave all his artists and their wives or girlfriends a leather telephone directory, the compilation of which he had personally supervised. It was Epstein's VIP visiting book for the hierarchy of the entertainment world, containing the addresses and telephone numbers of the best restaurants and clubs, as well as the phone numbers of such contemporaries as Mick Jagger.

Now he prepared to instal himself in his first London home, a flat at 15 Whaddon House, William Mews, Knightsbridge, a few hundred yards from Harrods. (Alistair Taylor received his first assignment as NEMS general manager in a postscript by Brian to his letter of appointment: "Don't forget to phone the carpet fitters about the underlay.") A tall black valet, Lonnie Trimble, was installed at the apartment.

❑

As his groups dominated the charts, the appearance fees of his top trio—the Beatles, Billy J. Kramer, and Gerry and the Pacemakers—rose to around £1000 per night for each act. And Brian's percentage increased on a sliding scale from 10 percent to 25 percent, as the contract stated. For some acts, the fee to their agent was 10 percent, but Brian felt justified in asking for more. He proudly told everyone that he was much more than an agent. He also gave his artists personal management, marketing strategies, press relations, and secretarial service; other acts had to pay their managements for these separately. What most of his acts realized, too, was Brian's utter dedication. He liked to be kept informed of the Beatles' whereabouts around the clock, and he became incensed when a Beatle was diverted for a few hours from his "schedule." None of his staff had the privilege of "steering" a Beatle without his advance approval. Brian had jettisoned his personal life to immerse himself in his new-found mission, and he unswervingly cared about his performers' welfare. Back in Liverpool, cynics believed he was suffering from megalomania. But those who fully understood him realized that Brian was deeply in his love at last . . . with his new vocation.

The strain of juggling the Beatles' careers alongside those of his other acts caused Brian much worry. His appetite for managing more artists was insatiable; yet he knew he would be unable to give them equal time. After Gerry had two hit singles, Brian called him to his office, saying: "Truthfully, Gerry, I cannot devote the same time to the Beatles and yourselves. Because the Beatles have become the biggest property Britain has ever known, and you come second at this moment." A London management agency had offered to take Gerry and the Pacemakers from Brian, increasing the singer's income overnight.

It could have been an explosive moment with Gerry Marsden, who had always had a keen rivalry with the Beatles. But Brian's forthrightness won his understanding. Recognizing Brian's qualities, he told him: "I don't want any other management. You've done what you've done for us with no problems. You'll just have to devote more time to the Beats,* Brian, because they're so massive. I understand." Flattered and flushed with pride, Epstein then said that in the long run he would make Gerry more money, but he would have to accept less attention.

---

*Throughout his life Gerry Marsden has called them the "Beats."

❏

Amazingly, there were still more acts ready to join Brian's "Nempire." Despite his failure to touch gold with some artists, his name carried an aura that few could resist, an imprimatur of style and flair. Merely to be under Epstein's baton was to step boldly outside the financial orientation of the "old" music industry, to which he had brought a hitherto scarce quality—integrity.

Epstein refused to become involved in the career of Marianne Faithfull, who had been discovered and launched by his old friend Andrew Oldham. Approached by Marianne's mother, Brian said he would not sign another girl singer as long as he managed Cilla Black—an illogical statement, really, since many of his groups were competitive. He and Cilla, "the Edith Piaf of the future," were inseparable, he told his friends. Clearly, she represented a significant personal as well as professional relationship for Brian; he glowed in her company, enjoying her unsophisticated Liverpudlian presence.

This devotion to Cilla lost him several potential girl stars. Of these, Marianne, launched with a hit composition by the Rolling Stones, "As Time Goes By," was to become not only a lasting success as a singer but also the visual epitome of the decade. Epstein admired her; she perfectly fulfilled his twin requirements of pop sensibility and theatricality. He carefully monitored her progress with the Stones, whom Oldham had positioned as the unkempt opposites of Epstein's clean-cut Beatles. The entire Stones camp was always high on Brian's list of party guests, and he developed a particularly close social friendship with its most sensitive musician, Brian Jones. Epstein also socialized with Marianne and her boyfriend for a spell, Mick Jagger. But even the persuasive tones of Marianne Faithfull's mother, an Austrian-born baroness, could not persuade him to cement a business relationship; Brian kept his distance professionally. Cilla would remain his proud, solitary female.

Yet he felt a need to balance her with a "leading man," a solo singer in the mold of Tom Jones, say, or Engelbert Humperdinck. And so began the puzzling case of Michael Haslam.

At twenty-four, this pub singer in Bolton, Lancashire, seemed an odd candidate for Epstein's attention. Playing guitar and singing robust ballads, he was a well-established local semiprofessional with slim prospects for entering show business full-time, since he worked by day in a tannery. But in the summer of 1964 he caught the eye of Godfrey Winn, a writer whose flamboyance matched his exaggerated prose. Over dinner in London with Cilla and Epstein, Winn enthused about his unlikely discovery, and within a few days Epstein, with Winn in tow, was driving his Silver Mercedes to Bolton to witness Haslam's Sunday night performance at the White Hart pub.

Arriving at the pub in his tuxedo, Haslam was stunned to see the man he had just seen at home on national television as part of the Beatles' first triumphant American visit. "What's *he* doing *here?*" Haslam asked his drummer, as they caught sight of Epstein in the car park.

Inside, Godfrey Winn made the introductions. Epstein saw Haslam's slick two-hour show, and taped his performance on a pocket-sized recorder. Just as he had found with the Beatles, Cilla, and so many more, Brian's excitement was immediate. Accompanying Haslam to his home after the show, he said he wanted to manage him; he would appear on the next Beatles concert tour in the autumn. To Michael Haslam, it was all unreal. The fantasy continued when, next day, a telegram arrived: "The tapes are great. Consider yourself under personal management. Brian Epstein." Recalls Haslam: "I was so excited I couldn't sleep for a couple of weeks. It was unbelievable."

Whisked to London, he quickly received his grooming. Brian chose his two mohair suits, made by Dougie Millings, instructing Haslam to wear one for stage work, the other for television; the singer's hair was styled by Brian's hairdresser, Ivan, in Jermyn Street; and he was told that his guitar playing had to stop. "It was difficult after ten years of having the instrument round my neck," Haslam says. "Suddenly, what to do with my hands was a problem. I felt like a man with no arms! But he explained to me: 'I know nothing about music but I know what I like!' He hadn't got a ballad singer and saw me as a straight leading man opposite Cilla. And I went along with it. It was difficult to cross him. He was so *nice*. I got the feeling that if you crossed him anyway, he'd find it difficult to tell you."

Despite his confidence, Epstein's financial investment in Michael Haslam was low. "He gave me a choice," the singer recalls. "I could have paid him twenty-five percent of my earnings, but when you come from Bolton, you go for money in your hand." Haslam opted for a flat salary of £60 a week, plus expenses.

Although powered by George Martin's producing talents and the musical direction of leading orchestra leader Johnnie Spence, the recording career of Haslam never bore fruit. Epstein gave Haslam about three hundred demonstration songs to listen to, but when he was unimpressed, Brian arrived with the song that he was "certain would make the top ten." Alas, Haslam's debut single, "Gotta Get a Hold of Myself," sold well but failed to reach the charts, as did his second, the prophetically titled "There Goes the Forgotten Man." Epstein was more disappointed than Haslam.

After two years, all the signs indicated that Michael Haslam would not measure up to his high potential as a recording artist. When the option on his NEMS contract came up for renewal, Brian treated it in a cavalier fashion. One day he talked to the singer about their next recording move, but quickly followed this up with an already drawn-up agreement ending their association "by mutual consent." Haslam signed it with no bitterness. Reflecting on a glorious magic carpet ride, he says: "He never raised my hopes. He was a good thing in my life."

❏

At his Knightsbridge flat, furnished in expensive ultramodern style, Brian settled into life in the capital with typical contradictions of moderation and extravagance. The apartment was neither huge nor ostentatiously furnished, and invitations there were issued to a favored few rather than to large crowds. Houseman Lonnie Trimble was a model of quiet discretion.

It was appropriate that Brian chose to locate NEMS's London offices next door to the London Palladium, almost synonymous with the glittering world of show business. Inside Sutherland House at 5-6 Argyll Street, however, things were far from plush. Brian oversaw all the office fittings and furniture. His own office, large and magisterial in style, featured a black leather settee and a mahogany desk, but for the most part the new hub of NEMS Enterprises had a somewhat cold atmosphere. The office partitions did not reach the ceiling, and the lack of conversational privacy irritated both the staff and visiting artists.

And there were larger tensions. The growing roster and the lack of a sound organizational structure, together with Brian's determination to be involved with every aspect of his artists' lives, meant that he was taking on far too much. And America, with all its promise of capitulation to the Beatles' sound, beckoned.

But most of the staff were happy with Brian's move to London. "The lower paid people in the organization, and the girls and clerks who came from Liverpool, held him in great awe," says Tony Barrow. Brian generated great loyalty, although it apparently was not unanimous.

A telephone call from someone at NEMS in London staggered television producer Johnny Hamp in Manchester. About two hours before he was to screen a Beatles trailer for the next edition of his popular show "Scene at 6:30," a voice told him: "The Beatles won't be in next week to do the song because they're too big to do local programs now." Hamp was both angry and mystified: as the man who had first televised the Beatles, on "People and Places" in August 1962, he had an excellent rapport with them, dating back to their Hamburg days. And he rated Brian very highly as a man of his word. He could not trace the identity of the telephone caller.

The trailer had to be revamped. The producer substituted these words: "The Beatles are good lads, but they're not coming on to the program to do their show next week. But don't forget, lads, you meet the same people on the way down that you met on the way up."

With about fifteen minutes to go before those words went on the air, Epstein telephoned Hamp from London. "Johnny, about the boys and next week. They'll definitely do the show on Thursday." Hamp, perplexed, said he had earlier received a cancelation and had prepared a statement. "I know," said Brian. "The message was rubbish. Take no notice." Hamp just had time to reintroduce the original trailer. To Epstein, it was disturbing confirmation that someone in his office, never identified, was a saboteur.

Sutherland House, his office, where a solitary black and white picture of the Beatles dominated the walls, was his sanctum. People were expected to knock on the door and wait for his invitation to enter. He carefully monitored his liquor cabinet, from which he took the occasional whisky but which was off-limits to others: he berated an executive for serving drinks to a visitor when he was out.

Brian was far too preoccupied to indulge in social discourse in the office. If it was somebody's birthday, he would greet them; his politeness in such situations was cosmetic, however. "He was immaculately mannered but totally uneasy with women, other people's secretaries," says Tony Barrow.

More surprising was his continuing conviction that he alone had a hot line to information about the private lives of his artists. Jealously protective of his relationship with the Beatles and Cilla, particularly, Brian would explode if someone casually mentioned that Paul McCartney was going away with his girlfriend, Jane Asher, on holiday.

"Who told you that?"

"Paul did."

"Really!"

The insecurity of Brian meant he wanted to possess all his artists' private information. Says Barrow: "He'd be really furious. He'd go puce. He made you feel embarrassed at knowing such a dreaded secret!"

❑

The year 1963 had brought Tony Barrow an avalanche of new acts to be projected to the press, radio, and television. With the national media screaming for Beatles interviews, he and Epstein agreed that the group needed a separate press officer.

In a Liverpool pub, Epstein met Brian Sommerville. He was thirty-two and balding, with all the pompous bearing that came from serving as a Lieutenant Commander in the Royal Navy. After fourteen years in the navy he joined Theo Cowan, a leading London film publicist. There, Sommerville handled press for Peter Sellers, Judy Garland, and the Royal Film Performance. When Epstein met him, he was working in the publicity department of the *Daily Express*. After a few drinks, they went to the Cavern. By then Brian had bought his own flat in Knightsbridge, and he and Sommerville later met a few times for dinner in London.

Impressed with his heavyweight connections in the film world, Epstein saw prestige in luring him to NEMS. Although Sommerville had no affinity with pop music, Brian offered him the job of Beatles press officer because he might bring just the right authority to a diplomatic role. Sommerville accepted the job on condition that he would not join the NEMS staff. Instead, he set up his own limited company, with Epstein as a shareholder and the Beatles as his only clients. His fee for handling their press was £100 a month.

Initially, the Beatles were pleased. Epstein told them they deserved a press officer of their own, but their relationship with Sommerville was never harmonious. They resented his regimental stance and his bossiness. He never grasped their humor or learned to accept their tardiness, as everyone around them was forced to do. George Harrison, particularly, took an instant dislike to him; in Paris at the George V Hotel, Sommerville's fearsome temper flared when, after a heavy night, the Beatle informed him that a journalist would have to wait an hour for the pleasure of interviewing him. Sommerville erupted: he would not keep an important writer waiting. Harrison threw a full jug of orange juice over Sommerville, who responded with a thump around George's ears. At that, they called a truce.

Sensing the Beatles' uneasiness, Epstein was in a quandary. He disliked certain of Sommerville's methods. At a New York airport press conference, for example, Sommerville had lost his cool and shouted at some of the journalists to shut up. Epstein told him that such a thing was not done. Conversely, he believed Sommerville's stiff collar, pin-striped suit, and bowler hat were the perfect image to represent him and the Beatles in the United States.

As press officer, Sommerville expected some autonomy but instead found himself undercut by Epstein, who would organize some media interviews himself, then blame others if they went wrong. And Sommerville grew tired of Epstein's insidious methods of making him uncomfortable. "He'd say he wanted a serious talk with me, but not right now—and he'd make a point of saying that in front of three or four people. It was embarrassing."

After a press conference in New York, there was another roasting for Sommerville. Said Epstein: "I *do* wish you would remember when you start the press conference, to say: 'Mr. Brian Epstein presents his compliments to the ladies and gentlemen of the press. . . .' " Sommerville told him the idea was twee.

As with other male friends whom he persuaded to work for him, Epstein found that being in a professional relationship changed his attitude toward them. Sommerville, in fact, became a whipping boy for the sometimes moody and capricious Epstein, who snubbed him at the office and at the television studios. "He screamed blue murder about my hotel bills before he signed them," says Sommerville. Once, leaving Sommerville's suite at the Plaza in New York to go to dinner with Geoffrey Ellis, Epstein caught sight of a waiter arriving with a trolley groaning with gourmet fare. Aghast at such lavishness, Epstein berated his press officer.

Finally, the showdown between the two came after Somerville had been on the job for only ten months. No letter of agreement had ever been exchanged. Now, said Brian, there was a need for a contract. Sommerville was livid. There had to be a basis of trust, he said. "And why should I restrict myself for the future if I want to earn my living writing a book or taking up journalism?" Epstein was rigid: there had to be a firm contract. Sommerville roared: "You must give me some credit for being a friend. I'm not going to wantonly embarrass you. Brian, you don't *trust* me." The two men were shouting over dinner at London's Grosvenor House Hotel. "No," said Epstein finally. "I don't trust *anyone*."

Later, red-faced and angry in his Argyll Street office, Epstein dug up a catalogue of complaints about Sommerville's performance, incidents long forgotten by the press officer. It was a no-win situation. Sommerville resigned.

When Sommerville had quit, he placed an ad in the personal column of *The Times:* "Ex-Beatles Publicity Manager looking for a job. . . ." This attracted lots of attention, and as his press relations office expanded and he represented such important acts as the Who, the Kinks, and Manfred Mann, Sommerville's relationship with Epstein healed. Over dinner at Chapel Street one night with Lionel Bart and Sommerville, Brian became emotional about his contretemps with his ex-press officer: "Of course I could have trusted you. . . ."

"I wasn't cut out for the job of Beatles press officer," says Sommerville now. "I was a square peg in a round hole. I liked Brian for the most part, but I would have been better staying just a friend." He scarcely respected him as an operator. "He was very bad at arranging financial matters. He allowed his heart to rule his head far too many times in too many areas. He wasn't honest. He didn't have integrity. I couldn't trust his word. I don't think he ever told a deliberate lie, but he would try to explain away something that was quite clear and unequivocal by saying he meant something else. He had a convoluted way of turning an argument round to his advantage when in fact it was he who had got himself into a knot."

Sommerville believes Epstein got rid of him because he had a new blue-eyed boy: Derek Taylor. "The Australian tour was about to start, and I discovered that the people there had been told that Derek would be the press man. My name had never been mentioned." The incident confirmed Sommerville's theory that Epstein was devious.

During his sojourn in Torquay working on his autobiography, Brian had struck up a good relationship with Taylor. He respected his vigor and style. They gambled and socialized together, exchanging conversation about the theater, enjoying drinks. Brian always liked to be soothed, and Taylor's confidence and persuasiveness came at a critical period in Epstein's evolution. Then, in a journalistic coup, Taylor persuaded Epstein to allow him to "ghost" George Harrison in a series of *Daily Express* articles for which the Beatle received £100 each. This outlet was particularly valuable to Brian at that time: John and Paul had their songwriting, Ringo was new, but George needed a spotlight.

In Torquay, Epstein offered the erudite Taylor a coveted job as his personal assistant.

Taylor was to represent another of Brian's many unhappy conversions of friendship to business. As with so many of these relationships, it would be punctuated not only by delight but by anguish and despair, stemming mostly from Epstein's wholly unreasonable demands on his staff.

Brian liked to assume a paternal role in nurturing people's careers, but it did not always work best for his organization. Taylor was, in his own words, a "Fleet Street chancer." Epstein had not thought through their future association but was prepared, as often, to gamble on instinct. "Brian had no idea how to deal with a fully unionized ex-reporter who was used to putting in what looked like embezzled expenses and taking his full National Union of Journalists holidays. He came from a world where you were 'Mr. Brian' or 'Mr. Clive' and you worked for your holidays. And if you were *wanted*, you didn't go on holiday," says Taylor. The hiring of a family man by a demanding boss who insisted on twenty-four-hour service was a mistake. Taylor was great company but a poor butler. "He expected the same kind of loyalty from me that he gave to the Beatles.

"When he said to me, 'You're always *disappearing* in the evening. I never know where to find you,' I said I was going home. He called it disappearing." Even with close associates like Taylor, Epstein fanatically guarded his relationship with the Beatles: "He wanted it to be just him and the group with nobody in between."

There were advantages. Taylor had a swagger and panache that gave Brian confidence. He knew the ins and outs of newspapers and coolly steered his boss through visits to the *Daily Mirror* offices and to television studios. Brian, though fond of the press, was always unsure how far he should trust journalists. He reveled in playing one reporter off against another: "Don't you think it's rather clever of me to give this story just to the *Daily* . . ." But this frequently caused him and his aides problems. "He was enormously good company but he could be very difficult. He was about the most unreasonable boss I ever had," Taylor reflects. Unlike Sommerville, however, Taylor found Epstein quick to recover from a tantrum. "He was most impulsive, but he didn't bear grudges." When Taylor let Brian down in Australia, failing to write a speech and also missing a plane, Brian had to appear alone before Australia's press. He was very angry but recovered quickly. "I don't think he was very good at cold fury," says Taylor. "It was 'on with the show.' "

Because of their joint realization that Derek could not stay in the job for long, the parting was without rancor. It happened at a hotel near Kennedy Airport, New York. Earlier, Derek had commandeered Brian's limousine when he urgently needed transportation for journalists. Brian erupted. Taylor felt he behaved churlishly. Derek resigned and Brian wept at the inevitability of losing a valued friend as a colleague too. Taylor went on to join the *Daily Mirror* briefly as a reporter and to consolidate his close friendship with George Harrison.

His friendship with Epstein continued, his admiration for him undiminished. "It was terribly frustrating," he reflects on his ten months with NEMS. "What I joined and what I wanted wasn't what I thought it was. This was not an easy gig. It looked like a lot of fun from the outside. It was not."

9

❑

AMERICA!

BEATLEMANIA CROSSES THE ATLANTIC

ALTHOUGH IT WAS only a year after the Beatles' debut on the charts, the tingle that Brian Epstein had felt in the grubby Cavern in Liverpool had been vindicated. Still, there was no solid evidence that he would be able to transmit that feeling to America, then the home of popular music. As he paced the Beatles' tours of Britain, he wondered how, if not when, he could ensure their becoming "bigger than Elvis."

Fortuitously for Epstein, 1963 brought with it profound social and political stirrings that worked to his advantage. In the United States, the Reverend Martin Luther King united black America and triggered the consciences of millions of whites with his "I have a dream" speech. Washington and Moscow established a telephone "hot line." President Kennedy made a momentous appearance at the Berlin Wall; five months later, he was assassinated. In Britain, the prospect of a government in disgrace loomed as the Profumo sex scandal began to unfold.

Popular music, as always, mirrored the changing national moods. Songwriters reflected the energy of youth and real social concerns, both elements often intertwining. In America, the lack of any discernible rock 'n' roll trend gave an opening to the articulate young singers and songwriters working in the folk clubs. Bob Dylan's classics, "Blowin' in the Wind" and "Don't Think Twice It's All Right," were given best-selling status by Peter, Paul and Mary; the Beach Boys and Jan and Dean began the California surf music sounds. British youth, conversely, was beginning the epidemic for Liverpool music that would soon engulf the world.

After 274 shows in the dingy cellar club that had shaped their music and sharpened their personalities, the Beatles made their last appearance at Liverpool's Cavern on August 3, 1963. This was Epstein's decision. He told Bob Wooler they would be back, but privately he knew they had outgrown the place forever. During the summer the Beatles had appeared in a series of Epstein-promoted "Mersey Beat Showcases," featuring several of his acts. Presented in a number of British movie theaters, they were sellouts, and the backstage scenes of fan fever caused Brian to make a crucial announcement to the Beatles. For their safety as well as prestige, the Beatles would no longer play small clubs or ballrooms, where they were too accessible to audiences and in danger of being mauled by overzealous fans. After existing contracts for ballroom shows had been fulfilled, he told them, they would play only in theaters with elevated stages.

The move carried a streak of Epstein panache as well as practicality. By the autumn, he had secured a TV booking that would make the biggest impact so far on their lives. The night of their appearance on "Sunday Night at the London Palladium," on October 13, two thousand teenage girls screaming "We want the Beatles" battled a police cordon outside the theater. Police vans sealed off the front of the Palladium so that the Beatles could be smuggled out the back. The stage doorman, George Cooper, commented to reporters that such riotous scenes had not occurred since American singer Johnny Ray's show in 1955. Next morning, Britain awoke to its morning newspapers and a new word: Beatlemania.

The Beatles had sung for only fifteen minutes on the Palladium TV show, performing "I Want to Hold Your Hand," "This Boy," "All My Loving," "Money," and "Twist and Shout." Their ecstatic reception transcended their music. And when the Beatles became the emblem for optimism, their elegant manager was vindicated in his forecast that they would be "bigger than Elvis." Without once gloating over his visionary flair, Epstein enjoyed being feted at their side.

A phone call from impresario Bernard Delfont was the first sign that the Beatles' appeal had broken down all age barriers. Traditionally, the Royal Variety Show starred family entertainers, ballad singers and classical musicians, jugglers and comedians. Inspired by his teenage daughter's enthusiasm for the Beatles, Delfont decided on the radical move of inviting them to perform in the show. But when the Beatles and a proud Brian went to the Prince of Wales Theatre, London, for the show on November 4, the iconoclastic Lennon had a shock for him. In the dressing room, John told Brian he wanted to debunk the show and introduce a light note to a stuffy, old-established tradition. He was sure the Queen Mother and Princess Margaret wouldn't mind if he said something like: "Those of you in the cheap seats clap your hands, all the others, rattle your fucking jewelery." Aghast, Brian was in yet another quandary. He didn't want to quell John's spirit, but at this, their finest hour, he could not incur the wrath of the entire population by having him swear before royalty. It took all of Brian's persuasive powers to get Lennon to drop "fucking" while leaving the rest of his aside intact. The censored remark was a highlight of the show, capturing the Beatles' antiestablishment bent. Brian breathed again.

❏

In the spring of that year, Epstein set his sights on conquering America with the Beatles. But it was too early for him to carry much clout. Fate, luck, and the prescience of a young Jewish pop watcher in New York gave Brian his break.

By day, Sid Bernstein worked as a $200-a-week agent at General Artists Corporation, more in tune with the world of adult cabaret artists than with the fickle rock 'n' roll set. By night, he was studying the music business at the New York School for Social Research. His teacher instructed him to read British newspapers. Bernstein noted British headlines carrying news of the Beatles. Before long, he found himself watching the Beatles story unfold daily from London; it was more riveting than his studies.

With considerable verve, he telephoned Epstein's home in Liverpool in mid-1963. Politely, he told Brian of his interest and asked what his American plans were. "We don't have any audience there yet. We can't get any radio airplay, but we've been trying to break through," Epstein said candidly. Bernstein, who had not heard a note of the Beatles' music, assured him he would succeed and asked what fees the Beatles were getting. "Brian said he was getting the equivalent of two thousand dollars a night for appearances in Britain," Bernstein remembers. "That was superstar money in those days."

Bernstein thought quickly, then announced: "I will offer you sixty-five hundred dollars for two shows in one day." It was a wild offer based on a gambler's instinct. Epstein was impressed: "Sixty-five hundred dollars? Wait till I tell the boys at Isow's about this." (Isow's was a Jewish restaurant in Soho, London, where agents gathered to discuss deals.) "But Mr. Bernstein, where would you present the Beatles in New York?"

"Our most prestigious hall. In fact, the most important concert hall in the entire *world*. It's Carnegie Hall."

Bernstein could only guess at the glowing pride Epstein was experiencing. "*You* want to play *my* boys at Carnegie Hall? But why would you want to commit suicide? They don't mean anything in your country." Bernstein again emphasized his confidence in them. Had Epstein heard of Carnegie Hall? he asked. Brian said yes, he had seen a BBC-TV program that emphasized its reputation as a home of classical music's big names. He brimmed with enthusiasm at the idea of the Beatles becoming the first pop group to entertain there. Quickly, his pragmatism and ideas for promotion got to work on the idea.

"When would you play them?" he asked Bernstein. "There's no airplay. It's not going to be next week."

"It could be six months from now," answered Bernstein.

"Oh no, that would be too soon," Brian said. "First of all, we need airplay and I'm not sure we're going to get it."

"Then let's make it next February," said Bernstein.

Comforted by this long-term confidence, Brian agreed—with one condition. If the Beatles did not have an American hit by the end of 1963, he could cancel the date. The two men agreed on a "telephone handshake." As with many agreements by Epstein, there was no letter of exchange.

Just as he had met a brick wall with the British record industry two years earlier, Brian was now about to face the antipathy of American record bosses. EMI Records in London automatically offered "Please Please Me" to its American company, Capitol. "They would not take it at any price," recalls Sir Joseph Lockwood. American ears, they insisted, were not attuned to this essentially British sound. Their rejection gave EMI and Epstein the right to offer it elsewhere. The option was picked up by Vee Jay, a small Chicago label, whose deal called for $20,000 per record, paid in stages. The record died. EMI switched to another label, Swan, for "She Loves You." That release, too, gave Brian no heart, failing as it did to make any national impact.

Brian's promotional thrust, which always outweighed his greed for early big money, now became the Beatles' greatest asset as they approached the formidable hurdle of conquering America. He remembered George Martin's contention that the Beatles did not come alive until they were seen; in Martin's case, their visual appeal had been the deciding factor. What they needed in America, Brian felt convinced, was an appearance on a major national television show. But that would be difficult to arrange without a hit record to their credit.

By then, Capitol Records had become interested. They dealt a knockout blow to Swan and launched an energetic sales plan for the next Beatles single, "I Want to Hold Your Hand." Epstein, pushing again on promotion, persuaded Capitol to spend $20,000 on advertising and also to manufacture five million "The Beatles Are Coming" badges to generate interest in the U.S. tour he was now planning.

It was a buoyant Epstein who returned to Liverpool from London for Christmas 1963. It had been an exhilarating year. Ahead lay a spring visit to New York, which would surely establish the Beatles as the world-beaters he had always predicted. Yet there were some cynics. When Brian popped into the White Star, near the Cavern, for a drink with Bob Wooler and proudly told one of the group's staunchest allies that they would be going to America in February, Wooler was apprehensive: "What on earth are they going to do for America?" He did not think their style was right. Epstein, his pride dented, became indignant.

There was immediate clear evidence, though, of the Beatles' leaping popularity. As Epstein stood drinking in the Liverpool pub, someone approached Wooler wanting to sell him a "Beatle Blanket," an ordinary sheet with their faces printed on it. Protective of them like a doting father, Brian was enraged at this unauthorized merchandising of the Beatles' faces. He threatened legal action unless the "Beatle Blanket" was withdrawn.

❏

Nothing less than the Beatles' appearance on a major national television show was Brian's ambition when he arrived in New York in November 1963 to lay the promotional groundwork for the group's assault on America. Sid Bernstein's confidence and advance planning had fired Epstein's enthusiasm. He decided to work well ahead on promotion plans.

He used his persuasiveness on the producers of "The Ed Sullivan Show," who agreed that the Beatles' British success was enough to warrant their appearance on three successive Sundays, February 9, 16, and 23, 1964. Each show would reach about seventy-three million viewers coast-to-coast. It was a triumphant break for Brian—but expensive. He had to agree to heavily subsidize the Beatles' appearances; further, the Beatles would be paid only $10,000 for all three performances. Measured against their huge earnings, it was a pittance. But Brian rationalized that the exposure on a prime television show was worth the less than optional terms.

Brian charmed the Americans with his essentially British presence, but Sullivan was aghast when Epstein said he always monitored the way in which the Beatles were projected. "I would like to know the exact wording of your introduction," Brian said to the doyen of TV variety shows. Sullivan replied tersely: "I would like *you* to get lost."

Now relocated in New York, Geoffrey Ellis received from his mother British newspaper articles that showed that "your friend Brian Epstein seems to be doing quite well." There followed a letter from Brian saying he would be visiting New York—just after the Beatles' appearance on the Royal Variety Show—to research the Beatles' U.S. prospects. He turned to Geoffrey for a little advice: "I don't know anything about New York. It has to be a good hotel to make the right impression." He did not care what he paid.

Brian checked into the prestigious Regency Hotel on Park Avenue. With him came Billy J. Kramer, "one of our top artists in England," as he introduced him to Geoffrey. The three went walking in Times Square, where Kramer enthused over some sports shirts. He was stopped from buying them by Brian. "No, you don't. Not your image at all." Ellis was surprised at Brian's assertiveness in managing a young artist. He was awestruck, too, when Brian, exuding confidence, started to drop famous names: "I saw Ed Sullivan today. . . ." Brian asked Ellis: "Do you know any good journalists who can help me with publicity for the Beatles?"

Geoffrey's only contact in the world of journalism was an erudite young man, fresh out of college, who phoned him regularly for publishing tips from the insurance field. David Garrard Lowe worked for *Look* magazine and a sister publication, the *Insider's Newsletter*. Geoffrey now phoned Lowe, his charm and Oxford University pedigree carrying irresistible persuasion: "David, I have this old friend from Liverpool who has a group of musical people. He says he has an idea they will be important, and they're called the Beatles."

Lowe remarked that Beatles was a strange name. Undeterred, Ellis said that Epstein, anxious for guidance, would contact him. Brian telephoned Lowe with an invitation to lunch, after which Lowe took him to see his editor at *Look*. The man glanced at Brian's pictures of the Beatles. "I'll never have pictures of boys with long hair in this magazine," he told Epstein. David Lowe, however, ameliorated the rejection with a short article introducing the Beatles in the smaller *Insider's Newsletter*.

Impressed, Brian quickly forged a friendship with Lowe. Had he any other ideas for publicity, he asked? "Yes," said Lowe. "I think you're so far out in a funny way that the *New Yorker* might do something in their 'Talk of the Town' section." He took Brian to meet a friend of his on the staff.

The *New Yorker* interviewed Epstein in his suite at the Regency Hotel. The article, published on December 28, 1963, began: "Intimations have lately been reaching us of a rapidly developing craze among young people in England for the music of, and public appearances by, a group of pop singers called the Beatles." Epstein, the magazine noted, "proved to be a polite, round-faced man, elegantly but conservatively dressed and with a quite conventional haircut."

Brian told the writer: "The Beatles have broken every conceivable entertainment record in England. They are the most worshipped, the most idolized boys in the country. They have tremendous style and a great effervescence which communicates itself in an extraordinary way. Their beat is something like rock 'n' roll but different from it. They are quite different from the big English rock 'n' rollers in that they are not phoney. They have none of that mean hardness about them. They are genuine. They have life, humor and strange, hand-some looks . . . they have been called a working class phenomenon but I disagree with the sometimes expressed notion that their appeal is sometimes to the working classes. The Beatles are classless. We get fan letters from public schools as well as from working class people. Mummies like the Beatles, too—that's the extraordinary thing. They think they are rather sweet. They *approve*."

The magazine noted that "for all Epstein's single-mindedness about the Beatles, his account of their allure was delivered with an air that we associated more with an English drawing room than with Tin Pan Alley." After describing his background and proudly pointing out that the Beatles had sold five million records, Brian uttered a parting proph-ecy. Riotous scenes had occurred all over Britain, he said, adding: "I think that America is ready for the Beatles. When they come, they will hit this country for six."

❏

During a marathon three-week season of nightly Beatles shows at the Paris Olympia which had begun on January 16, 1964, Brian received a stunning telegram from his London office. "I Want to Hold Your Hand" had jumped from 43 to 1 on the charts compiled by the Amer-ican music magazine *Cashbox*. It sold a million copies.

Coming only days before the Beatles' visit to New York to appear on "The Ed Sullivan Show," this was the breakthrough Epstein wanted. As the champagne flowed in Paris, Brian was approached by an American agent, Norman Weiss, the head of General Artists Cor-poration, from where Sid Bernstein had phoned him. Visiting Paris as manager of singer Trini Lopez, who was featured in the Beatles' show, Weiss asked Epstein if the provisional booking of New York concerts, as well as the Sullivan TV shows, could now be confirmed. Brian, sensing the time was ripe, made the deal with Weiss for the Beatles' concert debuts in New York and Washington.

Shrewdly, Sid Bernstein had acted well in advance of Brian's au-thority, setting the date of the Beatles' concert debut for February 12, 1964, a national holiday (Lincoln's birthday), when children would be out of school. He had to borrow the $500-dollar deposit to secure the rental of Carnegie Hall.

Bigger than Elvis Presley . . . Brian really did believe it. The cards were slowly falling into place. "I don't think the Beatles fully understand how lucky they were that they fell into the hands of Brian," says David Lowe. "He mixed with people very well. I found him articulate, with an enormous drive to succeed. He was very determined, not desperate, but with very few self-doubts that he let on in public. There were a lot of self-doubts in private in his life."

Bernstein knew very quickly that he was on to a winner. After a few months, he was ready to place his first advertisement for the Carnegie Hall concerts in the Sunday edition of the *New York Times*. He was assured a sellout: the Beatles then held the top three positions in the U.S. Hot 100 records charts. The tickets Bernstein had priced at the customary concert scale of $3.50, $4.50, and $5.50 were exchanging hands among the touts at $75, $100, and $140. "A whole new army of ticket scalpers was born," he recalls.

After the Beatles' triumphs at Carnegie Hall and on "The Ed Sullivan Show," Brian was besieged by American promoters. Sid Bernstein offered him $25,000 for one show at Madison Square Garden, and took Brian to visit the venue. But Brian said a solitary show in the 20,000-seat hall was not what he wanted; he needed a national tour to capitalize on his gamble with "The Ed Sullivan Show."

Within a month of that massive television exposure, Brian's brilliant stroke of targeting paid dividends. The April 4 edition of *Billboard*, the U.S. music magazine, showed the Beatles at 1, 2, 3, 4, 5, 31, 41, 46, 58, 65, 68, and 79 in its best-selling singles charts; in the albums charts, they were 1 and 2. Advance orders for "Can't Buy Me Love" had been two million. Beatlemania U.S.A. was secured. Capitol Records' switchboard proudly greeted all callers: "Good morning; Capitol Records, home of the Beatles!" In their summer tour, the Beatles would be en route to the posterity Brian had always predicted.

❑

Back in London, Brian decided on a spectacular event to mark the forthcoming long haul around America. On August 12, 1964, he hosted a glittering party—described as "Mr. Brian Epstein, At Home" on formal invitation cards—at his Knightsbridge apartment. The Beatles, Lionel Bart, Alma Cogan, and Mick Jagger mingled with Brian's family, friends, and favored members of his office staff. He was the omnipresent host. Seeing his grandmother in earnest conversation with Judy Garland, Brian was intrigued. When the American singer moved on, he anxiously asked his grandmother what they had been discussing. "How to make chocolate cake," she answered. He was aghast that such a great artist should be engaged in such mundane chatter, but quickly realized it was evidence of the relaxed atmosphere.

Harry and Queenie were delighted to see that a kosher selection had been added to Brian's carefully chosen array of food and champagne. But Queenie, who arrived ahead of the other guests, was horrified when she went to the roof and saw the centerpiece decoration for the huge marquee: hundreds of carnations shaped as a palm tree. It looked breathtaking, but Queenie pointed out that the flowers were red and white. "That is bad luck," she told Brian. He immediately ordered that they either be changed or removed before the guest arrived. Dozens of bottles of red ink were quickly sent for. Assistants dipped the white flowers into bowls of it, narrowly meeting the deadline for the start of the party.

❑

Brian's love of the theater continued unabated and largely unsatisfied. Although he had created for himself the ultimate lead role, he had no deep love of the world of pop music. He enjoyed its drama, its projection, and the moment when a good song came from an able performer. But now that it had given him success and a measure of clout, a little indulgence in the legitimate theater was surely all right.

The pop world into which Brian had arrived was predominantly heterosexual. Elvis Presley's revolution, continued by the Beatles, preached male sex appeal to girls, and the people who populated the music scene were largely on the same wavelength. It would be a full decade before the arrival of David Bowie and Elton John, heralding the "glam rock" era and its connotations of bisexuality. The theater, with its higher homosexual population, continued to beckon Brian.

Occasionally he was invited to dinner parties by theater folk. One followed his visit to London's Duchess Theatre in 1964 to see *The Reluctant Peer*, a William Douglas-Home play starring Dame Sybil Thorndike, Naunton Wayne, Imogen Hassall, and Frank Pettingle. At the lavish party in Eaton Terrace, Belgravia, Brian found himself sitting near the play's juvenile lead actor, Peter Bourne.* He was surprised to discover he was the brother of pop singer Mike Berry, the hit record star whom Brian had befriended in Liverpool. "Brian was the star of the evening, the most important person at the party," says Peter Bourne.

Peter was twenty-three, homosexual, and a rising actor. Brian admired his Pierre Cardin suits and ties and his articulateness. Immediately, Brian "quietly and shyly" confessed that more than anything he wanted to be an actor. He told Peter that he had left RADA unsuccessfully. Says Bourne: "I said, 'Well, *be* an actor! Look, you've got all this money, you can make a choice. Change your name and go into rep!'

"He was gentle, quietly spoken, a bit nervous. In the Belgravia situation, half of them were wealthy queens, the other half were pretty boys to dress the place. I didn't expect him there. It was quite a shock when somebody introduced me.

"At the dinner I played it very cool. I wanted him to be very impressed with me. And I instinctively knew how to play his game. And I didn't give him an inch, really. I played the femme fatale, keeping my mouth shut!

"I was among these very wealthy men and I was getting twenty-five or thirty pounds a week. They were all millionaires."

Brian went to the theater several nights to develop his friendship with Peter Bourne. They visited restaurants after the show and Brian introduced him to friends of his in the pop scene: Cilla Black and Peter Noone. "It was wonderful to be met at the theater by a Bentley, impressing all these actors," says Bourne.

Epstein was, says Bourne, "very afraid of being gay. I hadn't come out yet, and in the seventies I got involved with the Gay Liberation thing. But in those days, it was very discreet and quiet. There were plenty of bars and all the gays were having a good time; I was quite happy about it. I loved the gay world. But Brian was very frightened. He was very sort of discreet about it. At that point everybody was made to feel there was something wrong with being gay." Brian sometimes visited Peter's home in Gloucester Terrace, but he also trusted him sufficiently to give him a key to his Knightsbridge flat.

*He now works under the name Bette Bourne.

"I used to put on a really posh accent in those days to get into the theater," Bourne recalls. "John didn't like that at all. Ringo was always very sociable. I think I was very much the pretty boy of the moment, probably one of several people. Brian had a very beautiful American boyfriend and they'd been having a row. I think I was unconsciously being used as the usurper, in a way." Brian and Peter's conversation often swung round to the theater. "I felt sorry for him because he was so frustrated in acting. He thought it was silly I should try to persuade him to continue in the theater. I told him Laurence Olivier got chucked out of the Central School of Acting and Rex Harrison too."

Bourne was able to form solid opinions on Brian's reluctant homosexuality. Talking of their relationship, he says: "The sexual thing was practically nil. I liked him very much and tried to discuss some things with him. He wouldn't. He was afraid. I don't think he knew himself. He'd gone up a road that in a way he regretted. In spite of all this money and all his power, the Beatles got the adulation. He got the fame, he got the money, the extras, the frills, but he never really got what he wanted." That, says Bourne, was "to *be there*, on the stage, in the limelight."

Talking of Brian's torturous conscience as a homosexual, Bourne says: "The pressure of being gay in those years was enormous. Particularly for him. As well as delighting him, the situation he was in alarmed him. He couldn't afford, for instance, to have a feminine image of any kind, any indiscretion like that. Because the rock-world image was so heavily butch and male in those years. Even in the theater, if there was any indication from the stage that I was gay, I wouldn't have got the job, wouldn't be in work. Brian knew all this, instinctively, as far as his role was concerned.

"Being gay obviously made him lonely because he couldn't discuss it with his closest friends. They all knew. They were okay about it: 'Well, Brian is gay and that's it.' But they didn't want to know anything about that, really. I got the impression he didn't talk to people intimately very much. Lennon was probably the only one."

After two months of keen friendship, exchanging Christmas gifts, going to the theater, dinner dates, and parties together, Brian and Peter agreed to split. "It was probably clear to him that I wanted more intimacy, wanted to be more intense and more real, perhaps. I wasn't his type. That was really the truth. I was a bit upset. He asked me for the keys back, so I suppose he ended it."

❑

When he planned the Beatles' first American concert tour in 1964, Brian had been somewhat overzealous. In Britain, he had toured the Beatles two or three times a year and they had thrived on it. Not knowing the geography of the United States, Brian authorized a preposterous itinerary: thirty-two shows in twenty-four cities in thirty-four days.

On his arrival with the Beatles at the Hilton Hotel in San Francisco for the first concert, on August 18, Brian was handed a telegram from Colonel Tom Parker, manager of Elvis Presley. Offering his help "as a friend," Parker sent Presley's best wishes for a successful tour and asked Brian to phone him. For John, Paul, George, and Ringo, this was the beginning of a friendship with their idol that would have been unthinkable only nine months earlier.

The month-long visit to the United States brought wild scenes. Nine thousand fans greeted them at San Francisco airport, and from the Hollywood Bowl to Philadelphia, Chicago, Boston, Cleveland, and New Orleans, the Beatles had to be confined to hotel rooms, limousines, and planes. Prisoners of fame, they were on course for immortality: cans of Beatle breath were on sale alongside of swatches of their unlaundered hotel bed linen, which was chopped up and sold for $10 per three-inch square. Weeping with delight, a generation of American teenagers, as well as their parents, had clasped the Beatles to their hearts. For Brian, such excitement was merely the opening of a new chapter.

But as the magnitude of the Beatles' popularity became all-consuming, Epstein's care and possessiveness were to become his burden. His failure to delegate responsibility—from choosing a hotel or an airline to handling security, from drawing up the press itinerary to monitoring the Beatles' repertoire and social freedom—meant he had less time for the other acts he had signed up so enthusiastically. They still expected his full attention. But at the end of 1964, as he proudly promoted "Another Beatles Christmas Show" at London's Hammersmith Odeon, the world was at his feet. He could scarcely be blamed for believing that both his judgment and his organization were impregnable.

❑

On January 10, 1965, Sid Bernstein phoned Epstein with the most ambitious proposal ever for a pop group. The Beatles were immensely popular by then, but nothing could prepare their manager for this overture. "Brian," began Bernstein, "I would like to put the boys into Shea Stadium." Shea was a 55,600-seat baseball park, an awesome prospect compared with the 2870-seat Carnegie Hall.

There was a palpable pause from Brian. "Are you sure, Sid? I don't want to be embarrassed, or the boys embarrassed."

Berstein knew he had Epstein's confidence and friendship, but still, he had to work to push through this seemingly preposterous scheme. "Brian, the box office people at Carnegie Hall told me we could have sold out *two hundred thousand* seats, leave alone the 2870 each show. I'll tell you what: I'll pay *you* for every empty seat at Shea Stadium!"

Brian was worried about security. But the American assured him yet again: he could handle that aspect. Would Brian agree in principle to the giant concert? Bernstein wanted nothing in writing; just as with the Carnegie dates, Bernstein and Epstein did not have a contract drawn up but relied totally on each other's honesty and integrity. "He was rare, unique in that respect," says Bernstein. "If he said it was a deal on the phone, that word was true."

"Very well," said Brian. "If you are sure about security, let's agree with the Shea Stadium. It will be very exciting. I'd like a guaranteed payment of a hundred thousand dollars as an advance, against sixty percent of the gross receipts, whichever is the larger. Sid, I'll make it easy for you. You don't have to give me a hundred thousand right now. Send me fifty thousand now, and then give me the other fifty thousand just before they play the date. But I would like the money before the concert."

Bernstein was in a tight spot. He had just gone broke with a flop tour called Shindig at the New York Palladium. The weeklong show had featured several acts, including Gerry and the Pacemakers. He didn't want to tell Brian of this bad news, which partly reflected on one of the acts in his stable.

"Brian, my money is all tied up right now," Bernstein countered. He agreed with the two-payment request but asked for a few months' grace. Epstein said he would be in New York two months from then, around April 10: "I'll be staying at the Waldorf Towers. Why don't you call me and come up and give me a check then for fifty thousand, with fifty thousand due two months later on June 10?"

Bernstein was now accustomed to such precision. "Fine, Brian. By the way, can I advertise it?" He wanted some cash to flow in to meet Brian's demands.

"Oh *no*, Sid. Definitely not. It's not bona fide until I get your deposit. No interviews, no advertisements please, Sid."

"May I talk about it then, Brian?"

"How can I stop you talking about it?"

❏

Bernstein owed Epstein a big moral debt, and Bernstein knew it. Sure, Sid had demonstrated great vision with the flurry of expensive telephone calls from New York to Liverpool, which had ensured the Carnegie Hall concert. But Epstein's confidence in Bernstein, a poor boy from the East Bronx, had enabled him to become a significant New York impresario. Bernstein had Epstein's trust, and that was equity. No matter what the temptation, he could not now blow it by splashing "Beatles for Shea Stadium" across the media. Besides, there was a small matter of $100,000 to be found.

He was busy establishing other beachheads of the British pop invasion that gripped America's imagination in 1965. Because of his Beatles-Epstein liaison, Bernstein was able to present concerts by the Rolling Stones, the Dave Clark Five, the Animals, Manfred Mann, Herman's Hermits, the Moody Blues, the Kinks, and others. Now, he faced the very apogee of his life, as the originator of the greatest pop concert by the most important act in the world. And yet he couldn't do any more than talk about it, informally, until he had secured it with money he did not have!

He had also become a father for the first time. As Sid Bernstein wheeled Adam's pram around Washington Square near his home in Greenwich Village, young people recognized the man known as the precursor of the British pop invasion. The kids kept asking the same question as they walked along with him: "Sid, what's next?" He could tell them, without breaking his bond with Epstein: "The Beatles at Shea Stadium this summer."

"Where can we buy tickets?"

What a waste! All these kids wanting to spend money on tickets, he reflected, and I want to sell fifty-five thousand seats, but I can't tell them where to write to, and certainly can't direct them to the stadium or the ticket agencies. And Sid owed money: two months' rent, the grocer too.

Then he had an enterprising flash, one that could not possibly alienate Epstein. He rented a box at the post office on Nineteenth Street. Now he could tell the kids to pass the word around: they could send deposits for tickets to Sid Bernstein at P.O. Box 21.

Three weeks passed. Sid Bernstein walked the seven blocks from his house to the post office, expecting perhaps payment for thirty tickets, which would pay his rent arrears. If he got fifty, he could also pay the grocer. More than that, he said to himself, and, well, I'm not a drinking man but maybe I'll get drunk tonight.

The sight that greeted him at the post office was astonishing: his box was crammed full. He was sure he had more than fifty applications for tickets. "Hey, buddy, you got a lot of mail. What do you do?" said the attendant.

"I'm in the mail order business."

"Well, boy, you must have some hot item."

A second attendant came from the back, saying to Sid: "What's *your* racket? You're gonna need help." There followed three giant sacks full of mail, and Bernstein had to return home for his car to collect them.

There were more applications than tickets available. When April 10 came, Bernstein dutifully called Epstein at the Waldorf Towers. He walked into Brian's suite and wrote him a check for $100,000, double the amount initially due. With no advertising, Sid Bernstein had sold out Shea Stadium inside of three weeks, merely by word of mouth via the incomparable Beatles fans' grapevine.

Epstein was impressed with the check, but still concerned about security. "Just make sure it's tight," he told Sid. There were problems and pressures on this score, says Bernstein: "New York City police were not allowed inside the stadium. They could only come in if there was a riot. They were everywhere outside, but inside I brought in more ushers from Madison Square Garden and a team of detectives. There would be about seven or eight hundred security men, not counting the police outside. I oversecured it. Lloyds of London charged me twenty-five thousand dollars for insurance of the one night, which was an awful lot of money in 1965.''

The Beatles' purse, as negotiated by Brian, was good: receipts totaled more than $300,000, so the advance payment of $100,000 was topped up by $80,000. "For just twenty-eight minutes work—that's all they did onstage," reflects Bernstein. "Nobody knew how short it was, nobody cared. They got the money for just being there. It was magic.''

Only one hitch threatened to mar the big event. Intoxicated by his success as a promoter, Bernstein was to become manager of the Young Rascals, who would have a huge hit with "Groovin' (on a Sunny Afternoon)." With his keen eye for promotion, he used the Shea Stadium screen to alternate a crowd-safety message with Sid Bernstein hype: "The Rascals Are Coming." Sid did not know of Brian's disapproval of anything that attempted to ride on the backs of the Beatles. When Brian saw the Rascals plug, his tone became deadly serious: "Look, Sid, if you don't get that message off the air immediately, the boys will not play." Bernstein acted quickly. He had wanted to emulate Brian with the Rascals, but he was to learn, like hundreds of others, that there could never be another group such as the Beatles. "I saw the power, the excitement, the rewards, and I wanted to be the Brian of the U.S.," he admits now.

The security was perfect for the Shea concert on August 15. There were no casualties. But to keep faith with Epstein, Bernstein paid a price. His profit on the night was a mere $6500. So much had gone into oversecuring Shea Stadium that it eroded his benefits.

There was consolation from a loyal, emotional Brian. "The way you handled Carnegie Hall and this big event, Sid, I want to make a promise and commitment to you. As long as I live or the boys are around, you shall always have them for this territory." Bernstein rues the day he failed to ask Brian, during his initial approaches, for representation rights throughout America. "He was so impressed with the way Carnegie went down, and the security, America would have been mine for the asking.''

A summit meeting of the two most influential pop managers of all time took place over lunch at the Beverly Hills Hotel, Los Angeles, in August 1964, during a Beatles American tour.

Brian's meeting with Elvis Presley's manager, Colonel Tom Parker, emphasized to Brian how young he was to have achieved so much. It should also have made him realize that managing the Beatles was a full-time job and that he was already overreaching himself in continuing to build his empire. When Brian expressed his surprise that Parker had never managed another artist, the older man replied: "Elvis has required every moment of my time, and I think he would have suffered had I signed anyone else. But I admire you, Brian, for doing it. Obviously you have a different organization. But remember, too, that when Presley soared to fame I was forty-four. When the Beatles happened, you were twenty-eight. That helps."

The two men found useful comparisons in the attention they gave to their stars. When Epstein mentioned the tight security needed to protect the Beatles when they toured, the Colonel commented: "You don't have to protect the Beatles as we protected Elvis because with them there is no jealousy. You don't have to fear the boyfriends as we did, because your artists are characters loved in a different way. Your problem is to protect the small fans from getting hurt in the crush. We have never had them so little."

Recollections of their early days in management revealed their common tenacity: Parker said he had launched Presley by doing "rough jobs" like selling tickets in the dance halls where Elvis appeared. Brian replied: "So did I, in little Lancashire towns. I took around my own posters and sold tickets when they were earning less than twenty pounds a week."

When entering the pop world, Brian at least knew about selling records. He knew nothing whatever about the world of films. An overture from the movie world therefore seemed solid: the giant United Artists wanted to contract the Beatles to make their debut and nominated an American living in London, Walter Shenson, to produce it.

While *A Hard Day's Night* was made at a total cost of £200,000, including everyone's fees, and its successor, *Help!*, cost a mere £400,000, with neither movie giving the Beatles much money in advance, Brian proved surprisingly meek when discussing profit participation for the Beatles or NEMS.

Before meeting Epstein, Shenson had privately agreed with United Artists that they could offer Brian and the Beatles 25 percent of the profits for *A Hard Day's Night*. At their meeting, Brian agreed to the £25,000 salary for working on the movie. When the talk moved to percentage profits, Brian was the first to set a figure: "I couldn't accept anything less than seven and a half per cent," he told a puzzled Shenson.

"They made the pictures for very little cash," says Shenson, "because everybody wanted to make a low-budget comedy with the hope that the profits would be larger." And that is what happened: both Beatles films are still accruing profits for them through video and television rights.

❏

Whenever Brian planned to visit America, the first person he alerted there was Nat Weiss. A quintessential New Yorker, droll, witty, deceptively astute, Weiss was a divorce attorney dabbling in theatrical work when they first met at the suggestion of Weiss's London client Larry Parnes. Weiss became Epstein's most loyal friend, business partner, and confidant—certainly in America, perhaps in the world. Just before Brian went to New York, he would phone Weiss and ask him to confirm the reservation for his usual suite, 35E, at the Waldorf Towers. The same room was essential every time: Brian had to have that view of the East River. Brian's telephone call would also specify precisely the amount of liquor required for the bar in his suite, right down to the brands. And he would list the new American records that Weiss should program on a specially made cassette to be played during Brian's limousine ride from the airport to the city.

Their first meeting, at the end of 1964, came after the Beatles had made their big impact in America. Weiss was invited to see Brian at the hotel he then used, the Plaza. "It was a rather strange evening," Weiss remembers. "I got the impression he was very shy. Brian was smoking a joint as I arrived and he asked me if I'd read his book, *A Cellarful of Noise*. I said no."

In February 1965, Epstein was again at the Plaza, this time with

Gerry Marsden. He phoned to invite Weiss to breakfast. "I was preoccupied with having breakfast myself at the time. I was with a student
from Columbia University and I kept asking Brian about the Beatles,
and the student said to me: 'Is that *Brian Epstein?* I'd do *anything* to
meet Brian Epstein.' I'd never seen such a fantastic response from
someone who was normally quiet. It threw me."

At the Plaza, Epstein asked Weiss if he could get tickets to see the
movie *Zorba the Greek*. "Why he couldn't just go to the movies and
buy tickets I don't know," says Nat. But it was a first indication to
him that, for Brian, everything had to be a big production. Weiss got
him the tickets; after the show Brian went to his apartment. "Brian
and I and a couple of other people sat in my place and smoked all
night."

That night Weiss was impressed by something "strange and
unique" about Epstein. "His whole demeanor, his thinking, his approach, his insights, were amazing. Brian was not aggressive when he
met people but you knew you were being scrutinized personally. He
always wanted to be the one in pursuit of things."

Brian knew nothing of the bars to which Nat introduced him. "He
was fascinated with some of the places on Forty-fifth Street—the
Wagon Wheel Bar, Kelly's Bar. They were rough places with service-
men, prostitutes, and rough people. But they were fun places and he
just liked that type of atmosphere.

"Walking up Forty-fifth Street off Broadway one night, Brian said,
'You know, people might begin to recognize me. I'm on the TV show
"Hullabaloo" and I'm becoming a personality in my own right.' "

10

❑

STYLE

FAME, GRANDEUR—AND INSECURITY

THE ARCHETYPAL POP STAR'S MANAGER in the mid-1960s was not renowned for ethics, manners, honesty, taste, or style. The boom in record sales, in concerts and clubs, and in media interest had bred opportunistic spivs, confidence tricksters with an eye on quick, easy money. Many exploited their "discoveries" on the pretense of providing them with instant fame and fortune. They sacrificed any long-term career prospects for their artists in favor of overnight gains for themselves. Before the word "rip-off" had permeated the music scene, the manifestation of it was rife. Epstein was utterly different. If money had been his prime motivation, the Beatles might never have broken through.

In the entertainment world and beyond, Brian's name was a byword for class and integrity—and he cherished his reputation. His manners, sensitivity, and iron belief in all his acts were a constant topic of show business conversation, and this winning combination continued to set him apart after his move to London.

He enjoyed the speedy London life, "both the runaround discotheque thing and the luxury of good things." He recalled that when he was an army conscript in London, an uncle had taken him to dinner at the Savoy Grill. Observing Brian's demeanor in the restaurant, his uncle said to him: "*This* is what *you* really enjoy." Brian was able, though, to avoid being sucked into the whirlpool of Swinging London, to distance himself as a businessman when he found that essential. "There is a very grave danger," he said, referring to the mood of the mid-1960s, "that people will delude themselves into thinking that Swinging London is some sort of artistic progress. I think this 'Mod' thing is awful. I haven't had much to do with it. All this finger-snapping, hippy business is very contrived; so much nonsense in many ways."

His growing celebrity demanded appropriate surroundings. In December 1964, Brian moved into his new £40,000 home at 24 Chapel Street, Belgravia, London. A Georgian town house, it was stamped with the character lacking in his sterile fifth-floor Knightsbridge flat, where he had spent six rootless months. It was time for a move. Too many people knew the old address, and his privacy was repeatedly being invaded. With its silk wallpaper, a Lowry original, Chippendale furniture, and oak-paneled study, the four-story property in Chapel Street was the house in luxurious good taste which Brian had always craved. Now that he was an important name in show business, he could at last project his own personality without fear of being charged with egotism.

Ensconced in the air-conditioned comfort of his Chapel Street home, Brian was ready to indulge in the kind of London theatrical lifestyle about which he had fantasized as a frustrated Liverpool shop-keeper. He had three cars—a maroon Rolls-Royce, a gray Bentley convertible, and a white Mini. They were colored, he said, because he had previously been bored by the drabness of his "pre-Beatles" cars, which were usually black. He had a gigantic wardrobe, all kept in pristine condition by his valet. His tailored shirts now came in boxes, one of each color, from Turnbull and Asser in Jermyn Street, Picca-dilly; his suits came from Gieves and Hawkes in Savile Row. He was, he said, happier to have his hair cut by an expensive craftsman rather than by an ordinary barber. He took Cilla's suggestion that he go regularly to Raphael and Leonard, where they could more easily style his long sideburns.

In July 1964, he was named one of Britain's ten best-dressed men. The British Clothing Manufacturers' Federation presented him with a silver plaque citing his "exemplary standards in the choice and wearing of clothes. . . . His sartorial taste hits the mark as surely as his eye for talent . . . he is one of the moderates." With typical diffidence, he never mentioned the award, which seemed to embarrass him.

Though he was a gourmet with an exotic palate, his instructions to his resident butler and chef always specified simple fare: steak-and-kidney pie, cold cuts, ice cream. But he insisted on the best ingredients. With his keen eye for cost, Brian carried out spot checks on the grocery bills. When a butcher overcharged, he ordered that the meat come from elsewhere. (Yet he was lavish, generous, and extravagant in his spending on others at Asprey's and never once criticized his assistant Wendy Hanson's selection of his Christmas gifts.)

He developed a formidable knowledge of London and New York restaurants. Brian loved fine food, particularly oysters; he pored over wine lists and knew the vintages. And it was important to his vanity to be seen in the correct dining rooms. In the mid-1960's the Trattoria Terrazza in Romilly Street, Soho, established the popularity in London of Italian restaurants. It was heavily patronized by the stars of Swinging London: Terence Stamp, Jean Shrimpton, David Bailey, the Beatles, and the Rolling Stones. The restaurant's inner sanctum for these major stars was the Positano Room, where admission was strictly limited to VIPs.

When Wendy Hanson arrived in her office one morning, Brian casually asked: "What did you do last night?"

"I had dinner with Joan Baez," replied Wendy.

"Oh, where did you go?"

"We went to the Trat."

"You couldn't have done," Brian said, "because I was there."

"We were in the Positano Room. Where were you?" asked a puzzled Wendy.

Epstein was "genuinely furious," Wendy recalls. He raged at her: "You're just my *assistant*. And *Time* magazine says that you *can* get in the Positano Room if you're Brian Epstein. And last night I couldn't even get in."

Central to his lifestyle were frequent trips abroad, during which he could indulge not only his love of fine restaurants but one of his least publicized interests—bullfighting. His interest in the theatricality of bullfighting predated his meeting the Beatles. He discovered it on his solitary visits to Spain, principally in Madrid, Valencia, and Seville.

The life of El Cordobes, who was known as "The Spanish Beatle" because of his long hair, became a fixation with Brian, who was determined to become involved in the world of matadors. The bathroom of his new home was dominated by an eight-foot-tall blowup of El Cordobes's face.

(On one of his Spanish visits, often made en route back to London from the United States, he became manager of a British-born bull-fighter named Henry Higgins. At a bullfight in Barcelona, handicapped by two black eyes suffered from the bull, Higgins had delighted Brian with his triumph. A congratulatory telegram awaited Higgins afterward. Epstein believed that as well as being a talented matador, Higgins had a magnetic star quality. Brian's grandiose idea was that Higgins might star in a film of his creation. Hypnotized by the theater of bullfighting, Epstein wanted to combine it with the youthfulness of pop music in some way. It was another fancy that never reached fruition. And his interest in Higgins never generated much activity.)

Yet for all his outward panache and success, those close to Brian worried about the curious emptiness, the loneliness, of his world—this despite the coterie of music-business friends who telephoned and visited at all hours of the day and night. At work, he was either inspired and commanding or hopelessly unreliable. Privately, he was using drugs too much—either experimentally, as with LSD, or as medication with stimulants and downers. It became hard to predict Brian's moods or decisions, although he continued to function well when he was in the right frame of mind.

He still supervised money matters with what he considered a logical combination of frugality and extravagance. He spared no expense for his parties, where he would personally check that the silver had been cleaned, that the correct selection of cigarettes had been placed in holders for the guests. He soon forgot the many thousands of pounds he invested and lost in the career of Tommy Quickly. But with penny-pinching parsimony, he was often mean to his staff. He charged Derek Taylor for a ticket to take his wife to see the premiere of *A Hard Day's Night;* and the cost of the limousine home that night which Taylor charged to NEMS was arbitrarily deducted from his salary. The man juggling multimillion-pound deals for his artists, dominating the international charts, and commuting to America still found time to query his press officer Tony Barrow's reason for taking a journalist to lunch.

"It was his method of making sure the staff didn't take advantage," says Derek Taylor. "But I didn't see myself as staff, rather one of the gang. He saw me as one of the gang emotionally and spiritually but not when it came down to the books. That's why I saw him as a shopkeeper."

His artists, of course, knew of no such trait. When he took Cilla to the premiere of the film *Lawrence of Arabia*, she casually admired the wafting perfume of an actress sitting hearby. "Can you smell it, Brian? It's absolutely marvelous." Next morning at the Savoy Hotel, Cilla's breakfast tray held not a bottle but a complete box of the perfume, which Brian had identified as being by Christian Dior.

But if ever he suffered delusions about who had earned the fortune that was coming into NEMS daily, Lennon would correct him. Once when the Beatles went to dinner at Chapel Street, Ringo began absentmindedly picking away at the inlaid ormolu on the back of one of Brian's precious carved chairs. Epstein watched in horror for a few minutes before saying: "Oh don't do that, Ringo, you'll mess it up." John retorted: "He had to *buy* the fucking thing."

❏

By the time Brian arrived in America, the fame of the soft-spoken, pinstripe-suited Englishman who had so brilliantly marketed the Beatles preceded him. Their music and interviews dominated the airwaves, and Epstein was sought by disc jockeys and writers. In New York, Doubleday bought the American publishing rights for Brian's autobiography. At a meeting with an editor, Brian learned that there would have to be different pictures from those in the British edition. He seethed with anger. It was his book, he declared, and he would exercise a veto over which photographs went into it. Doubleday phoned Ernest Hecht in London: "This man is impossible, rude, shouting about the pictures."

Moments later, Epstein was on the phone to Hecht. "I have met an impossible person from Doubleday. I cannot possibly allow them to use the photos they want. Withdraw the book from them."

It was the middle of the night in London and Hecht was in bed. "Brian, we can't withdraw it. You've had the money. . . ."

"Well, give it back to them."

"But then there will be a lawsuit, Brian. Look, they're reasonable men. . . ."

Finally, Brian capitulated. Doubleday repackaged the book and he grudgingly agreed to some amendments.

❏

On one visit to New York, Brian became enamored of an aspiring actor/model named John Gillespie. Relocating to London, he darted in and out of Brian's life. Nicknamed "Dizz" Gillespie, he became known to the inner circle at NEMS as someone whom Brian was befriending, but nothing prepared them for their boss's bizarre move on his behalf in December 1964. With little evidence of his work, Brian signed Gillespie to NEMS with a £50-a-week retainer, to the astonishment of staff who queried his undisclosed track record. Nevertheless, a brief press statement was published confirming the latest name in Epstein's stable.

The relationship would turn dangerously sour within six months, causing Brian and his closest friends deep anguish. Moreover, the NEMS staff was baffled by the fact that nothing whatsoever was heard of Brian's involvement in Gillespie's career at NEMS. This was the only business episode, if it could be thus described, which he refused to discuss with his colleagues.

In early April 1965 Brian, in New York to see Cilla Black's crucial appearance on "The Ed Sullivan Show," dropped a bombshell on Nat Weiss. Brian revealed to Nat that a boyfriend of his named Dizz Gillespie had blackmailed him, threatening him with a knife. "Brian had a grandiose way of explaining something that was very simple," muses Weiss. "Brian started telling me that in England the boy had tried to put a knife to his throat and stole money from him.

"Brian was fascinated with him and emotionally very attached to him." But Weiss was puzzled: despite the danger to which Brian felt exposed, he was defensive of the boy. Brian's eloquent, romantic descriptions cut no ice with Weiss. "The more Brian spoke, the more this boy sounded like every other boy on Forty-fifth Street; he sounded like a ten-dollar hustler, an ilk I was familiar with. Because of Kelly's Bar, I'd known all these cheap kids for years."

But the very big Beatles 1965 tour, including an appearance at Shea

Stadium, was coming up. And Brian was worried. Brian and Nat were now friendly to the extent that Brian occasionally stayed in Weiss's apartment. "The Gillespie thing bothered Brian because the boy was in New York," recalls Weiss. "He didn't know what to do about the whole thing." Brian was worried about Gillespie's making trouble for the Beatles on their big tour. He asked Nat formally to be his lawyer and deal with the problem.

A confrontation between Weiss and Gillespie took place at the Warwick Hotel. "He was not a bad-looking boy but he was really, as I thought before, just a common hustler. And he started to tell me he'd been very nice to Brian and Brian had made all this money now . . . and he wasn't giving him a fair share. And I said: 'You're not Brian's partner.' " Gillespie replied: "Well, if he wants to get rid of me, at least he should take good care of me." He suggested ten thousand dollars and a car.

Nat Weiss, whose burly frame invited little argument, retorted: "You know, if I had my way, I'd just have you taken care of by some friends I know." (Weiss stresses that this was a frightening tactic—"I have no connection with people who do those sort of things.") "Trouble was," Weiss continues, "he got me angry. I told him: 'I think you're just a cheap ten-dollar hustler and I can't imagine what Brian sees in you.'"

Weiss went back to Brian with his views. Epstein wanted to gloss over the problem with as little fuss as possible. He had clearly been fond of Gillespie. And, most important, he did not want the problem affecting him on the Beatles' American tour. He took the attitude, says Weiss, that "we worship the gods we have created." Brian was very frightened of what might happen. However, Weiss reassured him that he should not worry: "Brian, if the worst comes to the worst, he'll never come near you!" Weiss says: "I always wanted to let loose with this person but Brian really put strong reins on me."

Finally, Brian's obsessive need for peace prevailed. "Well, why don't you give him something? Give him three thousand dollars and get rid of him." Back at the Warwick Hotel, Weiss presented Gillespie with the cash and an ultimatum. "This is it. Take it or leave it and just get lost. Whatever you think Brian owes you for all your time and friendship and everything like that . . . here's a gift. But if you're ever seen again, near Brian or the Beatles, Brian will have nothing to say about what I do because you'll be breaking your word to *me*." Gillespie concurred, signing papers of agreement.

He then said he would like to see Brian. "It's too late," Gillespie was told. "Brian is off." Weiss had kept him talking long enough for Brian to get out of town. Epstein pressed ahead on business, firmly believing that the Gillespie episode was closed. Later on, it would resurface in a much uglier confrontation. Brian was to rue the day he believed that "buying off" a problem would be so easy.

❏

The nonstop rise of the Beatles following their American success, plus the shining careers of Cilla, Gerry and the Pacemakers, and Billy J. Kramer, obscured Brian's lack of success with his other artists. To the public he was simply Mr. Entertainment, the "founder" of the Beatles, as one American described him.

Brian once confessed to the author that his very large ego could no longer be contained by pop management. To the role of "impresario" he wanted to add many more facets. He sought challenges, and areas in which to strengthen his belief in his Midas touch. Brian was able to conceal his ego through his quiet, self-effacing style.

But even his closest friends were aghast at his move into record production. As his debut act he chose, ironically, one of Liverpool's best-known groups, Rory Storm and the Hurricanes. The link came through Arthur Howes, the Beatles' concert promoter, who managed Storm, the group from which Ringo had transferred to the Beatles two years earlier.

In Liverpool, where Brian's helter-skelter rise to fame had left the city agape, news of Rory's recording session under Brian's baton was passed around the pubs and clubs with incredulity. How bizarre that Epstein should now choose to record one of the city's best-loved groups, which had been left behind in the stampede to London. On visits back to Liverpool, Brian had been asked by Storm to be his group's manager. "I want another group like I need a hole in the head," Epstein told Rory one night in the Blue Angel. His disinterest in Storm was hard to reconcile with his absorption in some lesser talent. Perhaps partly to throw the well-respected musician an olive branch, Brian was at the controls at London's IBC Studios as Rory recorded three tracks, notably "America" (from *West Side Story*). Alas, the record, issued on the Parlophone label (dominated by the Beatles), failed. Undeterred, Brian announced that he would continue in record production with one of his own acts.

And his signing of artists to NEMS continued: as a judge on a visit to a West Country talent contest, Brian sat alongside Dick Rowe of Decca, now known for eternity as the Man Who Turned Down the Beatles. The winning group was the Rustiks, and in a sudden spirit of largesse Brian capped their prize by announcing that they would be signed by NEMS and managed by him. In London he became the producer of their debut single. But virtually the same route as that traveled by Michael Haslam awaited them: they appeared in some of Brian's package shows, but never shone. And a folk group called the Silkie, whose look and sound came close to those of such successful 1960s acts as Peter, Paul and Mary and Britain's Seekers, came under Brian's wing after they sent him a tape of their music. This time he really did delegate responsibility—to Alistair Taylor, whom he chose as their manager. But Brian monitored his every move. Unlike most NEMS groups of this period, the Silkie scored with John Lennon's "You've Got to Hide Your Love Away."

But Epstein's magic wand could not bring automatic gold. The Paramounts, a musicianly group that was the genesis of an infinitely more successful band, Procol Harum, were next signed by NEMS, bringing the total acts under Brian's control to fifteen. "Brian didn't see these acts as sidelines to the Beatles and his other work," says Alistair Taylor. "They all had to be cared for. He did his darndest, but he was sensible enough to realize that he couldn't win them all."

Brian's interest would be genuine during the signing period, but if a group failed to take off quickly, he tended to look for new stimuli. Boredom was the flashpoint, just as it had been at the Liverpool record shop.

"When will the clear-out of Brian Epstein's stable begin?" asked the *New Musical Express* tartly on March 19, 1965. For the *Melody Maker*, I had asked Brian a similar question during a breakfast interview at his Knightsbridge flat. Under a headline which ran "Brian Epstein predicts: I Give the Beatles Two or Three Years More at the Top," the January 16 article reported that after a recent Beatles concert in Bradford, Brian had been mobbed by hundreds of autograph hunters. But while his and the Beatles' status was secure, people were asking pertinent questions about his other acts. Could Epstein and his team maintain their grip? "I want to prove my faith in these people," Brian told me defensively. "I'm absolutely certain that Gerry has a marvelous career ahead . . . he's not short of work. I've just had offers for him from Iceland and Toronto! As for Cilla, if anyone talks to me of her being on the wane, well, there will be very few doubts, if any, very soon. Her new record is coming out just at the right time with the public interest in Cilla just right; she is going to make the top ten.

"Billy J. has a very good record coming out and I think he will develop as a good singer."

On the Beatles' future, Brian was circumspect. "I think they will maintain strong teenage appeal for two or three years. After that maybe they will become really established film stars.* They have the talent. They are unique and they have a long way to go in films, something very few people expected.

"They would only get restless if their work, and interest in their work, was not allowed to develop properly. They're as much pleasure-loving as anyone else. They have no desire to give up and do nothing simply because they have made some money. They want to carry on creating for a long, long time.

"I hope they never get to the state where they think they are slipping. The last month or so has been marvellous for them, topping the single and LP charts in Britain and America. Can you call that slipping?"

In truth, the also-rans severely dented Brian's pride. "He just went quiet about them in the office," says Tony Barrow. Brian kept up the pressure on Barrow to get press coverage for them, even when it was obvious they were failing to get public acclaim. Faced with flop records by Tommy Quickly and other artists, Brian would struggle on with a final thrust, putting what Barrow considered unreasonable pressure on everybody around him to resuscitate a corpse. "If it was an act he felt strongly about, he would go on and on for a very long time."

Over at EMI, George Martin had no doubt that Brian had taken on too many acts. "Brian was always a bit flowery with his new people. He would say: 'It's such a wonderful group, George. I know you've got a

*This showed considerable vision by Brian. The Beatles had made only one film, *A Hard Day's Night;* his remark was made before they had made their more demanding film, *Help!*

lot on, but I would appreciate if you'd listen to them because I'm sure that with your talent you would do wonders for them.' I hated turning things down but eventually I had to. I could not do everything. I was at my wit's end in the studio. And if I had little faith in some of his artists, I'd have to say no. The standard of people he brought in deteriorated. After the Beatles, when he got to the stage of people like Tommy Quickly and Michael Haslam, we were going fairly well downhill.

"He took on too many. He wasn't very careful about what he did, thinking the formula would work every time. And it didn't." Part of the reason for the failures of some of Brian's other acts, Martin believes, was that at other record companies he did not find anyone as sympathetic as himself to supervise the sessions.

Whether they succeeded or not, all the acts enjoyed saying they were managed by Epstein. "He got a lot of stick on two scores," says Barrow. "They reckoned they were joining a man who did have enormous power. It was a myth among artists that this man could do magic things in the music business. So they thought success was assured." And they were baffled when they did not get Brian's personal attention. When he did begin delegating certain new acts within NEMS, and they failed to have lasting impact, the artists became disenchanted. And when anyone raised the subject of an artist who was struggling for commercial success, Brian skillfully changed the subject.

Brian's personal fame initially made him uncomfortable but he eventually accepted it relucantly. "I was very fierce about the management not being known at all . . . it just happened to me," he told Michael Charlton in an interview on BBC-TV's "Panorama" in 1964. "I was not conscious of being famous." In the first twelve months of management, he had tried to ensure that his name was not mentioned. Pressed to say if he envied his artists' popularity as individuals, he said that by 1964 he had grown to enjoy being interviewed: "I don't envy the Beatles. I could obviously not do what they do." His humility often surfaced unexpectedly: he would sign autographs: "Brian Epstein—BEATLES manager."

❏

Reviewing the individual Beatles in 1965, Brian said to me that John Lennon had a "great mind and is a great person. One of the best people I've ever met, an interesting character to watch develop." On

George, Brian said: "I always think of him as a friend. A somewhat inconsistent person who can be difficult. Never has been with me. Great personal charm but this goes for any Beatle." Ringo's arrival into the group was "one of the Beatles' most brilliant doings. It was something they wanted and that I carried out."

Paul McCartney was, said Epstein, "probably the most changed Beatle. He's mellowed in character and thought. A fascinating character and a very loyal person. Doesn't like changes very much. He, probably more than the others, finds it more difficult to accept that he is playing to a cross section of the public and not just to teenagers, or subteenagers, whom he feels are the Beatles' audience."

On the Beatles generally, Brian's views at the end of this exceptional year were succinct: "Any faults they are supposed to have are never apparent individually." Their faults surfaced only when they were together as a group—"when there is too much talent in one room."

Events had moved so swiftly that despite his grand lifestyle and high income, Brian had scarcely indulged himself in the two years since he and the Beatles had become national heroes. It was time to restructure his organization: the staff at Argyll Street rose to fifteen with the appointment of his old friend Geoffrey Ellis as executive director and Bernard Lee, an experienced man whom Brian had lured from the Grade Organisation, as head of the bookings agency.

It was time, too, to distance himself from the mayhem of that office. At Wendy Hanson's suggestion, he moved to his own separate office at Hille House, Stafford Street, off Piccadilly—an important move psychologically. Brian knew he could not personally control the new breadth of his company. He would revert to personal management of his pets—the Beatles, Cilla, and Gerry—and leave a well-oiled machine to take care of the rest.

As Wendy Hanson's role dovetailed into personal assistant to the Beatles as well as to Brian, she needed an extra secretary at Hille House. Joanne Newfield* was the twenty-year-old niece of bandleader Joe Loss, a connection that always impressed Brian. He delighted in mentioning her uncle's identity to whomever Joanne was with. One of her first jobs was to go to Epstein's house and, over a four-day

---

*In 1968 she became Joanne Petersen on her marriage to Colin, former drummer with the Bee Gees.

period, prepare and type his Christmas-card list. "At first I was in awe of him. He'd sweep through the office, terribly well-dressed, so handsome." The days he went to the office were nerve-wracking, she recalls; the days when he was absent were boring.

Joanne had bluffed her way into the £15-a-week job with no shorthand; when Brian discovered that, he gave her tapes of his letters. With her Chanel suits, minidresses from Biba, and white Mini car with a huge daisy painted on its roof, she was the epitome of Swinging London. Since Brian related to the mood of the era, his rapport with Joanne was excellent. And as he came to enjoy his home more, he appointed her his private secretary at Chapel Street, to the chagrin of Wendy Hanson.

With a live-in couple, Antonio and Maria Garcia, as housekeepers, and Joanne arriving at 10 a.m. every day from her Finchley home, this was the perfect setup for Brian. Joanne occupied a small room at the top of the house, overlooking the patio, while Wendy remained at Brian's office in Hille House. His visits there were erratic; he admitted that there were days when he could not face contracts or business decisions, days when all he wanted to do was simply talk to the Beatles or Cilla.

As her position became the link between Chapel Street, Hille House, and Argyll Street, the effervescent Joanne assumed a role of importance that belied her inexperience. Like so many who knew Brian closely, she gave him infinitely more than a working day. It was total devotion and dedication. "I was infatuated with the job," she says. "I adored him."

❏

In the vernacular of the world's press, Brian had been elevated to the title of Beatles Boss, a phrase that genuinely irritated him. Even in his new position as an entertainment mogul, the Beatles remained very special to Brian Epstein. "I hate to be called their boss; I am their *friend* and I happen to be their manager too," he said many times. Nor was he entitled to the fictitious position of Fifth Beatle, which some allocated to him.

There was no such figure, said Brian with his usual precision. But Tony Barrow recalls that Epstein once asked Barrow to describe him in a press release as the Fifth Beatle. Barrow declined, arguing that the media had already so described him and that it would be unwise to belabor the point. The request, though, did highlight how much Brian identified creatively with his artists—as much, in fact, as through the business end of their relationships. "I found it impossible to suss out his personal feelings for other artists," says Barrow. "I could tell when he talked about some that he had personal feelings: it glowed in his face and his words." But the Beatles were special, compartmentalized in his mind. Everyone around Brian, professional colleagues and social friends, quickly learned that only he could first raise their name in a conversation. The alternative often caused him to change the subject.

Amid the mayhem that surrounded Beatlemania, the program-hungry BBC had as much difficulty as the rest of the world media in confirming Epstein's plans. Their problem, described graphically in an internal memorandum, spoke of contact with Bernard Lee, the bookings director at NEMS. "He is extremely helpful and reliable," observed the BBC document, "but suffers from the same ailment as do all Mr Epstein's employees. That's to say, they are never in a position to say 'yes' or 'no' to anything without first going to Epstein. As Epstein spends a lot of his time (when he's not in China or Peru, that is) behind locked doors in his own office with his own staff not even being able to get him on the telephone this [meaning contact between the BBC and Bernard Lee] is not exactly satisfactory. (A point which I made to Epstein when I was vouchsafed the privilege of a personal interview in his office, during which time he went through an embarrassing routine of ticking off various members of his staff on the telephone.)"

❑

In London, surprisingly, Brian was a very rare visitor to the Beatles' homes. John and Cynthia found their first flat in Earls Court through a photographer friend, and Brian never visited them there. But encouraged by Lennon's interest in buying fine art and antiques, Brian did take delight in one particular request as John and Cynthia were moving into their new home. On a visit to Paris, John had seen an original Modigliani priced at £750,000. He asked Brian to arrange for a London viewing. With his customary panache, Brian flew to Paris and persuaded the art dealer to visit London for just a day with the painting.

Brian signed a letter to enable the dealer to get the export license. In London, Brian laid on a lavish buffet lunch in a room at Claridge's. At 1 p.m., with everyone in place, there was no Lennon. Two hours passed. Brian phoned Weybridge and roused a sleeping John, who had gone to bed at dawn. With no concern for the dealer's flight from Paris or Brian's lavish arrangements, Lennon said to Brian: "Oh, tell them to come back tomorrow." Flushed with embarrassment, Brian said he would buy the painting if necessary. But the dealer, expecting to meet a Beatle and feeling slighted, left London in a huff.

Paul McCartney always lived in central London: first with his girlfriend Jane Asher at her family home at 57 Wimpole Street, and later at 7 Cavendish Avenue, St. John's Wood; Brian was not a regular visitor to either place. George and Ringo initially shared a flat together in Green Street, Mayfair, and Brian encouraged them to move to his apartment block in Knightsbridge. The Beatles often visited his Knightsbridge flat and his Belgravia house but could not be described as part of Brian's social circle.

He did enjoy driving them around London, to restaurants and clubs, but his appalling driving was a standing joke. All his life, Brian had been an unnatural driver, having passed his driving test at age nineteen after three failed attempts. His attention wandered, and when he spoke to his passengers, he looked at them for too long. Animatedly, he swung his open-top Bentley around the city, parking dangerously and often knocking into cars as he tried to negotiate awkward spaces. Chided by his painstaking chauffeur, Brian Barrett, Epstein had a pat excuse: "What are bumpers *for*?" He was philosophical, too, about cruel carvings of the word "Queer"—evidently gouged with a key— on the door of his car when he parked it in the mews behind his Chapel Street house; the same inscription was once etched onto the door of his garage.

Pattie Boyd, George Harrison's girlfriend at that time, remembers Brian's bizarre driving: "I was a passenger in his Rolls driving to Sussex. Driving through London, we came across a green traffic light. To my absolute amazement Brian drove very slowly and then came to a stop until the lights changed to orange and then red. Then he shot off." Pattie and George rebuked him for his "outrageous" driving. "He had no idea what we were talking about. I think he was color blind. But Brian could get away with anything."

❑

As he continued to negotiate world tours for the Beatles, and as people looked with amazement at the outsized roster of artists he had now brought into NEMS, rumors grew of a sale of the Beatles by Brian. Bernard Delfont,* who with his brothers Lew and Leslie Grade dominated the London entertainment scene, had first met Brian when he put the Beatles in the Royal Variety Show in 1963. "We had some discussions about my purchasing his company and the Beatles, and we went pretty deeply into it," he recalls. "I think he was quite keen to have an associate and he wanted someone to share the load with him. I used to meet him in the South of France quite a bit. I think he needed the umbrella; we were always on the verge of completing a deal.

"I respected and admired him, but I always felt he had a look about him as if it was getting too much. I thought he was looking for guidance. I didn't press him, but I thought he might get into the hands of someone who might not be right. I thought it would be better with our organization. The Beatles, at their peak, were enough for any one man to concentrate on." Delfont offered £150,000 for 50 percent of Brian's companies, with Brian retaining a considerable creative involvement. In the early 1960s that huge sum, plus the colossal weight of the Delfont organization with its international network, was not to be dismissed overnight.

Over dinner at Liverpool's Rembrandt Club, Derek Taylor fixed Epstein with the direct question: Would he ever sell the Beatles? Brian admitted that Delfont had offered him £150,000 for a half share in all his artists and management companies, with guaranteed veto for Brian over any proposed project. He said he was considering this offer because the weight of work was becoming too heavy. When he consulted the Beatles, they were decisive. "They said they would rather break up than leave me. John told me to fuck off, which was *very* moving." It was the emotional commitment from them that Brian had waited for. Nine months later, in America, a syndicate of businessmen offered him *three and a half million pounds* for his business interests in

---

*Now Lord Delfont, chairman of the First Leisure Corporation, an entertainment monolith.

the Beatles. He enjoyed explaining that they could not be bought, because their relationship with him could not be severed. His role could never be diluted.

❏

In less than three years, Epstein's organization had grown like an octopus, artistically and administratively. As Northern Songs alone announced a profit of £621,000 in 1965, Brian's profile increased through his compering of all-star TV shows made in England for America's giant NBC. At Shepperton Studios he filmed interviews for the program "Hullabaloo" with the Searchers, the Moody Blues, Billy J. Kramer, and others. It whetted his appetite for the Moody Blues, who soon afterward signed with him for management.

Apart from the film deals and his company machinery, Brian needed to feel free to do what he did best: assert his personality, befriend his artists, attend their appearances. As the Beatles became feted by the Establishment, it was obvious that the future would get busier.

❏

Although Bob Dylan had been a Beatles favorite for about a year, his adoption by the British public as a major songwriting force and folk hero did not happen until mid-1965, when his album *Bringing It All Back Home* was released. Through American contacts, Brian was offered what would have been the ultimate coup: the promotion of Dylan's historic 1965 British concert tour. In February of that year he turned it down. For once, his creative foresight was not working. The tour was picked up by Tito Burns, now a firm friend and gambling companion of Brian's; Epstein quickly regretted passing over Dylan as his other artists emphasized the American singer's influence and importance.

Burns and Epstein were polar opposites in their approach to the entertainment business. Epstein was ruled chiefly by his heart, his impetus mostly artistic. Burns, a terrierlike negotiator, had been schooled by the toughest dealer in show business, Leslie Grade. Fast-talking, fast-thinking, with a twinkling Jewish sense of humor, he was always looking to the next deal. Brian liked him, respected his industriousness, and often reflected on Burns's interest in the Beatles as early as their "Love Me Do" period.

As well as representing Cliff Richard, Dusty Springfield, the Searchers, Eden Kane, and Gerry Dorsey (later renamed Engelbert Humperdinck), Burns had solid American names under his banner: to Dylan he added Peter, Paul and Mary, Dionne Warwick, Bobby Vee, Vicki Carr, and Tony Orlando. And his American business contacts were impressive.

The NEMS roster of artists, which represented merely the tip of Brian's frantically busy life as a manager and personality, was now huge. In 1965 Christmas greetings to fans in the entertainment papers, the list included the Beatles, Gerry and the Pacemakers, Cilla Black, Billy J. Kramer with the Dakotas, the Fourmost, Sounds Incorporated, the Moody Blues, Tommy Quickly, the Remo Four, Cliff Bennett and the Rebel Rousers, the Silkie, the Rustiks, Paddy, Klaus and Gibson, Michael Haslam, the Paramounts—"and Brian Epstein."

During one of his gambling evenings with Burns, Brian proposed taking over Burns's organization, and he found Tito receptive. "The idea was a good one because he wanted to be free to walk about and be the figurehead," says Burns, "which he was good at, but his business side wasn't that great." Epstein's plan was that Burns would be bought out and that Tito would join the combined company with part ownership of the agency side of it. Burns would be chairman, with Brian as managing director. Over about a dozen lunches and dinners, the two men enthused—Brian, as ever, relishing the grand plan, Burns typically hot on the deal itself. He said: "Brian, let's work out all the details *before* we go into it. Let's not say: We'll talk about it afterwards. If we can't settle the finer details before we sign, there's no way we'll sort it out later."

Burns enthusiastically anticipated a huge pop empire in which NEMS would be able to call the shots to theaters and television companies from a great power base. "We could have said to the theaters, for instance: 'You're asking thirty-five percent of the gross. That's too much. You're taking liberties. Let's make a deal. If you talk about twenty-five percent, then we'll come. If not . . .' Look what we could have deprived them of! We could go to another theater group."

Epstein and Burns ordered their lawyers and accountants to work out a deal, but there were problems even as Burns and Epstein continued their talks. Burns, a skilled negotiator, refused to have his role challenged. Brian refused to concede that he would not have veto power over any of Tito's deals on behalf of NEMS. "If I'm running the agency, then my word is in that agency," Burns told him. "Presumably having got this far, I know what I'm doing. Nobody tells me where and how to do the deal. You, Brian, quite rightly *manage* those acts. If I say to you I've got a hell of a thing here, a million-dollar commercial for Coca-Cola for the Beatles, tell me if you are interested or not. But don't ever tell me how to make a deal, right?"

Says Burns: "Brian couldn't quite agree that he would have no say in how I did the deal. I couldn't take that. I maintained that once the principle is agreed, I will make the deal." What Brian secretly wanted was someone to put his business in order and run it correctly, "and when it came to the crunch *he* wanted to walk into the Coca-Cola office and say yes, I accept. He couldn't bear the thought," says Tito, "that I would be there saying it's a deal."

Brian's insecure personality was again colliding with his best business interests, and not serving him well. In the midst of their talks, Burns said there would have to be a delay, since he planned a holiday in the south of France. Epstein said he was also going to Aix-en-Provence; they could meet there and make more progress than their respective lawyers. In the beach restaurant of the Hotel Provençale at Juan-les-Pins, at the prearranged time of 4 p.m., Tito sat waiting for Brian. An hour later, when he had not arrived, Burns adjourned to his room. Shortly afterward, Brian knocked on his room door. "What the hell happened?" Burns asked.

"I heard from London that news of our meeting got out," said Epstein. "It was known that we were meeting at four o'clock."

Who cares? Burns asked. "I can't understand you. What are you hiding?"

Brian was furtive, sheepish, but said he didn't want people in London reaching conclusions. Tito Burns was baffled. Recalls Burns now: "He felt he was a big star and nobody should know we were meeting. I said: 'What's the big deal? Don't you think someone could have seen you coming into this room here? That would be even worse!' " Realizing he had manufactured an artificial drama, Epstein said they could talk there and then. No, said Burns. He could not leave his daughter on her own while they sat and talked. They would have to wait until they returned to London.

Back in London, the talks continued at Brian's office in Argyll

Street. John Lennon, knowing the pressure on Epstein, told Burns he hoped the merger happened. Brian continued to balk at Burns's adamant contention that he needed autonomy over the deal-making machinery. "Nobody wanted to sell the Beatles over his head," says Burns, "but it made sense to use their power as a bargaining tool." All Burns sought was the right to go to Brian, ask for his acceptance of a good offer, and then go back and complete a deal. "He couldn't quite see that. He didn't want to lose that little bit of control he had with them."

Next, Burns said that the first thing he would do was open a NEMS office in New York. They would need only two people to staff it, an agent and a secretary, and they would get the 15 percent commission instead of giving it away. "Which is in fact our money, Brian . . . you never know what happens with another agent in America who perhaps is selling his crap off on the backs of our big stars." Burns's logical argument underlined various dangers that faced anyone in show business: a hired agent in America could easily "throw their rubbish on to the bill and get commission from them, as well as furthering the careers of their people instead of ours." Why not put the Beatles out in America with Cilla, Gerry, Billy J. Kramer, and others? he told Epstein. "Send them all in! Let them be seen! With a bit of luck they'll get picked up . . . but Brian couldn't see it."

"Don't you realize, Brian," Burns said to Epstein, "the office will not only pay for itself, it will make money, and you're in control! It's *ours*. They will do what we say. They won't say to us: Listen, this is the best we can get you. We tell them no, you go and get this amount."

Burns saw that Epstein was scared. Perhaps the confidence, the knowledge born of tough experience, and the sheer hardheadedness of Tito were too much for him. On the American question, it was clear that Brian did not want to relinquish his status as manager—the pride of walking into a major agency office in New York, such as General Artists Corporation, and getting the red carpet treatment. If he arrived at his own office, he would not be so feted. He might also have had to jettison his plan to go into business in New York with Nat Weiss, and Nat was a close friend. Where it was humanly possible, Brian wanted to be in business alongside real allies.

Flanked by their lawyers and accountants in Epstein's office one night, Brian and Tito became heated. Tito would not budge on a contract which he saw as essential to his working ethic. "I said: 'It looks as though we're not going to make it.' And Brian said: 'In that case I think we had better just forget it.' " There were too many fundamental problems. "We're going to hate each other and it's silly," Burns told Epstein. Shortly afterward, Tito's organization was absorbed by the mighty Grade Organisation, where Burns became a director. He later joined MAM, the organization that ran the successful careers of Tom Jones, Engelbert Humperdinck, and Gilbert O'Sullivan.

"He was telling me we were partners but he was the boss!" reflects Burns. "He was saying I was in charge until he said I wasn't. His intentions were all right but he couldn't let go.

"There was no bitterness. I loved him too much. I was sad. It could have been the beginning of a huge empire. But even when we were arguing, there were no daggers," says Tito Burns. "He was a likable, lovable, sweet person. He was naive, but that added to his likability."

Brian did not consider himself a good agent: the "money-collecting" role was too hard-edged for him. He conceded all his critics' points on the subject of money-making. "I don't think I'm very clever at making money. I'm not a fool but I'm not a financial genius. I'm sensitive, I think, and of all the things which hurt me, giving people bad advice hurts most. I'm much more careful about judging people now, and quite prepared to change my first opinion. I'm not easily conned."

The image and reputation he still craved was as "Eppy," his artists' friend and personal manager. The money would flow in naturally from their talent, the public demand, and his flair in planning career strategies. He also wanted to be able to give his artists proper attention, and big show business agencies with hundreds of artists on their books were devoid of the personal touch, he observed. "If you've got the gift, you can delegate, but you can't delegate and keep in personal touch." That was his reason for rejecting the role of agent for himself. But as his addictive streak brought more acts into his organization, his time became scarce, his behavior became erratic, and his performance became blurred. He clung firmly to his philosophy of excellence, however, and his enthusiasms remained undimmed.

He firmly believed that quality and commerciality won through, without hype. The same conviction that had fired him at the Cavern held true when in mid-1966 he had a letter published in the *Times*. "It is not entirely true that singles become favourites through highly commercialised exposure to the public," said Epstein in response to the newspaper's survey of the pop scene. "I believe that a disc of real merit, and here I mean of course one that genuinely appeals to the public buying such discs, will become a hit through just the minimum of plays on either the recognised or pirate wavelengths.

"And it is not difficult to obtain play for a disc of such merit even without the pressure of the interested parties. Possibly this sounds somewhat puristic and, in any event, when I am concerned with a record my organisation will pull out all the stops in order to promote. And such promotion will undoubtedly contribute to the artist generally. However, hit for hit, that is my belief."

A record promotion campaign in Britain in the 1960s was short and simple. It consisted of sending single records to television's "Juke Box Jury," "Thank Your Lucky Stars," and "Ready Steady Go!" and to the radio's "Housewives Choice," "Junior Choice," "Saturday Club," "Easy Beat," "Two-Way Family Favourites," and Radio Luxembourg. If any three played the record, it virtually resulted in a hit.

Brian's "hit intelligence" may have placed a touching faith in the ability of a hit to win through, but it was soundly based: he had the twofold experience of record retailing and artist management, as well as the social friendship of top disc jockeys: Kenny Everett, Alan Freeman, Brian Matthew, Chris Denning, and Tony Hall in Britain, and Murray the K in New York. In the innocence and enthusiasm of 1960s pop, their ears were finely attuned to potential hits, and they earned more power to create hits than their inane, musically bankrupt successors of the 1970s and '80s. Epstein kept their company and used them as an impeccable grapevine, never losing his enthusiasm for the medium of the single, whatever strides his artists made with albums. And once he had left Liverpool to live in London, he phoned his old Whitechapel shop on most Saturdays to check which records were the fastest sellers.

Television and radio producers, familiar with managers grumbling about their fees, noticed that Epstein was different: for him, the need for exposure was the prime consideration. Johnny Hamp at Granada TV in Manchester recalls that his first fee to the Beatles was a mere £12 each. "Brian was astute: he just wanted them on the show." Three years later, with the Beatles established as world-beaters, Epstein still considered presentational quality more important than money. He agreed with Hamp on a fee of £1000 for a program devoted to the music of Lennon and McCartney for which Brian could have named his price. The program went on to earn large sums internationally for twenty years, and to critics of Epstein in 1965 it had been deemed a weak giveaway, another example of his "soft" dealing. But driving tough bargains had been left behind in his early days in the Merseyside clubs. Quality and consolidation mattered most.

When new records were released, many managers appointed themselves promotion men, relentlessly plugging the product. Epstein never did this. It was, he maintained, beneath his dignity to do what the record company was paid and equipped to do. And he had contempt for most disc jockeys, whose banality was matched by self-importance and ignorance. The only British exceptions to Brian's disinterest in the breed as professionals were Alan Freeman, with his boyish, infectious enthusiasm, and Brian Matthew, a cool professional.

On the eve of the Beatles' first American visit, Brian phoned Freeman one Sunday and asked him to lunch en route to the BBC, where Freeman was presenting his weekly hit show "Pick of the Pops." Brian sent his chauffeured Bentley to collect a puzzled Freeman, who knew Brian chiefly by reputation. Brian asked Freeman if he would like to be the Beatles' personal disc jockey and compere during their forthcoming U.S. tour. Freeman, flattered, said that that would be "rather wild," but why him, in a land where thousands of disc jockeys would qualify? "Because the boys are so zany, and you are older, while you are mid-Atlantic in your style," Brian answered. "I love the way you disc-jockey and I think I could launch you in America." After a stunned silence, Alan said that since he had an agent, Bunny Lewis, any deal would have to be done through him. Brian said he would talk to him again about it, and his limousine took Freeman to the BBC after lunch. Nothing further was heard of the idea by Freeman, who believes his talk of a commercial deal may have squashed Brian's enthusiasm.

11

❑

THE SLOPE

"LIVING ON BORROWED ADRENALINE"

I<small>F</small> 1963 <small>AND</small> 1964 <small>WERE YEARS OF ACHIEVEMENT</small> and euphoria, the last two and a half years of his life were rife with frenzied, self-inflicted, and ultimately damaging pressure. Paradoxically, these same years were his artists' most creative. With their scuffling over, they were free to flower as songwriters and studio performers, charting the evolution of pop music into album-orientated rock.

Brian's forays into the world of gambling became habitual. The Bentley parked in Berkeley Square stayed there until the early hours as Brian won or lost thousands of pounds playing chemin de fer or baccarat in Mayfair's clubs. Tito Burns introduced him to such clubs as the Curzon House, a particular favorite. "He gambled pretty heavily and it wasn't fivers or tenners. But he wasn't a fool. If he comfortably lost maybe two or three hundred pounds, that was fine. It was a lot of money in those days." Significantly, Brian kept a physical distance from other gamblers, never sitting at the table as though entrenched for the night. "He always stood at the back and just called out," says Burns.

At other gambling centers, the Clermont and Crockford's, Brian's love of great food and wine became well known. "He would order the most tremendous meals," says Geoffrey Ellis, who accompanied him

241

several times. "Then he would affect great surprise when told there was no bill for the dinner. Because they knew he was going to lose a few thousand on the tables."

George Harrison and his wife Pattie, holiday guests of Brian and his parents at Cap d'Estelle in the south of France, saw a different gambler. "He was absolutely brilliant on the tables in Monte Carlo," Pattie remembers. "He played several games, a lot of roulette, and he'd win an absolute fortune." He was something of a Pied Piper: "A lot of people would see where Brian was placing his bets and follow him. Once he realized this, he would stop and go to another table."

Brian booked Pattie and George into a private villa attached to the beautiful hotel. "It was very romantic and I remember feeling very grown up," says Pattie. "Brian told us he had stayed there with his parents when he was a boy. He let me know that he really enjoyed life in the south of France."

His mother found his grand style incongruous. Queenie knew a Brian who enjoyed simple home comforts: "I was more used to seeing Brian picking at a chicken in the kitchen than ordering gourmet meals." Realizing his change, Queenie once jested to Harry on a trip to France that Brian would not approve of their chosen hotel "because it's only got one concierge." It seemed too simple for Brian's sophisticated taste, but he approved. His parents knew Brian enjoyed gambling; he visited casinos with his father. But they had little clue of the frequency of his habit.

Gerry Marsden warned Brian that his gambling was accelerating dangerously. "He'd win eleven thousand pounds one night and lose fifteen thousand the next. I used to tell him he was stupid but Brian got a kick out of it and it *was* his money!"

❑

Several observers ascribe the reason for Brian's depression and mood swings to one particular day: on October 26, 1965, the Queen invested the Beatles with their MBE medals at Buckingham Palace. Brian was not honored. He felt the reason could be that he was known to be a homosexual or that he was a Jew.

He had to endure jibes by people insensitive to his wounded pride.

A serious Epstein talking to impresarios Tom Arnold (left) and Bernard Delfont (now Lord Delfont) after becoming the controlling leaseholder of London's Saville Theatre. It was the start of a big financial problem for Brian; ironically the big deal was made on April 1, 1965, April Fool's Day. *(Times Newspapers)*

With Eamonn Andrews during a television interview on May 23, 1965. Asked his ambition, Brian said his greatest wish was to act in a play. He inscribed this print to his parents: "M and D: Thought you might like this one. Love, Brian." *(ABC Television)*

With his latest signing, the vocal-instrumental trio Paddy, Klaus and Gibson, in 1965. *(The Photo Source)*

Just off to the races, on the patio of his Knightsbridge flat in 1965.
(Epstein family collection)

Another hotel, another tour: John Lennon with Brian and his personal assistant Wendy Hanson in Genoa, Italy, 1965. *(Wendy Hanson)*

Brian's secretary Joanne Newfield. *(Joanne Newfield)*

At the world premiere of their film *Help!*, the Beatles and Brian are presented to Princess Margaret and Lord Snowdon at the London Pavilion, July 29, 1965. *(Press Association)*

Backstage at New York's Shea Stadium, on August 15, 1965, during the Beatles' triumph. Brian calmly reads a paper while police and officials plan to cope with the 55,600 fans. *(The Photo Source)*

At Shea Stadium, a pensive Brian makes a list of songs backstage; shares a dressing room drink with Ringo; and takes his frequent position alongside the stage. *(Keystone Press/The Photo Source)*

Gambling with hundred dollar bills while on tour in America with the Beatles, 1965.
(The Photo Source)

Holidaying in the south of France:
Brian strolling in Nice with his
guests Pattie Boyd and George
Harrison on September 18, 1965,
and photographing the action with
them at a bullfight in Arles.
(Associated Press/Rex Features)

As vice president of the Finchley (London) Jewish Youth Club, Brian receives an engraved trophy from the members on September 7, 1965.
(R. Brewster/Hendon Times)

The best man toasts Gerry Marsden and his bride Pauline Behan, his fan club secretary, after their wedding at St. Mary's Church, Woolton, Liverpool, on October 11, 1965.
(Gerry Marsden)

A break from making the promotional film for the record "Paperback Writer" at Chiswick House, London, May 19, 1966. *(Keystone Press)*

Arriving at New York's Kennedy airport, August 6, 1966, to "assess the situation" after John Lennon's statement that the Beatles were "more popular than Jesus" had caused an uproar. *(John Topham)*

In the office of his New York friend and partner Nat Weiss, Brian drafts his speech for the press conference to explain Lennon's controversial comment. *(Nat Weiss)*

With Beatles producer George Martin at Portmeirion, North Wales, in August 1966; Brian had gone there to recuperate from glandular fever. *(George and Judy Martin)*

The Beatles at a press conference at Brian's Saville Theatre on October 26, 1965, after receiving MBE medals from the Queen at Buckingham Palace. Brian is flanked by Neil Aspinall, the Beatles' road manager. *(Associated Press)*

At the end of a troubled year, Brian radiates happiness as he visits his beloved Cilla Black in her dressing room at London's Prince of Wales Theatre. She starred in the revue *Way Out in Piccadilly* in November 1966. *(David Magnus/Rex Features)*

America's Four Tops were one of Brian's favorite acts. He is pictured after presenting them at his Saville Theatre on November 10, 1966. *(Syndication International)*

Standing amid the debris of the Saville Theatre the day after fans rioted at a Chuck Berry concert on February 20, 1967. *(BBC Hulton Picture Library)*

Brian adopts the appearance of the flowerpower era, March 1967. *(John Topham)*

Outside his country house,
Kingsley Hill, near Uckfield,
Sussex, in July 1967. It was
a retreat Brian hardly had a
chance to visit.
(Syndication International)

A week before his death,
Brian entertains his New
York friend Nat Weiss at
the pub in the mews
behind his house.
(Nat Weiss)

Brian sent these two pictures, taken a few days before his death, to Nat Weiss. He looks debilitated and uncharacteristically unkempt, lying in the sun on the roof of his house at 24 Chapel Street, Belgravia, London. *(Nat Weiss)*

(Clive Epstein)

When Epstein went to dinner at the Mirabelle with Geoffrey Ellis, a leading actor at the next table, under the influence of drink, taunted: "Look at that little boy over there . . . he couldn't get an MBE!" Epstein coolly ignored it and the actor was hustled out of the restaurant. Unconsciously striking a chord that comforted Brian, Paul McCartney told a press conference that MBE stood for Mister Brian Epstein. Such delicious word-play was precisely in tune with Brian's sense of humor, and he enjoyed repeating the story to friends for months.

A month after the Beatles' award, Brian was confined to his bed for three weeks with yellow jaundice. This caused him to cancel a trip to the United States to negotiate the sale of the Beatles' Shea Stadium concert film to television companies.

Throughout 1965, Brian had been constantly in attendance on Beatles tours, darting in and out of towns to catch up with them. He stood at the side of the stage, arms folded, eyes transfixed, unwilling to exchange even a nod with anyone who came near. His concentration on every aspect of a Beatles show was total, from the lights to the sound, from the running order of the songs to their clothes, from their stage banter to the positioning of the microphones. The delighted, possessive smile on his face became a snapshot of the euphoria of the period. "But I noticed the difference in 1966," says Tony Barrow. "Then, he was steering clear. Apart from when he was indisposed, he was actually avoiding being around too much because there were more likely to be confrontations with the Beatles that year.

"Things were turning nasty. When he turned up and swept into a dressing room, instead of being greeted, he was usually turned upon. Quite often it was semifacetious but it became increasingly serious. He would make an entrance into a dressing room and hope to throw down a publication that had a Beatles front cover. He'd say 'I've got you this' or 'Here's the new album sleeve.' But far too often he'd now be cut off in his prime by somebody tackling him about something. And he hated to be *tackled*. He hated it on a one-to-one basis. He hated it even more on a three- or four-to-one basis."

Wendy Hanson, Brian's assistant for the Beatles' U.S. tours, believes he stayed away from his new personal office, in Mayfair, because he was frightened of making mistakes. His home became his base.

His secretary, Joanne Newfield, loyal and intuitive, loved her boss dearly but found his "mood swings" exasperating and worrying. She "covered" hundreds of times for his absences and inability to keep appointments. Says Tony Barrow: "If the Beatles hadn't seen him for a while for whatever reason, the more stick he got when he did come, because it had been piling up waiting for him."

Brian often went alone to the French or Italian Riviera for short holiday breaks. And be became lonely. Once he telephoned Wendy Hanson from Monte Carlo and, on the pretense of having some papers for her attention, invited her to the south of France. "He really was just very lonely," she recalls. "We went over to Monte Carlo, where he took me to Hermes and bought me a handbag." At night they went gambling. "He gave me a hundred pounds. When I made it up to three hundred from winnings, I said I was going home. He couldn't understand why I'd stopped gambling when I was winning."

Yet there was a contradictory streak in his nature, and when it got the upper hand, even a trusted aide like Wendy would sometimes be reduced to the rank of serf. "Who's going to come to the studio with me to help me sign by Christmas cards?" Brian asked a few months after Wendy had joined him.

"Well, I'm not," she replied tersely.

"What do you mean, you're *not?*"

"Well, I'm not your secretary. And you can sign your own cards, Brian. The envelopes are done and you don't need somebody there to *help* you."

Wendy Hanson became used to judging Brian's moods, which ranged from mercurial and ecstatic to despondent and inconsolably depressed. As Brian became less predictable and more irritable, Wendy found his "mood swings" very distressing. "I didn't understand about drugs," she says. In a hilarious faux pax, she said to Paul McCartney: "I don't know what's wrong with Brian."

"What do you mean?" asked Paul.

"Well, he's being *very* odd."

"He's on a trip," the Beatle explained.

"No, he's not. He's in London," Wendy said, innocently. Says Wendy now: "I didn't understand what a trip was."

The incident became a Beatles joke during their next American tour: "Where's Brian, Wendy? Is he on a trip or is he in London?"

High on adrenaline but needing sleep, Brian began taking sleeping pills to slow him down and stimulants to get him moving. The combination of these, together with a regular daily intake of wine and cognac, began to take its toll.

At Chapel Street, Joanne Newfield soon had to abolish her routine working schedule of 10 a.m. to 6 p.m. "Some mornings I'd arrive and he'd been up since eight. 'Where have you been? You're late for work,' he'd say. Other days, I'd get there early and he'd not rise until three in the afternoon and he'd have me working half the night. Sometimes it was obvious he was lonely and wanted company; I'd stay in the guest room. He'd obviously thought up reasons for me to work late and I'd end up having dinner with him. I knew from his diary why he was working late. It was empty."

Joanne and Wendy both knew he was homosexual. "I knew he was gay the minute I saw him," says Wendy. "He never told me, but he knew I knew. It bothered me when people came into his life and took advantage, making him unhappy. I would have liked for him to find somebody whom he could have lived with. He was frightened the Beatles would find out he was gay, which of course they knew."

Brian told Joanne about his homosexuality one night over dinner at Chapel Street. It made no difference in her adoration of her boss. There were times, she reflects, when she wondered what would happen to her young life. "I was totally hooked into being around him. It was really awful. I was hooked yet it wasn't always enjoyable or plain sailing."

So relaxed did Brian feel in Joanne's company that he took her to the Variety Club Ball at London's Dorchester Hotel. "He was absolutely the perfect escort. He became very comfortable with me." Much later, during one of their "after hours" dinners at Chapel Street, Brian became maudlin: "I don't know, I'm just no good with anyone. I just can't have a relationship." Adds Joanne: "I think that deep down he didn't want to be gay."

There were so few sympathetic ears. Brian had to confront most of his emotional crises privately or bury them. When he looked for someone to listen to his cris de coeur, rarely was anyone compassionate enough on hand at the right moment.

One such crisis occurred during his stay at the Beverly Hills Hotel in Los Angeles. Brian had struck up a particularly warm rapport in

London with Berenice Kinn, wife of the owner of the *New Musical Express*. An ebullient, intuitive Jewess, she and husband Maurice formed part of the core of London's 1960s show business hosts and partygoers. Brian was a frequent visitor to their flat in Lowndes Square, near his Knightsbridge home. At such functions, Brian stood apart from the cigar-toting egotists, fired primarily by profit, who formed the backbone of the British entertainment establishment until he broke the rules. "He did not have a very pushy personality," says Berenice Kinn. "There was something shrewd about him but he was completely different. He was also very shy." Later on, she would perceive his apparent shyness as a cover for his homosexuality.

That night in California, the phone call at 11 P.M. from Epstein's hotel bungalow to the Kinn suite in the main hotel was not for the influential Maurice, but for his wife. Brian had earlier escorted her to a private screening of *My Fair Lady* in Los Angeles. She was in bed when Brian asked her to go across and visit him. Approaching Brian's bungalow, running the gauntlet of security men and police hiding behind trees, Berenice was immediately struck by the pungent smell of marijuana wafting from his apartment. "Brian, what are you *doing?*" she asked on entering. "You are well known, an important man. Are you going to allow yourself to be busted *here?*"

It soon became obvious that that was his least significant worry. Red-faced and emotionally charged, he was "terribly sad, weeping as he sipped away at a drink." He told Berenice of a broken relationship that upset him deeply. And he needed a shoulder to cry on. Not for the first time, Berenice recalls, Brian unburdened to her his inner turmoil: "He was a very troubled person. I honestly felt that a lot of it came from the fact that he was gay and he came from a Jewish background. Indeed, he said so. I think he had Jewish guilt from the beginning, and because he was gay he reacted to it more like a woman does."

Loneliness, Brian once said, was his biggest fear—"although one inflicts loneliness on oneself to a great extent." In one of his most significant remarks, he observed that the Beatles "always make an effort to involve me in what they're doing." It was said with the air of pathos that was always audible when he touched upon one of his own raw nerves. Asked by interviewer Mike Hennessey in London's

Melody Maker if he had ever contemplated suicide, Brian replied: "Yes. But I think I've got over that period now."

❏

With his pop empire established faster than he dared hope, Brian reverted to his first love, the theater. His love of the stage had never faltered. Now, as an established impresario, he had an alternative to acting: owning a theater and having creative control over its presentations.

This move proved to be easier than expected. He now had good communication with Bernard Delfont, one of the czars of London show business, and on April 1, 1965, after short negotiations, Brian became the leaseholder the Saville Theatre in Shaftesbury Avenue.

Epstein was thrilled but slightly worried, the joy of running his own theater tempered by fears about its viability and the time it would demand of him. So he did not gleefully walk around announcing his latest project. He let news of the grand acquisition drift out, even to his staff. In a bizarre omission, Brian failed to tell John Lyndon, his production director, either that he planned to take over the Saville or that he had bought it. He waited for Lyndon to react to the national news of his venture, which would form a huge part of Lyndon's job.

Brian expected Lyndon to mention the project to him, but Lyndon played it coolly, remaining silent. Finally, one night, Brian phoned him: "Well, you know all about the Saville Theatre, that I've bought it?"

"I hope you've done a good deal on it," Lyndon said.

Brian was brusque. "That is beside the point. I want to present lovely things on Sunday nights. I want to make it *marvelous*. Just like the Apollo in Harlem.* That will be its image. I want Shaftesbury Avenue to really vibrate on Sunday nights and I know you can do it for me."

The Saville was a white elephant, a drain on Brian's resources from the start. To stand any chance of booking plays into it, he would have to visit the provinces and try to catch commercially viable shows before

*The New York theater that was the starting point for many major pop names in the 1960s.

other theaters did. But too often Brian's artistic preferences triumphed over his commercial instincts.

Gerry Marsden, advising him against his Saville investment, was as blunt as ever. "It's daft. You're going to screw yourself." Undeterred, Brian said it would be the grand mecca for pop music from Britain, which ruled the world.

Another project was a link with disc jockey Brian Matthew, who shared his love of the theater. They teamed up to propose a new theater at Farnborough, Kent, at a cost of £38,000. The main purpose would be a three-month festival of new and classic plays performed by leading players, intended for eventual transfer to London's West End. But the plan to build the two Brians' Pilgrim Theatre ended when the local council refused planning permission.

His appetite whetted by the Saville venture, Epstein wanted to confirm his talent for theatrical production. He decided to present *A Smashing Day*, a play by Alan Plater, at the New Arts Theatre Club, off Leicester Square, London, on February 16, 1966. He appointed as director John Fernald, the head of RADA, who had admitted Brian into the academy when he yearned to be an actor. Few projects had excited Brian so much as this play; his interest was so great that he told Joanne to take all his paperwork to the theater during rehearsals, since he would see every one.

The cast included Hywel Bennett, and the percussionists at the side of the stage were Robert Powell and Ben Kingsley, all three later to achieve fame. Just two days before the play's opening, when Fernald became ill, Brian readily agreed to take over the production and supervise final rehearsals.

At noon, with Brian due, the assembled cast was awaiting his arrival. By 3 p.m. he still had not arrived. Joanne, responding to an alarmed phone call from Vyvienne Moynihan, buzzed him on the intercom at Chapel Street. "Brian, you were meant to have been at the theater . . ."

"I'm sick," he answered, sounding tearful and emotional. "I'm very sick and I can't go. I have the flu. Please leave me alone."

Joanne told Vyvienne, who was facing a confused and demoralized cast. She was not prepared to accept Brian's withdrawal. Racing over to Chapel Street, she buzzed him on his intercom, to his astonishment. "What are *you* doing here?" he said.

"Brian, you can do it," she began. "We really need you badly."
He ended her pleas by switching off his intercom. But Joanne noticed
that he quickly turned it on again, that he would overhear her "play
acting" in an attempt to win him round: "What *are* we going to do
without him?" said Vyvienne.

The ploy worked. After a while, Brian appeared, immaculately
dressed but looking exhausted. "It had been utter fear," says Joanne.
"He was terrified of his big moment in the theater, and his body had
become so resistant to very strong pills. That caused him to feel zonked
out when he woke up." The thought of *A Smashing Day* landing in
his lap was too much for him. But Brian responded when assured that
he was essential to its existence.

His instructions to the actors were cogent and decisive. "Brian made
no sweeping changes. It was not a difficult play to produce," says
Bennett. "He liked the idea of taking it over. There seemed no
reluctance. It was, after all, his money that was invested in the play.
He saw it as a career step." ("Everything he touched was turning to
gold around that time," adds Bennett, who socialized with him at the
Pickwick Club.) Brian's enthusiasms were contagious among the press;
he persuaded Lennon and Ringo to attend the first night and filled
the theater with his friends from the pop world. The Beatles noted
that Eppy had rarely looked so happy.

The play was a creative high spot in Brian's life. At last he was
credibly involved in the legitimate stage. But the play was doomed
in the 300-seat theater. "Nothing had gone wrong for Brian until
that moment," says Bennett, reflecting on the immediate knowledge
that *A Smashing Day* was *not* going to be a smash. "Nobody knew
what the future held for him, but I knew he was a creature of
extremes who suffered depressions. It was all or nothing with
Brian."

Bennett witnessed an overnight change in Brian. At 2 a.m., after
the opening and the party, with everyone in a state of relief, Brian
insisted that someone drive him to Fleet Street to buy the morning
papers so that he could check the reviews. "They were not bad," says
Bennett, "but not unqualified raves. Brian was very naive; he did not
take failure well. When he read these, he was deeply distressed; he
had it all out of proportion. *A Smashing Day* was a very small play on
show in the right place. It was going to play to fairly small audiences."

Brian, as always, had delusions of theatrical power and saw his production as momentous.

After the lukewarm reviews, Epstein almost totally withdrew from the project. "On the second night," says Hywel Bennett, "he came into my dressing room and subjected me to an hour saying everything was my fault. One night he was giving me the world, the next he was really distressed, having a tantrum and saying he didn't *need* the theater. He had these extremes." Brian was unable to qualify the lack of success by writing it off as "good fun."

Next day the old Brian was back and he took Hywel to his hairdresser. Epstein's hair had been restyled, and Hywel, back at Chapel Street, had complimented Brian on it. "I actually said: 'That's great. You should wear your hair that way.' He blushed as red as a beetroot. I'd never seen that in a man. I realized it was a very dangerous thing to say to Brian. I was naive."

A Smashing Day ran for a month, during which Brian hardly showed up at the theater. "He was like a spoiled child when he realized it was not a great success," says Bennett. "He had no apparatus in himself to deal with it." So, on that opening night, faced with poor reviews, he "tried to apportion blame." It was, muses Bennett, "rather a feminine trait. There was a very feminine side to him—not bitchy, but he could not take failure well. He had a lot of success but he was subject to moods and depressions."

After the demise of *A Smashing Day*, Bennett did not encounter Brian until several months later, when Brian invited him to lunch. "I had made the film *The Family Way*, and they were approaching Paul McCartney to write the music. I think Brian wanted to show me he was still in charge; at lunch he was talking about whether he was going to allow Paul to write the music or not.

"I shall always think warmly of Brian Epstein. He was the kind of person one had to keep at arm's length, because our sexual preferences were very different. There was a weak side to him when things did not go his way. My brush with him was brief but I wouldn't have missed it."

❑

In his office or his home, in public or in private, the quiet tone of Brian's voice gave little away. Instantly identifiable on the telephone, it could be soporific during meetings or interviews. Only rarely could Brian's inner moods be detected from his posture. Only his blushing face, which he tried to hide, revealed his fundamental shyness, his exposed vulnerability.

And these symptoms increased. A uniquely powerful figure on the energetic and competitive 1960s pop scene, he felt at once intoxicated by the pleasure of his role and pressured by the multifaceted responsibilities he had inflicted on himself. Life at the helm was heady; for a man who had made his own wish come only too true, it was also threatening. For Brian, a patient strategist who was also attracted by life in the fast lane, the pace of his activities was too potent. He trusted few colleagues, yet retained the work ethic so forcefully that an internal battle with his hedonism was inevitable. How he wished that his brother had joined him in the move to London! Clive's stability would have provided the cornerstone of his complex network of companies. But he was needed to run the still-thriving Liverpool business.

Making deals, worrying about the smallest details of the concert and recording careers of his beloved artists, defusing their capriciousness while sitting atop his empire—all this gave Brian no respite. The self-inflicted intensity of his work was a hedge against his loneliness and the realization that what he cherished, his own family, was unattainable.

Some of Brian's friends and staff theorize that the crises surrounding the Beatles in 1966 were the biggest cause of his deepening malaise. Not only was their talent in full flower, but they were now experienced, wise, decisive: the superficiality of pop stardom had been absorbed and enjoyed, and it was a time for consolidation. Epstein's pioneering work, which had taken them from Hamburg and Liverpool to London and around the world, was complete. But it would be demonstrably inaccurate to say that the Beatles no longer needed him and that he felt rejected. Despite their lack of sentiment or expression, they leaned on him, albeit in a different way. He was one of the few people in the world they all trusted. They knew he was betrothed to them, that they were his substitute family. More than a manager, he had assumed the relationship of their older brother.

What really caused problems in the last eighteen months of his life was his own insecurity, which in turn caused him to fail to structure his new business satisfactorily. The work was mounting up, but Brian was uneasy about the people in his organization; and now that the Beatles had entered a new phase, he certainly had to reevaluate his role with them.

Coupled with these pressures was the inner loneliness. Whom could he turn to, apart from his mother, father, and brother? And even they could not be expected to penetrate the private wall Brian had built around himself. His lack of a lasting relationship, a cause of sadness to Queenie when she accepted Brian's homosexuality, meant that Brian faced all his worries in solitude.

The changes in his behavior began not as a result of the Beatles' changing tempo but at least six months earlier. At Chapel Street, his secretary knew he was taking slimming tablets as uppers and other pills as downers, hoping to balance the two but often failing; in fact, he had become a compulsive pill taker. Joanne remembers him taking more of the white slimming pills than she thought safe. "I had taken the same tablets myself, and I knew I would be up awake for two nights if I took a half. Brian took a whole one, often." He told her he took them to check his weight. "He was very weight-conscious. He could get heavy if he wasn't careful. He used to eat and drink a lot. I don't think he was fit; he used to put too much stuff into his body and never took any exercise." Joanne saw a man "living on borrowed adrenaline." And she became accustomed to his regular mood swings: "He would go from being really nice, with a lovely warm, benevolent, and kindly look on his face, to being cold, arrogant, and superior." Often this was the result of drug use.

Brian would often rub the enamel off his teeth when he rubbed blue tablets, uppers and downers, to grind them down. "He seemed to do that instead of chewing them," says John Lyndon, his production director. Yet Lyndon, like most of his staff, never saw him smoke marijuana. "When he knew certain people wouldn't approve, he kept them at a slight distance," says Lyndon. "With some of us he never wanted to be seen to be less than straight."

Brian's edginess about drugs was emphasized when Wendy Hanson once went with him and the Beatles to the Ad Lib club in Soho. "It was very late and I was very hungry. I took a handful of peanuts. Brian grabbed my hand and said: 'Don't *do* that!' " She thought he had gone mad. She asked: "What did you think it was?" Brian said he really thought she was swallowing a handful of pills.

He lived in fear of being "busted" for drugs, particularly after so many pop stars—including some of his friends, like members of the Rolling Stones—had been arrested. At Chapel Street, for a period, he feared the police were keeping watch or were about to arrive with a warrant; Brian ordered that the entire house, including all the drawers, be thoroughly vacuum-cleaned.

His mood fluctuations increased, Joanne remembers: "If he was in a black mood, you stayed out of his way. They were the worst and I'd close the door. I got to recognize the changes. First, he would not go into the office, or he'd come in simply to say I should cancel all appointments. And I could see quite easily that he had too much amphetamine in his system. He was speeding, overelated. And the other side would be deep depression. Brian's whole life was run by his moods, and everybody had to judge them."

Joanne never knew what to expect when she went to Chapel Street each morning. Would she find that dreaded note telling her to cancel all engagements? Would he be sleeping till early afternoon? The ritual of "covering" for him, plus her concern for his health, became a pressure. And there were uncharacteristic practical jokes. Joanne bounded up the stairs to her office one morning to be confronted by a life-size photo of Brian that he had fixed to the inside of her door. "When I closed the door, it was like he was standing there. I leapt out of my seat. He thought it was absolutely hilarious but I couldn't stand it." She had it painted over.

Some mornings, after a party, Joanne would spend hours putting records back in their sleeves, for while he admired tidiness, Brian certainly needed looking after. His notes to his secretary carried requests for attention to his needs but were often laced with an air of pathos:

> Jo
>
> What happened to crayons, charcoal, paints, board., etc. bought from Winsor and Newton?
>
> Good morning. Better late than never. Many happy returns of yesterday. Love, Brian. (Be a bit tolerant of me at my worst. Really, I don't like, or want, to hurt anybody.)
>
> Please inquire of a good photographic retailer if Polaroid camera techniques have improved. Can I have a camera that takes larger pictures . . . what advances have been made?

The latent but deep anger at himself for his tantrums was clear to Wendy Hanson. "The isolation, withdrawal from the world, and his feelings of guilt were terrible. Jewish guilt, homosexual guilt, and drugs guilt were all there."

It was the vacuum in his life that had provided the impetus to his magnificent obsessions: first the Beatles, who amply justified all his faith, and then his other artists and staff. "It wasn't that he was gay so much but that he was a bachelor—that's what allowed him the opportunity to fall in love with the lot of them and pour this passion into looking after their careers," says a friend, disc jockey Alan Freeman. "The manager needed to have no other ties, and all the love he would have given to anybody was given to the Beatles. That's why they really made their breakthrough."

Brian saw homosexuality "almost as a cause," says Nat Weiss. "In a way Brian thought New York had a certain amount of freedom, the people were much more liberal about it. And Brian was never attracted to other homosexuals. The people he liked were basically very macho, people like hard-hat construction workers and truck drivers."

New York homosexuals met in bars, in parks, in men's rooms, in subway stations. The bars were generally owned by very heavy-handed people, and homosexuality was illegal. Outside New York—which had Greenwich Village—the situation was probably worse.

"On his own he would like to go down to Times Square and have a look around. He went alone, which was dangerous. When I found out about it, I told him: 'Don't do that.' And so he stopped. He didn't like boys or men who were the slightest bit effeminate. He liked people who were basically straight, masculine men." Brian's attitude to his relationships surprised Weiss: "I'm amazed how forward he was."

Because he did not want to be publicly discovered to be a homosexual—and he worried about that—the legend of the Beatles may have rested on a very thin thread of luck. The adverse publicity would have been enormous.

"He was not a happy homosexual," says Joanne, his secretary. "In those days it was much harder to be gay: a stigma. It would have been great if he could have found someone to have a relationship with, and be happy. But he never found that. He was rich, young, famous, managing the Beatles, but basically a very lonely man." She saw turmoil and conflict inside him: "Deep down I think there was a real battle. When he had a really bad depression, he saw the collision happening and just headed straight towards it.

"He was always searching for love . . . and yet it was all around him. There was incredible love and loyalty for Brian. But he was so lonely, and he wasn't close to people. Maybe he didn't realize there were many people around him who did care for him. You could talk to him and sometimes you'd think he was on another planet, he was so aloof." Yet when he smiled, it was a warm smile. He told Joanne of the happiest moment of his life: standing at the side of the stage at Shea Stadium seeing the Beatles.

Alistair Taylor became saddened by the sight of Brian so obviously depressed. "Oh I'm so low, nothing is going right," Epstein said to him once. Taylor often found Brian transmitting such sad feelings. It affected him deeply "because I cared for him. He was a great man, and as a manager nobody came within a million miles of him."

"He seemed to be marginally lonely," says the British disc jockey David Jacobs, "but he was quiet, a gentlemanly sort of person, always correctly turned out and extremely well-mannered as only a well-to-do, middle-class, Jewish, provincial, successful businessman could be. Quite like a fish out of water with some of the managers who were around." Jacobs, compering functions that starred the Beatles, saw the protective Epstein enjoying the limelight, "but quite clearly it wasn't enough to make him happy."

He could afford to be open about his homosexuality with a trusted ally, like the London *Daily Mirror* reporter Don Short, because he knew there was no way, in the 1960s, that Short could write about it even if he wanted to. Among the Beatles, Short found Brian's private life a "nonconversational area," apart from inoffensive one-line jokes. Short, a confrontational reporter who often visited Chapel Street for evening vodkas to maintain his excellent relationship with Epstein, once asked Brian about the rumor of his affair with Lennon. "I've heard the story as well," Brian told him, "but it is simply not true, Don." Short, who darted in and out of most of the Beatles tours, observing the full extent of Lennon's heterosexuality, still discounts talk of a Brian-John liaison.

Brian was most comfortable with women when he knew they knew about his homosexuality, says Short. "But if there was another homosexual at the table, I sometimes found him slightly cloying. That's when I felt my time had expired and I should make my excuses and leave." A change overcame Epstein in those situations: "He became almost childish."

❑

Brian always made time for holidays, and within Europe no place eclipsed his beloved Spain, where he frequently went alone for a few days to attend bullfights. One such trip ignited a friendship with a Liverpool-born pianist who then lived in Rome. Dennis Wiley had first met Brian at a Merseyside party also attended by the actor Brian Bedford; on tour with a gospel-singing group, Wiley was reintroduced to Epstein in a gay bar in Barcelona. Telling Wiley of his immense pride in presenting James Baldwin's play *The Amen Corner* at the Saville Theatre, Brian enthused about Wiley's work with the black gospel-singing and dancing act. He would help them when he returned to London, he said.

The two men exchanged phone numbers, and the pianist next contacted Brian from his new home in Milan in 1966. Wiley, impressed by a "very pleasant, charming guy, socially awfully nice," arrived in London that Christmas and met Brian a few times, accompanying him to the Saville Theatre to see Georgie Fame and also going to his house for a pre–New Year's Eve party. The evening remains firmly in Wiley's memory: "I remember the fattest, most enormous hash cigarettes I have ever seen being passed round. I was on a 'downer' when I smoked one and it affected me badly. Brian had told me he had to take pills to get to sleep and also to get up in the morning. With the touring and the wild social life he led, it must have been a terrible strain."

If the pressure was apparent to a passing acquaintance like Dennis Wiley, it was glaringly obvious to Epstein's inner circle.

One of Brian's most emotional encounters was, uncharacteristically, with one of his artists. On their regular visits to the Pickwick Club in Great Newport Street, Leicester Square, the Beatles had been impressed with a trio named Paddy, Klaus and Gibson. The Beatles knew them as a melodic group who had also made the Hamburg club scene; individually, they were brighter than most musicians. Paddy Chambers, at twenty-three, was tall and rugged, an engaging conversationalist who had seen service with two top Liverpool Cavern bands, the Big Three and Faron's Flamingos. Klaus was Klaus Voormann, the accomplished Berlin-born artist who designed the cover for the Beatles *Revolver* album; he would later marry Astrid Kirchherr, the Hamburg girl who was engaged to Stuart Sutcliffe, known as the Fifth Beatle, who died before their fame. And Gibson Kemp was formerly with a major Liverpool band, King Size Taylor and the Dominoes; he would later become a key executive with a major record company in London.

Again, Epstein signed Paddy, Klaus and Gibson without considering whether he had time to cope. Although he negotiated them a contract with Pye Records and gave them each a £50-a-week retainer, he secured them very little live work. And yet he was proud, taking Queenie and Harry to see "my great new band."

"I basically don't think he gave the band *anything* in management. I don't think he had a clue," says Paddy Chambers. "But it was obvious after a while that he was getting emotionally very hung up on me, and I tried my best to cope with it." Chambers says that despite the fact that he was married, he was "quite sympathetic" to Brian's warmth while rejecting his advances. "I actually ended up in bed with him one day, but after about five minutes I said, 'Brian, I just can't handle this,' and I got up and walked out." Brian even asked Paddy and Joy Chambers to go and live with him at Chapel Street, in the basement apartment. They declined and stayed in Liverpool, but on his many visits to London, Paddy would see Brian and they remained "dead close friends."

One of Paddy's first meetings with Epstein was to serve as an example of Brian's tempestuous behavior. Before Brian bought the Chapel Street house, Paddy went to his Knightsbridge flat: "For some strange reason, and I suppose it had to be drugs, he was 'off his cake.' He just totally wrecked the whole, very expensive flat, ripped all the drapes down, smashed the cocktail cabinet to bits. He didn't tell me what it was all about but he freaked out. I didn't know him closely at the time."

Another tantrum occurred at the Chapel Street house, where one of the most unnerving aspects was the intercom in every room. Paddy, staying overnight in a spare bedroom, heard a furious row between Brian and a young drummer—not a member of one of Brian's acts but a regular friend. After hearing loud bangs, and records being smashed, through the audio system, Paddy decided he would have to investigate if the row continued for another minute. Then the front door slammed. The drummer was walking down the road with one of his shirtsleeves missing. "There had been a fight and Eppy had defended himself by ripping his shirtsleeve off."

While Voormann and Kemp "wanted to be as successful as they could in as short a time as possible," Brian found friendship in Chambers partly because they never talked business. "The reason Eppy chose me as a chum was the fact that I wasn't the slightest bit interested in that." Brian accepted him into the inner circle of friends and gave him a whiff of his lavish lifestyle. Recalls Chambers: "Once, Brian said: 'Oh, I had a bad night last night gambling. I lost twenty grand.' And I thought: Fucking hell, I'm skint! That could buy me a *house.*

"We got the fifty pounds a week from NEMS as a retainer whether we worked or not. And that's all we ever got because we never worked. It was a joke as far as the business was concerned, but I went along with the whole thing because I was having a hell of a lot of fun, socializing with the Beatles and Eppy in the clubs. Sad thing is, if Eppy had been around now I know he'd have been right behind me. I don't think we had enough time to do anything."

Brian had made no promises or statements about the group's potential. "He just tried his best with what he had available. But to be honest, the management side of things he completely cocked up. One thing's certain. When all that was going and he started to become a rich man, he started drinking heavily and taking drugs heavily and generally not keeping himself together. It may be that if you haven't got anything to fight for, you stop fighting."

During the period when the Beatles were making their *Sgt. Pepper* album, Paddy, visiting London, phoned Brian, who invited him to Chapel Street. "I've got a surprise for you," Epstein added.

"When I arrived the Beatles were there with their four respective wives or girlfriends. Eppy disappeared and came back with a big silver tray with a little sugar cube on it. Obviously I knew what it was." This was to be Paddy Chambers's first LSD trip. "When I popped my cube, Lennon was falling apart. They'd apparently been doing it for quite a while, and he said: 'I've got to see someone tripping for the first time.' "

Within a couple of hours, the party were hallucinating on the effects of LSD. "We were all ripping newspapers up and flung them all over the room." They talked dreamily about how beautiful the house was, particularly the huge lounge. Epstein disappeared and brought "tons of newspapers," and they were all "literally knee deep in newspaper, just falling about in it." Gradually, the Beatles party went home and Paddy stayed on in the spare room. "I was still tripping and there was only Eppy in the house. He pressed his intercom button. 'Are you still awake?' I said yes. I went to his room and we had several large vodkas and some sleeping tablets. We were trying to bring ourselves down a bit." It was apparently one of Brian's favorite methods of slowing himself down.

Another visitor to a small party in Chapel Street was Johnny Gustafson: "John Lennon was there and they were playing records. Everybody drifted off. Probably because I had to go back to my flat alone, I stayed the longest, hoping for another drink. I was looking out of the window and Brian put his arm around my shoulder. 'John,' he said, 'I could really help you, I could do a lot for you.' I said: 'I know that, Brian, but I couldn't do much for you though.' And I went.

"Next day I really felt guilty. Not because I hadn't done whatever he wanted or whatever he thought he wanted, but because I had just gone. I should have stayed and talked. A shame. He was a lonely person."

❑

It seemed typical of the turbulence of the whole year that on February 28, 1966, Liverpool's Cavern Club, where it had all started for Brian, should be closed by the Official Receiver for debts of £10,000. The Cavern was later bought by Liverpool Corporation to make way for an underground railway system, a plan that never reached fruition. The closure of the club was brief, and when it reopened within a few months, Brian sent a cheerful congratulatory telegram. He had been unsentimental about the club's problems, offering his lifelong conviction was that if anything was uncommercial, it should never expect philanthropy.

Artistically, Brian's music and theater interests blossomed that year. The Beatles hoisted their work to a new height, producing the album *Revolver*, which would stand forever as perhaps their finest. It featured classic songs like "Here, There and Everywhere," "Eleanor Rigby," "For No One," "Yellow Submarine," and the prophetically titled "Tomorrow Never Knows." To their original talent for making catchy singles, the Beatles had demonstrated stunning abilities as album makers, straddling the world of popular culture. Such was their frenzy, so frantically inventive and social were their days and nights, that the Beatles did not have time to stop and ponder the difference made in their lives by the status, poise, manner, and communicative skills of their manager. He could deal on a "street level" with the tough cookies of the entertainment world, deal sensitively with autograph hunters at concerts, and skillfully address the nobility who knocked on his door.

❑

With the Beatles' world popularity based partly on young girls' sexual fantasies, Brian had been proprietary about the women in their lives. Lennon had been married in Liverpool before the group's fame. Paul's romance with actress Jane Asher was impossible to banish from the world's media, as they stepped out so often together; but the relationship was not to result in marriage. That left George and Ringo.

Brian still clung to the notion that major pop stars should seem to be "available" to their young female fans, and initially he was not happy about Ringo's plans to marry Maureen Cox, his girlfriend from Liverpool. Brian's opposition was dented when she became pregnant, and he happily endorsed their wedding. He was best man at the ceremony at Caxton Hall, Westminster, on February 11, 1965. And to divert the nation's press, Brian arranged an unlikely honeymoon base for the couple—the home of Brian's lawyer David Jacobs in Hove, Sussex.

Later that year, the third Beatles marriage in Brian's lifetime was planned. George Harrison had met leading model Pattie Boyd on the set of the film A Hard Day's Night, and they had been close for more than a year. Just before Christmas 1965, Pattie remembers, she was driving George in London when he asked her to drop off at Chapel Street. "George jumped out, went to see Brian, came back ten minutes later and said: 'It's all right. Brian has said we can get married in January. Off we go!' I said: 'What?' I didn't have any idea that he wanted to marry me. He didn't actually consult me about it. But Brian had given his blessing and said it was quite all right. God had spoken! It was going to be fine."

At the wedding, on January 21, 1966, at Esher Register Office, Brian was joint best man with Paul McCartney, then the only bachelor Beatle.* That night, Brian hosted a small dinner party for the couple at Chapel Street. But the happiness of the wedding celebration provided a stark contrast to what Brian's inner circle learned of his priorities in life.

Present were Paul McCartney and Jane Asher, John and Cynthia Lennon, Geoffrey Ellis, Wendy Hanson, and George and Judy Martin. After dinner, the talk drifted to a question posed to everyone around the table: "What's your idea of perfect happiness?"

"It was rather sad," says Geoffrey. "Brian replied that his perfect idea of happiness was to have a number one record fifty-two weeks of the year." There was silence; everyone was shocked at the superficiality of Brian's reply. Here was more confirmation that work was the only true release in his life, to the exclusion of everything else. Once, asked on a BBC broadcast to name his favorite record of all time, he answered lamely: "The latest Beatles record."

Brian's homosexuality was rarely mentioned among the Beatles party, Pattie says. "It wasn't a serious or important point. If it was mentioned, it was a lighthearted joke. It was not detrimental to him because his personality was so strong.

"He influenced them all tremendously. They had a great amount of respect for him. He seemed to have almost a dual personality. They knew they could rely on him to look after and guide them; on the other side of his personality, when he wasn't working, he was ready to play. Whatever they would take or smoke, Brian would be there as well. So he could pull both sides together very well. When he relaxed, he relaxed completely. I just adored him."

Even when the Beatles enjoyed worldwide popularity, Brian never liked their women to be publicly visible. Initially, it was difficult to stop publicity about Paul's romance with Jane Asher, or George's romance with Pattie (until she became his wife). "His artists had to be totally available to the fans. To connect them with a private life,

---

*Pattie and George were divorced in 1977. Two years later she married Eric Clapton, whom she had first met at a party at Brian Epstein's Chapel Street house. They were divorced in 1988.

a love life or sex life, was detrimental, in his view," says Tony Barrow. Journalists seeking an interview with Paul and Jane, John and Cynthia, Ringo and Maureen, or George and Pattie were rebuffed. "Go and organize yourself with Jane Asher and separately ask me about Paul," said Barrow to reporters. "But don't try to interview the pair of them as a couple. It won't happen."

The jealousies that existed among Epstein's artists, fanned by their sudden fame and inflated egos, caused him anxiety. The Beatles publicity roller coaster was difficult to control, but even as late as 1965, Paul, John, George, and Ringo were monitoring their press. Throughout their ascent Brian had told the world that they were leaderless: "They don't have a leader. They are four people." He had instilled it into them and now it rebounded on Epstein. In the recording studios, where Lennon-McCartney songs dominated, there was growing resentment, particularly from George Harrison.

Since magazine publicity always favored John and Paul, the realization grew that they were indeed first among "equals." Brian naively believed that the press could be orchestrated to give the Beatles equal space individually. "You've used Paul again," he would tell Barrow. "I thought we'd agreed we were going to try to get something on George and Ringo." Barrow would explain that the journalist didn't *want* George or Ringo; he wanted to talk to Paul, perhaps about songwriting. Barrow remembers: "Brian couldn't understand or accept the inequality of exposure, that persuasion wasn't within my capability." It was finally decided that in joint interviews John would be partnered by George and Paul by Ringo, to try to "level off" the publicity. When the resulting coverage still gave more attention to John or Paul, Brian castigated Barrow. He could never comprehend the press attitude to the individual Beatles.

To Brian, they were a magnificent unit. Yet his relations with them individually went through several phases, reminding him of their nuances as well as the bond that made them indestructible. Because John had the swiftest tongue, most observers believed Brian found him the most difficult Beatle to handle. But John was expedient in his quest for success. Although he didn't enjoy Brian's smoothing of their image, putting them in suits and stopping them from swearing and drinking onstage, he accepted the fact that Epstein had a major plan. John grumbled about being marketed in suits and ties—but not until the

Beatles were established. Once Epstein had delivered the Beatles successfully as a package, Lennon still accepted most of his decisions, but that tolerance lasted only a few years. His horizons were far wider than those of the other Beatles.

The prickly George, described as the Money Beatle because he took more interest than the other three in Brian's business dealings, was to Brian a figure of some frustration. Edged out by John and Paul's supremacy as songwriters, he was acknowledged as the group's most fastidious musician, a rock-solid and inventive guitarist, but overall a testy character. His droll sense of humor was an asset.

Ringo, the perfect foil for all three, was to Brian affable and malleable.

Epstein's biggest pressures came, unexpectedly, from the disarming Paul, who applied himself more diligently than the others to the strategy of the Beatles' career. Brian bristled as Paul asked him the most questions—about concert tours around the world, about record release dates. Paul was the one who gave him the hardest time. "Brian was more ready to forgive John because John gave *everybody* a hard time," recalls Don Short. "But with Paul, the insults and arguments were more meaningful.

"Brian once asked me who out of the Beatles was the most difficult. I fell into the trap of saying Lennon because he always had a lot to say at press conferences. In fact, Brian's answer was McCartney. Paul wanted to project himself as the nice guy, but in terms of arranging Beatles business, Paul was the problem."

Faced by Paul's assertions and questions, and under the pressure of business, Brian was not able to defend himself so easily. "Paul learned to conduct himself quickly and Brian felt overpowered. He recognized Paul as very forceful and was, on a personal basis, a little scared and uncertain of him," says Tony Barrow. McCartney also gleaned from Epstein the art of sophistication. "Paul was very much a social climber in those days. He liked to learn the etiquette of life from Brian."

In the six years of his management, the Beatles never admitted their immeasurable debt to him. They believed that to speak glowingly of one so close would appear coy and weak. But Lennon, whose tough veneer concealed more sensitivity than the other three ever showed, went further than anyone to praise Brian. "He's the only one we take things from. He's one above us," John told Maureen Cleave in the *London Evening Standard*. "Everybody else packs it in when we start screaming at them because they're frightened. We wouldn't be run by anybody but him—not *anybody*, I tell you."

In their undemonstrative way, the Beatles returned his loyalty, never publicly criticizing him. But now they were becoming inquisitive. They talked to other pop stars and businessmen and gleaned an impression that Epstein had not maximized their earnings, had done "soft" deals, was not tough enough. Probing from George Harrison, as well as Paul McCartney's leadership aspirations, increased the heat. Despite all their criticisms of him, however, they knew they would never find a manager with such intuitive understanding of their personalities, or a man who so genuinely cared.

❑

Feeling the need for better business foundations, Brian cast his mind back to simpler days and the people he had admired when he was trying to "break" the Beatles out of Liverpool. He turned to Danny Betesh, the scrupulously ethical Manchester agent and promoter. Epstein's business now resembled an octopus and he felt strangely exposed. He told Betesh that his intelligence sources in New York showed that Allen Klein, the battling manager with an appetite for British pop acts, had set his eyes on the Beatles. Klein had infiltrated the record industry by persuading artists that they were being exploited by greedy record companies. He projected himself as their savior.*

Contact between Epstein and Betesh had been sporadic for three years, since the Beatles' 1963 concert tour. Now Brian invited Danny down to his Hille House office for lunch.

Danny's thriving management operation, Kennedy Street Enterprises, based in Manchester, controlled such top acts as Herman's Hermits, Wayne Fontana and the Mindbenders, and Freddie and the Dreamers. All had had big American success on the back of the British "invasion" begun by the Beatles. Brian was very impressed with Danny's achievement: he ran the only management and agency that could

---

*John Lennon appointed Klein his manager two years after Epstein's death, during the Beatles' argumentative period, when they ran Apple. Klein's arrival presaged the deep rift between Lennon and McCartney.

claim to have the top three places in the American charts for three consecutive weeks.

Over lunch, he quizzed Betesh about his company—its profitability, its development plans for the artists—and Danny's views of a takeover by NEMS. "I was flattered and interested," says Betesh.

Allen Klein was also a topic of conversation. Betesh had won a court battle in New York against him after Klein had attempted to lure Herman (alias Peter Noone) from his British management. "We had problems with Klein over the years," says Betesh, "and we discussed him at quite some length; he always thought Klein was a big threat to him; he was worried about interference."

Brian did not pursue his overture for a takeover of Betesh's Kennedy Street Enterprises. As his personal and business problems mounted during that period, he let the idea drop. Since their temperaments seemed well matched and their philosophies of management similar, it was both men's loss. Betesh has remained successfully in the music business.

❏

Another major business hurdle loomed for Brian. As he built up his empire and encountered the problems that always surround the signing of new artists, he could not ignore a vital date in his diary: EMI Records' contract with the Beatles expired on June 3, 1966. Talks between Brian and EMI, increasingly involving their lawyers, had begun in 1965. Brian said he could not be a party to a deal with the company beyond September 1967 because his own contract with the Beatles expired at that time.

There were many meetings between Epstein and EMI's Len Wood, Brian always telling him that he could not agree to anything, that he wanted to go back and discuss the position with "the boys." The cordial Wood, in New York in the midst of the 1966 renegotiations, discovered that Brian was in town and phoned him at the Waldorf Towers. Stressing that the time and place were wrong for talking about contracts, Wood said there were still several things he would like to discuss, including promotion plans of the next Beatles album, *Revolver*. Brian invited him over for tea. To Wood's surprise, it was almost impossible to discuss anything with Epstein in his suite. The phones rang incessantly; Brian was preoccupied with a number of airlines that were competing for his return flight to London. "There was I, trying to talk about promotion plans, and there he was answering the phone to airlines," says Wood. Sometimes, observed the EMI boss, Brian allowed his popularity, his position, and his prestige to take precedence over important priorities.

Partly because of Brian's busy schedule, an interim recording agreement was drawn up while the lawyers set to work with proposals on Epstein's behalf.

Dominating Brian's thoughts on that New York trip was, as ever, his next move. In what was probably his most comfortable business venture, he joined forces with Nat Weiss to form Nemperor Artists, launched with a $10,000 loan from JAEP (James-Epstein Music). Brian was astonished at the quickness with which the debt was repaid—the result of Nat's first signing. On a trip to Atlantic City, Weiss stumbled across a bar band called the Rhondelles, who impressed him with their imitations of the Beatles and the Beach Boys. New to signing artists, Weiss told them he had a friend, Brian Epstein, who might be able to help them. They laughed in disbelief. Next, he managed to get them work in a New York club, the Downtown, and a recording audition. Record executives again thought Weiss was bluffing when he dropped Brian's name. Finally, Brian was impressed with the demonstration tape. He disliked their name and wrote on a piece of paper: "CYRKLE." "That's their new name," he told Nat triumphantly.

Nat then showed Brian the record contract he had acquired for them. Brian read it and tossed it across the floor of Weiss's apartment. "If they have a hit record, I'll renegotiate it," he said, smiling. Within five months they had topped the American best-seller lists with "Red Rubber Ball," and Brian put them on the Beatles' 1966 American tour.

❏

Nothing was allowed to interfere with Brian's enjoyment of the good life, no matter what the pressures. Brian loved New York. He sensed that its energy and expansiveness paralleled his own. And he always preferred a metropolis to suburbia. Manhattan's speed and the eclecticism of his new friends in the music business had a profound effect on him. His picture postcards home to his parents described "the skyline of my favorite city." He reveled in New York's fine restaurants, choosing each outing with care and adoring the French oysters at La

Caravelle. Clothes shopping was essential on every trip; friends re-marked that he was never seen twice in the same suit. And with Nemperor Artists established in America, he turned his thoughts to buying his own apartment in Manhattan. It would have to face the river, he told Weiss, just like his regular suite at the Waldorf Towers. They inspected several and brought the shortlist down to two: one at Seventy-second Street and Third Avenue; the other, Brian's favorite, at the St. Tropez on Sixty-fourth Street and First Avenue. For tax reasons, they agreed, it would be best for the apartment to be in Weiss's name. Brian eagerly anticipated moving into his New York residence after the Beatles' 1966 American tour. There was no inkling that matters of much greater importance than a New York home would hit him like a tornado as the year's events spiraled from dangers to disasters.

❑

Back in London, he was confronted by major and minor crises. And his staff, faced with Brian's difficulty in delegating responsibility, ran into a string of brickbats and bouquets as they tried to unravel his intentions; nobody was quite sure at any moment whether he or she would be complimented or berated.

At London airport, Alistair Taylor dutifully went to meet a dawn flight that would carry two unknown musicians from New York whom Brian was befriending. When they arrived, penniless but with guitars, they faced an immigration ban because they had no work permit. Taylor phoned a grumpy Epstein, sleepy after a late night. He agreed to go to London airport to vouch for their authenticity as musicians. Just over half an hour later, dressed immaculately, Epstein arrived, went into the immigration office and gained accreditation for the vis-itors. Emerging triumphant with them, he tore into Taylor for failing to do likewise. "*You* should have done that," he asserted. "And look at the state of you," he continued, inspecting Alistair's unshaven face, casual sweater and slacks. Dress should be formal on company busi-ness, he reminded him,

Taylor bellowed that he had been at the airport since dawn, pre-venting the repatriation of two scruffy hippy musicians who had arrived without documents or cash. And how could he be expected to sway immigration officials as much as Epstein personally?

"I am surrounded by idiots," Brian raged as they stalked out of the airport. He went to the phone and angrily called three senior colleagues to berate them for failing to arrange smooth immigration for his guests: "This is the most disgraceful occurrence that has ever happened in my company."

"That's it! I've finished!" Taylor stated. "You can stick your job. I've been here since six o'clock trying to sort out a mess created by you and these musicians." He stomped off but Brian caught up with him, insisting on a drink. "You know what I'm like. . . ." he said apologetically.

Taylor was fired several times, notably for double-booking an engagement for one of Brian's favorite groups, the Four Tops. "For somebody in your position to make such an elementary mistake is quite outrageous," Epstein said. "It warrants your resignation." Stoney-faced, he turned on his heel and left his office.

As Taylor began clearing his desk, his phone rang. "Can you come in, Alistair?" No, he replied, he was busy. He had been sacked and was clearing his possessions. "Come in here *this minute*," intoned Brian. "Now, it's a lovely day. The sun's shining. We *are* kidding each other, aren't we?"

"He was the boss, and not a relaxed boss," says Joanne Newfield. "He moved purposefully around the office. People were fairly scared of him. When he swept through that office, everyone jumped to attention. He didn't stop and chat to people at their desks. I was terrified of him when I joined the staff because he seemed to have everything under control. If the papers were not on his desk the moment he arrived, he'd be beside himself with fury." He was a creature of habit. Staff would wait for the regular signal that he was free: he would drop his pile of newspapers and magazines on the floor outside his office.

Bad-temperedness was one of his failings and he admitted it. He reproached himself often for such behavior "and for being mean from time to time," he told the *Melody Maker*. "When I'm rude or mean to somebody it takes me days to get over it." He disliked ignorance, pettiness and prejudice. "But egomaniacs don't put me off. I think I, myself, have overcome a very large ego so I'm very forgiving and tolerant of egomaniacs. There are a lot of them about and some of them are very brilliant and clever. I also dislike dictatorship and I've never tried to dictate to my artists, although I'm aware that I command quite a bit of respect."

That respect held steadfast through the final eighteen months of his life, even though his aids caught the full force of what Wendy Hanson described as his "horrendous mood swings." And that was just and proper, as he saw it. Confrontations with his artists had to be eliminated. Had he not, right back from Liverpool days, acted as the protector of the Beatles, Cilla, Gerry et al.? They could all understand, and even enjoy, Brian's sensitivity and mercurial moods, but they didn't want *him* coming on like a performer. He was there to be a friend and a manager in equal proportions.

Yet his antics often matched those of an actor. While in the Bahamas watching the Beatles film *Help!*, Brian became bored with the daily routine and decided to go with Wendy Hanson to New York. Reservations were difficult to find on short notice, and when they finally got on a Pan Am jet, Brian was separated from Wendy in the first-class section. He complained to a stewardess, who retorted: "You're lucky to be on this flight." Immediately Brian hand-wrote a letter of complaint covering the seating imperfection and what he construed as rudeness, pompously telling the chief steward: "I want this message conveyed by radio to the head of Pan Am in New York so that he receives it by the time we arrive." When he arrived at Kennedy airport, a posse of VIPs was there to greet him and apologize.

Brian's travel behavior became the bête noir of his associates. Returning a week later to London, Brian was scheduled to take Pan Am's 10 a.m. flight. As a valued client, he was offered a car. Wendy declined the offer, saying they had their own limousine. At 8:30 a.m. a porter went to Epstein's room to collect his twelve pieces of luggage; Brian, still in bed, had not packed anything. They breathlessly left the hotel at 9:10 a.m., and after a hair-raising race to the airport, scrambled aboard the plane only a few minutes before take-off, the luggage at their feet at the front of the first-class cabin. The plane took off at 10:10 a.m. Epstein looked at his watch. "Goodness gracious, ten minutes late in takeoff," he said cynically and too loudly. "Typical Pan Am!" His audacity caused muttering among his fellow travelers and embarrassed Wendy.

"He was always losing his luggage," she recalls. To make it more recognizable, she ordered a set of Gucci cases. Brian asked: "Why is it all green and red?" Accepting her advice that it would be distinctive, he went with it to Bermuda. On arrival he was immediately on the phone to London "in an absolute fit." When Wendy asked calmly what was wrong, Brian spluttered: "I got here, grabbed my suitcase at the airport and . . . well, the key worked, which is very *bad*, Wendy, because it wasn't my case at all. It was full of *bought, ready-made shirts*! So Gucci luggage is not just for rich people. . . ."

❏

Coupled with the resentment many of his staff felt regarding Brian's absences and erratic behavior were an affection and admiration that exceeded those in any boss-employee relationship. Brian's innate charm proved an asset in his demands. Phoning their homes at two in the morning or during holiday periods, he would say: "Are you sure I'm not interrupting? Terribly sorry for ringing you at this time." When something concerned him, he had a compulsion to act immediately; his profuse apology would win through. "I felt quite sorry for him," says one associate, "but there was nothing whatsoever one could do. The last thing he wanted was any kind of therapeutic help from those around him. He didn't think his friends and colleagues knew or could see what was happening to him in his personal life, or through drugs. Looking back, he deserves pity rather than anger. Like everybody else, he had his weaknesses and failings. But unfortunately, his were in the limelight, because that's where he'd put the Beatles."

Brian's peak moment of elation came at a successful performance, not necessarily a huge one. Radiant as a bridegroom, he showed joy as he stood in the wings or at the back of the theater, his eyes literally twinkling. Rubbing his nose with the back of his right hand, he was in heaven. Such behavior was mimicked by some of his colleagues, but not in mockery. Despite all his blemishes and weaknesses, most people who knew him returned the intensity of his affection.

"I saw him with tears in his eyes when he saw the Fab Four a lot, but those were tears of joy," says Derek Taylor. "I don't want to be coy, but he always looked like a chap crying on the inside. He always looked, despite his radiance, a sensitive man. He would say things like: 'Never mind *that*—we're going to have a lovely party. Let's sit down and plan it.'

"He did pride himself on being a good judge of people. That was a fair self-assessment. In terms of business relationships, he sometimes made mistakes and they could be costly."

❏

Inevitably, during his temperamental period, Brian managed to alienate some of the hundreds of people with whom he had to do business. His inability to delegate well, plus the juggling act he had now assumed with his a multitude of interests, meant severe pressure on his time and patience. There was conflict with even the most well-meaning of operators.

Brian had a fractious relationship with Al Brodax, a thirty-five-year-old New York film entrepreneur. In 1964, Epstein granted him a license to produce thirty-nine half-hour shows, each featuring three Beatles songs, for coast-to-coast Saturday morning transmission on ABC-TV. Brodax was the writer-producer of the series, in which an animated story was concocted around Beatles lyrics: for example, an octopus fell in love with the Beatles in their song "I Want to Hold Your Hand." The series ran for three years, profitably for Epstein, who took 50 percent of the fees. He was delighted with the deal and the creative aspects of the films. "Brian's promise," says Brodax, "was that if that was successful, he would allow me to make a full-length feature." But Brian had signed a three-picture deal with United Artists. After *A Hard Day's Night* in 1964 and *Help!* in 1965, they "went to India instead of making their third picture," according to Brodax. Brian reluctantly agreed that Brodax should get some scripts written for his approval. Epstein stalled Brodax, canceling meetings.

Brian kept Brodax waiting in London for ten days for an appointment. After one all-day wait, Brodax found it incomprehensible that a man of Epstein's stature did not go to his office even to sign his mail. "We had drafted a dozen treatments for the project," remembers Brodax. "I even had top writers like Joseph Heller (author of *Catch-22*) write some and they were not cheap! Brian dismissed them all out of hand." When Brodax asked him if he had actually read the Heller treatment, Epstein answered: "Was that the purple cover? That's not my favorite color." Did that mean, Brodax pressed, that he hadn't read it? There was no answer.

"Brian Epstein was very officious and rude, a pain in the ass," says Brodax. "My belief is that if you take no for an answer in my job, you're out of work. So I persisted."

United Artists, meanwhile, were getting impatient for a signature, and Brodax was not prepared to leave London without Brian's agreement. Wendy Hanson, sensing it was an important deal that Brian should honor, finally ensnared him at Hille House. Brian was so incensed with Wendy's plot that he threatened to fire her. Brodax got his agreement. Brian liked the title *Yellow Submarine* and Ringo liked the idea, which was written by Erich Segal.

Brodax was the head of King Features, which had been responsible for movies of the caliber of *Popeye*. When the Beatles heard this, they were scathing about *Yellow Submarine*. Epstein, however, saw the commercial potential in the project and was prepared to submerge his personal antipathy toward Brodax. "The Beatles feared the worst," says George Martin, "but in truth the project was in the hands of very good artists. If Brian hadn't stuck to his guns, that classic would never have happened."

Epstein had committed the Beatles to write four original songs for the film. Their aversion to the whole idea manifested itself with the new forcefulness that Brian had learned to accept from them in 1966 and beyond: they tried to dump their inferior material into the movie. Says Martin: "If they had any rubbish, as they considered it, at the end of a session, that would be one of the songs. There used to be a standing joke: 'Ah, good enough for *Yellow Submarine* . . . let them have *that* one.' Of course, when *Yellow Submarine* became a big success, it was a different story." Suddenly, the project had been approved as a Beatles idea from the start, rather than something Brian had agreed to against their wishes.

There was a bitter row about the countries for which Brodax sought rights. "Britain is *mine!*" roared Epstein finally, insisting on home distribution for himself. Brian never saw the film, though; it was not shown until a year after his death.

"My meetings with Brian were not convivial," says Brodax. "He was cavalier. There was some resentment of me; when the Beatles were in the room, they looked towards me and he somehow disliked that." Such an admonishment, implying that Brian was childishly defensive of his role, is difficult to comprehend, since he had spent four years enthusing about the Beatles' articulateness and intelligence. He was protective, but never denied their assertiveness.

❏

The signing of the Moody Blues to Brian's company seemed to herald a massively successful coup, adding an extremely "hot" group to his bursting stable. After four years as an impresario, Brian saw the need to strengthen his operation with durable acts that would produce immediate prestige. The Moody Blues' single "Go Now," at the top of the charts in 1965, was a huge Paul McCartney favorite and established them as strong musicians. The gifted group from Birmingham, which then featured Denny Laine,* seemed to be on their way.

But Brian failed to show the patience or strategy necessary to realize their potential. Although he knew they could scale the heights, he seemed unable or unwilling to devote the time necessary to reposition them for the golden future that surely awaited them. He met them in New York with Nat Weiss, who recalls that Brian quickly "thought the group should be doing more for themselves." They seemed to expect Beatles-level attention immediately, and Brian always disliked such presumptuousness to be shown by artists. In London, Brian rapidly lost interest and patience and appointed Alistair Taylor as their personal manager. To Epstein, the group seemed unreliable and undisciplined. Defending them, Taylor pointed out that they were young to the business and needed supervising. Brian, furious, again threatened to fire Taylor, this time for backing a group that was behaving unprofessionally. It was, he reminded Taylor, unbecoming behavior for a NEMS act.

*Denny Laine joined Paul McCartney's Wings group in 1971 and co-wrote with him the big-selling British single "Mull of Kintyre." Laine's successor in the Moody Blues, Justin Hayward, wrote a multimillion seller, "Nights in White Satin," which established the group internationally in 1967. They remain very successful.

12

❑

DANGERS

THE END OF AN ERA

THE BEATLES, INTERNATIONAL HEROES after a series of hit records, were now lauded as bright actors—as Epstein had predicted—through two films, *A Hard Day's Night* and *Help!* Their majestic concert before 55,600 at New York's Shea Stadium had been the zenith of their career as live performers. John Lennon had written two books to wide critical acclaim, confirming Brian's conviction that he was the fulcrum of the group's talent; Brian was especially proud when John asked him to be a director of the newly launched Lennon Books Ltd. Against such a solid backdrop, there was no reason for anything but excitement. Nobody was to know that the Beatles' show at the Glasgow Odeon on December 3, 1965, would mark the start of their *final* British tour. But a series of catastrophic events in 1966 would give Brian his first reversals.

It was to be a year of tension, traumas, and hoaxes. In America, Brian's profile was so high that people impersonated him to gain media attention. A report in the *Palladium* newspaper in Richmond, Indiana, on May 16, 1966, particularly aroused Epstein's ire.

Brian had just seen Cilla's important appearance in cabaret at London's Savoy Hotel, then went to his beloved Spain for a holiday. The American paper reported him as being interviewed at the town's Leland Motor Inn during a visit to plan the Beatles' August tour of America.

Under the headline "Beatles Will Slip in Couple of Years Manager Says During Stopover in City," Epstein was quoted as admitting they would fade. "In perhaps two years people will say: Beatles? Oh yes, they are good. But they will not be the tops." The fabrication continued with wild inaccuracies: he had met the Beatles in "August 1963"; he had won some money on the stock market, enabling him to invest in the group; tickets for the coming tour had not sold so quickly as for the 1965 tour; and when asked if he got tired, Brian was reported as saying: "I'm 42 years old."

"He said he prefers not to have his picture taken because he wants to stay in the background," reported the paper. Even so, it continued, he was being asked for autographs.

The report reached Brian's desk on June 11. He immediately fired off this letter to Nat Weiss in New York, reflecting his pique:

Dear Nat,

Quite obviously, someone has been posing as myself. There are often inaccurate reports in the American newspapers about myself and my activities, to which I very rarely take exception. This one, however, I feel I must protest against, principally because I would not like other newspapers in America, to say nothing of the rest of the world, to "lift" its content.

Principally, I object to the quote "inferring that the Beatles will slip in couple of years" contained in the headline.

I have never visited Richmond, Indiana and would certainly *never* stay anywhere called "Leland Motor Inn"!

I usually allow press to take my pictures.

I have never suggested that the Beatles may, at any time, fade from the top.

I have never dabbled in the stock market. To suggest that Paul "owns the firm which makes all the group's records in England and licences U.S. firms to make them" is utter rubbish.

I have never said "Ringo spends all of his money."

Paul being a jokester and the bit about the favourite stunt is rubbish. As you know, I would *never* suggest that the Beatles owe their success in America to Ed Sullivan. They will *not* be doing another Sullivan show during the upcoming tour.

It is certainly not true that all the tickets are sold and to add a final insult to an unjust wound, I am not and would not suggest, infer or say to anyone "I am 42 years old."

Would you please protest, in the strongest possible terms, to the newspaper concerned and ensure a properly presented apology.

Yours sincerely,
Brian Epstein

When in June 1966 the Beatles went back to Germany, the country that had once nurtured them, Epstein and I joined them on the train that took them from city to city—and to the thirty thousand fans who saw them in four days. There was understandable sentimentality in such a triumphant return to Munich, Essen, and Hamburg. Epstein preened like a peacock over his all-conquering "boys," resplendent in their new uniforms: green velvet suits and yellow silk shirts.

By then, the Beatles and Brian had become accustomed to the cranks and weirdos who harass the famous. Death threats, phoney paternity suits, and demands for money had become part of the pressure of being a Beatle. So when an anonymous telegram arrived in their Hamburg dressing room, saying simply, "Please don't fly to Tokyo. Your career is in danger," they took little notice. Only George Harrison, who regarded fame as an intrusion on his role as a musician, commented drily that the Beatles evidently had enemies as well as friends.

When they flew on to Tokyo, it turned out that the death threat was serious. The Beatles were to play five concerts from June 30 to July 2 at the Budokan, a hall regarded by some, particularly students, as sacred for martial arts and sports tournaments; for a pop group to play there was "sacrilegious." The Beatles and their entourage were surprised to learn that they would occupy an entire floor of the Tokyo Hilton, including the Presidential Suite, and only realized why when they arrived there: every alternate room was occupied by armed security guards. Brian and the Beatles thought the authorities were overdoing it until they were told they would not be allowed out of the hotel to sightsee.

Their only exits from the Tokyo Hilton during the week were for the journeys to the Budokan in a convoy heavily escorted by outriders. Marksmen stood on the concrete bridges. In the Budokan, where the crowds were all on upper levels looking down on the Beatles in the center of the hexagonal hall, a huge number of cameramen with powerful lenses scanned the audience looking for potential assassins. The Beatles, still not appreciating the seriousness of the death threats, joked about the high security. Brian, following his lifelong rule that the Beatles should never be bothered by bad news, would not tell them of the intensity of the police concern, or of the real dangers. It was not until the concert promoter arranged for shopkeepers to visit the hotel, transforming their rooms into a bazaar offering cameras, kimonos, silks, that the group finally realized the extent of their isolation.

The tight security in Japan was as much a surprise to Brian as to the Beatles. When the Japanese visit passed without incident, Brian could perhaps be forgiven for believing that the Beatles were unassailable.

But other events of 1966 would increase the pressures on him. From Tokyo they moved to the Philippines, where the Beatles' two appearances on July 4 had been arranged by Epstein's colleague Vic Lewis. The Beatles were to appear before 100,000 at a Manila football stadium, their biggest-ever one-day audience.

The two shows were scheduled for 4 p.m. and 8.30 p.m. There was a suggestion that, en route to the afternoon show, the Beatles might pay a courtesy call on the wife of President Ferdinand Marcos, subject to final approval by Brian and the Beatles party. The proposed time was 3 p.m. but Epstein did not confirm it.

Astonishingly, the president's wife expected the Beatles party for a prelunch reception. The first lady had invited the aristocracy of the Philippines to bring their children, totaling about two hundred, to the reception, which had place cards at tables, as for a formal event. At 11 a.m. military escorts arrived from the palace at the hotel to take the Beatles to the reception. "This is nonsense," said Brian. "Nothing like this has been organized." The officials told him to consult his itinerary, which in fact said nothing of a morning engagement. "The Beatles are still sleeping," Brian told the escorts. "Why didn't anybody discuss this with me? When the Beatles get up, it will be to go to the show. This might have been able to happen at three o'clock on the way to the show, but there's no way I'm going to get them out of their beds now to go to the palace and come back again." He repeated that he had not confirmed the appointment.

The escorts left and the afternoon show went ahead. Brian returned to the hotel before the evening show and sat with his press officer watching television, expecting a report on the successful first concert. Instead, Epstein was horrified with a news item saying the Beatles had snubbed the Philippine first lady. There were shots of place cards being removed from the lunch tables.

"From the palace's point of view they were being let down by the Beatles from eleven o'clock onwards," says Barrow. "Brian was absolutely appalled. The escorts who had come in the morning hadn't made the size of the event clear. So Brian didn't realize the significance of it and neither did I. We went through the day not knowing what was happening, until that newscast. Then we knew the enormity of the so-called snub."

From the tone of the broadcast Epstein sensed how the denigration of the Beatles could be orchestrated by the authorities. Worried about any escalation of the problem, Brian instructed Barrow to phone the television channel and offer a statement. The TV editors agreed and sent a crew to the hotel within an hour. Barrow drafted a speech and Brian was filmed making his statement, in which he explained that the Beatles had no intention of snubbing anyone. No formal invitation had been relayed to him, to the Beatles, or to any of his party, said Epstein. But when the item went out on the television news later, the gathering crisis became obvious: Brian's voice had been obliterated, while the rest of the program had perfect sound quality.

"His voice was not dubbed out but intentionally scrambled," says Barrow. "I could make out what he was saying with great difficulty because I scripted it. But if you didn't know, you could not understand a word." Meanwhile, death threats to the Beatles were being phoned to the hotel and the British Embassy.

(Later, Brian admitted that he had no real regret about the Beatles' failure to appear at the Presidential Palace. It was not as if the heads of state or their guests had any real desire to talk to the Beatles about their lives, he pointed out. "They're there simply to gawk at them, and to be able to tell their kids that they actually spoke to the Beatles. Frankly, we find this embarrassing.")

The next day, with the Beatlés due to fly to New Delhi en route to London, the Filipinos vented their full fury. It began in the hotel, where the staff said they could not touch the Beatles' baggage. Their limousine suddenly became unavailable to them, locked behind gates. Taxis taking them to the airport took an absurdly long route, presumably in the hope that the Beatles party would miss its flight. At the airport, they faced not only a spirit of noncooperation but physical danger: all security services had been withdrawn, and the near-deserted airport looked as if it had been hit by a strike. The airport manager decreed that the Beatles should fend for themselves. The escalator was not moving. At the KLM airline desk, the Beatles' huge amounts of luggage, as well as instruments and equipment, had to be loaded by the Beatles party.

Lewis and Barrow, part of the advance party who had loaded the Beatles' baggage, phoned Epstein back at the hotel: "Don't bring the Beatles yet. It's dangerous out here. We'll ask KLM what's the absolute longest they can hold the plane back." The receptionists referred them to the pilot and he agreed to hold the plane for forty-five minutes. When the pilot told them the plane could wait no longer, Epstein and the Beatles raced to the airport to be met by a hostile, jeering crowd. Between the departure lounge and the plane, they had to run the gauntlet; on the tarmac the Beatles and their advance team were jostled and punched. Since the entourage did as much as they could to protect John, Paul, George, and Ringo, Brian caught most of the mob's fury. He was hit in the face and kicked as he ran from the airport building to the apron.

As Brian nursed his injuries, Lewis walked up the gangway of the plane and leaned over his seat. "Did you sort out the tax problem? Did you get the money?" he asked. Brian flew into a rage, shouting: "Is that all you can bloody think about at a time like this?" Lewis was angry at what he considered Brian's hypocrisy, for if they had come away without money as well as having endured such humiliation, the trip would have been even more disastrous. But Lewis's timing was appalling. Brian had not secured any receipts before departure and had agreed that the Beatles' fees, minus tax, could be posted to London. A physical punch-up between the two men was averted only by the applause of the happy Beatles as the plane took off. But the division in outlook and priorities was perfectly highlighted by the incident.

Lewis, ever the professional agent and businessman, saw his role in black and white. The sensitive and vulnerable Epstein felt, as ever, that there were issues at stake wider than mere money.

On the stopover in New Delhi, the family man deep inside Brian found time to cable his worried parents, assuring them of his safety despite the alarming reports they had read of the Philippines chaos.

❏

For Brian and the Beatles, the Far East tour had been a great strain. Never again, the Beatles and Epstein chorused. Brian immediately canceled a visit to the Philippines by Cilla Black. At a 6.30 a.m. press conference at London Airport, John Lennon confessed that he had been petrified; George Harrison said they had been subjected to Gestapo-like tactics. Back at his Chapel Street house, Brian paid the price for his mounting worries: a rash covered his body and it was diagnosed as glandular fever. The doctor said it would be about two weeks before he could travel.

Epstein first phoned Nat Weiss to postpone a visit to New York, where he was to coordinate the forthcoming tour by the Beatles. Brian was disappointed. He loved the prospect of organizing American tours: it was safe territory, with lots of friends and Beatlemania.

"What's glandular fever?" asked Weiss.

"Oh, here we call that mononucleosis." Repeating the word to his secretary, Brian told her to use it officially to British people who inquired about him. "It sounds most impressive!"

Convalescing in Portmeiron, North Wales, Brian told his mother by telephone that he was bored but that a break was essential before his forthcoming American trip. His boredom and enforced rest had lasted only a weekend, however, when a phone call from Nat Weiss in New York forced him back to reality.

"Brian, you know I would never ask you to come to America, but something is happening that is *so* serious. . . ." Weiss had just received a phone call from a Birmingham, Alabama, disc jockey: "Is that the Beatles office? We are *burning* Beatles records!" Three other similar calls came in quick succession, followed by a newsflash from Memphis saying the city council was considering a ban on the visit by the Beatles during their forthcoming concert tour.

For the third time in as many months, the Beatles and Brian were in trouble. This time, it was an interview that John Lennon had given to the *London Evening Standard* five months earlier which began the crisis.

John had said: "Christianity will go. It will vanish and shrink. I needn't argue with that; I'm right and I will be proved right. We're more popular than Jesus now. I don't know which will go first, rock 'n' roll or Christianity. Jesus was all right but his disciples were thick and ordinary. It's them twisting it that ruins it for me." In Britain the article, by one of the Beatles' regular commentators, Maureen Cleave, was accepted as another outspoken interview with the most thoughtful and articulate Beatle. Now, unexpectedly, it was reprinted under a syndication agreement with an American magazine, *Datebook*. And it was featured on the front cover.

America, which had canonized the Beatles for two heady years, was about to deal them a most devastating blow. Weiss's office was inundated with calls from the Deep South's Bible Belt saying that Lennon's sacrilegious remarks would be punished. As the Ku Klux Klan marched, Beatles records were thrown on bonfires, and thirty-five radio stations banned their music. It was the start of the "holy war" Weiss had reported by telephone from Manhattan to Portmeirion.

Though he was ill, Brian decided he had to fly to New York immediately. He called Alistair Taylor, who made most of the travel arrangements at NEMS. "Get me on a plane tomorrow to the States."

In New York, Kennedy Airport was packed with reporters. "I grabbed Brian and got him into the car," says Weiss. Then Brian said: "How much will it cost to cancel the Beatles tour?" A million dollars, Weiss answered. "Well, I'll do it," Brian said. "I can't let anything happen to anyone. This tour is not going out. Now, let's go out and have a good time and we will deal with it tomorrow."

Weiss was stunned, horrified by Epstein's flippancy. He wanted an immediate debate on the crisis. "This is *serious*, Brian."

Yes, Brian agreed, it was important. "But let's go out and have a good dinner, find some people, and have fun."

At Manhattan's Sheraton Hotel, Brian was anxious for a good atmosphere at his personal press conference there next day. He asked about the hors d'oeuvres that would be served to the journalists and asked Nat to charter a boat for a two-day vacation when the furore had subsided. With Brian, it often seemed that the ugliest news or situations had to be balanced by sunshine on the horizon.

Before he gave his own press conference, Epstein called Lennon at his home in Weybridge, Surrey. The only way to preserve the tour, Brian told him, was for John to apologize. Otherwise, there was no way their safety could be guaranteed. Lennon's reply was succinct: "Tell them to get stuffed. I've got nothing to apologize for. Cancel the tour. I'd rather that than have to get up and lie. What I said stands."

Epstein pursued his own explanation to the press. "The quote which John Lennon made to a London columnist nearly three months ago [sic] has been quoted and misrepresented entirely out of the context of the article, which was in fact highly complimentary to Lennon as a person and was understood by him to be exclusive to the *Evening Standard*. It was not anticipated that it would be displayed out of context and in such a manner as it was in an American teenage magazine." This was inadequate. Brian had failed to make the subtle but crucial point that John was not being blasphemous and was not claiming Beatle superiority over the church. He should have stressed John's characterization of the Beatles as "more popular," not "bigger." Lennon was making a social observation. But Epstein would not accept this recommended explanation—it was not for him ever, he said, to interpret a Beatle's words.

Brian's press conference was purely cosmetic and he knew it. What America now wanted, needed, demanded was John Lennon. Brian called him again. Now that he had heard the sinister death threats and saw the other problems surrounding the tour, Epstein was convinced that John *had* to explain himself. The Beatles always did pretour public relations in America, and John agreed to face the media at the Chicago press conference already scheduled a few days later at the city's Astor Towers Hotel.

Meanwhile, the American promoters had virtually persuaded Brian to let the tour continue. A Lennon explanation would calm the controversy. Epstein still had genuine fears, after Japan and the Philippines, that the problem might get out of hand. Uncharacteristically, he felt that the final decision about this tour should be made with John. In an emotionally charged Chicago hotel room, he spelled out the danger to Lennon but said he had been assured that America did, after all, love the Beatles and that with a fair press the tour could go ahead. A cancelation would present enormous difficulties. John broke down and wept, his head in his hands. He was full of remorse for having got the Beatles into such a mess on the eve of what should have been their finest American tour. Brian turned away. He could not bear to see Lennon, of all people, in tears.

There had been times when Brian had rebuked John for his outspokenness to the press, but this was an occasion for repair rather than remonstration. They were in a no-win situation: John didn't want to apologize, Brian wanted the tour to go ahead; but both decisions were fraught with ramifications. Brian wanted to go over John's speech but Lennon was in no state to discuss it. They went into the conference virtually unprepared.

If it had been any event other than a big American tour, Brian would certainly have canceled it. "Brian said to me just before the press conference that John was the one who was at risk," says Tony Barrow. "Unless John doesn't want it to go ahead, Brian said, the tour is on. The only thing that would alter that now is if John decides . . . it's in his hands.' "

Facing the newsmen, John was conciliatory. "If I had said television is more popular than Jesus, I might have got away with it. But I just happened to be talking to a friend and I used the words 'Beatles' as a remote thing . . . I'm not anti-God, anti-Christ or antireligion. I was not saying we're greater or better. I believe in God but not as an old man in the sky . . . I used 'Beatles' because it was easier for me to talk about Beatles.

"I wasn't saying whatever they're saying I was saying. I'm sorry I said it really. I never meant it to be a lousy antireligious thing. I apologize if that will make you happy."

After a few exchanges with journalists, John ended the conference with "There's nothing more to be said." And the tour went ahead.

The Bible Belt of the Deep South was the danger zone, and as Brian stood by the side of the stage in Memphis, a loud firecracker from the audience frightened everyone. His head spun round to fix on John, but the band played on. While the Memphis concert took place, a religious meeting was held in the town to pray for the forgiveness of the audience. But the tour was a huge success, the Beatles revisiting Shea Stadium in New York and going on to Dodger Stadium in Los Angeles, attracting more fans than during their 1965 tour. But for Brian, it signaled a massive change in his behavior: on the 1965 U.S. tour, he had stood alongside the Beatles at press conferences, and at concerts usually took up his position in the wings; in 1966, he was hardly there.

❑

The Beatles' concert at Candlestick Park, San Francisco, on August 29, 1966, proved to be their last anywhere. Lennon and Harrison were the chief proponents of the decision to stop touring. George had long maintained that going on the road was a charade, that their music, unheard above the screaming thousands, was suffering. He wanted the Beatles to spend more time in the recording studio. John needed little persuasion; he found touring uncomfortable and tiring. Paul McCartney asked Tony Barrow to tape the concert—a sure omen that it was special. Even though Brian knew that San Francisco would mark the end of the Beatles' tours, he could not bring himself to go to the show. He did not want to have the night become a special event, or a finale. It was not, after all, the end of the Beatles; nor would Brian concede to anyone that this was their concert "exit."

The warning signs had been there on the few occasions when he caught up with the group on the U.S. tour. "This is *it*," John and George would say to Brian after a difficult show or when their equipment had caused problems. Their manager, believing their tetchiness could be traced to the "Jesus Christ" controversy, or to plain irritability on a given night, was hopeful that it might not be the end of the road. When the dust settles and they are back in London, he told himself, they will hanker after live audiences again. He knew better, though, than to try to persuade them to change their minds in the middle of the tour, and he never replied to their contention that this would be the last tour. It was not surprising, then, that Brian was not at the San Francisco concert, for to him it was just another end-of-tour appearance. Had he boarded their charter plane back to Los Angeles after the show, he would have seen George Harrison flop into his seat and, with a broad grin, announce: "Well, that's it. I'm not a Beatle anymore."

Told of their decision, and asked about it by Tony Barrow, who now faced questions from the world's press, Brian remained utterly convinced that they would tour Britain later that year. He showed a provisional itinerary to Barrow, who asked if he could announce such plans to the clamoring media. No, said Brian firmly. "There would be hell to pay if this goes out."

Epstein derived great joy from planning Beatles tours, but it became obvious that his "leaking" of the British tour idea to Barrow was a subterfuge to keep the press officer from taking the Beatles' decision seriously. Brian adamantly refused to allow Barrow to say that there would be no more tours or that the Beatles planned to concentrate on making records and films. Epstein told me at this time that he was considering four solo film parts for the Beatles, but this never happened either.

To Brian it was incomprehensible that the raw excitement of the Beatles "live," the very essence of their original attraction for him, was gone forever. His method of accepting the decision was to continue as if it had not been made. That was always Brian's way of dealing with unpalatable truths.

❏

As the Beatles played their final concert in San Francisco that night, a far greater drama was about to hit Epstein's private life. Earlier that day at the Beverly Hills Hotel in Los Angeles, where Brian had been staying with Nat Weiss, he had met up again with Dizz Gillespie, the man Weiss thought he had vanquished a year earlier in New York. Against Weiss's wishes, Brian had agreed to allow Gillespie to visit him at the hotel. Gillespie was staying with a friend in California and had called Brian saying he would like to see him again. Brian was flattered; he was still fond of Dizz and they spent the afternoon swimming in the hotel pool. "Oh he's changed," Brian assured Nat.

"He *hasn't* changed," Nat Weiss insisted. "Get rid of him."

"Oh, you don't understand . . . he really loves me."

"Yes, he really loves you and all your money," retorted Nat. "Stay away from him. He's a cheap hustler. If you wanted to keep your beer cold, you'd put it next to his heart. I don't trust him."

Says Weiss: "Brian was always fascinated by the dangerous aspects of this person. He had an amazing control over Brian. This boy's attitude was that Brian had made so much money and he wanted to get his share of the way things were going. And Brian used to tell me the Beatles used to like Dizz." This was untrue, probably a ploy by Brian to persuade Nat to be more tolerant of Gillespie. In fact, he was the only boyfriend of Brian's whom the Beatles knew, and with their renowned antennae for problem people, they made it known to all their "insiders" that they felt uncomfortable in Gillespie's company. "All four Beatles really disliked him," says one of the Beatles' coterie.

Weiss told Brian he was sure the Beatles would say they liked anyone who was with Brian, "just as a polite person would show civility to anyone's partner before perhaps going home and saying they were terrible!" Weiss continued to warn Brian, emphasizing the fact that Gillespie was a hustler: "Don't tell me about those kind of people, Brian, because I know what they're all about."

After that sociable afternoon reunion with Dizz, Epstein firmly believed their relationship was on again. As the Beatles began their farewell concert, Brian and Nat went together to dinner in the Beverly Hills Hotel. When Weiss returned to his room, he noticed his briefcase was missing. He walked in to tell Brian, who quickly realized that his was gone too. There was little of value in Weiss's case, but Brian's contained $20,000, contracts for the Beatles' tour, plus a bottle of Seconal barbiturates, which were illegal. They did not have to wait long to know the identity of the thief. A ransom note arrived from Gillespie to Weiss asking for $10,000 for the return of the briefcases. The threat was that Epstein's possession of barbiturates would be revealed. By now, says Weiss, "I hated him. I really was out to get him."

After two days of anguish, Brian flew back to London. He told Nat not to act, to "let it go." When he asked Wendy Hanson to buy him a new briefcase from Asprey's, her heart sank when Brian gave her the news. She knew what was in the stolen case. Says Weiss: "Brian just didn't want the publicity, and didn't want to get Dizz into trouble because he was afraid of the scandal." But Weiss was determined to pursue it. "My logic," says the lawyer, "was that if he stole my briefcase, I wanted him arrested." Weiss hired a private detective to arrange a meeting with Gillespie at a railway station. The rendezvous was a trap; Gillespie was arrested by the police.

Weiss sent Brian's briefcase on to London. About half of the $20,000 it had contained was returned, and the contracts were intact. The bottle that contained the Seconal pills was empty. Brian, amazingly, was "very upset that I had him arrested," says Weiss. "He was very depressed by the whole thing. The whole betrayal is what really destroyed him." The incident deeply affected Brian, whose life code was based on trust. And the later realization that he had been so humiliated on the final night of what became the last-ever Beatles tour was the ultimate personal devastation.

❑

The end of the Beatles' touring days was dispiriting in every way for Brian: emotionally, professionally, and financially. The Shea Stadium concert was eleven thousand seats undersold and the tickets to fill the venue had been given away; a Beatles concert had been "papered." A year earlier, Shea had had a genuine capacity crowd. When receipts were totted for their appearance there on August 23, 1966, promoter Sid Bernstein presented Brian with a bill, which Epstein was bound to pay because of his guarantee to the promoter. The show had grossed $292,000, of which the Beatles received 65 percent ($189,000). But such was the nature of Brian's deal with Bernstein that he owed him $800. For Brian, it was a bitter finale to the Beatles' days of touring.

13

❏

LONELY HEART

BLIND FAITH AND BAD DEALS

WITH THE CATACLYSMIC DECISION by the Beatles never to tour again, 1966 became Brian Epstein's year of high tide. By the middle of the year many of his staff deduced that "Eppy" had big business problems. Characteristically, he did not talk about them with his colleagues. A British economic recession was having a marked effect on bookings fees of some of his lesser artists, and Brian made his first essential surgical moves—a process painful for him to confront. His loyalties would have to be compromised.

With Tommy Quickly out of NEMS, signed by another agency, Epstein passed on his option to re-sign Michael Haslam and the Rustiks. Two other groups, Tony Rivers and the Castaways and the Paramounts, went to other companies: neither had had the impact anticipated by Brian. He was finally showing clear signs of tightening his organization. With regret, he told colleagues, he would henceforth have to act decisively when all attempts at promoting certain artists had failed.

About forty musicians, with the Beatles and Cilla way out in front, had earning potential. The rest were rather small profit-makers or were being subsidized. Some eighty staff members now occupied five NEMS-rented offices around London.

Astonishingly, though beset by business problems that seemed insurmountable, Brian never lost his smiling confidence. He predicted that new singles by Billy J. Kramer ("You Make Me Feel Like Someone") and Gerry and the Pacemakers ("A Girl on a Swing") would be Top 10 British hits. Neither even reached the charts, severely bruising Brian's pride and his pocket. Easily hurt but too dignified to let it show, Brian stepped out as a "leading man," a role he had so coveted ten years earlier at the acting academy. Still, as the monarch of London's artistic revelry, his instincts were those of a frustrated thespian. He would swap his role, he admitted, to be able to write songs like Lennon and McCartney, "because that is basically a creative talent." But though he cast his net wider than the field of pop music, to be heralded as the manager of the Beatles was no handicap, even in the company of more highbrow tastes. He was never embarrassed by such a connection: "If I'm at the opera or theater, I find the English are too sensitive to say anything about the boys."

And there was the Saville Theatre, that aesthetic joy but financial albatross. As a young boy, one of Brian's favorite books had been *The Swish of the Curtain* by Pamela Brown. The charming novel, in which seven boys and girls run their own Blue Door Theatre Company, struck a chord deep inside him, and there were uncanny parallels now for him, twenty years later. The core of the story was so apt:

> "How glorious," exclaimed Lyn. "A theatre of our own! Oh, it's a dream come true." But that was only the very beginning. The boys and girls had many problems to overcome if they were to be taken seriously by their parents and friends. . . .

Brian's instinct had guided him gloriously in 1961, and his tenacity had produced stunning results during the next year and beyond. But now, burdened with the logistics of running a theater, he faced a costly penalty for his self-indulgence. In what he considered a prestigious venture, he imported the musical *Amen Corner* to the Saville from the Edinburgh Festival, but it lost money. Brian's dramatic judgment was sound enough, for more than twenty years later, after his death, the show would be a theatrical success. But despite big television exposure for the Saville leading lady, Claudia McNeill, and although Epstein's name yielded big press publicity, the show did not fill the 2,800-seat theater after three nights. And even the full houses had scores of free guests. Brian's next presentation, *On the Level*, adapted from a Ronald Miller book with music by Ron Grainer, was expensive to stage. That, too, failed to attract the crowds. Next, he tried a ten-week season of the D'Oyly Carte Opera. Truly, the Saville was proving a magnificent but expensive substitute for Brian's failed acting ambitions. .

His difficulties caught the eye of the media. A cartoon by Neil Smith in the *New Musical Express* depicted the Saville as Epstein's toy doll's house. "I don't care much for the three chins he's given me," Brian commented, "and I'm not sure that I like the theme of all the artists appearing as puppets with me as the manipulator. That's not strictly true." To friends, though, Brian admitted the cleverness and accuracy of the theme.

For the first nine months of his Saville control, Brian's possessiveness was as evident as when he launched any of his acts. He gave little leeway to John Lyndon as production director. Brian immersed himself in every facet of the theater, checking the running order of the shows, concerning himself with the precise amount of time allotted to each act onstage. "He would argue for two minutes more or less for the artists because he considered he was safeguarding the interests of his acts," says Lyndon. When Brian went to the performances, he could never sit through the entire two hours; he stalked the theater. Yet somehow, at the end of the evening, he would know who had cheated on the clock by overstaying the time allotted onstage.

Lyndon, a strong-minded man the same age as Brian, joined Epstein with plenty of experience in theater direction. "When he crossed the boundary of complaints against me, and saw my pique and petulance, he would know and he'd leave immediately," says Lyndon. "He could never face people's anger and have a stand-up argument."

"Brian found the Saville even more of a problem than he expected," says Geoffrey Ellis. "He knew he was going to have to spend more money on it than he could stand. It needed a total refurbishment, pulling out twelve hundred seats and replacing them; new carpets. He was upset that he couldn't afford to revamp the Saville as he would have liked. But he spent a lot of time there. For a while, he had confidence. He'd say to me: 'I'm determined to turn it round, but my God, what a lot it's costing. What a lot of effort and trouble.' "

But always there was the conflict between Brian's pride and his commercial judiciousness. A classic case was the British tour of Gaumonts and Odeon theaters by the Four Tops, a leading American act; arranged by Vic Lewis in his role as NEMS managing director, it was scheduled to begin in January 1967. Lewis's skill as an agent meant that if the tour attracted the fans, as expected, NEMS would show a profit. If it was not a huge success, it should at least break even. Brian, wanting to stamp his own personality on the prestigious event, flew to Detroit and gave away concessions: he agreed to pay the group's tax, first-class air fares, and other unnecessary bonuses. The result was an amended contract that guaranteed trouble. Even if the tour went well and sold out, NEMS would lose about £10,000. And it did. Just as Tito Burns had predicted, Brian's meddling with deals once they had been closed was causing havoc.

The Four Tops, one of the Tamla Motown label's greatest acts, were also booked by Brian into the Saville. This engagement, too, lost money, but Brian glowed in the wings; the concert was an exhilarating triumph, musically justifying Brian's decision to reserve Sunday nights for grand pop events. For a man who had not warmed to pop until his late twenties, he quickly gained a sense of excellence, and his adoption of the Four Tops, inevitably as friends as well as a golden act, was seen by the music fraternity as one of Brian's finest hours. He was justifiably proud. Shortly after the Saville show, writing to a Liverpool musician friend from New York's Waldorf Towers, Brian said: "By the time you get this you'll have heard of my great coup to present Tops in England. Very proud of this indeed. Hope you are proud of me too."

The Four Tops show crystallized Brian's plan to stage significant pop events every Sunday at the ailing theater. He wanted it to be similar to the Olympia in Paris, with artists booked for a week. His bookings for the beginning of 1967 were adventurous, including stars who would endure as legends: Little Richard; Cream, featuring Eric Clapton; the Who; and Fats Domino.

The Saville deal with Delfont gave Brian control over the lease for two years, since he had bought 60 percent of the company that ran the theater. Delfont and Tom Arnold each retained 20 percent.* They confidently expected that Brian's fresh ideas would benefit the venture and that they would reap some of the benefit. But Epstein rapidly discovered that a cartel in theaterland controlled what shows went into each house. And nonmembers of that cartel, himself included, found it very difficult to get profitable shows into an isolated theater. "It simply wasn't possible," says Geoffrey Ellis, "to snap your fingers and say: 'As from today, I'm going to put on my own productions.' We didn't have any productions to put on. So we had to pursue a policy of attracting conventional shows. Brian worked very hard at it, invested a lot of money, but this was a terrible financial drain from the beginning."

There was a positive pleasure in the Saville for Brian: he loved being responsible to the Lord Chamberlain for its correct operation. And pop shows of a high caliber made it a Sunday night mecca for Swinging London. But one full night a week did not make a profitable theater: too often the place was closed for six nights.

❏

To compound a tough year, Brian's worries paled beside the news that came in a phone call from Clive in Liverpool: their father Harry had been rushed to Sefton General Hospital. Harry and Queenie had recently moved from Queens Drive to a smaller home, Treetops, Glenrose Road, Woolton. Preparing to go out for a dinner one night, Harry had suffered a massive heart attack. Brian raced to his father's side to be given the news that Harry would be in hospital for six weeks. When he did leave the hospital, Harry was so ill he had to return, making it an eleven-week stay altogether. There was excitement among the other patients when his famous son arrived. "Go and wave to the ladies," Harry urged Brian, pointing out the chattering fans. Brian's modesty prevailed: he was not a star, he said.

That Christmas, Brian went home to stay with the parents he still addressed as Mummy and Daddy. He took his father a box of flowered shirts and ties and was thrilled to see his father mobile. The grim news for Harry, to whom work was therapy, was that he had to slow

*Brian bought out their shares to gain complete control of the lease on July 11, 1966.

down. But Brian was pleased that at least his father was out of a hospital bed, and planning a holiday in Bournemouth.

As he faced the renegotiation of the Beatles' recording contract with EMI, Brian faced the wrath of British fans, who had not seen them perform in concert for a year. They demanded to know what was happening when America had just enjoyed a long concert tour (even against the background of death threats) but British supporters were being deprived of live appearances. Brian deflected the attack by emphasizing the need to ensure the group's safety.

But the same question faced him wherever he turned: Had the Beatles really split? John Lennon was in Spain making his solo film debut in *How I Won the War.* George Harrison was in Bombay studying the sitar. Ringo was merely paying a social visit to John on the film set. There were no plans for a follow-up single to "Yellow Submarine" and certainly no British tour plans. Demonstrating his tough veneer when under fire, Epstein told *Disc and Music Echo:* "There's no real question of the Beatles retiring. They're simmering down, making films, writing music, making records. That's their future."

This defense was not enough to silence vociferous fans, who picketed outside his home while he was out seeing his group Sounds Incorporated support the Beach Boys in concert.

"While I know live appearances are of permanent importance to many people," he explained, "the Beatles find themselves open to so much interpretation, like that appalling debacle in Manila and the comments about Christ.

"Be sure the Beatles themselves like singing and playing to a public, but it's become so difficult and so tense that their enjoyment and pleasure, let alone their finance, is taken away.

"Still, while they are creating albums like *Revolver,* I doubt if the public are entitled to expect much more of them. Their future together lies as far as the moon. I'm not thinking of theaters but a big record-buying market. With this and more good films, they can only keep developing.

"I know the main contention is that they have become too flippant, but I don't think many of the fans really feel this. Those that do just don't consider the difficulties that the Beatles encounter through being who they are."

Who besides such an accomplished public relations man could say nothing with such disarming candor? Brian's measured tone and control had soothed so many crises in this fashion. It was left to Cilla Black to introduce a note of levity into what was becoming an almost pious question. Asked if the Beatles would retire in any way, she gasped: "They can't! I've got my shares in them."

❑

With a combination of negativism and envy, people inside show business began asking two rhetorical questions: How long can the Beatles last? And: Has Epstein lost his touch?

Brian was phlegmatic in his responses. "All I can say is that I hope their artists are as happy and successful as mine in three years' time. After twenty-nine years of no hits, I did produce the Beatles, Cilla, Gerry, Billy J., and the others." He pointed to his new hit American group, the Cyrkle; his plans to expand Gerry into the theater (which did materialize); and the Fourmost's growth in cabaret.

"Just because some people aren't having hits doesn't mean they are not doing well. Or that I'm gradually withdrawing from pop. I'm as keen as ever. They place their faith in me and I'm deeply aware of the responsibility."

Of the gossip that scoffed at him, he told *Disc and Music Echo* in a rare broadside: "It's extraordinary what sharks there are at work in the pop business. I'm appalled at some of the people in it. I just won't barter with these people. My advice to any new artist would be to take a course in mathematics and economics before entering show business. The only trouble is that the 'know-all' artists become mistrusting and uncooperative so that they're as bad in their own way as the agents themselves."

He was doubtful if another Epstein would emerge in pop. "There is room for someone. But apparently pop doesn't attract straightforward people who also have some artistic integrity. Most of the new people who turn up seem to be unfair and ephemeral types."

The events of the autumn of 1966 were turbulent. On September 27, Brian entered the Priory Hospital, Roehampton Lane, Putney, for a complete checkup, emerging after ten days with instructions to coast a little. The charisma of his name was still potent, however, and nothing could shield him from the questions from fans, the press, and his staff. Despite a year in which the Beatles had been harangued in

America because of Lennon's "Jesus" remark, despite the Philippines debacle, and however great the rumblings inside NEMS, Brian was still the golden figurehead of world pop management.

The revolution he had marshaled four years earlier out of Liverpool was still seen as the popular music industry's finest hour, a motive force. As the Beatles embraced the drug culture, profoundly and impressively changing their music, Brian experimented alongside them.

❑

While his public utterances were as comprehensible and smooth as ever, his business and private lives were uneasy as Christmas loomed in 1966. "There was no pattern to his working life. He was getting very foggy and seemed to hibernate at Chapel Street," says Wendy Hanson. "I was covering for him a lot."

Brian's need for attention, and lack of permanent company, became clear to even the most junior of his staff. At Hille House, the receptionist, twenty-year-old Jill Forbes, talked about the weekend parties at the Marble Arch flat she shared with Laurie McCaffrey, the NEMS receptionist. The rambunctious events reached the pages of the national newspapers. When Brian called Jill into his office, she expected a severe admonishment for contravening the secrecy agreement that all Brian's employees had signed.

"I understand this is the second weekend that you have been having these parties," Brian began. "I think it's pretty miserable . . ."

Feeling guilty, Jill intervened: "I'm terribly sorry, we shouldn't have done . . ."

". . . I think it's pretty miserable," Brian continued, "that nobody should think of inviting *me*. I would really love to have come."

Jill sensed a man "in dire need of a good friend." His emptiness was obvious to her when he asked her to go into Hille House on Saturday mornings. There was no work for her to do. She quickly realized she was there to provide him with company, place his racing bets with the bookmaker, or be sent to buy his after-shave from Galeries Lafayette in Regent Street. Her loyalty to him, even as a junior, was instinctive: "He was a nice, kind man who gave an incredible quality to my life. He was fantastically perceptive, generous, thoughtful, sad, pathetic. I couldn't fault him, but now I can see that he was desperately lonely and needed a stable partner."

Wendy Hanson had quit several times as his personal assistant. On one occasion Brian, refusing to accept her letter, rejected it with a ploy. "Why don't we have an evening out? And I'm not accepting your resignation. Let me take you to dinner." The evening began with a typically exaggerated Epstein gesture of cajoling charm. He sent his chauffeur to Wendy's flat in Conduit Street with the evening paper. At Les Ambassadeurs, Wendy inspired Brian to concentrate on the theatrical aspect of his life. "Look Brian, just because the Beatles aren't going to perform, your life hasn't come to an end. You have such potential. You have imagination. You wanted to be an actor, and now you have working for you Vyvienne Moynihan and John Lyndon . . . and your own theater! Why not stand London on its ear? Put on a season of young British playwrights, people who have talent but who are not yet commercial. Do it! Get on with it! You can't spend your life in pop music."

With Brian warming to the idea, Wendy then tackled the most serious issue. "You've got to do something with your life. And first of all, you've got to stop taking drugs." She recalls: "I talked him into it but he did a trick which I now know about. He said: 'I'm too famous to go to a clinic so I'll have to do it at home.' "

Chapel Street was swept clean of all Brian's substances, and nurses were drafted in for a few days. "They really did clean out the apartment," says Wendy, "but Brian had tremendous charm and one day talked one of the nurses into letting him go for a little walk. And we lost him for two days. You can't just clean up and go back to life. You have to join a follow-up group. Nobody mentioned this to Brian."

As with all other staff, Wendy Hanson found his seesaw behavior unpredictable. Once, she had planned a private trip to Paris for the weekend. On her return Brian asked: "Well, what *are* we going to do about a Christmas party?"

"I asked you about that last week," Wendy rebuked him.

"Absolute nonsense. You never discussed it with me. We'll have a Christmas party. Arrange it!"

Recalls Wendy: "He was often difficult, demanding, impossible like that."

With only days to go, Wendy had to find a bartender and pull out all the stops to arrange the lavish office party down to the last detail.

"It finally worked but it was a nightmare. He sent me a card but he didn't give me a Christmas present that year. I was miffed."

Geoffrey Ellis believes Brian did not like his own company. "He would love to have had a stable relationship, a marriage of any sort, which he didn't receive. There's a difference between loneliness and solitude: I think he was lonely rather than solitary."

"It was like he was onstage, playing a part, giving a performance, twenty-four hours a day," says John Lyndon of Brian's continual theatricality. "He put up this tremendous veneer; the only moments in his life when he didn't give a performance were when he found something he was lusting for. They were the only moments of honesty. He was a very lonely man."

Wendy's patience was finally exhausted when Brian phoned her at home at ten one night. He had lost the address of a recording studio where he had been due four hours earlier. He began shouting. "You ought to *know* where to find it. You're my assistant." In Wendy Hanson, at her most glacial, he met a dead end: "Brian, I'm really not your nanny. I'm really not putting up with this any longer. I'm going to lead a normal life. And goodbye." She resigned by letter next day and went to join film producer David Puttnam.*

While she worked off her notice, Brian was mysteriously absent for days. Finally, he arrived at Hille House, slammed his door, buzzed her on his intercom, and said frostily: "Will you come in, Miss Hanson?"

"Good morning, Mr. Epstein," she said, returning the formality.

Brian looked sheepishly at her when she entered his office. "I suppose it's too late to ask you to do my Christmas shopping," he began.

Wendy said no, she had nothing else to do, having passed all the office work to Joanne. She spent the next morning at Asprey's buying decanters and silverware within Brian's set budgets of £10 for most gifts. The only people Brian shopped for personally every birthday, anniversary, and Christmas were his parents.

*A few months after she left, Brian telephoned Wendy and told her she was the only person who could unravel a Herculean international task for him: getting permission from many world-famous figures to use their images on the cover of the Beatles' *Sgt. Pepper* album. She did it.

The Beatles sent her a farewell gift, and Brian refused to part from her without a promise of continuing friendship.

Writing on December 20, 1966, to accept her departure, Brian confessed to his personal problems:

> Dear Wendy,
>   Now that it's happening I'm truly sorry to see you leave. How can I say thank you enough? I do sincerely want you to know that I have appreciated so much your help, co-operation, patience and kindness.
>   I'm sorry that I've been gone most of the last few weeks. I'm sure you thought otherwise; it had nothing to do with yourself. I've had some difficult personal problems and also been a little pre-occupied with a new development businesswise. The former I really believe I've solved and I'm looking forward to a bright future.
>   Don't let this be goodbye. Please keep in touch, and I do mean it. And don't hesitate to allow me to be of help to you in the future if you think I can.
>   You'll be missed by many at NEMS, but most by me.
>   Love, Brian.

Wendy Hanson, too, left with affection for the impossible man she had almost tamed. "There was something very lost about him. . . ."

❑

Christmas 1966 epitomized the highs and lows of Brian's life. "I think we should look a little festive here," he said to Joanne, walking around his house. He beamed with cheer when she went out and returned with cards and decorations to adorn the elegant lounge and his study. His holiday would be spent, as often, back in Liverpool with his family. He enthusiastically set about signing his four hundred Christmas cards with the flourishing, distinctively formal signature now known so well throughout show business and beyond.

They went to artists and staff, past and present business associates, and friends and contacts, some of whose names showed a surprise "link" to people not associated with Brian. The list included Allan Williams in Liverpool; David Frost; Princess Margaret; the Buckingham Palace press officer, Sir Richard Colville; all the Rolling Stones, individually; Peter Sellers; Elvis Presley; the Four Tops; top British photographer David Bailey; Bridget D'Oyly Carte. There, too, with private addresses indicating more than a nodding acquaintanceship, were Sir John Gielgud; Manuel Benitez (El Cordobes, the bullfighting star) in Córdoba, Spain; Henry Higgins, his own bullfighting protégé; Dean Martin in Beverly Hills; Orson Welles in Madrid; and Daniel Farson, licensee of the Waterman's Arms on the Isle of Dogs.

The joyfulness of the season was marred by his private worries, so multifaceted and complex that a friend once remarked to his secretary that Brian was on a collision course with himself. The Beatles had stopped touring, but still he could tell nobody. People would panic, expecting them to split. And if the reality became "hard news," then morale at the office, already a problem, would plummet. The subtlety of remaining a recording group was, in 1966, too fanciful for most observers.

In Britain with his hit group the Young Rascals, Sid Bernstein met Brian for dinner. Unaware that the Beatles had stopped giving live shows, he offered £350,000 for two concerts in one day at New York's Shea Stadium in 1967. With world television rights, Sid enthused, it would make millions. Brian shook his head. "I can make no plans for next year," he said, somberly and significantly.

John, Paul, George, and Ringo were manifestly maturing as men. "Eppy" was concerned that they might become disaffected with his business management because of the pop world's grapevine from American musicians. Was Allen Klein still a threat to him? The Beatles, with Paul McCartney's thrust, were talking about launching their *own* company, Apple, to run in tandem with Brian's management and with NEMS. It was absurd, Brian thought privately. *They* should stick to music just as Lennon had once told *him* to stick to counting the percentages. But Brian could not, and did not, want to stop them. It was clear, though, that a dilution of their relationship was on the horizon, however much togetherness still existed between them.

And there were other worries. The Saville was a problem that could not easily be cast off.

Epstein displayed the soothing calm that had marked his style from Liverpool to London, from the Cavern to the Hollywood Bowl. If his friends and colleagues did not see a relaxed Brian, he reasoned, alarm bells would ring far and wide. But there was no hiding from his discreet staff the debility under which he was working. Increasingly, Joanne Newfield found herself to be a secretary under siege. A typical hand-written note would be on her desk as she arrived at Chapel Street:

> Joanne—
> Under no circumstances am I to be disturbed. I will announce myself when I'm available. I'm aware that I may miss the Shea press showing . . . under no circumstances suggest to anyone I'm asleep.
>
> B.E.

In another, asking for the butler to deliver him breakfast promptly at 3 p.m., Brian wrote to Joanne:

> In strict confidence I've decided to be "officially" unwell. Please do not tell *anyone* it is untrue except family (tell my brother if he calls that I'll explain why I'm unavailable later).

"I tried to ring him several times, but half the time couldn't get him," says Alistair Taylor. "He was either in bed or Joanne was block-ing his calls."

His appearances at Argyll Street became events. "Sometimes the door would open and there he'd be, to surprise us," says Taylor. "Standing grinning, looking slightly flabby around the gills, but never out of his head. I never saw him smashed. I knew what was going on but there was no point in me saying: Brian, pull yourself together. What happened is that he became virtually a recluse."

Yet when Brian was fully operational, he could be as cohesive, alert, and flamboyant as the man who, five long years before, had galvanized Liverpool and the world with his methodical determination. On Jan-uary 24, 1967, Brian's letter to "My dear Nat" in New York began:

> Enjoyed our telephone conversation the other evening and hope that you took note of the various matters on my personal behalf, which you undertook to arrange.
> As you will remember it was my decision to fly to Mexico on March 1st and you were going to arrange the best accommoda-tion. . . . I do hope that this is the sort of hotel which I will like and that it will be completely private and beautiful. Perhaps you

would ask the travel agents or the hotel to send me a brochure
giving me some idea of what it looks like and its facilities.
Very much looking forward to seeing you on 24th February.

He flew to New York en route to Mexico. "I have a great surprise
for you," Nat Weiss said to Brian when he arrived in Manhattan. "I've
arranged for you to have lunch today with Dominguín." Brian could
scarcely contain his elation at the prospect of actually meeting such a
legendary Spanish bullfighter. Weiss had never seen Brian so boyishly
enthusiastic. He upgraded his rented limousine to a new Lincoln
Continental, which took him to the Regency Hotel for cocktails to
meet Dominguín and then on to a top French restaurant. "Brian was
almost in tears as they talked about bullfighting," recalls Weiss. He
said he'd never wanted anybody's autograph before, but this was an
exception.

Dominguín and his friend had little knowledge of whom they were
meeting. "What exactly do you do?" they asked, inviting Brian to a
bull farm in Spain.

"I am the Beatles' manager. . . ."

"Well, bring them with you."

Brian said meeting the great matador was one of the high points of
his life.

The holiday in Mexico imbued him with optimism, energy, and
comparative good health. He avoided narcotics. There was, however, an expensive bill for Brian's forgetfulness. He hired a car and
abandoned it; months later, Nat Weiss received a $3000 bill from
the rental company when they finally discovered the "lost" car on
a roadside.

Back in London, uncertainty and depression engulfed Brian. Anxious to tighten up his amorphous business, he decided to privately
explore the possibility of pulling himself out of NEMS in some way,
perhaps arranging a financial takeover. Above all, he wanted to rid
himself of the chores of chairmanship and simply be the personal
manager of the Beatles, Cilla, and Gerry.

He phoned Larry Parnes with an invitation to tea at Chapel Street.
Brian, in bed, wearing a dressing gown over his pyjamas, looked ill,
with a yellow complexion suggesting he had been suffering from hep-
atitis. Proudly he played Cilla's new single; Parnes played the new

release by Billy Fury, the Liverpool singer Brian would have liked to manage. But his mind was on wider issues.

"Brian said he wanted to retire," says Parnes. "He said he was fed up, worn out, and couldn't control the empire which NEMS had become." In an escapist mood, Epstein said he wanted to get away on a long cruise. He offered Parnes a senior role inside NEMS, which was declined. "The moment you leave that company," Parnes told him prophetically, "it will fragment and then break up." Brian became despondent. After three hours of trying to persuade Brian to unwind, Parnes left. It was the last time they met.

Yet most of Brian's letters were anticipatory and many featured his laconic humor. Writing to Derek Taylor in Los Angeles early in 1967, by hand on his personal notepaper with "From Brian Epstein" printed at the top, he appended his own description of himself: "Manager and frequent looner." He wrote of how he was "very busy but I must have a few days rest (to prepare myself to receive the Four Tops), but in great form. Very happy about my Stigwood deal."

He enthused about the Beatles' new single, due out on February 17. "Super smash, without question one of their best. Titles: 'Penny Lane' and 'Strawberry Fields Forever.' " Years after the Beatles and Epstein had been accused by Liverpudlians of deserting their roots, Lennon and McCartney had returned to their teenage memories for songwriting inspiration and given their home city immortality with two songs that brilliantly evoked its unique atmosphere.

Brian continued in his letter, referring to Strawberry Fields: "John tells me the latter is between Menlove Avenue and Beaconsfield Road. Do you think it'll help our image in Liverpool? I used to get the tram (number 46) from Penny Lane to the Epstein's, Walton Road, when I overslept and was too late to accompany Daddy to work in his Triumph at 9 o'clock." The record, Brian mused, would "probably kill fifteen birds with one stone."

❑

"Brown paper bag money" was a phrase so furtive and undignified that it never existed in Epstein's vocabulary. It was coined by those around him to camouflage undercover tactics used by Brian and various concert promoters, particularly in America, for cash payments that would circumvent the tax authorities. Booking the Beatles was a profitable coup for many of them; a few thousand dollars or a few hundred pounds in cash, handed to Epstein after some shows, was their way of helping Brian reduce the effect of the monumental tax bills that followed each tour.

Brian's lifelong attitude to money reflected the artist inside him. He was often cavalier and carefree, perhaps because real money problems had never surfaced in his pre-Beatles life. Although at NEMS he was ever conscious about not leaving too many taps turned on for his staff to squander, his own handling of big money had always been almost at odds with his meticulous persona. And yet he often drove the toughest bargains.

Even at NEMS in Whitechapel, as sales of Beatles records sent his cash receipts soaring, he was strangely casual. He walked through the Liverpool streets with wads of notes in his pockets to the Charlotte Street branch of NEMS. There, he handed the cash to Edith Yates, the bookkeeper, saying, "Will you please count these and look after them?"

Against such flamboyant contrasts ran Brian's central core of integrity. While he was prepared to accept cash for the Beatles, he was never prepared to pay it to "oil the wheels" for any of his artists or staff.

His supreme test came when one of his acts, the Silkie, the folk group who cruised to success with the John Lennon composition "You've Got to Hide Your Love Away," gained a Top 10 American hit. In New York to arrange a promotional tour for the group, Alistair Taylor was told the good news and the bad: they could do nine television shows for a thousand dollars each performance; but they could not get a work permit. Epstein was due into Manhattan shortly after Taylor received the double-edged message.

By the time Brian arrived at Kennedy Airport, Taylor met him with a solution to the dilemma facing his hit group. "I had been told that if I gave a certain person a thousand dollars to oil the wheels, a work permit would be arranged," says Taylor. "But Brian flatly refused to lend me a thousand dollars for this purpose. He said he had never bought his artists into anything with cash and did not intend to start." Taylor argued that they had the Ed Sullivan TV show and eight others on offer. An income of $9000 in fees, plus such enormous exposure, surely justified the method. Epstein was adamant.

The Silkie were furious with Brian for his unswerving refusal to lend the cash to Taylor, whom he had appointed their personal manager. In London waiting for details of their flight to New York, they were told to return to Liverpool for Christmas. They never forgave Epstein for what they saw as an effective curtailment of their career. They broke up shortly afterward.

❑

To the astonishment of those around him, Brian began to distance himself from the machinery of his central business. He seemed incapable of juggling his activities, a major failing that may explain some of the problems that plagued his growing empire. For the manager of so many artists and the instigator of so many projects, it was ultimately self-defeating: he could be consumed by only one topic at a time. He gave each subject, each meeting, each artist, his undivided attention in turn; he could seldom be diverted. He hated his meetings interrupted. Nothing was more urgent than the matter under discussion.

Not even a telephone offer of a vast sum for literally a few seconds' work by the Beatles was allowed to steer his thoughts away from a domestic meeting with one of his staff. Don Black, the quiet, astute manager of ballad singer Matt Monro, who joined NEMS with Vic Lewis, took the call from an American TV station. Brian had a particular affinity with Black, who had just won an Oscar for writing the title song to the film *Born Free*. Epstein admired Black's ability to combine creative talent and business knowhow.

The Americans wanted an immediate answer to a request: Would Brian allow the Beatles to appear on the Lucille Ball show? All the Fab Four had to do was stand on a corner in Piccadilly Circus while Miss Ball walked past them and did a double take. Black thought it worth breaking into Epstein's meeting. "Excuse me, Brian, I've got a network TV station in America on the phone. They want to know can they . . ."

"Please, not now," Brian interrupted. "Don't bother me. I'm too busy."

Black returned to the phone: "It's impossible to get an answer. The man is in a meeting."

The TV man persisted: "This is terribly, terribly important." He explained how little it would tax the Beatles' energy or time. "For that, we will pay a *hundred thousand dollars*. But we must know now. We need him for five seconds; we have to arrange film crews."

Black went back into the meeting. "Brian, they won't take no for an answer. And they're offering . . ." He had written the vast sum on a piece of paper that he handed to Epstein.

Brian remained unfazed. "Oh, just tell them not to bother. For goodness sake! No, no, no, no." He dismissed it, says Black, as if rejecting the offer of a cup of tea.

❏

A postmortem on Brian's complex web of company affairs shows a man better at visualizing, promotion, sales, and marketing than at hard dealing. The seeds of Brian's thinking can be traced back to his family business background, where everything was geared to retailing and marketing. NEMS was a typical Jewish immigrant furniture company in which just about every member of the family had shares; Brian's adoption of this technique began from the moment he realized the need for a separate company to operate his pop events. NEMS Enterprises, launched in June 1962, demonstrated a degree of trust few family members show for each other: Brian and Clive each owned half of the company.

NEMS Enterprises, the master company handling the affairs of the Beatles and other acts, had to be reshaped after the incredibly successful year of 1963, which culminated with the Beatles' appearance on the Royal Variety Show. On April 27, 1964, the capital was increased from £100 in shares to £10,000; Brian made his shareholding £5000 and Clive's shareholding £4000, giving the Epstein brothers 90 percent, with the rest divided among Lennon, McCartney, Harrison, and Starr.

Bringing the clients into the business showed Brian's sense of fair play. "Nowadays, that would be anathema," observes Sam Alder, a noted British rock manager and record company owner. "The advice would be that the manager must keep his business one hundred percent owned and the artists should own their business." Subsequent show business history has shown that it is unhealthy for both parties to receive advice from the same lawyers and accountants.

By the 1970s, a rock band successful in Britain did not make the same inroads in America until a year or two later. So the manager had time to put the business in order before the bigger receipts arrived. Epstein had no such advance warning of the Beatles' earnings. After his energetic local work for them in Liverpool, their British success was meteoric and their American and international funds flowed rapidly. And what Brian could not call on—something that became readily available in the 1970s—was a large body of professional opinion, in accountancy and law, to guide him and help maximize his and the Beatles' income. In the mid-1960s, the music business was hardly an industry.

To many, Epstein's handling of the songs of Lennon and Mc-Cartney deserves censure. Northern Songs was registered on February 22, 1963, with Dick James and Brian its first directors. A month later, the shares were split into A and B shares. Dick James had forty-nine of the A shares, and the B shares were divided between Lennon and McCartney: nineteen to John and twenty to Paul, with ten going to NEMS Enterprises. In February 1965, the company went public on the London Stock Exchange, with the issue of five million shares. Upon Brian's death, his brother Clive became a director of Northern Songs (in October 1967), but in June 1969, Dick James sold the company to ATV for £10 million. It was the single most contentious deal arising from the Epstein-James era. The Beatles were angry at what they regarded as a betrayal.

James claimed that since the Beatles were by then divided in business, with Allen Klein representing three of them and Lee Eastman representing McCartney, he was acting in their future interest in ensuring a strong sale of the song catalogue rather than having the company torn apart by the Stock Exchange. By the 1980s, when Michael Jackson had acquired the company owning the Beatles' catalogue, it was hinted that Brian's naiveté in giving the songs to James was the first fundamental mistake made in losing John and Paul possession of their "birthrights," the songs they wrote.

With hindsight, Brian could have set up his own publishing company rather than giving the publishing license to Dick James. He could then have asked James to administer it. And he could have launched his own record production company and leased the tapes to EMI. But Brian was bound by enormous loyalties, and the escalator was moving far too quickly for him to backtrack from contracts already signed with these two parties. And the music business was far less industrialized and wise than it became in the 1970s. Moreover, James did a first-class promotion job.

Had Epstein been motivated purely by money, he would have renegotiated in 1966 along those lines.

"But Brian can't be blamed completely," says Sam Alder, "for not having conceived the sheer size of the Beatles' success and the way it would continue, years later, in songwriting. He was operating twenty years ago. In those years, there weren't the accountants, lawyers, and administrators around who could help him to do it. Brian did everything needed by a director. There is no sign of the companies he was involved with being in default on filing, or their accounts not being clean.

"If Brian had been a more selfish, greedy man," notes Alder, "there would be an edifice which would now possibly be owned by the conglomerates. Because the whole point of building that sort of edifice is that you eventually sell it after putting lots of properties into it. Comparing Epstein of the sixties with Robert Stigwood in the seventies and Richard Branson in the eighties—the difference was that Epstein was not looking for methods of earning the next million. He and his major artists had made enough money to live on. He never ever wanted to be the richest or the biggest, but to be the best and then turn to something else and be the best at that too.

"A manager can delude himself into thinking the artist is only successful because the manager has brought that about. But I don't think Brian was that sort of person. He was too close to his artists to think of himself as being separate from them. The way the Beatles story unfolded after his death shows the degree to which he held them or the structure together. The destructive forces in a band after its initial period of success are always best held together by the manager who grew with them through their period of early success.

"Brian's business dealings looked rather like an orchestra without a conductor. The people playing in the orchestra were good, but they weren't being led at the speed a conductor would have led them."

Although naiveté and loyalty shaped Brian's attitude to business in the five frantic pop years, he could scarcely be charged with nepotism. "What Brian did," says Alder, "was form NEMS and run the Beatles business in the way he knew from his grandfather's furniture firm. In such families, the home centers on business: if the family business does well, the home runs well. They sit at home and talk about business, so as you're all working together out of official hours, you incorporate a company together. What Brian did was effective and still functions perfectly well for many businesses."

And there is a theory that Brian's absences from the office were more disorienting than damaging to his staff. Entertainment is one industry that often allows casual management to flourish. "Many managers of very successful rock acts stay incommunicado," says Alder. "It's possible that by not going to meetings Brian allowed the Beatles' business to build up its own momentum and he avoided wrong decisions being made. If an act is so strong and its image untarnished, a manager will get away with not attending to business. This is the one business [in which] he can do it and add to the image.

"I don't see Brian as an unfair or dishonest man. Definitely not. I see him as all too human a guy, much too vulnerable to be a businessman. What he should have done is allowed the Beatles to get a business manager and stayed on the creative side."

By December 1965, the NEMS Enterprises company split was seven thousand shares to Brian, two thousand to Clive, and 10 percent in the hands of the Beatles.

Despite Lennon's reputation as the dilettante and iconoclast of the Beatles, his sense of business appears, from the records of the companies, to have been the most attentive of the four. He was usually the first Beatle to sign business documents, and his fascination with Allen Klein in 1969 reflected his interest in commercial returns for his artistry. There are instances in the rosters of the companies where Lennon would become a director a month or two before McCartney. When the Beatles as a quartet owned a company, and two directors were needed first, John's name was usually one of them. "John had a keenly developed sense of ownership," says Alder. "Many people who play in a band for the first time don't realize it is a business and partnership, that something tangible is being owned, namely shares in a company. Lennon appears to have perceived that more than most." McCartney, who tried to unify the Beatles upon Brian's death, emerged as a masterly controller of his own financial destiny.

In terms of ownership, at least, Brian was virtually the Fifth Beatle: they split most of the companies five ways.

Having earned something like £5 million in the fiscal year 1963–64, Brian was asked by Cliff Michelmore on BBC-TV's "Tonight" if he felt exposed to charges of exploitation and being parasitic. Brian replied that he was "desperately careful" not to exploit his artists. Even if they did not want to know the fine details of his contracts, "it is my duty to inform them of the contents, even if they throw the paper away." He developed teenage talent rather than exploited it, he maintained. And every artist had bettered himself by signing an agreement with him.

How ruthless did Epstein think he had to be? asked Michael Charlton on BBC television's "Panorama."

"Not very," was the reply. "It may even be a fault of mine in the business that I am not ruthless enough." Any manager who tried to get big money quickly would be "absolutely wrong. . . . I looked at things without money initially in mind. It is important, but at first not the most important factor."

Epstein's business activities should not be judged harshly. In the five years of his stewardship of a fast-moving empire, he made far more inspired decisions than mistakes. He gave a pop scene in its infancy just what it needed: emotional commitment. To be managed by Epstein was an accolade in itself. His outstanding strength was as a personal manager and creative director rather than as a chairman or managing director of NEMS Enterprises. Once the Beatles had arrived, he did not want to immerse himself in what he saw as the gray world of finance. Any businessman's transactions and decisions, closely dissected, could expose weaknesses. Epstein's massive contribution, transcending management, was his ear, his eye, his style.

His biggest miscalculation was to stem from the merchandising of paraphernalia like Beatles wigs, watches, shirts, pillows.

By the 1970s, the "pop boom" that Brian had helped to begin had transmogrified into the "rock industry." Running parallel with the music, often eclipsing it in impact, were the ephemera of correlated business interests. Multinational soft drink corporations, as well as audiotape and tobacco manufacturers, poured huge sums of money into the pop music scene by sponsoring major events. It was a guaranteed method of reaching the rich teenage audience. The offshoots like T-shirts, badges, and clothing, as well as the arrival of cassettes as a major force, commercialized pop as never before. Managers, promoters, and record companies enjoyed rich pickings, often regardless of the originality or quality of the music they were promoting.

Back in the 1960s, when pop was young and the Beatles and Brian were pioneering the route to profits for many thousands of lesser artists and managers, the word "merchandising" was unheard of in relation to pop. But it was to enter their lives with a vengeance. Merchandising spurred greed and rivalry and became one of Brian's biggest problems as the cult of Beatlemania swept Britain.

From the start of his association with the Beatles, Brian had abhorred even a threatened exploitation of them. Their image and marketability were projected and protected by him alone. He vetoed every attempt to profit from them unless he was personally able to supervise "quality control."

When they sang "She Loves You" and shook their ample heads of hair, the Beatles gave credence to long hair among young men. The merchandising signals were immediately apparent, even if their ultimate ramifications could not have been anticipated: Brian was inundated with opportunists wanting permission from him to make Beatles wigs. And as the group's popularity soared in the next few months, Brian resisted requests by unknown manufacturers wanting to merchandise Beatles-endorsed boots, dolls, pillowcases, towels, pens. Finally, however, as it became clear that the Beatles were not a passing success and as the inquiries for merchandising approval increased, Brian felt that he could no longer contain the problem within NEMS. In 1964 he turned to his solicitor, David Jacobs, for advice.

Jacobs, originally introduced to Brian by Larry Parnes, had an impeccable pedigree and represented such stars as Liberace, Judy Garland, Lionel Bart, Zsa Zsa Gabor, Laurence Olivier, Shirley Bassey, and Eartha Kitt. Logically, Jacobs told Epstein that he should properly structure the licensing of Beatles merchandising and that as his lawyer he (Jacobs) would willingly supervise the companies involved in the actual operations. Brian was relieved to have unloaded the problem on a friend he could trust. The companies running Beatles merchandising were thus launched as Stramsact in Britain and Seltaeb (Beatles spelled backward) in the United States.

One enterprise that Epstein immediately approved originated with his cousin Raymond, who proposed that he and his brother Peter should make and sell Beatles sweaters and badges. They were licensed for world sales of sweaters at 30s. each, badges at 3s. 6d. each, and with a mail order arrangement they sold about fifteen thousand sweaters and some fifty thousand badges. Brian put an advertisement in *The Beatles Monthly Book* and ensured that Raymond and Peter got very good exposure for their goods in Paris when the Beatles visited the city. But the Beatles were not enormously successful in France, and the stores returned the merchandise. Brian's cautious cousins did not want to risk pursuing their interests in America, and their involvement fizzled out, losing them a little money.

Brian's attention to merchandising, meanwhile, had been forced to focus on the wider issues. Within months, merchandising was a seven-figure industry in Britain alone. Brian's occasional inquiry to David Jacobs was met with the assurance of a lawyer adept at bestowing calmness on troubled, frantically busy clients. And to the outside world, Jacobs became possessive about the lucrative offshoots, steadfastly refusing to discuss figures with anyone.

His stonewalling was, in one sense, understandable. Merchandising activity was so vast, so competitive, that it needed the full-time attention of one lawyer in Jacobs's Pall Mall offices. There was a deal with Mobil Oil to distribute photographs of the Beatles at garages throughout Australia, for a lump sum payment of £2000. That seemed a ludicrously small fee as the merchandising and licensing arenas exploded, and companies began to jealously guard their territorial rights. In Liverpool, a bakery was granted a license to market "Ringo Rolls." Within two days, a hundred thousand were sold at a royalty to the Beatles of a penny each. When the Beatles conquered America, a Blackpool company received orders for ten million sticks of licorice rock with the Beatles' name imprinted in the center.

Sales mushroomed to unprecedented levels, and it had happened almost overnight. About 150,000 toy guitars with the Beatles' picture on them were sold, for example. Here was a commercial world in which the sharks swam fin to fin, and unavoidably, pirated goods bearing the Beatles imprint came on the market. Jacobs's office issued proceedings about a dozen times and sent hundreds of warning letters, but litigation on so potentially huge a scale would have been difficult to instigate and control. It was more expedient to carefully grant licenses.

The contracts authorized by Jacobs, and shown to an approving Brian, included Beatles metal trays selling at 5s. 9d. The London manufacturer's first order was fifty thousand, with royalties for the Beatles at about 2½d. per tray. In Manchester, Beatles wallpaper costing 14s. 6d. per roll quickly sold a hundred thousand rolls, and there was a sublicense to the United States. A Somerset company produced Beatles ottomans at £8. 10s. and record cabinets at £7 15s. 6d., giving the Beatles royalties on gross sales. They had a one-year contract, with a renewal option, granting them exclusive rights to produce these and other items of household furniture in the United Kingdom and Eire. Production ran into the thousands.

Beatles chewing gum costing 2d. or 6d. was manufactured under a five-year license by a firm in Ingrebourne. Seven Beatles photos went into the sixpenny packet, two photos into the twopenny packet. Within six months, a hundred million photos had been used and royalties totaled more than £50,000 to the Beatles. With such success, the company gained a license to produce gum in the United States and Canada.

Bedspreads were made in Ashton-under-Lyne, with a world-rights contract for one year to the company. Production ran to five thousand single or double bedspreads a week. A London firm had world rights for peaked caps (in the John Lennon style) at 18s. 11d. each and berets at 14s. 11d. They produced thousands a week and gave the Beatles royalties.

There were children's guitars from 8s. 11d. to 75s., Ringo Starr drums at 99s. 6d., disc racks at 7s. 11d., with 130,000 guitars and "hundreds of thousands" of Beatles disc racks produced each month. It was claimed that on Merseyside, sales of switchblade knives declined at precisely the time that Beatles guitar sales boomed.

In America, licenses were assigned to one Nicky Byrne and three partners, but signed away by David Jacobs at staggeringly small returns to NEMS: 10 percent, against 90 percent of income to Seltaeb. Quickly, as income from licensing the Beatles' name ran into millions of dollars, the scene was set for an ugly confrontation.

The American licenses were administered for Brian by a lawyer named Walter Hofer, who had been introduced to him by Dick James. There were early problems, recalls Geoffrey Ellis, who was working in Hofer's office in New York in late 1964, when Seltaeb was launched.

"We would issue to somebody, for example, a license to make Beatles watches exclusively for the U.K., and then to another manufacturer a license would be issued to make jewelery worldwide. And the two could obviously conflict. The chap who had got the U.K. would claim it, and the other would say he'd got worldwide authority for jewelery which included watches in the U.K."

Those problems existed before the arrival of Nicky Byrne and his three partners. "The business was far less sophisticated than it is now," says Ellis. "Brian virtually said: 'I don't know anything about this . . . David Jacobs will handle it for me.' And the license granted to Seltaeb was supposed to exclude the existing licenses."

When Brian realized the enormity of the percentage signed away by David Jacobs, he felt sick at heart. "He felt he'd let the Beatles down," says Ellis. In reality he was being conscientiously critical of himself: it was perhaps the first time he had delegated anything of significance to anyone, and it had rebounded on him through poor advice. And who could have predicted the scale of merchandise sales?

Brian needed as many sympathetic ears as he could find. He suddenly invited John Lyndon to supper. Brian was worried over the deals he had sanctioned in America. "How do you know," Brian began during their meal, "when you've made the right financial investments? How do you know when your legal advice is good?" It was a recurring, evidently worrisome question, one not amenable to an easy solution. Lyndon, in an invidious position, ventured that if Brian was going to be carved up, he might as well be carved up by people he liked. "And if it's by the brethren . . ." Lyndon continued, referring to Brian's fellow Jews.

"He rather bristled at that, anything that cast him as the Jewish entertainment entrepreneur," says Lyndon. "If you didn't tell him what he wanted to hear, he didn't like it."

Merchandising developed into the most litigious worry of his management. The first salvo was from Seltaeb, which in the autumn of 1965 sued NEMS Enterprises, Brian, and the Beatles collectively on the grounds of conflicting licenses. The lawsuits then flew thick and fast. NEMS said that unless Seltaeb agreed to substantial increases in the Beatles' percentages, it would attempt to cancel the agreement on grounds that it was inequitable. NEMS also asked for an accounting of money that it alleged was owed to the company. By December 31,

1966, NEMS Enterprises was being sued for $60 million in the United States; as well as contesting this figure, NEMS was counterclaiming for damages.

With the stage set for a legal showdown, there followed an episode that, like many in big courtroom dramas, bore the ingredients of a comedy. At its root was the American civil procedure in which each contesting party has a right to examine the other party before trial, usually with sworn testimony. Notices for Epstein and his NEMS colleagues to appear in New York arrived several times at the office of Walter Hofer.* Hofer mentioned them to Brian by phone, but with no commanding urgency. He believed he could handle the problem, whereas he should have mounted an immediate rebuttal and alerted Brian and NEMS that they had to provide statements in advance of the case, as required by U.S. law. But Hofer did not want to alarm Brian.

As the legal notices to appear and answer questions went unattended, the Supreme Court granted a judgment against the Beatles, NEMS, and Brian for default. The news trickled out almost casually from a court friend of Nat Weiss's who had seen the judgment being entered: "Your friends the Beatles have judgment of five million dollars against them . . . default judgment!" Weiss phoned Epstein.

"Is that good or bad?" Brian asked him naively.

"It's *terrible*," Nat answered. "It's a *nightmare*!" He added that Brian should have been in court to answer the charges. Epstein had complete confidence in Nat's ability to reverse the judgment, but Weiss said it would not be easy. "I'll have to have a very strong lawyer to vacate a judgment on default." He demanded that Brian come to America immediately.

On the plane to New York with Geoffrey Ellis, Brian said: "You know, Geoffrey, I really don't remember much about this Seltaeb affair. I admit I was far too busy doing what seemed to be much more important things about the Beatles' career, their records, tours, and so on and so forth. . . ."

"Well look, Brian," said Ellis, "I don't know either. I should know more about it myself."

---

*The U.S. music publishing associate of Dick James, he launched the Beatles' fan club in America.

In New York, a worried Weiss said that the most famous trial lawyer in the city, Louis Nizer, would be interested in meeting Brian with a view to handling his difficult case. A short, rather theatrical man with an office rather like a cathedral, he sat on a raised platform so that anyone entering immediately looked up to him. "Mr. Epstein, have you read my book?" he began upon introduction.

"No, have you read mine?" Epstein countered.

"My retainer is fifty thousand dollars," Nizer continued. Brian did not blink. He knew from Weiss that a heavyweight lawyer was essential, and with the millions of dollars at stake, Nizer's fee seemed tiny.

The rapport between the two men was clinched by Nizer's fine sense of showmanship. Upon his arrival back at the Waldorf Towers from their meeting, Brian found in his room a gift-wrapped copy of Nizer's book.

Louis Nizer assigned Epstein's case to an energetic Englishman living in New York. Simon Rose had qualified for the New York bar but was still impeccably British, eccentrically wearing a bowler hat around Manhattan. He waded into the complexities of the case with tenacity and enthusiasm, but nothing could camouflage Brian's lack of knowledge about his own affairs. This time, his chronic inability to delegate came back to haunt him. For two exhausting days in January 1967, he gave evidence in chambers at the New York Supreme Court, with tape recorders menacingly whirring away. Brian bristled as he was repeatedly addressed formally as "Brian Samuel Epstein." His face reddened with irritation, he was flustered by his own poor preparation. Never before had he faced an inquisition about his accountability.

"Brian was made to look an awful fool by the Seltaeb attorneys," says Geoffrey Ellis. As he honestly pleaded a lack of knowledge, his weakness was exploited. The tone of questioning was tough: "But *surely*, Mr. Epstein, you *must* have realized that there were millions of dollars involved? You can't sit down there, Mr. Epstein, and say that in the matter of a million-dollar advance to the Beatles, you were unaware. Was it not your *duty*, under your management contract with the Beatles . . . A million dollars, and you were footling about with an appearance in Brighton that evening?"

In the heated atmosphere, Brian became intensely flushed. His charm won through on one count, however: after testifying on the second day, Brian gave the judge a lift in his limousine.

In the midst of the battle, on March 19, 1966, Seltaeb issued a writ for libel against Brian, NEMS, Geoffrey Ellis, and Walter Hofer, claiming $3 million in damages. The allegation was that the Beatles party had written to certain Seltaeb merchandising licensees saying that the licenses Seltaeb had issued were not valid. A worried Geoffrey Ellis, who had joined forces with Simon Rose to provide the bedrock of the NEMS case against Seltaeb, told Brian he didn't have even a fifth of $3 million. "Hold on Geoffrey . . . never mind . . . it will all sort itself out," said Epstein calmly.

And it did. Brian was forced to post a bond, a form of guarantee, tying up his assets for a short time, and the vacation of the default judgment was eventually won. Finally NEMS paid off Seltaeb with $90,000. Brian incurred $85,000 in legal fees, which he insisted on bearing personally. The payoff to Seltaeb, to eliminate them from the merchandising arena, was infinitesimal compared with the potential millions of dollars that should have accrued to the Beatles and NEMS. It was a triumph for the tenacity of Louis Nizer and Simon Rose.

But the merchandising debacle cost Brian dearly emotionally. "It was a very embarrassing, awkward case and Brian was upset about it," says Ellis. "I don't think Brian had a great deal to be ashamed of because he had put it in the hands of his professional advisers. They had let him down. Perhaps he should have found out more about it. . . ."

When the Beatles heard about the merchandising chaos, during their American tour, they turned their heat on Epstein. Don Short recalls Paul, especially, berating Brian: "We should be making millions out of this . . . it's your fault that the contracts were not signed up properly." Epstein said to Short later: "It's so hard to keep the whole bloody empire going. I am just a manager. . . ." Short adds: "John and Paul especially, and George, who later got into the act, felt that Brian had not been negligent but careless."

"I don't think the Beatles really appreciated him as they should have done," says George Martin. "Once they had success, they tended to blame Brian for not getting what was due to them, rather than applaud him for the success. They developed a very negative attitude. When it came to light that he had mishandled certain things, they were very vocal in their criticism that he was a rotten manager. Forgetting that without him they would not have existed in the first place."

Brian was not a clever businessman, Weiss says. "But then, a good businessman could not have done what he did. Because Brian did not think in terms of coming out commercially good. He thought in terms of *grandeur*. Versailles was not a good investment when it was built. But over a long period of time it ended up being something the country has been proud of for hundreds of years! Very often, it's not the best businessmen who have the most profound influence on history."

14

❏

DRUGS

THE EMBRACE OF A CULTURE

"ONE OF THE BIGGEST HANG-UPS I ever had was to categorize people," Brian said a few months before he died. "And one of the things the Beatles have taught me is not to. They do not categorize people, things or music."

He was pontificating, during a long American radio interview early in 1967, about many aspects of the Beatles' role and attitudes. There had been rumors of a Beatles split. Brian said neither he nor the group could comprehend how or why this should be said: "I'm personally hurt by it." Their new single, "Strawberry Fields Forever" and "Penny Lane," would show their unity and new musical horizons. They were working on a new album that would "prove more than a thing or two." "I don't like to be particularly swanky about it," Brian said of the *Sgt. Pepper* LP the Beatles were recording as he spoke. "But it is going to be great.

"They really are working every single night in the studio . . . there's no reason why they shouldn't appear in public again, but I don't think it will be in the concept we've known previously . . . how creatively satisfactory for them are those tours except in terms of finance? And they don't think too much about that. They leave that to me. But I

318

don't think you would get any one of them or me to categorically state
that they will never appear in public again."

It was as if Epstein felt he ought to reintroduce the new, meticulous
Beatles to American audiences during the radio interview. For six
tumultuous years he had unfailingly defended them, and now, with
their career tilting slightly out of his orbit into mature self-determination, Epstein was still their best ambassador. He tried hard to mask
his disappointment at their decision to end touring, but those close
to him saw he was jittery on the subject. "The Beatles' taking control
of themselves after 1966 was Brian's biggest fear," says one aide. "He
knew their music would move on with a wonderful future, but if they
had no enthusiasm for performing, his role was weakened."

His uncertainty about their next phase was paradoxically out of
character. Brian's threshold of boredom had always been low, and
theoretically he should have welcomed the change of tempo. As it
happened, it became another unsettling chapter for a man who had
endured two years of buffeting: business mergers, physical threats on
the road, self-inflicted debility, and criticism on all fronts for manifestly
taking on too many artists. The Beatles were at the top of his tree; it
would have been more comfortable if they had not swayed while he
attended to some of the branches. Yet there was something deep inside
Brian that would act alternately as their best friend, salesman, and
world's number one fan, whatever the level of flak from outside and
inside. That tolerance, his total acceptance of their foibles, had always
been his hallmark. Who but a unique loyalist—some would say a
sponge—would have endured the taunts, the insults, the humiliations
he had faced from the Beatles, only to walk away and sing their praises?
He was the conformist who never properly tamed four mavericks, for
he realized that to do so would have been to tamper with their special
chemistry.

The Beatles' treatment of him was crushing. John Lennon, in particular, found an easy target in Brian's vulnerabilities. John enjoyed
exploiting minorities, and as a Jew and a homosexual, Epstein was
wide open to attack. At Dublin airport, a reporter asked John where
Brian was. "In America, sorting himself out a new rhythm-and-Jews
group," said Lennon. When he wrote the words to his song "Baby,
You're a Rich Man Too," John paraphrased the title in one conversation with Brian as "Baby, You're a Rich Fag Jew." Answering the

door to Epstein's flat one night to a male friend of Brian's, John leered: "Have you come to blackmail him? If not, you're the only bugger in London who hasn't." And on a plane once, in jest but hurtfully, Lennon looked at Brian's passport and said: "Oh look—he's a Jew and he's got a British passport!"

Brian tolerated Lennon's viciousness because he considered it part of the price one had to pay for nurturing a genius. "If Brian had not been homosexual, he would have struck out," says Bob Wooler of Epstein's passivity. "He would not have tolerated Lennon and his whims and waywardness."

Lionel Bart says Epstein was "extremely manipulated" by Lennon. "It was almost like a slave-master relationship." In Bart's flat once, Lennon brought a German girl to tears. Pointing to Epstein, Lennon said to her: "Your people killed six million of his relatives." Says Lionel: "This tall blonde Fräulein was weeping and I said to John this wasn't necessary. But John said she *wanted* to have a cry. But really, John was a very caring person. When he was being cynical about anybody or towards anybody, he really cared for them. But Brian was forever apologizing for John."

Despite the jibes, Brian's communication with John was better than with any other Beatle. Lennon had the vision to see that the goal of Brian's dreams justified his methods, and Brian always felt grateful for John's awareness when things were tough. Lennon trusted Brian's instincts, and Epstein always valued that loyalty.

Nat Weiss says Brian "genuinely loved John Lennon. I think John's attraction to Brian really motivated him towards getting involved with the Beatles. Lennon's very image—his caustic wit, his attitude, and his mentality—is what attracted Brian. I know he found him attractive.

"It was more than a sexual attraction. It was a sort of love which he felt. I don't think this manifested itself in any sexual way. In Cincinnati in 1967, Brian told me he was going to redo *A Cellarful of Noise* and told me of the time he spent in Spain with John. I think he enjoyed the fantasy of that trip but I think it would have been spoiled by anything physical. I don't believe it was consummated. But it was genuine."

In a Cleveland hotel after a particularly riotous concert in 1966, Brian and Nat sat up all night. Using his hands as a means of flowery self-expression, Epstein gave a rare précis of the Beatles as he saw them. "He went through them in the finest detail. It sounded to me as if he was on top of every one of their personalities. He had great insight into all of them."

Brian said his relationship with Paul McCartney, who had been the most combative right from their earliest association, was then improving. Brian related more to McCartney's music than to John's, which was a little more personal.

Brian's harshest words were reserved for George. Says Weiss: "He felt he was okay but not that talented, and he was being too pushy when he did the sitar thing."

"I wish George would stop making such a big issue of the sitar and just *use* it instead of getting it out of context," said Brian. Adds Weiss: "Brian thought George was demanding too much for contributing so little. Also George was a bit too paranoid, wanting to know how much is NEMS getting. And Brian said: 'I know George really loves me, so it's all right; you have to understand him.'

"But what he was really saying is that he's a sort of pain in the arse, pushing everything all the time. And George was always—because George is basically a paranoid person—always worried about who's ripping him off. And maybe he had good reason to. I personally like George."

George made Brian's job of policing the Beatles difficult. When Harrison was visiting Los Angeles in 1967, staying in a rented house which Nat Weiss had arranged on Blue Jay Way, a concerned Epstein phoned Weiss. Harrison was the Beatle who proselytized most about the benefits of marijuana, and Brian worried about the backlash and aggravation. "Now, remember, when he lands, make sure he does not say anything," Brian told Weiss, who met the Beatle at the airport. Says Nat: "The press were there. I told George not to say anything. Someone asked him about marijuana and George said: 'Oh, it's the same as drinking Seagrams.' Brian was furious." Brian considered that Harrison's reputation as the Money Beatle was fair, as he asked more questions than the others about their earnings.

Ringo, meanwhile, posed no problem as the passive foil for the other three. "Ringo is a lovely boy," said Brian. "One of the great assets of Ringo is that even though he's the least talented he's not uptight about it."

Pressed often by interviewers to name his favorite Beatle, Brian had the bland answer of the perfect diplomat: "The last one I was with."

As an entity, they were indivisible and Brian knew it more than anyone. When their dressing room, hotel, or limousine door closed with the four of them inside, they were beyond penetration, physically or mentally. It was a barrier, Epstein realized, that he would find increasingly difficult to cut through as they grew older, but his defense of their privacy was a major priority from the moment he met them until his death.

That concern was an extension of his own need for a screen around his life. "His own situation made him overprotective of other people," says Tony Barrow. "If details of *his* private affairs got out, that would have been his downfall and, as he saw it, the downfall of his artists. So he had to protect his own image in order to protect that of the artists. They had to be super squeaky-clean, which is why he took great exception to a lot of the remarks by Lennon." Brian preferred the antiseptic image of the Beatles loyally presented by Sean O'Mahony in *The Beatles Monthly Book*. But even that portrayal erupted into a controversy.

Entering a new phase as serious studio musicians rather than publicity-seeking pop stars, and increasingly making their own daily decisions and diary engagements, the Beatles would do no more formal photo sessions during that troubled year of 1966. This posed immediate problems for Sean O'Mahony, whose job was to mirror the group's ever-changing appearance. Epstein had not involved himself in the *Beatles Monthly*'s editorial content; he was far too busy to monitor the detailed coverage offered by the magazine. It generated publicity, was a useful platform to the fans, and gave him a healthy profit. He settled for a check and the monthly sales reports.

O'Mahony had behaved honorably, although he had failed to penetrate the enormous American market with the magazine. A publisher there had told him, pre-1964, that the Beatles would never make it in the United States; when they did, the American publishing monopolies saw to it that O'Mahony didn't get a foothold to challenge their own Beatles glossies. O'Mahony did, however, send pictures of the Beatles to America's powerful *16* magazine, fulfilling an Epstein need for publicity.

The Beatles' vital decision to change tempo away from fan appeal might have stifled some entrepreneurs, but O'Mahony, a dogged, opportunistic warrior, was determined to protect his investment. When the Beatles grew mustaches, and he was faced with no new pictures, he decided to ride out the problem. His retouch artist had often removed the spots from their faces and bags from under their eyes so that the fans' images of their heroes would be unblemished by reality. "They were cleaned up if necessary so they became the sort of pictures Brian wanted the fans to see," says O'Mahony. Now, the same creativity went into drawing mustaches on their faces in photos already in stock.

"This was, in a way, a message to the Beatles to say: What are you going to do now?" says O'Mahony. "The result was a bit of an explosion." Epstein summoned him to a meeting at Hille House. O'Mahony, sensing a heavy confrontation, took his lawyer.

"Who is that with you?" Brian asked after the initial exchanges.

"He's my adviser," Sean answered.

"Do you mean that he's your solicitor?"

"Yes, he is, Brian."

Epstein, flanked by two lieutenants, Tony Barrow and Neil Aspinall, announced: "The meeting is ended until I have my advisers with me."

A week later the meeting was reconvened, this time with Brian accompanied by his lawyer David Jacobs. Epstein had grave news for O'Mahony. The Beatles were no longer happy with what he was doing and he should cease publication very shortly. Asked by O'Mahony to explain, Brian said the Beatles felt that their new image didn't need a fan magazine of the type he was producing and therefore Epstein wanted it to stop. "They feel you don't tell the truth. You're not reporting them as they are. . . ."

O'Mahony exploded with anger. "The *truth*? What do you mean? Do you mean for example when we were in Blackpool, John Lennon flinging open the window of the dressing room and shouting to the fans below: 'Fuck off and buy more records'?" Was *that* the level of revelation Epstein and the Beatles expected from their authorized mouthpiece? Should the Beatles be reported as they *really* were? Or were there no-go areas?

There was a deathly hush. Epstein and Jacobs looked at each other. This was not going to be a walkover; the lawyer began the process of conciliation. If Mr. O'Mahony would agree to editorial changes . . .

O'Mahony said he would be delighted, if the Beatles were willing to give interviews and photographs, to accommodate their new attitudes, and he would publish up-to-date information. Tony Barrow, always the malleable buffer, told Brian that *Beatles Monthly* did an excellent job—"a means of communication between the Beatles, NEMS, and their fans; otherwise they just have to rely upon people like Ray Coleman at the *Melody Maker*." The meeting ended amicably, a tactical victory by Sean O'Mahony against an attempt by Epstein to bulldoze the magazine out of existence.*

Any attempt to present the Beatles as immature pop stars would have been laughable. They had smoked marijuana for two years. And a large part of their interest and attraction lay in their thrusting outspokenness which contrasted with the vacuous mumblings of so many pop people. Since he had once been rebuffed by Tony Barrow for trying to project himself to the media as the Fifth Beatle, Brian rarely strayed into that hazardous route again. He also gave scant recognition to the Brian Epstein Fan Club, formed in America. It received his cursory endorsement, "but he did not want to pursue it and was not interested in that path for himself," says Debbie Gendler, who promoted the club on U.S. national television. Brian seemed rather embarrassed by that.

❏

Brian was always insecure about the fact that his contract with the Beatles did not run forever. It was due for renegotiation in September 1967, the month after his death. Although he was confident they would stay together, the terms might change and diminish his income from 25 percent to 10 percent. And Brian believed that that would be absolutely fair. The Beatles, now older and wiser, rightly intended to exert artistic control over themselves. If they were not touring, NEMS

The Beatles Monthly Book is still successfully published by Sean O'Mahony, in the same format. With a healthy circulation, it has nourished the enduring interest in the Beatles, combining memories of yesteryear with, ironically, a policy of presenting the Beatles as rarely controversial adult mop-tops. To adopt a more vituperative approach would, says O'Mahony, be "like shooting myself in the foot."

would have no agency function for them. Brian would be happy to be their personal manager in the strictest sense.

The Beatles, Cilla, and Gerry would be enough. How he wished he could rid himself of the remainder of his cumbersome, largely unprofitable empire. Relations with Vic Lewis had soured since the Philippines debacle, and Brian no longer enjoyed watching much of the operation inside NEMS, where the artists' bookings were handled by Bernard Lee, a superbly efficient recruit from the Grade Organisation. The office ran smoothly enough under Geoffrey Ellis, executive director for administration; his personal assistant Peter Brown acted as a liaison; Alistair Taylor was the reliable general manager; and with Brian Sommerville and Derek Taylor gone, Tony Barrow conducted "negative press relations," deflecting most Beatles inquiries. It appeared, on the surface, a well-oiled machine, and it did in fact perform with few hiccups. But Brian knew of its inner problems.

The drain of the Saville Theatre, now losing about £3000 a week, preyed on Brian's mind. It was accelerated when Bernard Delfont persuaded Epstein to buy out his 20 percent share in the unprofitable theater. This shrewd move by Delfont merely increased Brian's responsibilities, but he was still attached to the idea of being a theatrical impresario. Brian's business moves, aside from his special care with anything relating to the Beatles and Cilla, were getting very shaky. The year 1967 was about to begin as catastrophically for him as it would end.

❑

Everyone in British show business knew of Robert Stigwood. The ginger-haired Australian sharpshooter had arrived in pop in the early 1960s and with entrepreneurial flash successfully launched actor/singers John Leyton and Mike Sarne. With offices in Edgware Road, London, he also ran a music paper, *Pop Weekly*. He had mushroomed into an antiestablishment independent with his own adventurous record imprint, Reaction. It was one of the first labels to be leased to a major company, maximizing profits for the owner and artists, an example of profit control Brian might have emulated.

Diversification by Stigwood into the theater followed, with management of such household names as comedian Frankie Howerd and Ray Galton and Alan Simpson (who wrote for Tony Hancock). Stigwood had ridden out financial crises to emerge, by 1967, with Cream, featuring Eric Clapton; the Who; and the lesser talents Crispian St. Peters, Screaming Lord Sutch, and Oscar. Stigwood had a huge act on the horizon, not yet hatched: the Bee Gees. But they had not been announced when, on January 13, 1967, the merger of Brian's NEMS with the Robert Stigwood Organisation was made public.

To all observers, this seemed Epstein's most bizarre business move. From his senior director, Geoffrey Ellis, to his secretary, Joanne, heads shook in stunned outrage. *"Why?"* Brian had imposed the merger on his team with no consultation, which was unusual. He knew it would be received with gaping mouths. Ellis, who heard rumblings, had made known his displeasure a few weeks before the public announcement: "Brian knew I didn't like Stigwood or the deal."

In the bar at the Saville just before Christmas, Brian said casually to Geoffrey: "Oh, by the way, I've got your Christmas present here." The two friends had exchanged modest gifts each year since their first meeting in 1958. This time, the scale of Brian's gift broke their unwritten rule: a beautiful white gold evening watch from Kutchinsky. "It was way out of the league of gifts we had exchanged before. I gasped," says Ellis. Brian said immediately: "I'm not doing this because of the Stigwood deal." It was, however, a transparent act of conscience.

The new order meant that Epstein would remain chairman of NEMS, with Robert becoming joint managing director alongside Vic Lewis. The anger of Brian's staff and artists would have been fueled to the breaking point if they had known the financial background of the merger.

Stigwood's business methods and reputation were the exact opposite of Epstein's. He was as ruthless and as cavalier as Brian was sensitive and nonexploitative. Robert's panache, in contrast with Brian's, stemmed from an inbred ability to sell refrigerators to Eskimos. Somehow, he had managed to persuade Brian that with his flair for management and his roster of rising acts, including Cream and the Bee Gees, their two companies would benefit from a merger.

Originally, he had wanted to buy out NEMS, including all its contracts. Brian said this would be impossible with the Beatles, since he was their personal manager. That takeover did not materialize. Instead, NEMS bought out Stigwood's organization, but with a hugely advantageous option to Robert. This gave him access to buy 51 percent of NEMS at a cost of £500,000 within a year.*

Of all the cauldrons into which Brian could have pitched himself, this was the most incongruous. Particularly weird was his inclination to give such a positive deal to Stigwood, whose track record came nowhere near his own, while demurring in his talks with heavyweight long-term successes like Tito Burns, Danny Betesh, and Bernard Delfont. Stoutly, Brian made his expansive statement: "Although Mr. Stigwood will share with me in the general managing of NEMS's widening interests, I shall continue to be personally responsible for the Beatles and Cilla Black. . . . There is no question of NEMS's existing artists transferring to the Reaction label, but it does give us an excellent outlet for new talent."

The relationship was doomed. Into NEMS with Stigwood came David Shaw, his financial director. It was soon apparent that the two management styles were entirely different. As his staff bristled, irritated at taking orders from the new men, Epstein quickly realized his mistake. He flared at the frequent sight of Stigwood's white Rolls-Royce outside the NEMS Argyll Street office, bedecked with parking tickets and blocking the path of Brian's own chauffeured silver Bentley convertible. His irritation was somewhat assuaged by a cluster of fans who regularly waited outside the office hoping to see the Beatles. Angry at their nonarrival, the fans put a knife through the hood of Stigwood's car. Brian walked past pretending he had not noticed but upstairs told a friend of the incident. Smilingly, he remarked that Stigwood would not thwart his car parking space again.

"There was anger," says Joanne Newfield, describing the arrival of Stigwood in NEMS. "Overnight, the company was split into two camps. It was awful. Everyone asked: 'How could it happen?' George Martin called Brian in horror." All Brian's diehards, their loyalty now stretched to its limit, registered disbelief when they saw Stigwood sitting at Epstein's desk during his absence. Even Brian raised the roof at the news that Stigwood had occupied his box at the Saville

*Although the NEMS-Stigwood deal was announced to the public on January 13, 1967, it had been agreed to three months previously. This meant that Stigwood's option had to be exercised shortly after Brian's death. The Beatles then told Stigwood they did not want him to manage them. He did not exercise the option and withdrew from NEMS, where Clive Epstein became chairman.

Theatre. "Brian went off his head," Joanne recalls. Audaciously, she confronted Brian about it: "Why? Why is this happening?" She says: "He got on his high horse and said: 'Oh it will be wonderful. Robert is going to run things for me. It will be fine.' " In a rare confrontation, Joanne said simply: "No. It's wrong. It won't work." Privately, he knew she was right. And the evidence increased.

All the staff's minds "boggled" at the news, confirms Geoffrey Ellis. "Vic Lewis was incensed. I was very unhappy; I didn't want Brian to have to give up. And I thought it was probably not a good financial deal for Brian in the long run. When Stigwood and his people moved in, it was oil and water, really. Because we may not have been the most efficient company in the world, but we were bright, young, enthusiastic."

As everyone predicted, the partnership did not work. Although "Eppy" and "Stig" continued to romance each other in a business sense, Brian was immediately regretting his blunder, looking elsewhere for solace and satisfaction.

Despite the problems surrounding Stigwood's arrival, he certainly imported some noble talent into Brian's organization, giving NEMS wider credibility as a home for the rock greats. As well as the Bee Gees and Cream, the Who came into the company for agency representation. To many, Pete Townshend's great group ranked second only to the Beatles in the rock hierarchy. Some placed them ahead of the Rolling Stones because they carried a social message—not with mere energy and sex appeal but with Townshend's articulateness, which Epstein respected. The Who were co-managed by Kit Lambert, an upper-class son of the classical composer Constant Lambert, and Chris Stamp, brother of the actor Terence. Lambert, an ex-public schoolboy, became an occasional visitor to Brian's home. He made no secret of his obsessive admiration of Epstein's unflappable style and exemplary manners, characteristics that the emotional, well-modulated, homosexual Lambert found lacking in the pop business. While Kit studied Epstein's panache, Brian admired the marketing strategy that had made the Who heroes of the "mod" cult in Britain. When they met, often at London's Cromwellian Club, they would play a verbal sparring game. Brian was fascinated by what motivated Lambert, who shared his artistic bent but was slightly more money-orientated.

When news of his partnership with Robert Stigwood reached America, it was interpreted as signaling Brian's retirement. "I'm too gregarious a person to go and sit on the grass," Epstein told Murray the K during a radio interview in 1967. There were signs that Brian sought challenges outside pop management. He planned to produce a film in Spain, based on his beloved bullfighting and focusing on the Seville Fair. "You can hardly believe the offers and propositions which are made to me," he said, referring to Beatles takeovers. "By people with a complete lack of comprehension." Denying a rift or split in his association with the Beatles, Brian lapsed into the dreamy jargon of the flower-power period: "There was not even a row. That's the ridiculous thing. Everything is, and everything was . . ."

When Brian told John Lyndon of the new association with Stigwood, he was met with the expected sarcastic retort. "Well, at least we should have an office full of statues," commented the acerbic production director in a tilt at Stigwood's scorned gimmick of sending statuettes of one of his lesser artists throughout the music business. Brian was upset, much more so when he found that the energy of his staff, as well as the funds of NEMS, was being dissipated by Stigwood in connection with the Bee Gees. Trouble began when Lyndon refused to attend an inaugural lunch party with Stigwood and his colleagues at Chapel Street. "I do not wish to sit down at the table with them," Lyndon told a hapless Epstein. Very soon, Stigwood insisted that Lyndon should accompany the Bee Gees on a three-week European promotion tour. "Brian didn't have the guts to say no. He wanted *me* to say no to Stigwood," says Lyndon.

The daily role of Brian's own team became fuzzy. To whom were they reporting? To Epstein, Stigwood, Lewis, Ellis, Shaw? When a visit by Cream to San Francisco to appear at the famous Fillmore West fell into the organizational lap of Alistair Taylor, Stigwood asked him to accompany them. Brian's general manager said he would go only if Epstein authorized it. Robert said he would get that sanction. Still awaiting approval, Taylor was packing for his morning flight, and insisted by phone to Stigwood that he would not fly without Brian's authority. Brian could not be located. That evening a telegram arrived at Taylor's home. "Under no circumstances will you leave for America. Brian Epstein."

A livid Taylor finally phoned Brian to complain about his inertia.

He had not planned to get on a plane without his approval, and the cold addition of his surname on a telegram was the last straw! Brian said: "I'm sorry you're upset, Alistair, but I was trying to save money." He was decisive: "You are definitely not to go." Taylor settled down for dinner. At 2:15 in the morning, Brian phoned back. There was music in the background as Brian, under the influence of something, said: "Alistair, it's Brian. You will simply adore San Francisco. You will have such a wonderful time. Stay the week. See you when you get back. Bye-bye." Epstein then hung up.

At London airport next morning, a Pan Am official told Alistair Taylor his boss was downstairs. "Not a chance," replied Taylor. "I spoke to him at three this morning and he was out of his head. He wouldn't come here. He's nothing to do with Cream." Intrigued, Taylor went downstairs. There, indeed, was Brian, immaculately dressed, looking for the Clipper Club. "I have just come to wish you a good trip and apologize to you personally for last night. And I'll just meet the boys before they go." Sober and ebullient, Brian was in perfect spirits as he shared a farewell drink with Taylor and Eric Clapton, Jack Bruce, and Ginger Baker, who, as Cream, would become one of rock's legendary forces.

Initially deferential to Stigwood, Brian quickly realized he had made a business error in allowing him inside NEMS. What he feared next was the development of an even bigger schism than that which existed between Vic Lewis and himself. His two partners were totally different: while Lewis thought the Saville was a loser from the start, and disliked Brian's indulgences, at least Stigwood was theatrical enough to understand Brian's creative whims. "Stig" was at least a *performer*.

Brian had been offered representation of the Bee Gees early in 1967, but he felt too beleaguered by problems to concentrate on launching the group that would eventually score resounding successes as singers and songwriters. The Bee Gees were passed to Stigwood, who saw their potential and, to the intense annoyance of Epstein, said of them: "They'll be bigger than the Beatles." Inside NEMS, a power play began, caused by Brian's frequent absence. Stigwood began to push Ellis aside in all decisions; when Brian heard of that, he was displeased.

Like Brian, Stigwood laid grandiose plans for his operations. Launching the Bee Gees with an enormous press party in New York,

he asked Nat Weiss to rent a yacht and stage a glamorous all-day party.
"Who are you going to charge it to?" asked Weiss. Stigwood replied:
"Bill it to my personal account."

Epstein phoned Weiss from London that night. He had heard of
the extravagant shindig. "Who is paying for this?" he asked tartly.

"Oh, Robert told me to charge it to his personal account," Weiss
answered. "Those were his words."

There was a silence before Epstein spoke icily. "Number one, he
only works for *me*," Brian began. "You're *my* partner. Number two,
you're going to have to pay for this. Number three, Robert owes me
ten thousand pounds on a personal loan already. Number four, when
the Bee Gees have come to America and earned a million dollars, *then*
they can take a yachting trip." Then he hung up.

Brian always admired artists other than those he managed or discovered, particularly Cream and Georgie Fame. But he resented Stigwood's hustle with the Bee Gees. "He liked their music, and liked
them personally," says Weiss, "but when Robert described them as
the next Beatles, Brian was furious."

❑

Against all the odds, Brian remained capable of important and successful business activities. The stress on his health and the visible and
hidden problems at the office, not least the renegotiation of the Beatles
contract with EMI, did not dissuade him from intense bursts of energy.
The work ethic instilled by his family remained a motive force. Flexing
the muscle of the new-look NEMS, he flew with Vic Lewis to New
York on February 27, 1967, and secured the right to present concerts in Britain that summer by the Monkees, the manufactured-for-
television group hilariously touted as "successors" to the Beatles.
While there, Epstein arranged a first New York visit by Cream, sched-
uling them to play with the Who during Murray the K's concert week
at the RKO Theatre; and he began negotiation for another British tour
for the Four Tops. Keen as ever on promotional tactics, he chaired a
press conference that surprised New York's media: at the unheard-of-
hour of 10 a.m. at Max's Kansas City club, he spoke of his company's
new interests in Cream, the Who, the Bee Gees. He blushed with
pride when the media people showed more interest in him than in his
sales talk about unknown pop groups.

When he began taking barbiturates back in his Waldorf Towers suite, Brian faced an angry Nat Weiss. "Don't take those things," Nat urged him again, seeing the path down which Epstein was going and knowing the hostility that built up when he overindulged. Says Weiss: "When he took too many he became really very nasty and very aggressive."

When Brian's assistant Peter Brown returned after spending money to an extent Epstein did not approve, Brian rounded on him. Remembers Weiss: "Brian took the change, threw it in Peter's face, and said: 'You're fired, Peter. And I want you to go back to London immediately. Economy class.' " Next day, Weiss interceded and cooled down the row. The outburst had been caused by Brian's ingestion of drugs. Weiss had wrestled him to the floor of the hotel suite, forcing a bottle out of his hand, throwing the pills out the window.

In New York, Brian always seemed at his most celebratory, living the champagne life most Sunday nights at Lüchow's restaurant on Fourteenth Street, enjoying conversations with strangers across the tables, and dining regularly at Quo Vadis, La Caravelle, the Chauberon, or Maude Chez Elle. Eating out was never spontaneous: the restaurant was as carefully selected as the wine and the cognac. Often, a chauffeured limousine ride round Manhattan and Central Park, with Brian smoking filter-tipped marijuana from a cigarette case full of ready-rolled joints, would be a favorite pastime. "Brian never rolled his own joints," says Weiss. "He wouldn't know how to begin. Brian could not even fold an envelope!" During the motor cruises Brian would invariably ask for the same song to be placed on repeat on the music system: the Four Tops' "It's the Same Old Song."

❑

The overriding qualities of Brian Epstein, which became his legacy to his artists, were his caring, kindness, and generosity of spirit. When John Lyndon was in Great Yarmouth supervising a dress rehearsal for a series of concerts starring Gerry and the Pacemakers and others, Brian suddenly discovered that Cilla was unhappy with the routine surrounding her show at Blackpool. Brian phoned his production director from London. "You must go to Cilla in Blackpool tomorrow. Cilla is unhappy." An airplane had been arranged by Brian to fly Lyndon over for the afternoon.

Lyndon protested that he was busy, but Brian said his flying visit was essential. He flew north for a few hours, later reassuring Epstein by phone from the stage door at Blackpool that Cilla was happy, and saying that he was now returning by air to Great Yarmouth. "Moments like that are to be cherished," says Lyndon. "If Cilla was unhappy, or any of his artists, then out of his pocket he would have taken the last ten quid to make sure that they weren't. This is what was so lovely about him." It therefore wounded Brian's pride and ego, and severely dented his emotional vulnerability, when Cilla became the most difficult of his artists at the time of his weakest physical state.

"You could tell Brian really cared for Cilla Black," says Debbie Gendler, one of the Beatles' American fan club secretaries. She saw Brian "brimming with pride" as he watched, arms folded in familiar position, as Cilla performed in the Persian Room of New York's Plaza Hotel. But empty seats proved what many show business insiders feared: the prestigious venue was far too sophisticated for Cilla, who was scarcely known in America. In not strategically planning her entry into the United States, Epstein for once had erred. Yet Cilla articulated her recognition of what Brian achieved: "I wouldn't have got to the top without him," she told BBC television's "Panorama." "Because I come from Liverpool; nobody wanted to know about Liverpudlians. It was a handicap because of the way we spoke!"

Problems with Cilla had begun in the autumn of 1966. During a demanding period, with his health threatened and his working pattern notoriously unsynchronized with his artists' diaries, Brian had been strangely neglectful of the girl singer he admired and loved. This became painfully apparent when, on November 3, Cilla opened along-side Frankie Howerd in the revue "Way Out in Piccadilly" at the Prince of Wales Theatre. Where once he would have visited the show at least once a week, Brian's visits after opening night became sporadic. A whole month went by without his appearance. Only a year before, Brian himself would have considered this a heinous crime.

Cilla felt ignored during the show's nine-month run and saw Brian's absence as a crushing insult at a stage in her career when she was full of youthful self-importance. Says Cilla now: "It's a terrible regret to me that he did not tell me more about his depressions, because I could have been a bit more understanding. In those days I was full of 'What's happening to *me*?' I was so very young. . . ."

Cilla and her husband Bobby also resented their treatment at the NEMS office—their requests to speak to Brian were diverted to others. With the old interaction gone and with so many non-Liverpudlians now on Brian's roster of artists, they felt deprived of the old "family" atmosphere. "We all thought Brian was a superman," says Cilla. "Suddenly we discovered he was vulnerable. It was quite a shock."

The time had come to leave Brian, Cilla decided. When Bobby phoned him with the decision, Brian was distraught. He knew he had been inattentive and that Joanne had stonewalled them on the phone many times. Immediately, Epstein invited them to lunch at Chapel Street. There he explained that he had been under pressure and also unwell. "We went on the roof garden of his house and there he broke down," recalls Cilla. "He said: 'Please don't leave me. Don't do this . . . think again.'" Cilla and Bobby wept, too, when a tearful Brian said: "There are only five people in the world I care about other than my family: the Beatles and you. *Please* don't leave me, Cilla. . . .'" She hugged him. Epstein felt she had previously shown a lack of compassion about his problems; now he knew she had no true conception that he had any.

"So how could I leave a fellow who said that?" she says now. "He did not make any excuses. He said he was on top of everything at his work. We decided to give it another go."

When Brian was with Cilla, his secretary noticed he always assumed a look of benign affection. The only day it deserted him was on that day. "Cilla felt neglected by Brian," says Joanne. "Robert Stigwood had called her about something and she went off her nut. She only ever wanted to discuss her work with one person—Brian. Brian was terribly fraught about this. But by the time they came down from the roof garden, they were all smiles. He'd weathered the storm."

It was, Cilla reflects, wrong not to accept the fact that Brian had to delegate some of his work. "Being totally naive and very selfish, I didn't put two and two together. I said enough's enough. There was no row." She was joining the long list of people close to Brian who realized, from his daily behavior, that inside the man of calm charm was a complex figure of lonely vulnerability. How many other managers or show-biz agents would show such genuine emotion, unlinked to money, over a relationship with one of their acts?

It was not the final contretemps in Cilla's relations with Brian. As he indulged more frequently in narcotics and admitted it to the media, Cilla was to be one of the few artists in whom he later confided.

The impact and heartache caused by his fracas with Cilla went deep. Brian rarely allowed the world to know of any internal strife. But backstage at the *New Musical Express* Pollwinners' Concert at Wembley, Brian met Tito Burns, then manager of Dusty Springfield. The two men exchanged pleasantries, but Burns noticed that Brian had come from Cilla's dressing room "looking white." "He said he was having a hard time."

"I'll do a swap with you," Brian joked. "You give me Dusty and I'll give you Cilla."

"Thank you, Brian, but I like the way Dusty sings."

❏

Neither the Beatles nor his closest staff experienced Brian's daily condition as clearly as Nat Weiss, to whom he spoke nearly every day.

In mid-June 1967, just as the *Sgt. Pepper* album ran into controversy with a BBC ban on the song "A Day in the Life" for its drug connotations, the Beatles were back in the studio. Confirming their embrace of the psychedelic and flower-power movement, they recorded "All You Need Is Love," a song by Lennon and McCartney. In a world satellite television link the Beatles, plus such pop luminaries as Mick Jagger, Keith Richard, Eric Clapton, Keith Moon, and Marianne Faithfull, sang the song that would become a world anthem before about 400 million international viewers. For Brian, too, it was a clarion call to his oft-concealed sentiments. The Beatles had actually capped a stunning album with a mesmerizing single.

"Tell Nat to call me immediately," Brian told a guest by phone to Weiss's New York apartment late at night. Nat called him from a pay phone. Clearly under the influence of something, Brian intoned his brief message to Nat: "All you need is love. Love is all you need. Tell Capitol Records Monday morning, that's the single. That says it all." Then he hung up. It was characteristic of his sometimes dreamy behavior that flower-power summer, when his inner discipline clashed with his outer posture.

❑

In midsummer 1967, two men's eyes met in the psychedelic clothes shop Granny Takes a Trip in Kings Road, Chelsea. Brian Epstein and the eminent songwriter Lionel Bart had been close friends since meeting in Liverpool three years earlier; Bart had gone there to absorb the atmosphere of the city for his play *Maggie May*. When Brian attended the opening of the show in Manchester, he was enormously impressed that Bart had taken along as his guest Judy Garland, whom he introduced to Brian.

Epstein had been a fan of Bart's work since the days when he ran the NEMS record store. Lionel's talent for writing music for the theater in shows like *Oliver!* and also Cliff Richard's early pop hit "Livin' Doll" was, to Brian, the perfect, brilliant marriage of his own twin interests.

That sunny day in Chelsea, both were with other company. They nodded to each other. Bart bought cowboy shirts and Brian indulged in his favorite apparel of the period, psychedelically patterned shirts. "I looked like a ragamuffin," Bart recalls. "Stoned out of my mind. We did not talk; we both knew we were both wrecked and on the road to nowhere."

It was not until Brian moved to London that they became close. Their friendship centered on a group of entertainment figures who met regularly at the home of singer Alma Cogan.* The singer with an infectious laugh in her voice wore notoriously flamboyant dresses, which Brian loved. She was famous in show business circles as much for her gregariousness as for her successful singing career.

Brian's friendship with Alma was one of the few enduring connections he made. The male-female aspect was irrelevant: she was a forceful, imaginative, naturally enthusiastic woman who loved her show business life. Brian admired the theatrical flair deep inside her. They socialized and spoke by phone extensively. Seen together, they seemed perfectly at ease, a couple destined to be together. Watching them enjoy a tête-à-tête dinner at Liverpool's Rembrandt Club, Bill

---

*Alma Cogan died, aged thirty-four, of cancer on October 26, 1966. Brian, who had only intermittent contact with her in the preceding few months because of his world travel schedule, was morose at the loss of one of his closest friends.

Harry firmly believed it was a permanent, significant relationship. "They looked so right for each other. I thought they were going to get married. I thought: 'He's fallen in love. Isn't that great?' They had a common sophistication that was absolutely fantastic." Virginia Harry adds: "They were unarguably *together*."

Alma's first-floor flat in Stafford Court, Kensington, shared with her mother Fay and sister Sandra Caron, a rising young actress, was a regular rendezvous for the clique led by Bart and Epstein. "That flat," remembers Bart, "was the sort of place that you could go to at three in the morning, throw coins up at the window, and eventually a face would come out and throw the keys down." Brian often arrived after a Beatles concert, either alone or with John Lennon, who, with his penchant for satire, addressed Alma's mother as Mrs. McCogie and sent her a Christmas card in that name.

To Brian, the particular attraction of the evenings was that guests were not restricted to pop people. Here he met such celebrities as Noël Coward, Sammy Davis Jr., Michael Caine, Ethel Merman, Danny Kaye, Tommy Steele, Cary Grant, Stanley Baker, and Terence Stamp, as well as theatrical folk invited by Sandra. Not all the visitors carried themselves with as much grace as Epstein. "Isn't it nice to see a real gentleman?" said Fay Cogan, to whom Brian usually took flowers.

"Alma was a very finely attuned, mystical person and she thought Brian was too," says Sandra Caron. "Alma went to his home many times and was bemused by his collection of hundreds of suits. They spoke often on the phone; Brian valued Alma's thoughts on many things." Whatever Fay's knowledge of Brian's and Alma's private lives, she visualized and hoped for a true romance. In the old days of arranged marriages, a Jewish mother like Alma's would have taken the initiative and pushed for it. But she was dealing with two fiercely independent adults.

Alma was a headstrong woman, difficult to cajole, and Epstein was one of the few men she would have wanted to manage her career. Alas, he could never do that: he had long ago made the pact with himself that the only girl singer he would manage was Cilla. But Brian's attraction to Alma was so special that he took her to Liverpool and introduced her to his parents; he sent her postcards whenever he traveled; he brought her a gift from each trip. Alma's extrovert, bubbling personality and keen interest in clothes struck a chord in him,

and if Brian was ever to have married, Alma seemed the perfect partner. Brian and Alma's affection for each other was never to be clouded
with talk of his homosexuality. "That was swept under the mat," says
Sandra Caron.

Brian and Lionel Bart were also "very thick." They went on a
bullfighting holiday together in Torremolinos, Spain; when they went
away independently, they exchanged holiday gifts. And when Noël
Coward complained to Bart that he was having trouble in America
getting together with "your friends the Beatles," Epstein instantly
smoothed a way for that meeting. Brian's friendship with Bart, though,
went beyond such meetings. Together they experimented with drugs.
"The flower-power thing was happening," says Lionel Bart, "and Brian
and I felt it necessary to be a part of it in many ways. We had to be
in touch with what was going on in the world of pop music. You could
say we were emotionally immature. But it was a courageous thing for
that man to do. He and I were experimenting, trying to find something
good in life but using oneself as a test tube. We all did it together
occasionally."

The use of drugs attracted Brian partly as a means of relaxation and
of extending his perception, as he believed it; and also to experience
how the Beatles were changing.

"It was the done thing," Bart continues. "I was into meditation
with the Maharishi, one of the first to do that about three years before
the Beatles got involved. We were all trying to find a universal theme
to touch the world with, and in a way, during Brian's lifetime, it came
off."

There was no hiding Brian's use of drugs from most of his staff.
But at the slightest mention that he should take care of himself, he
fobbed them off. Brian dropped the curtain on his private habits, just
as he had always done.

Early in 1967, when he was medically advised to get more rest, he
seized on the idea of buying a country home. Kingsley Hill, at War-
bleton, near Heathfield in Sussex, cost £25,000. A modest country
home with sunken fireplaces, sweeping drive, spacious gardens, and
a cottage atmosphere, it would be a regular weekend retreat, one that
Brian hoped would help him back to better health. While buying it,
he stayed with Geoffrey Ellis at the home of his lawyer, David Jacobs,
at 2 Princes Crescent, Hove. As Jacobs completed the purchase, Brian

immersed himself in buying antiques, furniture, and kitchen equipment from shops in nearby Brighton. He enjoyed haggling over prices for such items as a collection of cutlery. Kingsley Hill, he told friends, would not be a show business rendezvous but his haven of tranquility. His visits there were, however, infrequent.

Brian's behavior worried even Geoffrey Ellis. Never a participant in Brian's encounters with drugs, he had nevertheless become used to his friend's polarized moods. "He became appallingly unreliable and late. At some meetings with accountants, he just wasn't making any sense at all but would suddenly latch on to a relatively unimportant point and make a terrible scene about it, shouting and screaming 'Why wasn't this done'—but without seeming to grasp the whole course of the meeting." Ellis assumed Brian's irrational behavior was caused by his being "under some external influence."

His staff became frantic for his attention. John Lyndon, who as production director needed immediate decisions, would find important appointments suddenly canceled by a phone call from Brian. The matter would have to be dealt with now, briefly, by phone, he said. Tony Barrow, under pressure from printers to authorize artwork for concert programs, waited for days past deadlines for Brian's approval. Eventually, the staff came up with the speediest method of getting a response from Chapel Street. Memos to Brian carried two alternative messages for his action: either, "If I don't hear from you at midday on [a date], I will assume it is all right to go ahead"; or, increasingly, an "option box" at the foot of his mounting internal mail: "Yes/No/Let's Discuss—please tick as appropriate." The mere need for such missives was evidence of his unreliability. Yet Brian was confident that careful use of drugs was inseparable from the cultural stage on which he played a leading role.

That summer of love in 1967, as the Beatles sang "All You Need Is Love" as a soundtrack to the hippy dream, it did seem that the pop music revolution to which Epstein had provided the litmus test had indeed changed the world. "The Beatles were part of the shrinking of the world as much as jet travel," says Derek Taylor, a fellow traveler in drug experimentation.

"One knew," says Lionel Bart, "that the whole world was seeing things together for the first time ever. The Beatles sang a song of love and it was *good*. You can't say anything was bad except that a few people from that period aren't with us anymore. And a few people burned their brains out and are walking wounded, or dead. I was one of the lucky ones who survived with a few brain cells. . . ."

A full-page advertisement in the *Times*, London, on July 24, 1967, was headlined: "The Law Against Marijuana Is Immoral in Principle and Unworkable in Practice." Sixty-four prominent signatories called for the government to encourage research into all aspects of cannabis use, including its medical applications. They asked that cannabis smoking on private premises should no longer be an offence; that it should be taken off the dangerous drugs list and controlled rather than prohibited; that possession of cannabis should either be legally permitted or at most be considered a misdemeanor; and that all persons "now imprisoned for possession of cannabis or for allowing cannabis to be smoked on private premises should have their sentences commuted."

Brian Epstein signed it, as did all four Beatles, using their MBE appendages. Other prominent names supporting the reforms were Jonathan Aitken, David Bailey, David Dimbleby, Graham Greene, David Hockney, Herbert Kretzmer, George Melly, Dr. Jonathan Miller, Adrian Mitchell, Kenneth Tynan, and Brian Walden. Several doctors supported the motion, and the advertisement cited medical opinion that marijuana "is not a drug of addiction and has no harmful effects."

"I really believe that pot, marijuana or hash—whatever you like to call it—is less harmful, without question, than alcohol," Brian told the *Melody Maker* shortly after the advertisement appeared. "I think there is a terrific misunderstanding about marijuana and its effects. So many people have said it must be bad that this verdict is accepted without question. And of course there is the malicious association between drugs and pop music. I think society's whole attitude to soft drugs must eventually change.

"There is a parallel with homosexuality when that was a cardinal sin. Isn't it silly that we have had to wait all this time for the reforming legislation to go through? You hear of very few prosecutions for homosexual offences these days."

On the question of whether suppliers of marijuana would try to turn their customers on to heroin and cocaine, Brian said: "The laws governing soft drugs principally create the danger. But the danger exists already with alcoholics who turn on to hard drugs. I think, however, that the danger is remote in the present context. None of the people I know who smoke pot are interested in harder drugs. They are certainly aware of the dangers involved." He said he had been apprehensive that he might become addicted "but I took that risk. It was a calculated risk. But then I am in no way addicted to alcohol and seldom smoke cigarettes."

Brian was adamant that his statements on drugs should not be construed as advocacy that everyone should experiment with them. This particularly applied to his admission that he had tried LSD. (Brian took LSD about six times from mid-1966 until the end of his life.) He felt that its effect was profound. "I think LSD has probably lessened my ego. People who have had a bad experience are few and far between—certainly not as numerous as the people who have died from overdoses of alcohol. And in any case we don't know the details of these cases. They may have mixed alcohol with LSD.

"I certainly didn't feel I wanted to fly or jump off a ledge. The feeling is too impressive and personal to convey in words. I know that I have sometimes had too much to drink and felt awful and unpleasant the morning after. But I have never had a hangover from smoking pot or taking LSD.

"I think LSD helped me to know myself better and I think it helped me to become less bad-tempered."

But while hallucinatory drugs like LSD certainly curbed Brian's ego, a sensation he enjoyed, they also eliminated the necessity to compete. The drugs induced a sense of "the world is one," and in the opinion of Lionel Bart, "that was no good for a businessman like Brian."

15

❑

PEACE

PACIFISM AND FLOWER POWER

THE BEATLES' CONTRACT WITH EMI, which had expired in mid-1966, was finally re-signed by Brian on January 27, 1967. After six months of complex negotiation by Epstein and his lawyer—on this occasion Alan Leighton Davis of the prestigious firm of Goodman Derrick—EMI's Len Wood was glad to be able to give his astute chairman Sir Joseph Lockwood something he could recommend.*

Traveling to EMI's Manchester Square, London, office in his chauffeured Bentley, with Geoffrey Ellis at his side, Brian allowed himself a moment of self-satisfaction. "It does give me a great deal of pleasure," he remarked, "to arrive here like this, being ushered into the board room, as opposed to a few years ago, when I was crawling round the record companies trying to see an A&R man to get the tapes played."

*Lord Goodman was consulted by Brian when he considered floating NEMS as a public company, meaning that the public would have been offered shares in the Beatles. The plan never reached fruition. Lord Goodman's memory is of "an attractive young man. I was impressed with his unexpected youth . . . courteous, tactful, and seemingly exercising a very considerable influence over four remarkable temperaments."

Wood had been concerned lest he be outbid by another company. "Until that contract was finally signed, somebody might have come along and my arithmetic might be such that I couldn't meet it. . . ." The Beatles had been recording for the company under an interim agreement. The new deal was unique, giving the Beatles 10 percent of the retail price of their records, double the normal royalty.

At that time it was the highest royalty ever given to any artists. While many had criticized his soft attitudes to business, Brian had patiently dug in for a remarkable deal that would serve the Beatles well long after his death. At his insistence, they were obligated to produce only seventy single sides for the nine-year duration of the contract. This, in effect, meant five or six albums. At the end of the first four years of the contract, they would not need to produce any records; their work could be condensed into less than half of the contract's life.

Brian's rationale to Wood showed considerable vision and also disproved the theory that he could not regain his business mettle. It was, for him, like returning to 1962: nothing mattered more than the Beatles' future. While he wanted a nine-year link with EMI, "how do I know that in eight or nine years' time the boys will still want to record? But certainly they'll produce the minimum they are required to do within four years. There will be another five years in the contract where they don't have to produce anything, but at least you'll know they won't produce anything for anybody else."

Wood was worried: "What they could also do is produce those seventy sides in one year and then I've had it!"

Unlikely, said Epstein, adamant. "They're not prepared to sign anything that commits them to going on working in the recording field after four years. What they *are* prepared to say to you is that whatever happens, they won't record for anybody else for nine years."

No other contract had been requested with such an exclusion clause; to Epstein it was clear the issue was a "deal breaker." Although the Beatles split in 1970, the contract proved valuable to EMI: their solo work was considerable right through the four years.

For Epstein, that EMI deal was a triumphant beginning to what would be eight months of problems ending in his death.

❏

"The more successful he got, the more lonely he became," remarks Larry Parnes. "He bought the Saville for something to do in the evenings, because not a lot of work, except for a business dinner, takes place if your artists are not working. And the evenings are the worst time. He was a sensitive person who bottled up his emotions; but all the success and money in the world could not make up for his loneliness."

As he confronted the nettles of his business life, plunging himself into the artistic aspects of pop shows at the Saville, his private dilemma seemed to grow. The dreadful inner conflict of reluctant homosexuality, relationships nobody knew about, and a deep desire to have been married and been a father, surfaced in his candid conversation.

That wish to be a family man was "slightly unrealistic and unlikely to be fulfilled," he told the *Melody Maker*. "But it is one of the biggest disappointments to me because I must be missing out somewhere not having a wife and children. I would love to have children." On his visits to Liverpool, Brian doted on his niece Joanne, born to his brother Clive and wife Barbara on October 24, 1964.

❏

Nor was Brian especially allured by kindred homosexuals when it came to business. Joe Orton, an anarchic playwright then being acclaimed for his play *Loot*, was asked early in 1967 by Walter Shenson if he might be interested in working on the Beatles' third movie script. Orton, an admirer of the Beatles' work, was quietly enthusiastic. But over lunch with Walter, he rebuffed two ideas: that *The Three Musketeers* should be the theme and that Brigitte Bardot should play in it. Both ideas were poor, Orton said. Shenson and Epstein, both believing the maturing Beatles fancied a new direction from the comedy of *A Hard Day's Night* and *Help!*, anticipated that the tough edge of Orton's writing might be an excellent point of departure.

Orton was summoned to Chapel Street to meet Epstein and "the boys" in late January 1967. Not wanting to display either his enthusiasm or trepidation, Orton had formed a negative view of Brian. "I'd expected Epstein to be florid, Jewish, dark-haired and overbearing," he wrote later. "Instead I was face to face with a mousey-haired, slight young man. Washed out in a way. He had a suburban accent." (Orton was from Leicester.) Brian introduced a star-struck Orton to Paul McCartney over dinner.

The playwright's script, entitled *Up Against It,* was generally regarded as brilliant. Shenson thought it fascinating but warned Orton against exposing the Beatles to their fans in a story too raw. Walter promised to contact Epstein, who by then, early March, was in America negotiating for the British visit of the pop group the Monkees. The procrastination angered Orton, who believed Epstein to be blocking progress. "An amateur and a fool! He isn't equipped to judge the quality of a script," wrote Orton of the manager he now patently dismissed. "Probably he will never say 'yes,' equally hasn't the courage to say 'no.' A thoroughly weak, flaccid type."

The script was finally returned, rejected and with no explanation, early in April. It was a blow to the ego of Orton, who did not even have the satisfaction of knowing that a Beatle had read it. The decision had been Epstein's. It is possible that, just as Walter Shenson had predicted, Brian deemed the theme of *Up Against It* too much of a leap from the Beatles' previous two films: Orton had said his script had them "caught in flagrante, become involved in dubious activity, dressed as women, committed murder, have been put in prison and committed adultery."

The flirtation between Orton and the Beatles camp, brief and negative up to this point, had no chance to develop. On August 9, 1967, just eighteen days before Brian's accidental death, Orton was beaten to death with a hammer by his homosexual lover, Kenneth Halliwell, who then committed suicide. At Orton's funeral, they played his favorite song, the Beatles' "A Day in the Life."

❑

During Israel's Six-Day War with the Arabs in June 1967, the Jews who sensed that Brian was ambivalent about his faith had intimations that they could be correct. As world Jewry rallied to provide financial support, Bernard Delfont and London music publisher Cyril Shane contacted the hierarchy of British show business. They were astonished at Brian's negative action; he said he would prefer not to be involved. "Religion doesn't appeal to me now," he said. "I can't take it. I'm respectful when I should be, no more. It doesn't worry my parents." He was decisively neutral, he declared.

Brian's secretary argued with him over his refusal to give financial aid to Israel at the time of the Six-Day War. "He received many letters of protest from Jews," says Joanne, "but he wouldn't budge. I thought he was wrong. I got the feeling that he didn't want to stand up and be counted." Brian told her that he could get no guarantee from the Israeli authorities that any money he donated would be used for medical supplies only, rather than the war effort.

Those close to Brian said that if religion was reflected in concern for one's fellow man, then Epstein scored highly: he was deeply committed to humanitarian values, other people's welfare, and treating people fairly. Epstein himself said: "I refused to help Israel's war effort because I'm as sorry for a wounded Arab as I am for a wounded Israeli. People fundamentally are all the same and I can't discriminate. People should have no greater concern for the suffering of one race than they have for any other. I believe in, and want to help as far as I can, to understand mankind and whatever color, creed, religion, or nationality. And I think this sort of philosophy, however broad and general it sounds, is the only basic one that the leaders of the world can work from to attain world peace."

His views reflected his lifelong pacifism but might also have been conditioned by the view of orthodox Judaism towards homosexuality. While some members of his faith regarded it as an abnormality, a sickness deserving sympathy, most orthodox ministers condemned it, saying it was their duty to interpret the Bible unequivocally. Brian could therefore have felt ostracized by the faith into which he was born.

Although the orthodox view remains, Brian could have found acceptance, had he lived, because attitudes towards homosexuality have changed in some Jewish circles. Some rabbis in the Reform Synagogues of Great Britain consider that a meaningful relationship that brings two people together is better than no love, and should be viewed compassionately. In her book *Jewish and Homosexual*, Dr. Wendy Greengross writes: "Traditional Judaism has always frowned on homosexual behaviour, citing scriptural texts . . . but recently traditional attitudes have been questioned on many fronts and new interpretations given to Biblical passages and Talmudic commentary.

"Many rabbis and scholars now believe that the voluntary and mutual loving and caring of two adults who are free to commit themselves to each other is good and brings happiness to the whole community.

"Jews are born Jews. Homosexuals who are Jews have the same rights as any others to choose to be a member of a religious congregation, to give support where it is required, to receive help if necessary. If we deny these basic rights to our fellow Jews, we may find that we ultimately have to pay a heavy price.

"The families of homosexuals very often feel alone and uncertain, and afraid of asking for help, lest they be castigated and blamed for circumstances over which they have no control. We have moved out of the age, which shuts away those like the mentally ill who do not conform, into a more enlightened society."

Rabbi Tony Bayfield writes: "Jewish experience has led us to recognise a special obligation to embattled and oppressed minority groups . . . Judaism may have condemned homosexuals in the past but we can no longer continue to do so. It is time to welcome our fellow Jews into the community of which they have as much right as we to be a part."

Brian Epstein died some twenty years before such views were advanced.

Brian undoubtedly felt the pressure of being a Jew who was homosexual. As a schoolboy he had suffered anti-Semitism, and throughout his life his orthodox family background made him acutely aware of his religion. He knew that his private life was frowned upon—if not by his loving family, then by the community of Jews whose whispering condemnation was absolute. The inner emptiness, a feeling of rejection by his own people, never left Brian. And it showed.

Although Brian's secretary was not a practicing Jewess, his perverse attitude to his faith puzzled her. Once, he realized that he had reserved a flight to New York on Yom Kippur, the holiest day in the Jewish year. "Oh, that's really pushing my luck," he said to Joanne. She rarely discussed their Jewish roots, but suggested he should cancel the flight. Brian said it was essential to travel. She told him: "That's really bringing the wrath of God on your head."

Judaism figured in his thoughts, he said—"there are many beautiful, true, and good things written in the scriptures and prayers"—but Brian found it difficult to accept religion of any kind in a ritualistic form. "I find myself uneasy and unable to comprehend so much within the precincts of a Jewish house of worship." The same would apply, he emphasized, to any specific house of worship. Belief in life and God, he felt, was better than ritualistic, religious praying. On prejudice toward Jews, Epstein said: "A lot of it is occasioned not by people who are anti-Semitic but by those who are affected by it. Jewish people sometimes have a defensive attitude because they *expect* a hostile reception."

Summing up his views in the *Melody Maker*, Brian added: "Because I'm of Jewish parentage, I find myself respectful and tolerant. I love my family dearly."

Brian also incurred the anger of Anglo-Jewish organizations when NEMS was involved in the British presentation of a German passion play about the trial and crucifixion of Jesus. Vic Lewis was in charge of the acquisition negotiations. The play, condemned by the Board of Deputies of British Jews, was to be presented in England by a company led by another Jewish impresario, Philip Solomon. The *Jewish Chronicle* weighed in with an editorial criticizing Jewish involvement in the play. "For Jews to promote a specifically Christian religious spectacle as a commercial venture will be as distasteful to sensitive Christians as it will be to most Jews," the paper opined.

As the storm grew over Jewish managers' tacit endorsement of a play regarded as anti-Semitic, Epstein and Lewis withdrew their involvement. Brian said in a statement that it was an issue in which he found himself involved through no fault of his own. "Under no circumstances did I myself or my organization wish to give offense to Jewish communities here or elsewhere," he added.

Whatever his private thoughts on religion, Brian responded compassionately to some requests from Jews for help. He joined Rabbi Dr. Israel Brodie, industrialist Charles Clore, and government minister Lord Mancroft on a committee to aid destitute children. And in November 1966, at the height of his personal and professional traumas, Brian became vice president of the East Finchley (London) Jewish Youth Club, playing table tennis with its president, singer Frankie Vaughan, and visiting the club to immerse himself in its activities.

While none of his performing artists were Jewish, Brian veered towards the company of Jews in the music business, and some of his senior colleagues were Jews: Nat Weiss, Dick James, Don Black, Vic Lewis, Bernard Lee.

Politically, Brian was a socialist at heart and a lifelong Labour voter, even though "it's not very good for me because they take most of the money I make. You just don't believe they can take so much." Labour was more humanitarian than the other parties, he reasoned. That conviction, too, isolated him from most show business industrialists.

❏

Beyond his family and relatives—as well as his second family, which stemmed from his work—Brian had very few friends. His work was all-consuming, his hobby as well as his job. He liked throwing parties but became bored once he had seen to every detail: the wines, the food, the brands of cigarettes, the flowers.

Not even a roomful of people could conceal Brian's unease. He disliked small talk, always giving the impression that his mind was elsewhere. And since there was a social cachet in being seen in the company of the Beatles' manager, Brian became unsure of people who sought his attention or issued invitations. Did they want his personal company, or that of the most famous pop manager in the world?

For a man so adept in social exchanges, he was curiously unsure of himself. "He'd shown the boys the way to great achievement and success, and he thought all his friendships, love, and companionship would follow automatically," says Vyvienne Moynihan. "But these grow slowly. Brian never matured enough to realize that. He also didn't realize that the boys themselves would grow. Suddenly, there he was, poor little rich boy, all the success in the world, everybody accepting him. But he still didn't have any foundation.

"He needed friends more than most, because of his background. And he had certain emotional problems. Yet there were so few people. When he was well known, when the Beatles had made it, he received tons of invitations. And not one of them was from a friend. It was terrible."

"There was a tremendous loneliness and searching in him," says John Lyndon. "There was a gut emptiness. He searched and searched outside for something to fill it, but never ever could."

His regular haunts included the Cromwellian in South Kensington. A favorite of the pop scene, it had a minicasino that Brian occasionally visited with Robert Stigwood; and in the basement he shared drinks with disc jockey Mike Berry.*

"I think it was Brian who invented Scotch and Coke as a drink combination, which the Beatles later took up," says Berry. "He was quite a heavy drinker but you'd never really notice. I always found him very lonely. He was very frightened of being who he was, very shy. It was easy to embarrass him; he'd be more frightened of meeting somebody than they were of meeting him." From the Cromwellian, Brian would sometimes move on to the Scotch of the St. James Club off Piccadilly; his drinking companions would note that he never left alone, without a companion in his chauffeured Bentley. Brian's nighttime wanderings around London worried them all. Perhaps, they reflected, he liked finding companions who neither knew nor cared about his identity.

Of all the people who came to London with him, Brian found the most male comfort from Gerry Marsden. Ebullient and soft-hearted, Gerry remained a gritty Liverpudlian disinterested in the drug culture that attracted Brian and the Beatles. As a workaholic, he grew impatient with his manager's excesses. "He'd ring me at ridiculous times, four and five in the morning, asking me to go round to his home, which I did, to talk him out of his terrible depressions," says Gerry. "He was a lonely guy. He didn't have many friends except us, the bands, and Cilla. And we were working lots of times when he maybe needed company. Sometimes he'd ring and we'd say: 'Sorry, Brian, we're knackered.' "

And so continued the nightly cycle of a solitary man who sought solace alternately in the seedy pubs of London's dockland, in the Old Kent Road, or in the ritzy gambling clubs of Mayfair. The drain on his emotions was poignantly reflected once in a note left to his secretary with the familiar instructions not to disturb him until the afternoon. After a particularly good night at the tables, and feeling the need to prove it, he wrote on an envelope containing hundreds of pounds: "Dear Joanne. Please bank my happiness. . . ."

That summer of 1967, Brian's friends saw a man whose moods and

*Unrelated to the singer of the same name whom Brian befriended at the Cavern.

appearances "seesawed." Paddy Chambers, a guest one weekend at Brian's home in Sussex, saw his old friend looking sad. "It was almost as if he knew what was coming." The carefree, happy, and smiling Eppy whom Chambers had known in his Knightsbridge and Belgravia homes had deteriorated. "There was something on his mind. He'd bought this luxury home but money couldn't buy him happiness."

"The change in Brian within the last couple of months was a terrible thing to see," says Tito Burns. "Whereas before he was nearly always smiling and looked rosy, he was suddenly nothing like that." Burns tried tactfully to warn Epstein of the downward spiral he seemed to be on: "Brian, did you read about so-and-so? Killed himself on drugs. What a schmuck. Had his life in front of him. . . ." The remarks went unheeded.

"Brian never seemed to have any close friends like we all did," says Johnny Gustafson. "I noticed that any men we saw him with we would never see him with again. Generally it was the wrong period for that man. He was too naive. He learned about life in general later than the bands did. The musicians were very down-to-earth; we'd learned how to cope with the world partly through the Hamburg scene. But Brian had no grounding: he stepped right in at the deep end and was sucked into the whirlpool of drugs. And he had neither the experience to know how to escape from it nor the stamina to do anything about it. It was very sad and really upset me."

❏

For all his inner pressures, Brian's flashes of insight and decisive actions reminded the cynics around him that he was still a commanding presence. But he felt exposed inside the NEMS office in London, alienated from his own company by Stigwood's self-serving bustle and Lewis's conflicting personality. Now he disliked going to his company headquarters in Argyll Street because he didn't enjoy what he saw there.

Only two people in the world understood him, he mused: his mother and Nat Weiss. The compassionate, ultrasensitive Queenie showed her concern about his loneliness and rootlessness. Nat Weiss, on the phone from New York most days, would tolerate none of Epstein's tantrums but demonstrated a telepathic reading of his best friend's thoughts. Brian liked his strengths.

In the spring of 1967, Brian made a brilliant move to cement his business link with Weiss and to ensure that nobody at NEMS could strengthen a grip on the company by appointing American representation of his or her own choice. Inside his suite at New York's Waldorf Towers, Brian began talking to Nat about improving their association: "We have three choices. Either we could be involved together legally and work together, which means you would handle the boys with me in America and Canada; or you could do whatever you want to do and I'd be glad to help you; or we stay friends, whatever you like." Weiss said he was flattered . . . at which point Brian pressed a bell and an aide came in with a contract for Weiss to sign. Brian said, smiling: "I thought you'd say that."

The three-year pact, signed on May 16, 1967, gave Nemperor Artists in New York exclusive representation of all NEMS artists in the United States and Canada. For a first year's payment of $1000 a week, Nemperor became "the American and Canadian office of NEMS," while the contract made Nemperor the management office of all the artists under NEMS's control. The arrangement was reciprocal with all Nat Weiss's acts, which were expected to gain in number.

The significance of the deal went unheralded and largely unnoticed by Brian's colleagues. It seemed to simply consummate the business link that had already existed between Epstein and Weiss since 1965. But its formal binding of the two companies was more resolute than most recognized, making Weiss Brian's official American representative.

Brian acted only just in time. A day after signing the agreement, his doctor suggested he enter the Priory Hospital in Roehampton for a complete rest.

❏

Luckily, his attendance at the Priory was flexible. He was able to leave the clinic frequently; this meant that nobody outside his tight circle of friends and colleagues knew he has having hospital treatment. Two days after his admission, on May 19, he hosted at Chapel Street the launching party for the Beatles' new album, *Sgt. Pepper's Lonely Hearts Club Band*. All four Beatles were among the small gathering of media people. Brian looked sanguine, with no sign of the debility for which he was being treated. He was perhaps quieter than usual but circulated smoothly among his guests, who animatedly enjoyed discussing the

new album with him. He had personally checked the exquisite catering: the fine champagne, vintage wines, glazed poached salmon,
and caviar.

The music, unlike anything the Beatles had done before, heralded
a new era in popular music. When the author took out a notebook
to take down some comments by John Lennon, Brian moved in immediately to ensure that nothing controversial was being reported.
He had been played a tape of the new album while at the Priory,
and was immensely proud of the Beatles' major leap into mature
music.

The sleeve for the *Sgt. Pepper* album was planned by the Beatles
as a montage of the world-famous personalities who had helped shape
their lives, including Marilyn Monroe, Karl Marx, Edgar Allan Poe,
Albert Einstein, and Mae West. The idea worried Epstein, and he
insisted that permission be sought from every living person whom the
Beatles wanted to feature. The Beatles thought he was being too
pedantic. Paul McCartney interceded, visiting Sir Joseph Lockwood
at his Manchester Square office. The EMI boss warned: "You'll get
a lawsuit from every one of these people unless you get their permission
to use their photograph. It could cost us millions."

McCartney was confident that they would all say it was fine.
"They'll love it: they'll do anything to please us."

"Under no circumstances will I allow Ghandi to appear," Sir Joseph
retorted. "He's a great holy man in India and we have a monopoly
over there." Later that day, Lord Shawcross, the former Attorney
General, and Lord Goodman coincidentally visited Sir Joseph's office.
Two of Britain's top lawyers, they said the album cover was loaded
with danger. Sir Joseph returned to McCartney with an ultimatum:
EMI would require indemnification to the figure of £50 million against
any legal action that arose from the *Sgt. Pepper* album cover. "I said
we will have the right to deduct that from all your takings," recalls
Sir Joseph. "Paul said: 'Oh well, that's all right.' "

The crisis was averted by the industriousness of Wendy Hanson,
who, although she had left his staff, returned at Brian's impassioned
request, solely to take charge of the problem. She made scores of
international phone calls and obtained all the necessary permissions.
Brian was not thrilled with the concept. And the episode was a further
reminder of Paul's ascendancy.

Despite his personal condition, Epstein still seemed enthusiastic bout extending his management functions.

In the middle of recording *Sgt. Pepper*—with George Martin at a Cilla Black session—McCartney had phoned Mike Leander, then a staff producer at Decca but known for his striking musical arrangements for the Rolling Stones and Marianne Faithfull. At the Abbey Road studios, Leander had scored the arrangement for "She's Leaving Home." Epstein, impressed with the song's unique arrangement, invited Leander to Chapel Street. "He was lying in bed, a charming man, very serious and sensible. He said he'd like to manage me," recalls Leander. The arranger could not accept. As a staff producer at Decca, working extensively for EMI as a freelance, he had to content himself with a flat-fee payment of £18 for his work on "She's Leaving Home," one of the Beatles' most successful album tracks.

Brian's offer showed how he still wanted a management stable that was multifaceted in its scope. And yet, two years earlier, the thought of Brian conducting a business appointment from his bed would have been unthinkable—the sort of casual conduct for which he would have fired a subordinate.

After the Chapel Street party, and unknown to most of the guests, Brian returned to the clinic. Next morning, he wrote lucidly by hand to Weiss in New York:

> Nat dear,
>   I feel so much better, I really wish you were here for another night in Swinging London!
>   Last night I went into London (and out of here for the first time since I came) to attend/host the boys' press party at Chapel Street.
>   It all went very well and I came back here to be provided with my most solid sleep so far (albeit only five hours). But they're doing well for me here by and large and I'm happy to be put straight.
>   I expect to go home about Thursday or Friday. It'll be a week or two before I'll be able to come to the States but I trust all is well in the meantime. I really hope Eric* is being looked after

---

*Eric Anderson, a twenty-four-year-old New York folk singer whom Nat and Brian planned to manage. He was signed by Weiss to Nemperor after Brian's death. The company remained the North American management representative of the Beatles, Bee Gees, Cream, Gerry, Cilla, and the Cyrkle.

because I do sincerely believe he can be most important and rewarding to us from all points of view. . . .

I hear fantastic reports of the Bee Gees' U.S. acclaim—and Beatles album cover is beautiful (although I rather think the Capitol cover may be even better because it will be stiffer) and it's on its way to you.

Will speak to, and see you, soon.

Love, Brian.

There were other outings from the Priory during his nine-day treatment. On the Sunday following the *Sgt. Pepper* party, he hosted lunch for his parents at Chapel Street and then returned to the nursing home. Brian seemed freshly stimulated by life itself, for in a letter to Nat Weiss he wrote:

I'm really sure this place is doing me a lot of good. For the first time really in six years I'm having some rest and feeling some peace. Of course I've not been completely bound to the place. On Saturday I went to tea and to spend a few hours at Ringo's where John, Cyn, Julian and George all showed up and that was really nice.

Last Friday evening I hosted the press party for the boys at my house. This went very well. The photography session in my drawing room verged on an American press conference scene—so I did some holding of my breath as everyone bounced around my antiques. And all seemed pleased.

I hope the house in Sussex will be ready for a shortish convalescence when I leave here which should be about next Sunday or so.

Well, Nat, it is a bright, sunny, beautiful morning (6:30 a.m.) and as I can hear the early jets coming in I'm thinking of you all. . . .

At the Priory, where one of his biggest hurdles was his problem with insomnia, Brian's moods dipped and soared. He swung from total command of his business to quick-to-tears sentimentality. But his instincts, commercial acumen, and enthusiasm for music never deserted him: he said to George Martin that he was slightly concerned that the Beatles might be slipping in popularity on records. That remark proved the springboard for their going into the studios and making "Strawberry Fields Forever" and "Penny Lane."

He asked his office to deliver to him at the Priory a list of his artists' positions on the American best-selling record charts. When a member of staff arrived with only the Beatles' positions, Brian was livid: "What about the other artists?" The man did not have them. "If you really were interested in music and our artists, you would have wanted to know. You are fired."

There was elation when a bouquet of flowers arrived from John Lennon with a get-well card that the Beatle had signed: "You know I love you and I really mean it, love John." Says Weiss, who had stopped off at the Priory on a visit to London: "It brought Brian to tears." But when Weiss said he had to return to New York from his quick trip, Brian panicked. He beseeched his friend to stay at Chapel Street until he was released from the nursing home. Weiss stayed in England long enough to attend a party that only Epstein could have masterminded.

Part of Brian's therapy on leaving the Priory was to make more use of his Sussex country home. Upon his discharge, on May 25, he announced a grand "house-warming" event at Kingsley Hill for three days later—an event that proved to be right in keeping with the flower-power and drug-induced psychedelic summer of 1967.

Brian greeted three Beatles and their wives at the door with the beaming pride of a proud father welcoming home newly married children: his role was certainly evolving as they grew, but there was the thrill of knowing that as musicians they were about to reassert their genius with the release of the *Sgt. Pepper* album. To Brian's intense sadness, Paul McCartney could not attend; since Brian was never happier than when all four Beatles and he were in the same room, Paul's absence upset him emotionally. But the party went ahead, a hallucinatory event of epic proportions, some of the guests being met at the entrance with LSD and marijuana.

George Harrison, who had one of his best non-Beatle conversations with Brian at the party, recalls that just before he died, Brian was "on the verge of possible realization which might have brought him to another level." He showed a healthy interest in George's enthusiasm for Indian cultures.

And Brian was among his closest friends: Lionel Bart, John Pritchard (former conductor of the Liverpool Philharmonic), disc jockey Kenny Everett, Nat Weiss, Mick Jagger, Marianne Faithfull, and Robert

Stigwood. Brian even paid for an air ticket for his former assistant Derek Taylor and his wife Joan to fly in from California; Taylor, who recalls taking LSD at the party, led the sing-along at the grand piano, deputizing in the role that Brian had hoped Paul McCartney would take. "Paul should have come," intoned Epstein to many guests. Brian was high on mixed substances, but he clearly missed Paul. "He knew it meant a lot to me," he added.

The day after the party, Rolling Stone Brian Jones, a special friend of Brian's, arrived with Georgie Fame. With Nat Weiss and others, Brian drove them to a rural setting for lunch. At the coffee stage, Epstein offered Nat a sugar cube. "No, I don't need sugar in my coffee Brian," said Weiss, realizing it was LSD. Recalls Weiss: "I've never taken acid and I didn't want to start there." Brian smiled as the two men ruminated on Epstein's excesses. Later, he drove Weiss to the railway station to get a train for London. In a typical flash of Epstein extravagance, when he caught sight of Nat's purchase of an ordinary ticket, he took it back to the booking office and changed it to a first-class ticket.

Brian believed sincerely in the philosophy of flower power, of love and peace and bells. Often he dressed in a psychedelically patterned shirt, and frequently referred to his friends in letters as "beautiful people." This was not merely an affectation of the period. Before entering the army he had talked of being a conscientious objector; he had always evangelized for world peace.

Pacifism was preached by many who adopted the counterculture philosophy of flower power and peace. Brian, who had been to see the important film *The War Game*, wrote to friends urging them to see it. Directed by Peter Watkins, the simulated documentary showed what could happen in the event of a nuclear war. The film had a profound effect on Lennon, influencing him greatly in his peace campaign, which he began in 1969 with "Give Peace a Chance." McCartney also spoke strongly of the film's significance. Epstein obtained a copy of *The War Game*, which he screened for many visitors to Chapel Street.

He had an affinity with the hippy dream but his departure point from it was, predictably, in business. The budget-conscious Liverpool shopkeeper deep inside him maintained that to be able to indulge, to be able to buy good dope, one had to make a profit at work and ensure that business was on a financially sound footing. Although he had made big mistakes, none had occurred in embryonic Liverpool, where he ran a "tight ship."

The need for stability in the euphoric atmosphere of the free-spending entertainment world, and the danger of converting hippy philosophies into a business ethic, were, alas, lost on the Beatles. Intoxicated by wealth, largesse, and unworkable ideals, they were busy planning a financially suicidal venture outside Epstein's direct orbit. With Paul as the driving force, they decided to launch their own company and call it Apple. The name symbolized, to Paul, starting afresh—"A is for Apple" was one of the first phrases every child learned on encountering the alphabet—and it heralded a new era for the Beatles. "Paul was the one who conceived Apple and he was the Beatle who gave Brian the most worry," says Joanne Newfield. "Paul was the one who would get on the phone and create. Brian had to explain and battle longer with him. On social occasions they were fine together, but whenever there was a worry from the Beatles, it always came from Paul. Apple was highly indicative of how difficult it was for Brian to cope with Paul at times."

Defying Brian's instincts and judgment, but under the aegis of lawyers who worked with Brian (Alan Leighton Davis) and his accountant (Harry Pinsker), the Beatles registered Apple Music Limited on May 25, 1967. Brian was an opening director, as was his brother Clive, and the first shares were held by Lennon and McCartney (twenty-four each) and Harrison and Starr (twenty-five each), with four left unplaced.*

While Paul pushed the Apple scheme through, Epstein had an ally in Lennon, who saw its pitfalls. "John had dreadful misgivings about Apple," says Joanne.

Brian believed Apple would be the Beatles' folly. How absurd, he told friends, that the Beatles, who had wisely steered *him* away from their music-making since their earliest days together, should now believe *they* had sound business sense. As evolving musicians on the threshold of an exciting, innovative, and important era in pop, they should continue to be artists, he firmly believed, and leave the administration to experts.

---

*After Brian's death, the company changed its name, on December 4, 1967, to The Beatles Limited. The company remains active.

Another Beatles project tantalized him. As part of their new interest in ecology, they planned to buy a Greek island for £100,000 and to develop it into an idyllic home for the Beatles, their families, and friends. As John and George went off to research it, Brian wrote to Nat Weiss: "A dotty idea, but they're no longer children. . . ."

❏

For two months after his country-home party, Brian improved mentally and physically, and appeared more able to submerge his business worries with good cheer. When Geoffrey Ellis casually mentioned that he was planning to visit the opera at Glyndebourne with William Cavendish, the personal assistant to Sir Joseph Lockwood, Brian said that the place was only fifteen minutes' drive from Kingsley Hill, where he was spending the weekend alone. "It's ridiculous driving all the way back to London after the performance. You must both spend the night at Kingsley Hill. And what are you doing about eating?" said Brian, warming to the idea of playing host. Having arranged to meet them during the interval, Epstein arrived in his Rolls-Royce. To Ellis's astonishment, in the trunk was a magnificent champagne picnic that his housekeeper had prepared. Epstein took delight in presenting it and cleaning up afterward, leaving his two friends to reenter the opera and join him that night at his house. To Geoffrey, it signaled the reemergence of the Brian he had known years before, full of similarly thoughtful gestures.

The final evidence, if needed, that the Beatles had changed from pop star mop-tops with hummable songs and family appeal into mature adventurers came when Paul McCartney admitted in an interview with *Life* magazine that he had taken LSD. The story was seized on by British Sunday papers and splashed across their front pages on June 18, 1967, Paul's twenty-fifth birthday.

Paul phoned Brian at Kingsley Hill the night before, saying he had told a journalist he had sampled the drug. After a sleepless night and after worrying throughout Sunday about the ramifications, Brian drove back to London on Monday knowing he would be asked to comment. "I finally decided to admit I had taken LSD as well," he said later. "There were several reasons for this. One was certainly to make things easier for Paul. People don't particularly enjoy being lone wolves, and

I didn't feel like being dishonest and covering up, especially as I believe that an awful lot of good has come from hallucinatory drugs. People tend to think of the San Francisco hippies as dirty and unhappy, but in fact they are doing rather better things than the people who lead our nation."

Coupled with Brian's admission was the warning that neither Paul nor he advocated the general use of LSD "by all and sundry." So he intended, he added, to warn people as well as to own up. They also wanted to help the cause of the Rolling Stones, he declared. "It is particularly unfortunate that they should have been scapegoats."*

His own decision to sample LSD was made because "I'd heard a lot of good about it and I had sufficient understanding of it to know what I was doing. I had also read a lot about it." He took it after the Beatles had tried it. "We are a closely knit circle and we influence each other." He emphasized that he did not "turn on" at first because he felt the need for drugs. "It was an experiment."

The Beatles could always handle themselves with the media. But Brian's first thoughts went to his other artists, who would be exposed by his personal LSD admission. That Monday, he took Cilla to lunch at Les Ambassadeurs in Park Lane. The purpose of the hurried meeting, he told her, was to clear the air over Paul's admission that he had taken LSD and pot. "I want you to know before the news is published that I've taken it as well," Brian told Cilla.

Cilla remembers how she "went berserk." "You're my *manager*! How can you be so irresponsible? They'll think I'm taking pot, now. And *you* tell *me* not to smoke on television, 'Juke Box Jury.' " During their tetchy meeting, Epstein said he thought Cilla would like to know what he was saying so that she could alert her mother and tell her not to worry about her. Brian needed all his persuasive powers to calm

---

*A reference to the trial on drugs charges of Mick Jagger, Keith Richards, and art gallery owner Robert Fraser, from June 27 to 29 at West Sussex Quarter Sessions. They were convicted, fined, and sentenced to jail. On June 30 the *Times*'s editorial, headlined "Who Breaks a Butterfly on a Wheel?," led a strong public outcry. On July 31 the Lord Chief Justice dismissed the charges against Richards and gave Jagger a conditional discharge. Only Fraser went to jail. On August 18 the Stones released "We Love You" to thank the public for their support. Lennon and McCartney sang on the record.

down a girl who distanced herself from the unreal world that Brian and the Beatles had entered.

Nat Weiss recalls bizarre drug-induced behavior by Brian at his New York apartment: "Brian was witty and very engaging, very charming, but if he smoked a joint or two, he'd take all the furniture and move into the center of the room and pile it up into one heap, almost like a tombstone. We'd talk all night, and then around four or five in the morning he'd go into the kitchen and bake a cake." Brian slept little, only about two hours a night. "I was amazed when I'd get up in the morning," says Weiss. "I could hardly see straight, but there would be Brian making notes of what was to be done in the day."

Brian's suits had specially made inside pockets that contained amphetamines. "I saw him taking Dexedrine. They were not illegal but an accepted medication for people like students who had exams, people who had a lot of work to do. They're now prohibited because people abuse them. They were normal medication for anyone overweight and I used them; they depressed your appetite. They kept you awake and you couldn't seek oblivion," says Weiss.

"Brian used to have all the people I knew roll all his joints, twenty or thirty, because Brian couldn't roll a joint! He was the least mechanical human being I've ever known." At Weiss's apartment building, when he stepped into the elevator, Brian often accidentally pushed the alarm button instead of the floor button.

Nat never saw his friend with circles under his eyes, "nor wasted, nor anything like that. He was always *up* but he wasn't speedy. He was taking all these pills, and it wasn't until I saw that that I imagined why this man slept so little. He had enormous energy. And when he wanted relaxing, the pot did it." The habitual drinking was replaced by marijuana. "Brian occasionally drank a vodka but I never saw him drunk," says Weiss.

"He was fascinated with trying things but he wasn't dependent on them. Brian tried acid because he thought it would give him further insights, and then he finally came to the conclusion that acid wasn't the answer.

"He thought it would widen his scope and comprehension. And there was the fascination with the glamour of something surreptitious. But he was never addicted or attached to anything. If the downers took hold of him, it was only to come back from the cumulative effect of all those amphetamines, so he could rest. Because he'd gotten to the point where he never slept. And consequently he found himself on this terrible seesaw of uppers and downers.

"So one was combating the other, and it began to take a toll on him physically.

"He was not a manic depressive but there was a psychological thing: there were times he would just fall into depression. But it was indigenous to him. Brian was not a guy who made heavy use of mythium and mood elevators, things like that. They could have kept the balance in his chemistry.

"But he had strange fascinations. What made him great destroyed him."

16

❏

BOREDOM

"LOVE, FLOWERS, BELLS, BE HAPPY"

THE CUMULATIVE EFFECT of LSD had been to reduce his ego, Brian told me in mid-1967. Yet with his relationship with the Beatles in a new phase, Cilla's departure only barely averted, and very few of his other acts enjoying the success of yesteryear, Brian needed to refuel his confidence. If 1966 had been a troubled year, 1967 had begun even more disturbingly, for he now bitterly regretted the deal he had given to Robert Stigwood.

Despite all his problems, however, Brian was showing resilience. On July 12 he flew to Belgium, where NEMS was fielding the British team in the Knokke-le-Zoute song festival. His spirits received a boost when Britain's team beat France to win the European Cup, with singer Roger Whittaker named the best individual act for his version of "If I Were a Rich Man."

❏

At first sight, Brian's next move, the appointment of a manager of *himself*, seemed incomprehensible, a ludicrous massaging of his ego. But the more he considered it, the more logical and practical it seemed. Nat Weiss was the obvious choice, since Brian wanted to increase his activities in America. "Let Nemperor Artists manage me, you can manage my career, and I'll pay a commission," Epstein said to Weiss a month before he died. "And you'll become the manager's manager!"

Enthused, Weiss set to work immediately, planning for Brian to host a television program for the Canadian Broadcasting Company, which would pay for his trip to the States on September 2, 1967. There would be a much-needed holiday in the Hamptons and some meetings in New York to raise Epstein's profile. Then Nat would take Brian on to California to discuss a film and other possibilities. This was to be the grand trip Brian relished.

"I had everything planned for a month's stay," says Weiss, "setting up this whole new career. It was the selling of Brian Epstein and it was to be a lot of fun. Brian was so 'up' about it. He couldn't wait to get here. Unfortunately, it never happened."

The trip was expected to yield an important management signing for Epstein and Weiss. During a visit to Los Angeles, Nat had heard the singer-songwriter Harry Nilsson and recommended him to Brian as a potentially exciting addition to their stable. Nilsson had recorded an elegant album, *Pandemonium Shadow Show*, which contained a Beatles medley, and he was beginning a close friendship with John Lennon and George Harrison. Epstein was anxious to meet him and strike a business venture during that proposed U.S. visit. It would have been the second signing to Nemperor for Weiss and Epstein and a creative coup.

Just as Brian seemed to be regaining a little optimism, the phone call on July 17, 1967, from Clive in Liverpool to Chapel Street gave devastating news: their father was dead. In Bournemouth, sixty-three-year-old Harry had rented a flat so that he could recuperate completely from his heart attack a year earlier. He and Queenie had enjoyed three months by the sea and were so relaxed that they even talked of buying a flat and living there, to Brian's delight. Harry talked about opening a small shop to interest him during a quieter life. That morning, Queenie woke to find her husband dead.

The tragedy was intensified by the fact that Queenie knew nobody in Bournemouth. It was astonishing and heartwarming for her when Brian, who she thought was abroad, arrived by her side a few hours after Harry's death. He was the first on the scene, having arrived back in Britain the previous night from the song festival in Belgium.

The loss of his father shattered Brian. The years of pre-Beatles misunderstanding had long since been replaced by Harry's pride in his eldest son's achievements and fame. As he joined Clive in comforting his mother, and arranging for Harry's body to be taken back to Liverpool, Brian pondered on their great days together, visiting the races at Chester, and the zeal for work that his father had instilled in him. He mused, also, on his parents' blissfully happy thirty-four years of marriage. During the return from the cemetery to the new Epstein home in Woolton, he sobbed uncontrollably.

Brian stayed at his mother's house for the weeklong period of mourning (sitting shiva) required by the Jewish faith. Queenie needed little persuading that she should soon leave Liverpool and take a flat in London not far from his Chapel Street house. Knowing how his gregarious mother would enjoy the theater and restaurants, he said that she should stay with him in the meantime, as soon as she felt physically fit enough to travel. They made plans to buy an apartment for her in Whaddon House, the block in Knightsbridge that had been Brian's first London home. He also suggested she should go with him to America on September 2. No, said Queenie, that would be too soon after Harry's death.

While in Liverpool, he went to Queens Drive to visit his old friend Rex Makin. Sitting in his garden, eating raspberry sorbet on a hot summer's day, Brian reflected that the Beatles story had become so monumental, far more difficult to grapple with than it had been six years earlier, when Makin had refused to draw up Brian's contract with them. Brian gazed nostalgically at his old home next door. "You must come and see my home in Chelsea," he said to Makin. "And I have a country home. . . ."

Makin demurred. "What would I want to go and see them for, Brian?" he asked testily.

"Well, use them whenever you want to," Epstein offered. The world traveler seemed oddly morose as he pondered on the people and things he had left behind.

His forthcoming American trip, as well as waves of varying emotions, was on his mind in a letter he hand-wrote from Liverpool on July 25 to Nat Weiss:

My dear Nat

Thanks so much for the cable. It was nice of you and very comforting. I'm coming to N.Y. on September 2. I'd have come earlier but my father's passing has given me the added responsibility of my mother.

The week of Shiva is up tonight and I feel a bit strange. Probably been good for me in a way. Time to think and note that at least now I'm really needed by mother. Also time to note that the unworldly Jewish circle of my parents and brother's friends are not so bad. Provincial, maybe, but warm, sincere and basic.

I'm going back to London tomorrow Monday and returning Friday. I'll have to spend a lot of time with her. After all, although my father was sixty three (a little young to die, I think) she's only fifty two and must find a new life. They were very devoted. She knew nothing else (married him at eighteen) and had nearly thirty four years' happy marriage (must be good). So you see I must do all I can.

Anyway I'll come in September for a couple of weeks or so. Should be able to fit in a trip to California (maybe Vegas en route).

The boys've gone to Greece to buy an island. I think it's a dotty idea but they're no longer children and must have their own sweet way. A few weeks ago they all (with wives, Neil and Mal) came to Sussex for a weekend. Mick and Marianne joined us on the Sunday. It was a divine time. Poor Mick (he looked beautiful). I hope he gets off when the appeal comes up at the end of the month. Of course the whole thing from the beginning was stupidly handled. I'll tell you all when I see you.

Beatles maintaining number one here for some weeks. I'm very pleased. Should be OK in U.S.

Can you put things in motion for September 2nd?

S'pose I'd better stay at the Waldorf for about eight days and then L.A. for about seven.

Well, can't think of anything else now. I'll relate some tittle tattle when I see you.

> Love to all my friends . . . take care.
> Brian

For the next three weekends, Brian traveled from London to Liverpool to be close to his mother. When he was not with her, he phoned her every night. Worried about her solitude, he arranged for her to have a housekeeper. He dutifully went to Bournemouth with Clive and his mother to help pack the belongings that had been left in the flat. "If I hadn't been coming here today," Brian told her there over lunch at the Green Park Hotel, "I'd have gone to the memorial service for Vivien Leigh." When he had been training for RADA, Brian had escorted his tutor, actress Helen Lindsay, to the first night of Vivien Leigh's show *South Sea Bubble* at Liverpool Playhouse. Her personality enthralled him, and as a lifelong fan of the actress, he had delighted in a conversation with her during the Beatles' Australian tour in 1964.

Queenie's arrival at Chapel Street on August 14 for a ten-day break totally inspired Brian. He comforted and entertained her handsomely. They took breakfast together, went to dinners at the finest restaurants: Carrier's in Islington and Le Gavroche in Mayfair. He rose at normal morning times and went to bed fairly early—a routine refreshingly different for him. He went to Hille House to work on most days. At night they went to the theater; they also saw the film *A Man for All Seasons*. Brian drove his mother to her brother's and sister's homes in London, and they all enthused about Brian's plan to move his mother south from Liverpool permanently.

He didn't miss a promotional opportunity, slipping a copy of Gerry Marsden's new single, "Gilbert Green," through the letterbox of disc jockey Pete Murray's flat, which was located in the same block where Aunt Frida lived.

A week before Brian died, he hosted a small family dinner at his Chapel Street home. The guests were Aunt Frida and her sons Peter and Raymond. The only difference they noticed from the Brian of yesteryear was that he opened the door dressed in yellow trousers and multicolored psychedelic shirt; and the dinner was served by a butler. "He was so normal," reflects Raymond. "He was adamant that since his father had died he should be closer to his mother. They'd always been very close, but he wanted her to move down to London to be near him." Brian seemed in perfect spirits.

That week, Brian also went gambling in Mayfair. There he met a casual acquaintance who had attended Wrekin College with his brother Clive. "He was in an affable mood," remembers Peter Scott. "He might have staked five hundred or a thousand pounds on chemin de fer, but he could obviously afford it. He wasn't foolhardy, wasn't a show-off. . . ." And Brian was not drinking heavily. Scott detected a "very warm, generous and kindhearted person." His demeanor, only a few days before his death, gave Scott no clue of impending disaster: "He was laughing and joking with all of us in the room."

The days preceding Queenie's arrival in London had been marred by Brian's tantrums on the phone to Nat Weiss in New York. Brian had taken hold of himself and steered fairly clear of barbiturates since his father's death, but the abstinence had left his nerves frayed. He was pompous and rude to Weiss in discussing his coming trip, and his friend had again castigated him for his manner. On August 14, Brian wrote to "My dear Nat":

> This is to say again and confirm what I said earlier on the telephone. That I'm very and sincerely apologetic for having offended you the other day. I really didn't mean to be personally offensive and certainly not officious. I cannot say how distressed I was to receive your letter and to realise how unpleasant I must have seemed.
>
> I'm truly relieved that you were still not angry on the phone and I hope you will accept my sincere and humble apologies in the spirit with which they were meant. Thank you anyway for making me feel easier. Please give my best to all and particularly remember me to Eric and say that I'm looking forward very much to seeing and working with him.
>
> But most of all I'm looking forward to seeing you in New York.
>
> > Love, Brian.

❑

As Queenie Epstein and Joanne Newfield sat in Brian's lounge in Chapel Street, Paul McCartney arrived with his sheepdog Martha. He asked if they would look after the dog for a short time; that night, he said, he was going to be inducted into the world of transcendental meditation, along with the other Beatles. The Maharishi Mahesh Yogi was giving a lecture at the Hilton Hotel. Queenie looked bemused. "What on earth do you want to bother with a stupid thing like that for?" she remarked. "I mean, Paul, you have so much talent, the world at your feet. . . ." But the Beatles, led by Pattie Harrison's enthusiasm, were hooked into spiritual awareness. Nothing would divert them from yet another phase of their evolution.

Although they had interested Brian in meditation, his mind was occupied by more earthly happenings. Besides the distractions of the Beatles' nonmeditative activities—indulging in Apple, buying a Greek island, planning the ill-conceived *Magical Mystery Tour* television film—Brian had to rededicate himself to Cilla's career. And he was excited about his impending American visit. On August 23 he again hand-wrote a letter to Nat Weiss, saying he would fancy a yachting trip during his visit to New York.

> Maybe on the Sunday we could have all manner of all pretty persons aboard and then on Monday we could mix the company a bit with the likes of Eric Anderson, etc., Bobby Colomby, the odd Cyrkle and other celebrated beautiful people.
>
> Actually I'll leave all this in your hands because provided I don't have to sleep at a place other than the Towers I'm sure I'll enjoy whatever entertainment you provide or arrange.
>
> Incidentally I hear from Geoffrey that my dear old friend Brian Bedford is appearing in something with Peter Ustinov at the Lincoln Centre—could you arrange for us to see it while I'm in NY? Apart from that I'm not aware of anything else to see at the theatre—are you?
>
> Maybe it might be fun to see Judy Garland one night (if tickets are difficult try her or her people directly—I do know her).
>
> Assuming the Royal York (hotel) is the very top in Toronto I'll be happy. I don't think it's the same hotel I've stayed at on my two previous visits to Toronto with the Beatles. But then I don't remember its name and it was huge, not very good. When you requested Jarvis to arrange the accommodation I trust you asked him to include reservations for yourself.
>
> Hope that we've got a lovely place in L.A. to stay in so that we can entertain all the beautiful people suitably. And I hope you managed to confer with Derek. [Taylor].
>
> I also hope that I'm not asking for too many things. But I'm anxious for this to be a good trip for us both. Anyway (say I indignantly) you are my manager.
>
> Eric's album makes lovely, happy, contented, dreamy listening. I'm very addicted to Anderson.
>> Till the 2nd—
>> Love, flowers, bells, be happy and look forward to the future.
>
>> With love, Brian.

Nat Weiss would never hear from Brian again.

❏

The news that came by telephone to Brian on August 25, 1967, was a fillip: BBC television was offering Cilla Black her own series. She had earlier refused Brian's suggestion that she should be the U.K. singer in the Eurovision Song Contest. "Sandie Shaw won it for Britain this year and there's no way we'll win again," she told Brian. Instead, he had aggressively sought the TV series. Here was tangible evidence for his leading lady that he had renewed his vigorous plans to expand her career, as she wanted, out of purely pop music and into show business. He could not wait to tell her, but could not locate her on holiday in Portugal. As he busily prepared himself for the weekend at Kingsley Hill with Geoffrey Ellis and Peter Brown, Brian wrote a note to his secretary:

> Joanne:
>   Please send suitable cable to Cilla requesting she calls me where I am (Sussex or here) S.A.P. as I've tried to contact her but impossible. Urgent matter.

He drove the fifty miles to Kingsley Hill that Friday afternoon anticipating a convivial weekend with friends, his first real outing since his father's death. Upon arrival in the early evening, he telephoned his mother in Liverpool, just as he had done every night since she became a widow. He sounded fine, Queenie recalls. He told her of his imminent restful two days and his plan to go to Bangor, North Wales, the following Monday to join the Beatles in their transcendental meditation studies with the Maharishi; he would probably visit her in Liverpool afterward, en route back to London.

At Kingsley Hill on that fateful Friday, Brian was puzzled by the nonarrival of friends from London whom he had casually invited to dinner. Geoffrey Ellis remembers that Brian, Peter, and he had consumed a few bottles of red wine and a couple of ports when Brian went to the telephone to invite other friends in London to join them. But it was a holiday weekend: people were either unavailable or away. He decided, nevertheless, to drive to London to seek some "action."

He was clearly disappointed that this eagerly awaited weekend in Sussex was not going to be stimulating enough with only two familiar friends. Although he had consumed a fair amount of wine, Brian was not drunk, Ellis says. Brian was yet again leaving his own party early, bored by its predictability.

Boredom, that motivating factor in Brian's life, was again coming into play. It was boredom that had pointed him towards Liverpool's Cavern when he outgrew record retailing. It was boredom with success, even on the monumental scale of the Beatles, that caused him to adopt far too many artists. It was boredom that persuaded him to buy the Saville Theatre, which, for all the pleasure it gave to Brian and thousands of others, was a sponge on his resources and his nerves. It was boredom with the predictable, safe way in which NEMS was operating by 1966 that encouraged him to bring in first Vic Lewis and then Robert Stigwood, decisions that brought on self-doubt.

Now, a social occasion in the idyllic Sussex countryside was boring him. His route out of this boredom would prove fatal.

The first person to feel that something strange was happening that weekend was Brian's intuitive mother. At 7 p.m. on Saturday, she was surprised not to have received the customary nightly phone call from Brian. "I rang up Kingsley Hill and spoke to Peter and Geoffrey. They said: 'Brian had to go back to London.' I then rang up the house at Chapel Street. Antonio said: 'Mr Epstein is sleeping.' I shall blame myself all my life for what I said next: 'Well, don't disturb him.' You see, that wasn't an unusual thing for Brian to do. Brian did keep funny hours. Even in Liverpool he would often leave me a note saying 'Don't disturb, I'm asleep.' So I didn't worry. Both Peter and Geoffrey told me he was in good spirits. They didn't seem unduly concerned." Queenie, nevertheless, had a nagging worry that something was curiously amiss. "Brian was erratic in some things. He *could* walk out of his own parties if he got bored. That was nothing for Brian to do . . . so when they told me he was sleeping at seven o'clock I thought he'd gone for an early night."

By 2 p.m. on Sunday, a worried Queenie again phoned Chapel Street to be told by Maria that Brian was still sleeping. Shortly after she phoned, Alistair Taylor's phone call to Clive gave him the news: "Clive, this is really terrible. We're at the house and Brian is dead."

"You're *lying*. You're *lying*," an enraged Clive said before hanging up the phone in disbelief. His distressed wife Barbara called back soon afterward to have the news confirmed.

A doctor and family friend, armed with sedatives, went with Clive to break the news to Queenie, who had not yet adjusted to the loss of Harry only six weeks earlier. It was beyond her wildest fear that she should now lose the son who shared her interests. She and Clive went immediately to London.

❏

Two hundred miles away in Bangor, North Wales, the Beatles found the news hard to reconcile with their new spiritual education. The Maharishi told them that if they harbored negative, sad feelings, these would be transmitted to Brian's spirit, so they should think positively. To the newspapermen who arrived at Bangor as they prepared to leave for London, the Beatles were too numbed to marshal their thoughts. Paul said it was a great shock and he was very upset; and George said there was no such thing as death, only in the physical sense.

In Portugal on holiday, visiting a night club with Tom Jones, Cilla Black and her husband Bobby Willis were approached by a waiter. "Your manager is dead," he said. Bobby, angry at what they thought was a sick joke, was furious. Tom Jones phoned a local newspaper. "It's true," he said, returning to the table. Cilla flew home the next day. She felt "desolate."

In Anglesey, only seven miles away from the meditating Beatles, Gerry Marsden was at his holiday home. He had no telephone. A local farmer brought a message: Norman Cowan, doctor of Gerry and Brian, needed to speak to him urgently. The news was what Gerry dreaded. Even in shock, he was annoyed with his manager and friend for not listening to his sound Liverpool advice to curb his excesses. If *only* he had seen him more recently, he repeatedly told himself. But Brian had stalled him. "He knew I'd say: 'What the bleeding hell are you doing, Brian?' We never made it. I felt a bit shallow. I should have really grabbed him. When you're that far down, it's lonely to get back up."

As Brian lay in bed on that Saturday night, three thousand miles away in New York his best friend was enthusiastically anticipating his arrival a week later. At his apartment at 301 East Sixty-third Street, where Brian had often stayed, Nat Weiss was checking with Brian's chauffeur about the music cassette Weiss had prepared, as always, for the car that would meet Brian at the airport. Such attention to small details endeared Weiss to Epstein.

Twelve hours later, mid-morning on Sunday, New York time, a phone call from Geoffrey Ellis halted Weiss's plans for the coming week. "I've got something terrible to tell you. Brian is dead. The press doesn't know about it yet. . . ." Weiss was dumbfounded, speechless. The tears would flow later. Within an hour, American journalists were phoning him as he packed his bags for the night flight to London.

In Newcastle-on-Tyne, Vic Lewis had just gone to bat during a charity cricket match. A man ran toward him saying he must phone his wife immediately. Convinced it was a family tragedy, he phoned his sobbing wife Jill. "Brian is dead," she said.

"Thank God," said Vic Lewis. It was an instinctive reaction, he said, to hearing that nobody truly close to him had passed away. He continued his cricket match before driving back to London for a Monday morning board meeting. He went to London Airport to drive Nat Weiss into London. Weiss was "disgusted" by Lewis's talk of how he was already planning to take over NEMS.

In Wiltshire, where they had gone to their cottage with their newly born daughter, George and Judy Martin were parking their car when someone walked across and said: "Your friend is dead." To mark the birth of Lucy on August 9, Brian had sent a huge teddy bear made of flowers to the hospital. When George and Judy returned to their London home, a further bouquet from Brian was waiting for Judy on the doorstep; the flowers were dead.

At the Saville Theatre that night, the audience leaving the first of two scheduled performances by Jimi Hendrix heard the news from the ingoing crowd that Brian had died a few hours earlier. Adorned with the flower-power uniform—jangling bells and beads and gaily colored clothes—they might have been expected to generate peaceful, compassionate vibrations. But amid talk of the second concert being canceled to mark the death of the theater owner, many became noisily angry and callous. "What difference does it make? I've paid for my tickets and want to see Jimi Hendrix play"—such was the mood of the second-show crowd. Production director John Lyndon recalls:

"The last thing Brian would have said was cancel my show. So I purposely didn't with the first house. It went on as an epitaph." The second show was canceled on the insistence of the musicians.

On the day after Brian's death, five red carnations were spread in a row on the top step at Chapel Street. Written on a rough piece of paper was the message "We love you too." The admirers were anonymous.

John, Paul, George, and Ringo went to Chapel Street on Tuesday to see Queenie. "They were very distressed, and said they'd do anything I wanted about the funeral." They wanted to attend, but Queenie, fearing it could turn into a circus with television cameras, said it would be best if they stayed away. "They were like four lost children," she remembers. John Lennon said to her: "Come to India with us and meditate."

What, Queenie asked, did the Beatles *do* when they indulged in meditation? "Well, you think of something—like, say, a carrot," John replied. Brian's mother raised a smile and brought reality into the brooding atmosphere. "Whenever I think of a carrot," she remarked, "I think of tomorrow's lunch." Cynthia Lennon gave her a single red rose.

Jewish law decrees that a body be buried within forty-eight hours of death. Because of the impending inquest, the coroner could not release Brian's body until a postmortem had been carried out.

The next evening, Brian's body arrived at the synagogue in Greenbank Drive, Liverpool, where he had impressed everyone, including his tutor, at his bar mitzvah nineteen years earlier, and where he had stood alongside his family on the Sabbaths and High Holidays. From there he was taken to the Jewish Cemetry, Long Lane, Aintree, and buried in Section A, Grave H12, near his father, in a ceremony that began at 7 p.m.

Gerry and Cilla and Nat Weiss and Peter Brown were there, along with the family; Cilla, upset at the Jewish law which discourages women from attending the actual burial, had been so distraught at the synagogue that Queenie had to give her a Valium. Compounding the gloom at the graveside was the tactless theme of the officiating rabbi, Dr. Norman Solomon. Ignoring all Brian's achievements and fame, he said that the man he scarcely knew was a symbol of the malaise of the 1960s generation.

This was the final crushing exit for a tearful Nat Weiss. Defying the Jewish rule of no flowers at funerals, he felt compelled to honor George Harrison's request that he toss on top of Brian's coffin a farewell on behalf of the Beatles: a solitary white chrysanthemum concealed in a newspaper.

All four Beatles wore black paper yarmulkes at the memorial service; their ample heads of hair caused the hats to blow away repeatedly, to the amusement of the congregation gathered at the New London Synagogue, Abbey Road, St. John's Wood, on October 17. They planned to wear psychedelic clothes but, in deference to Queenie, finally went in suits.

It was a fitting, ironic memorial setting. The synagogue is five minutes' walk from the telephone outside the St. Johns Wood Underground station. From there, five years earlier, an elated Brian had cabled the Beatles in Hamburg with the most important message of his and their lives: "EMI contract signed, sealed. Tremendous importance to us all. Wonderful." And only a minute's walk away from the synagogue lies the recording studios in which John, Paul, George, and Ringo realized his dreams.

"He encouraged young people to sing of love and peace rather than war and hatred," said Rabbi Louis Jacobs, who officiated at the service. Possibly no other person had achieved so much in so short a time, he continued. Through his remarkable ability to discern and nurture talent, Mr. Epstein had brought happiness into the lives of millions.

❏

Despite the inquest verdict of accidental death, a myth has persisted about the death of Brian Epstein. The public view, dramatic and almost heroic in concept, is that the faintly remembered manager of the Beatles committed suicide—a view perpetuated by commentators anxious to exploit the man's complexities and frailties. The theory is abetted by a streak of envy; in Britain particularly, the frequent resentment of success is enough to deny happiness to wealthy artists. Money cannot buy them love and happiness. To many, Epstein fell neatly into the compartment reserved for rich depressives who want to end it all.

Aside from the medical evidence and the inquest verdict, there were many reasons why Brian Epstein would not have planned suicide in August 1967. Six weeks before Brian's death, his father's demise had traumatized the whole family, especially Queenie Epstein. Brian was particularly close to his mother, and on his father's passing, he rose to his responsibilities as her eldest son with loyalty and devotion. For him to intentionally give Queenie any more heartache, still less a tragedy of this magnitude, would have been unthinkable. In addition, he was actively involved in buying her a London flat in the Knightsbridge block where he had once lived, and was relishing the prospect of living near to the person he described as "the most beautiful woman in the world."

Brian, too, was a meticulous man. He led an orderly, well-structured life. Yet he died intestate. He would not have wanted to die without leaving a will; such a lack of precision would have been completely uncharacteristic. None of his actions or words in the weeks, days, and hours leading up to his death resembled those of a man who intended to take his own life.

Finally, and crucially, Epstein was enthusiastically planning his future. Ten days before his death, I went to lunch with Brian at one of his favorite restaurants, Wheelers in Dover Street, Mayfair. I was then editor of the weekly music paper *Disc and Music Echo*, in which Epstein had shares, and he was anxious to help secure exclusive interviews for me. On August 17, 1967, Epstein wrote to Derek Taylor, his former personal assistant who was then living in California and was my hired columnist on the U.S. pop scene:

> Dear Derek
>
> Thought you would like to know that I am coming Stateside next month. I will arrive in New York on 2 September and will stay at the Waldorf Towers until the 11th or 12th. Then I am going to Toronto to host a television show for Canadian Broadcasting Company. (I hope it is going to be rather good; understand the Doors and Jefferson Airplane are among those booked. Anyway more later.)
>
> After that, about the 17th, I am coming out to California to look you all over. . . . I will be staying about a week (at the moment I know not where).
>
> I have just had a long chat with Ray Coleman and we both agreed there was far more interest in this country in some of the groups on the West Coast than most people here suspect. We

wondered therefore if you would be willing to help us by obtaining some decent interviews with them.

Ray would like to devote four pages to interviews with each of the following: Jefferson Airplane, Doors, Love and the Electric Prunes. He says he has mentioned this to you before but not had any luck. . . . I would like to help Ray and the paper if I can.

If you feel unable to undertake any of this could you let me know by return because I think I could write to some other contacts in Los Angeles. But naturally, Ray and myself would both prefer you to do them. Either four pages in one edition or I think actually Ray would prefer a page on each group spread over four editions.

Nice piece on George.* Very much looking forward to seeing you.

> Love to Joan and family and everyone else.
> Brian Epstein.

❏

Asked for tributes in the few days after Brian's death, his artists were understandably at a loss for words.

"There will never be another manager like Brian," said Gerry Marsden. "When I heard the news, I was completely shattered."

Predictably, Cilla Black was the most visibly shaken. "When I heard the news of Brian's death, I just felt utterly alone. I've never lost anyone so close or been to a funeral before Brian's. Anyone who was really close to him loved him." Her first reaction was to give up her work. "I was a coward. I didn't want to go on. But that's not what Brian would have wanted. He was so much more than a manager to me. He was a friend and adviser."

The Beatles' remarks reflected their adoption of a meditative philosophy:

George Harrison: "He dedicated so much of his life to the Beatles. We liked and loved him. He was one of us. There is no such thing as death. It is a comfort to us all to know that he is OK."

Paul: "This is a great shock. I am terribly upset."

---

*This referred to a report by Derek Taylor in *Disc and Music Echo* on his pilgrimage with George Harrison to the famous hippie district of Haight-Ashbury in San Francisco on August 7.

Ringo: "We loved Brian. He was a generous man. We owe so much to him. We have come a long way with Brian along the same road."

Of the Beatles, it was Lennon, the abrasive one, who was the most eloquent. The day after Epstein's death, I visited John and Ringo at Lennon's house in Weybridge, Surrey. Robed in white toweling beside his pool, John said the Beatles' induction into the calmness of transcendental meditation at the behest of the Maharishi Mahesh Yogi would help them withstand the loss of Brian. "We all feel very sad but it's controlled grief, controlled emotion. As soon as I find myself feeling depressed, I think of something nice about him. But you can't hide the hurt. I went to the phone book and saw his name and it hit me a few minutes ago. The memory must be kept nice, but of course something inside us tells us that Brian's death is sad.

"It hurts when someone close dies and Brian was very close. You know we've all been through that feeling of wanting a good cry . . . we all feel it but these talks on transcendental meditation have helped us to stand up to it so much better. You don't get upset, do you, when a young kid becomes a teenager or a teenager becomes an adult or when an adult gets old? Well, Brian is just passing into the next phase.

"His spirit is still around and always will be. It's a physical memory we have of him, and as men we will build on that memory. It's a loss of genius but other geniuses' bodies have died as well, and the world still gains from their spirits.

"It is up to us, now, to sort out the way we and Brian wanted things to go. He might be dead physically but that's a negative way of thinking. He helped to give us the strength to do what we did and the same urge is still alive."

Would the Beatles be where they are today if it weren't for Epstein? "Not the same as we know it, no. But the question doesn't apply because we met him and what happened happened. We all knew what we wanted to get over, and he helped us and we helped him.

"If Brian had been in on the lectures in meditation—and it's a drag he didn't make it to Bangor—he would have understood. This is the biggest thing in our lives at the moment and it's come at a time when we need it.

"Brian has died only in body, and his spirit will always be working with us. His power and force were everything, and his power and force will linger on. When we were on the right track, he knew it; and when we were on the wrong track, he told us so and he was usually right. But anyway, he isn't really dead."

Ringo, espousing the benefits of meditation and the teachings of the Maharishi, said he had already been criticized for not wearing a black tie. "It isn't disrespectful just because we don't wear black ties. It's what's in your mind that counts. You can be wearing a flowered shirt or black tie but neither governs what you're thinking. Brian's spirit is still here and it will always be here. Of course it's a big personal loss."

The Beatles were not merely the apex of Brian's life—artistically, commercially, and as a symbiotic partnership; they were, Nat Weiss avers, the alter ego of his entire being. "This was not a part-time, twenty-five percent commission job. It was sacred to him.

"He was so sensitive that the slightest degree of failure would plunge him into depression. Because he really felt he had such a high responsibility, to maintain what he was supposed to be to them.

"He thought of himself as an inspiring, creative manager. And because of that intensity, added to a loss of perspective, he was incapable of getting that relationship from any other source. So he found himself a very lonely person most of the time. He may have found other outlets, but nothing equaled that emotional intensity, to give him meaning."

Although Brian was recognized as an integral part of the Beatles and their story, he lived in their shadow. And however great the shadow, it was still a shadow.

George Martin believes the Beatles and Brian were growing apart as a natural process. There was nothing rancorous about it, but he says: "One of the awful things is that, if Brian had lived, he would have lost the Beatles. He wouldn't have survived as their manager. Because they would have split up anyway. They would probably have sought their own, younger, different people to look after their affairs.

"Brian, by his own design, had become too fragmented and the Beatles were too selfish to ever have someone like that. They wanted someone who did nothing else but the Beatles. Even more than that: by that time, Paul wanted someone who did nothing but Paul, John wanted someone exclusively, and so on. So it would have become an impossible situation. I cannot see that Brian could have retained man-agership of the Beatles. One hesitates to know how the future might have gone if Brian had not died."

❑

These days, the Beatles hardly ever mention Epstein's name. In the twenty-two years since his death, they have never fairly or adequately acknowledged the importance of his role, his tireless energy that de-livered them out of Liverpool. As individuals and as a group, they have given scant recognition to the man who devoted six years of his life to their careers, their creative freedom, and their personal hap-piness.

The mentions of Epstein's name in Beatles songs were obtuse, and never reached the public. There was no moral obligation to write lyrics about their manager, of course, but the only two attempts proved to be curiously indirect, particularly since they were written after Brian's death.

On July 19, 1968, Lennon—during a day of rehearsals at the Abbey Road recording studios, where he was preparing the song "Sexy Sa-die," a satire on the Beatles' meditation guru, Maharishi Mahesh Yogi—launched into a spoof song with uncomplimentary lines about Brian and his brother Clive, ending with the words: "Queenie's the queen of them all." But the trite, spur-of-the-moment lyrics never formed a completed song. Even after Brian's death, it seemed, Lennon could not refrain from frontal assaults.

George Harrison was, as ever, more oblique. In his 1970 song "The Art of Dying," he initially wrote: "There'll come a time when all of us must leave here—then nothing Mr. Epstein can do will keep me here with you." Depending on interpretation, it meant either that even Brian was not superhuman, or that he could not be expected to transcend the act of death. But when George recorded the song on his spiritually aware album *All Things Must Pass*, Epstein's name was replaced by "Sister Mary."

The world of pop has bred its own, often ungracious ethics, and the Beatles have always been no more or less personally expressive than most; but it is to their discredit that to the rising generation of the 1970s and '80s, Epstein's name means little or nothing. In their sad failure to honor the memory of their mentor and best ally, they apparently fail to accept a moral responsibility to express their profound debt to a man who helped them make history.

❏

In the month of his death, Brian Epstein estimated his own wealth on paper to be nearly £7 million. And the Beatles and he together had earned more than £25 million; since he had often laughed away the fact that he suffered a net loss on the Beatles in the first year of his management, the figures were spectacular. But the estate duty, chargeable at the rate of 80 percent on assets exceeding £800,000, meant that the final value of Brian's estate was about £500,000.

His holdings in Northern Songs, which had gone public with only partial success in February 1965, were estimated to be worth £342,000 at the time of his death. Within a day of his death, shares of Northern Songs fell by a shilling on the Stock Exchange as a result of the news. This wiped £250,000 from the songs' market value.

And in the days, weeks, months, and years after Brian's death, NEMS became a battleground that brought chaos to the Beatles' business affairs.

The personal effect of his absence, however, would be much more profound. For all Brian's periods of disorientation, he remained the truest friend of the Beatles, and without him they had no anchor. Needing each other, they had met at a point when ambition, kinship, and business merged into a kaleidoscope of shared dreams. Fun-loving or troubled, relaxed or tense, Brian had always been *there* for a solo Beatle or for the group. On his death, they were doomed as a group as warring factions within it surfaced.

Lennon had met Yoko Ono ten months before Brian's death, and his marriage to Cynthia was creaking. So, too, was John's empathy with Paul McCartney, who grasped the reins in an attempt to hold the Beatles together.

The Beatles decided they would not be managed by anybody else. In what became the nearest to a public show of recognition, McCartney declared: "No one could possibly replace Brian." The Beatles, whose personal management contract with Epstein had been described by him as "friendship and twenty-five percent," decided to manage themselves. Their agency contact with NEMS was due to expire on September 30, 1967.

On December 8, 1967, Robert Stigwood and David Shaw resigned their directorships; and on the last day of the year, the shareholding in NEMS owned by Brian was transferred to Queenie's possession. In February 1968 the company changed its name to Nemperor Holdings, and on April 24, 1969, Clive and Queenie sold their shares to the Triumph Investment Trust, which by then already had two directors on the board: Leonard Richenberg and Gabriel Whyte. An extraordinary general meeting on October 24, 1975, decreed that Triumph be wound up, although at this stage vast royalties were being paid to the company by EMI Ltd. and others.

The Beatles, meanwhile, headed irreversibly for their Armageddon. When Brian Epstein was alive, nothing went wrong for the Beatles; when he died, little went right for them outside of music. Brian had kept them in an enclosure, as hermetically sealed as possible. Now his protection, invisible though it sometimes had been, was gone and there was palpable disintegration. His management had its structural weaknesses, but they were allowed to do what they did best: make music and films.

Brian had always been aware, too, that if his role with the Beatles was diminished by the creation of Apple, then Allen Klein would be waiting in the wings to pounce on them. It wasn't that Brian was so much worried about losing the Beatles; their loyalty was understood, if unspoken. He was wary that their self-government would end in disarray or, worse, destruction. His vision of the Beatles as unsuited to business, and of Apple as a disaster, proved correct.

Now, leaderless, they sank themselves into the utopian dream of Apple. Planned during the last few months of Brian's life as a small company through which they could comfortably control their destiny, Apple rapidly became a monster. With hopelessly overstaffed luxury offices at 3 Savile Row, London, Apple was launched with a philanthropic policy that would have given Brian apoplexy: refrigerators overloaded with drinks, some employees charging even their clothes and home food bills to company accounts. Its aim was to help embryonic artistic talent. But for every promising signing, there were hundreds of hopeless cases draining the Beatles' time and cash. Unlike Brian's NEMS, it did not have a rising group like the Beatles as its foundation.

Ironically, this cavalier attitude toward money was championed by the Beatles, who had muttered about Brian Epstein's ineptitude as a businessman on their behalf! But if Epstein was "green" in business, as Paul McCartney has said, he at least balanced that failing with a fine ear for talent and strategy. And he never knowingly risked the fortune earned by his artists. Apple exposed the Beatles as hopelessly naive when it came to handling their own affairs. On January 2, 1969, John Lennon said in an interview with me that Apple was costing the Beatles £50,000 a week. Apple "needs a new broom and a lot of people there will have to go," he said in reference to the overstaffing. "It doesn't have to make vast profits, but if it carries on like this all of us will be broke within six months."

John admitted that he and the Beatles missed Brian's guidance. "Sure we miss him," Lennon said. "His death was a loss. That's probably what's the matter with Apple or the Beatles at the moment. Brian's death left us on our own. He handled the business and we find it hard to."

There were signs inside Apple that the presence of an Epstein-like figure was sorely missed by others. In the November 1968 Apple newsletter, someone wrote anonymously: "Brian Epstein is still a topic of everyday Apple conversation. No ordinary man and never to be replaced or disestablished. Is he around? We sometimes wonder."

Paul McCartney tried to weather the storm. Traveling into the office most days from St. John's Wood by London bus, he found himself confronted by three Beatles who had signed into business management with Allen Klein, the bête noire of Epstein's life. From the moment that contract was signed, on May 8, 1969, there was no turning back.

McCartney opposed Klein's arrival and refused to have him as his manager. The group quickly disintegrated amid bitter sparring between John and Paul. The Beatles, who had preached brotherly love, peace and togetherness, and a gentle philosophy of meditation, exuded vitriol toward each other and made it public. Lennon, divorced from Cynthia a year after Brian's death and immersed in a world peace campaign with his second wife, Yoko Ono, said he wanted another divorce—from the Beatles.

Paul, who appointed his father-in-law, top New York attorney Lee Eastman, as his representative, announced his resignation from the Beatles on April 10, 1970. And on March 12, 1971, after brooding miserably on the prospect of suing his "best mates," McCartney successfully launched a High Court action in London winding up the

Beatles. A receiver was appointed to look after the group's business and financial affairs, superseding Allen Klein, who by then had moved into Apple but faced the divided Beatles and a dispirited staff.

It was a sour end to a glorious decade. The beginnings of the Beatles had resembled a fairy tale. Their youthful tilt at the Establishment and their pioneering sounds had generated infectious happiness—and music that would stand as the touchstone of its time. Their official ending in litigation was grotesque. For all the heartfelt sadness at Brian Epstein's death, at least he was spared the misery of seeing "the boys" split up in such a debacle.

❑

It is simplistic to write of Brian Epstein as the Beatles' manager who suffered a tragically premature accidental death. His legacy is deeper. Through his insight and his fantasy, his awesome achievement in transforming four raucous rock 'n' rollers into the idols of millions, Epstein provided the springboard for a social revolution.

His more tangible epitaphs span the world. In England, Paul McCartney, George Harrison, and Ringo make music, run successful companies, and have finally accepted that—whatever their considerable solo achievements—they are frozen forever in the world's view as "ex-Beatles." In New York, Yoko Ono Lennon presides over the estate of the Beatle whom Brian regarded as the genius. Dotted around the world, from the Buckinghamshire home of television star Cilla Black to the Cheshire home of Gerry Marsden, from the California home of fan club secretary Debbie Gendler to the Australian home of his Chapel Street secretary, Joanne Petersen, hundreds of people speak warmly, tearfully, glowingly, of the man admired as vulnerable, charming, caring . . . the antithesis of the deal-hungry entertainment moguls who succeeded him.

And in his Manhattan office, Nat Weiss looks up at a framed piece of his best friend's handwriting. Brian gave it to Nat with a combination of fear and practicality. Perpetually scared of dying in a plane crash, Epstein handed the note to Weiss in mid-1967 as his friend saw him to the departure gate at Kennedy Airport. Worried about the problems surrounding the Beatles' imminent album cover, Brian instructed Nat to hand it to the Beatles if he should die on the journey. The message reads simply: "Brown paper bags for Sgt Pepper."

Author's Note

This biography could not, and would not, have been prepared without the encouragement and assistance of the Epstein family. I am particularly grateful to Brian's mother, Queenie Epstein, for her unfailing support for this project since its inception and for her grace and patience, especially in the subject's areas of sensitivity.

The late Clive Epstein's practical help, guidance, and loan of valuable documents and photographs were invaluable throughout my research. Clive's appallingly premature death at the age of fifty-one came on February 1, 1988, during the book's final preparation. He always distanced himself from Brian's private life and therefore had misgivings about my focus on it when necessary to the story. Since Clive was a man of absolute integrity, he understood the need for the truth, painful though it sometimes is. We shall miss him.

A paramount feature of Brian's life was that his professional associates were also his only friends and therefore were able to observe him from two perspectives. Nat Weiss in New York, Brian's closest confidant and a working partner for the last three years of his life, gave generously of his time, his memories, crucial insights, letters, documents, and photographs. The book would be infinitely poorer without his spirited help. Nat Weiss's honesty and loyalty to Epstein shine through and surely gave him strength in many difficult days.

In five years of life in the limelight, Epstein's fuse burned quickly and his position of great influence could have caused him to assume the mantle of a despot. Yet Brian died with a golden reputation for integrity and charm intact. His personal frailties and a certain naiveté in business were his chief vulnerabilities; weighed against his monumental achievement of discovering, nurturing, and launching the Beatles, they are insignificant. In the minefield of show business, rarely has anyone climbed so high while retaining such genuine respect.

Three women worked particularly closely with him and saw his personality under a microscope: Cilla Black, the artist whose talent Brian correctly envisioned as long-lasting and whose affection he cherished; Joanne Petersen, his devoted private secretary, who now lives in Australia; and Wendy Hanson, his compassionate personal assistant, formerly of New York and now living in Italy. Their warm protective memory of Brian Epstein will remain forever; I am indebted to them for sharing their thoughts and for providing important signposts.

My special thanks are due to Geoffrey Ellis, George Martin, Alistair Taylor, Gerry Marsden, Pattie Clapton, Cynthia Lennon, Tony Barrow, Sonia Stevens, and Bill and Virginia Harry. The knowledge, formidable memory, and interest of Bob Wooler in Liverpool, who observed Epstein during vital early meetings with the Beatles and others, have been an irreplaceable asset in grasping the period.

Mark Lewisohn, the world's foremost Beatles historian, has been a staunch supporter of this book as well as its researcher. I thank him warmly for his help in assembling the illustrations. For his experience and wisdom in helping to dissect Epstein's performance as a businessman, I thank Sam Alder.

My appreciation is recorded to people whose lives touched Epstein's either extensively or fleetingly and who all provided significant recollections and observations:

In Liverpool and the North: Beryl Adams, Helen Anderson, Don Andrew, Ken Ashcroft, John Banks, Walter Beaver, Danny Betesh, Peter Bevan, Vera Brown, Dave Carden, Paddy Chambers, Ray Cobb, Ric Dixon, Joe Flannery, Dennis Goodrum, Johnny Hamp, David Harris, Billy Hatton, George Hayes, Alma Johnson, Brian Johnson, Shelagh Johnston, Sue Johnston, the late Ted Knibbs, Sam Leach, Rex Makin, John McNally, Bernard Michaelson, Max Nathan, Rod and Christine Pont, Monica Shannon, Rita Shaw, Alan Swerdlow, Janice Troup, Allan Williams, Beryl Williams, the Reverend Samuel Wolfson, Edith Yates.

In London and the South: Jeffrey Archer, Lionel Bart, Hywel Bennett, Mike Berry (singer), Mike Berry (record company executive), Don Black, Robert Boast, Colin Borland, Peter Bourne, Tony Bramwell, Tito Burns, Sandra Caron, William Cavendish, Judy Coles, Lord Delfont, Joanna Dunham, Georgie Fame, Yankel Feather, Jill Forbes, Alan Freeman, Dr. Wendy Greengross, John Gustafson, Tony Hall, Michael Haslam, Ernest Hecht, Raymond Horricks, Keith Howell, the late Dick James, Stephen James, David Jacobs, Maurice and Berenice Kinn, Mike Leander, Helen Lindsay, Sir Joseph Lockwood, John Lyndon, Dougie and Gordon Millings, Vyvienne Moynihan, Sean O'Mahony, Alun Owen, Larry Parnes, Robin Ray, Peter Scott, Hal Shaper, Malcolm Shifrin, Don Short, Rabbi Daniel Smith, the late Tony Stratton Smith, Brian Sommerville, Brian Southall, Peter String-fellow, Derek Taylor, Raymond Weldon, Ron White, Dennis Wiley, Brian Wolfson, Len Wood.

In the United States: Al Brodax, Sid Bernstein, Billy J. Kramer, David Lowe, and Sue Weiner in New York; Debbie Gendler and Walter Shenson in Los Angeles.

Thanks to London's *Melody Maker* and *New Musical Express* for permission to reproduce parts of interviews with Brian Epstein; also to the *New Yorker* magazine for use of quotations from the first interview with Epstein in any American publication.

Eleo Gordon, Tony Lacey, and Annie Lee at Viking in London and Tom Miller, Lisa Frost, and Robert Daniels at McGraw-Hill in New York have been my fervent editors and supporters; so too has been my agent, Merrilee Heifetz at Writers House in New York. Their encouragement and advice have been greatly appreciated, as have those of my lawyer, Roger Samuels, and the Epstein family lawyer, Sally Hamwee.

The people who appear on a stage finally are acknowledged to be top of the bill, the rightful reservation for my wife Pamela and my sons Miles and Mark. For nearly three years they suffered my irascibility and absences during the pressures of preparation. For tolerating the unacceptable and for always being there, heartfelt thanks.

Ray Coleman
Richmond, Surrey, England
Autumn 1988

INDEX

389